Rite, Flesh, and Stone

Rite, Flesh, and Stone

The Matter of Death in Contemporary Spanish Culture

*Edited by Antonio Córdoba and
Daniel García-Donoso*

Vanderbilt University Press

NASHVILLE, TENNESSEE

Library of Congress Cataloging-in-Publication Data

Names: Cordoba, Antonio, editor. | García-Donoso, Daniel, editor.
Title: Rite, flesh, and stone : cultures of death in contemporary Spain,
    1959-2021 / edited by Antonio Córdoba and Daniel García-Donoso.
Description: Nashville, Tennessee : Vanderbilt University Press, [2021] |
    Series: Hispanic issues ; volume 45 | Includes bibliographical
    references and index.
Identifiers: LCCN 2021031090 (print) | LCCN 2021031091 (ebook) | ISBN
    9780826502193 (hardcover) | ISBN 9780826502186 (paperback) | ISBN
    9780826502209 (epub) | ISBN 9780826502216 (pdf)
Subjects: LCSH: Death—Spain—History—20th century. | Funeral rites and
    ceremonies—Spain—History—20th century. | Death—Spain—History—21st
    century. | Funeral rites and ceremonies—Spain—History—21st century.
Classification: LCC HQ1073.5.S7 R57 2021 (print) | LCC HQ1073.5.S7
    (ebook) | DDC 306.90946—dc23
LC record available at https://lccn.loc.gov/2021031090
LC ebook record available at https://lccn.loc.gov/2021031091

CONTENTS

First of all, we would like to thank the editors of Hispanic Issues, Luis Martín-Estudillo and Nicholas Spadaccini, for their support of this project from very early in the process. At Vanderbilt University Press, Zachary Gresham's guidance was fundamental to take this volume to the finishing line. We are also very grateful to the two anonymous readers for their careful evaluation of the manuscript and their suggestions, and to those artists, companies, and associations that have granted us permission to reproduce the illustrations that appear in this volume. And most of all, this book would not have been possible without the generosity of time and mind of each and every one of our contributors—we owe much to the company that you have provided in this unforgettable journey.

The prehistory of this volume takes place in New Haven, Connecticut, where the editors met without knowing that the opening of its beautiful Grove Street Cemetery in 1796 had commenced what Thomas W. Laqueur calls the "Age of the Cemetery." Laqueur's monumental *The Work of the Dead* is a cornerstone of this book. This project started in earnest in the fall of 2016 and greatly benefitted from the kind of formal and informal communication that only academic conferences can provide. We would like to thank Ignacio Infante and Tabea Linhard, organizers of the 2017 Mid-American Conference on Hispanic Literatures, for kindly giving us a chance to hold a panel with some of the contributors to this volume in Saint Louis in October. We are also grateful to the organizers of the Modern Languages Association annual convention for the opportunity to talk about death in a panel that met in Midtown Manhattan one freezing afternoon in January of 2018. Dean Allbritton and Germán Labrador Méndez were exceptional interlocutors on that occasion.

We gratefully acknowledge the assistance of our respective institutions. Antonio Cordoba would like to thank his colleagues at the Department of Modern Languages and Literatures at Manhattan College: Joan Cammarata, Marlene Gottlieb, Samira Hassa, Laura Redruello, Luisianna Sardu, Evelyn Scaramella, and

Nonie Wanger. He is also grateful to dean of the School of Liberal Arts, Keith Brower, for his support over the years. Daniel García-Donoso thanks his students and colleagues in the Department of Modern Languages and Literatures at The Catholic University of America, especially the invaluable feedback they provided in the fall 2018 Research-in-Progress seminar where he presented some of his individual work in this volume. He is also indebted to the staff at Mullen Library at Catholic for their tireless support, and to Duília de Mello and Ralph Albano of the University Institutional Grants Committee for believing in this project with a grant-in-aid to cover some of the costs associated with the publication of this book. He completed part of the preparation of the manuscript while on a sabbatical leave as a visiting researcher at the Universidad Complutense de Madrid—he thanks his extraordinary hosts in Spain, Esther Borrego, Santiago López-Ríos, and Rebeca Sanmartín.

Finally, Antonio also thanks Erika for her patience and love. Daniel thanks Alejandra and Emilia—your presence and unconditional love and support is what gives meaning to all this.

Materiality, Culture, and Death in Contemporary Spain

Antonio Córdoba and Daniel García-Donoso

"Death *then* was not what it is now; that death has passed away, although its ghostly traces remain, in the form of vestigial practices or unassimilated iterations of customs prevalent at other times," wrote Jacques Lezra in 2010 about death in the early modern Hispanic world (192). Death is complex and historically bound. Death in 1600 was certainly not the same as it is in the late twentieth century, or in 2010, or in the first half of 2020, when the COVID-19 pandemic changed the way people live and die all over the world. Most victims of the disease died alone, or surrounded only by trained professionals in public places such as hospitals, seemingly reinforcing and taking to its extreme conclusion the different narratives that support the secularization and medicalization of death—what Thomas Laqueur critically describes as "the evacuation of enchantment." But as Laqueur himself counterpoints, "[h]istory, memory, and politics, with the deep time of the dead as their resource, created a new enchantment of the dead" (186). This creativity can be seen at work in the early twenty-first century. "Social distancing" (that term that defines collective life in much of the world as we write this in the fall of 2020) drove mourners to engage in hitherto unseen forms of disembodiment and "modernization" of death by celebrating funerary rites via videoconference applications. In a funeral described in the *Washington Post*, the Jewish tradition of immediate burial (ideally within twenty-four hours) was supplemented by children of the deceased holding their phones next to the grave for the sake of 150 online viewers; for the three main mourners, the service "wasn't lonely at all," but rather it "felt pretty tremendous" (Alexander and Boorstein). For a few Americans in the *Post* article, the immaterial presence of virtual attendants and the intangible (but palpable) feeling of community and tradition were enabled by new material means of recording and transmission (cell phones) and all the material infrastructure that makes online communication possible. Meanwhile in Spain, one of the countries with the highest mortality rates in the first months of the pandemic, funerals were restricted to five attendants or fewer, the lack of physical presence was felt as one more devastating blow to the mourners, and relatives bought increasingly less expensive coffins for the deceased, abandoning the capitalist mirage of enchantment that comes from luxury and excessive spending (Martín; Congostrina). Death in capitalist modernity is certainly a mixed bag, and even the supposedly secularized funerary rituals of 2020 are meaningful in ways that are sorely missed when these rituals are absent. The living and the dead must be closer than a century of cultural discourse on death has wanted to see them. In 1916, in bustling, commercial downtown Manhattan, Juan Ramón Jiménez stumbles upon an old cemetery and sees it as "un único hermano gemelo del ocaso inmenso, trasparente y silencioso, de cuya hermosura sin fin queda la ciudad viva desterrada" (173) (the only twin of the immense, transparent and silent sunset from whose endless beauty the living city is exiled).[1] The realities of death and funerary rites in the early months of 2020 show that the old and the new, the non-secularized death and commerce, the old forms of enchantment and the new ones are not as opposed as Juan Ramón saw them. But they do not easily coexist, either. Tensions and contradictions shape the rites around the deceased, our understanding of their dead flesh and what eventually remains of it, and the production of the material and immaterial environments (the "stone" of our title for this volume of Hispanic Issues) in which they are laid, remembered, and commemorated.

Faced with the ever-receding nature of the experience of death ("death refuses itself as such to testimony," in the words of Jacques Derrida [37]), the scholar keen on seeing the face of death usually turns to matter and materiality to find the locus where mortality takes shape and becomes communicable. Forensic science provides information and data behind the circumstances of a particular death, but it is culture that provides death with meaning. With this in mind, we propose cultural matters of death—rite, flesh, stone—as this compilation's structuring principle, operating as frames of the expression of mortality within a distinct set of coordinates. The essays in this volume offer original approaches to how human remains are handled in the embodied rituals and social performances of contemporary funeral rites of all kinds; furthermore, they explore how dying flesh and corpses are processed by means of biopolitical technologies and the ethics of (self-)care, and how the vibrant and breathing materiality of the living is transformed into stone and analogous kinds of tangible, empirical presence that engender new cartographies of memory. Each from a specific disciplinary perspective, contributors problematize conventional ideas about the place of death in contemporary Western societies and cultures using Spain as a case study. Materials analyzed here—ranging from cinematic and literary fictions to historical archives and anthropological and ethnographic sources—make explicit a dynamic scenario in which actors embody a variety of positions toward death and dying, the political production of mortality, and the commemoration of the dead. Ultimately, the goal of this collaborative effort is to chart the complex network in which the disenchantment of death and its re-enchantment coexist, and biopolitical control over secularized bodies overlaps with new avatars of the religious and non-theistic desires for memorialization and transcendence.

Death, Culture, and Nation in Spain

As the title of this collection suggests, death and culture are concepts that bear an inextricable relationship to each other. Mortality and the obligation upon the living to mourn the dead constitute a fundamental precondition for cultural behavior. As Derrida has argued, culture itself

> is essentially, before anything, even a priori, the culture of death. . . . There is no culture without a cult of ancestors, a ritualization of mourning and sacrifice, institutional places and modes of burial. . . . The very concept of culture may seem to be synonymous with the culture of death, as if the expression "culture of death" were ultimately a pleonasm or a tautology. (43)

Culture pulls death out of the realm of the natural and seeks to normalize a phenomenon with profound consequences at the affective level. The very fact that humans deal with death in distinct and diverse ways is for Derrida a defining factor: "The difference between nature and culture . . ., between the animal and the human is the relation *to* death. . . . The true border would be there" (43–44). In addition, culture marks the threshold that separates *perishing* (that is, the mere cessation of biological life) from *dying*, in which death becomes artificial inasmuch as it can be instrumentalized to create, maintain, and strengthen social bonds.

But the malleable matter of death transcends the realm of social immediacy. As Michael Taussig explains, "In the making of modern nations, the dead do double duty. Out of nowhere, it seems, people conjure up a slice of deadness and bor-row from it their names, battle cries, and costumes, in order to present the new scene of world history in dazzling form" (10). Deaths offer an opportunity for sovereignty to manifest itself and engage in performance that goes beyond ter-ritorial states to include all kinds of "sub-, trans- and supra-national entities that seek to claim or produce autonomous domains of power" (Stepputtat 5). From nations and international peace missions to religious communities and insurgent social networks, the different ways in which the dead body is managed produce effects of sovereignty that do not necessarily coincide, and oftentimes conflict, with practices sanctioned by the state.

The present volume analyzes specific ways in which death is conceived of and represented in Spanish culture starting in the second half of the twentieth century. One must tread carefully when linking the concepts of death and Spain. On the one hand, as Federico García Lorca memorably said, "Un muerto en España está más vivo como muerto que en ningún otro sitio del mundo" (180) (a dead man/ person in Spain is more alive as dead than anywhere else in the world). This is the kind of bold pronouncement that leads foreign media such as the *New York Times* to print articles in which Spain is called "the most death-conscious country in Western tradition" (Josephs). As Katarzyna Beilin and William Viestenz point out, twentieth-century Hispanism contributed to shaping a cultural discourse that envisions Spain as a country with a privileged connection to death, to "a violence-ridden spirituality" (x). At work here is the problematic self-interiorization of a Northern European Orientalist gaze that constructs Spain as an anthropological space out of sync with modernity, frozen in a gesture of mis-encounter. Attempts to turn this intimate connection of Spain and death on its head, or to rearticulate it as some kind of alternative modernity, do nothing to erase the original othering move, and only validate political violence, social hierarchies, and "a generalized indifference toward suffering" (xi).

On the other hand, contemporary Spain allows us to study general trends in the cultural construction of death in Western capitalist societies, while it also offers specific, local inflections of these trends that can be acknowledged without buying into essentialist traps. Genocides were committed all over the world dur-ing the twentieth century, but the victims of the genocidal violence in Franco's National-Catholic state have not been the object of commemoration and truth-seeking initiatives that have taken place elsewhere, which has led to practices of recuperation and remembrance that occur "on the margins of existing memory politics" (Aragüete-Toribio 23). In the 1960s, the effects of modern capitalism on cultural attitudes toward death are shaped by Francoist developmentalist dis-courses, top-down approaches to the construction of social imaginaries, and the brand-crafting strategies of the Spanish tourist industry. The late 1970s and 1980s saw how the Spanish heroin outbreak decimated a generation of young people in Madrid (Fernández de Alba 69) and reached epidemic proportions in cities like Vigo, Sevilla, Barcelona, and San Sebastián, when it was estimated that one in five hundred people in the country were heroin consumers (Fuente Lafuente). But the young died in Madrid and elsewhere in specific circumstances that were still comparable to those in Berlin, Italy, or Thatcherite England, as Germán Labrador Méndez has pointed out: "son muchas las transiciones que sacuden la Europa de los años setenta y ochenta, y muchas las metamorfosis políticas y culturales del momento. Todas tienen sus costes. Los jóvenes tienden siempre a pagar precios muy altos por su participación en tales procesos de cambios" (152–53) (there are many transitions shaking the Europe of the 1970s and 1980s, and there are many political and cultural metamorphoses taking place at that moment. All of them have a cost. The young always tend to pay a very high price for participating in such processes of change). And finally, in the twenty-first century, white supremacist anxieties about migration in the Global North that have led to Brexit, the electoral victory of Donald Trump in the United States, and rising Far Right nationalist movements across Europe, put vulnerability, expendability, and death at the center of cultural representations of migration to Spain, as Jeffrey K. Coleman identifies in Spanish theater (4). That Spanish death may be specific does not make it exceptional.

Death, History, and Dis-Jointed Time

Flesh, rites, and stone call upon the individual and the collective in manners that demand distinct avenues of theorization, and dying bodies, ashes, and bones conjure up their own untimely temporality. In a series of lectures delivered at Johns Hopkins University in 1973 and collected and translated as *Western Attitudes toward Death: From the Middle Ages to the Present* the next year, Philippe Ariès addressed what he saw as an exceptional moment in European history. The French historian argued that

> In our day, in approximately a third of a century, we have witnessed a brutal revolution in traditional ideas and feelings, a revolution so brutal that social observers have not failed to be struck by it. It is really an absolutely unheard-of phenomenon. Death, so omnipresent in the past that it was familiar, would be effaced, would disappear. It would become shameful and forbidden. (85)

According to Ariès, modernity requires to avoid "the disturbance and the overly strong and unbearable emotion caused by the ugliness of dying" (87). Death gets "dissected" into a myriad of tiny medical acts, and evident sorrow does not elicit pity, but disgust (88, 90). For the French historian, Americans are to blame for these developments: "It seems that the modern attitude toward death, that is to say the interdiction of death in order to preserve happiness, was born in the United States around the beginning of the twentieth century" (94). Almost a decade later, his compatriot Michel Vovelle concurred. In a chapter of his book *Ideologies and Mentalities* that adapted papers delivered at conferences in the United States and Europe, he wrote, "Our own age has become aware, first in the United States and then in Western Europe, of a taboo which has made death a new category of obscenity. One thinks, among other things, of the hidden death of hospital wards and of private mourning" (70). In monumental monographs about the history of death, Ariès and Vovelle would insist on the points made on these public occasions. By the end of *The Hour of Our Death*, Ariès concludes, "A heavy silence has fallen over the subject of death. . . . Neither the individual nor the community is strong enough to recognize the existence of death" (608). As for Vovelle, in his *La mort et l'Occident de 1300 à nos jours*, he would connect this modern emergence of this "hidden death" to the ways in which the Christian religion loses its almost exclusive hold over the cultural processes revolving around death (532).

Ariès and Vovelle are only two of the most prominent names in a 1970s academic phenomenon that Mexican anthropologist Claudio Lomnitz describes as "the development of a cottage industry dedicated to the history and anthropology of death," a program devoted to "[t]he critique of Western denial of death" (12). A "conventional view of death" would arise in those years, according to Lyn Lofland, one that held that "America is a death-denying society, that death is a taboo, that death makes Americans uncomfortable so they run from it, that death is hidden in America because Americans deny it, and so forth" (72–73). In the 1970s and early 1980s, it seems, death was nowhere to be openly found in the Western world.

Hollywood seemed to agree with these French scholars. In *Poltergeist* (1982), cowritten by Steven Spielberg, the developer of the planned community where the protagonists live had moved only the headstones of the cemetery upon which their house now stands, leaving the corpses behind, under the ground. Supernatural mayhem ensues. The living and the dead cannot coexist in such close proximity, and when the capitalist modernity of the early Reagan years charges at full speed through the landscape, crossing some untouchable cultural lines, we get one more example of what Clive Bloom describes as a horror film trend in which audiences encounter "a happy nuclear family moving in only to be traumatized by a past that cannot be exorcised" (17). Keep the living and the dead apart, Hollywood says, seemingly confirming Ariès's and Vovelle's assertions. And yet the explosion of affect, the gothic terror conjured up by contact with the dead, the inability to erase "a past that cannot be exorcised" may invite us to question that straight-forward story about the evacuation of death from Western consciousness and Western social life. The complex fascination with death in modern times that *Poltergeist* plays upon suggests that death has not been merely put aside, successfully hidden after being sequestered by biopolitical governance and the medical-industrial complex.

Perhaps because we are not in the 1970s and 1980s any more, because the Western denial of death never really existed, and/or because the narrative of modernity-as-secularization does not sound so true in our post-secular times, cultural historians and social scientists have been identifying all kinds of coexistence and continuities between the living and the deceased. Modern technological developments are at the heart of "a trend towards the return of the dead to the spaces inhabited by the living" (Hockey et al. 17). Sites for the disposal of the ashes of the deceased include pubs, football fields, and, mostly, "mundane destinations . . . [that] carried associations with lives previously lived, whether everyday life or key life course transitions such as weddings" (Kellaher et al. 134). The porousness between humans and environment that twenty-first-century posthumanism encourages can be seen in tree burials, in which the buried corpse provides nourishment to the tree planted above it, so that the decomposing human matter under earth "becomes" vegetable matter in the sun, visible in its transformation to those visiting the tomb or just passing by. And all kinds of digital modes of public commemoration become available and more and more common, from the disembodied memorial sites on the Internet to "QR codes or steel-cased computer chips embedded in tombstones," full of information about the deceased (Boret et al. 10).

It would be a mistake to restrict this technology-enabled visibility and the presence of the dead to the twenty-first century, however. One can make a career devoting yourself to "understand[ing] all the invisible technologies humans use to make modern death and dying visible. Defined. Knowable. Experienced," as John Troyer does recently in a crucially important book (xxiii). This visibility begins with the industrialization of the dead body in the nineteenth century, in which embalming and photographic technologies that disguised decomposition and prevented visual degradation invented "a new concept of the dead body" (2). This was a body that was fit for public consumption and presence, one that technology allowed to be openly shown and thus become the center of those public gatherings known as funerals, one that could be easily memorialized in a portable, durable, and easy-to-display medium such as the printed photograph. New social practices and legal frameworks went along with technical developments, posing questions that involved technologies that are as much conceptual as material (xxxii). In the present, the corpse, "thus legally recognized as a body with some rights under the law, enters a state of existence where the seemingly normalized rules of scientific, legal, and medical 'life' become entirely destabilized" (xxxvii). Corpses are not simple, death is not simple, and the simple narrative of American-born modern concealment of death put together by Ariès and others may not be that simple. After all, as Lomnitz warns us, the social construction of death simultaneously refers to subjective, collective, and trans-collective horizons that bring about with them their own temporal orientations, which results in the "*coexistence* of various formulations of life and time" (19; Lomnitz's emphasis). Death is complicated, and we will be better served by focusing on the transformation and reinvention of traditions that Thomas Laqueur invoked in the passage cited above, rather than to assume clear-cut divisions and historical chasms.

For both practical and thematic reasons, it is essential that we establish a chronological framework that allows this volume to offer a cohesive and coherent understanding of the place of death in Spanish culture that is also inclusive of a productive plurality. As per the title of this collection, we cover the period from 1959 to 2020. Although the topic of death extends its reach across very disparate historical moments and geographical contexts, we believe that a series of key events and processes that either culminated or started around the 1950s in Spain produced a rapid shift in cultural attitudes toward death. It was then that a series of scientific advances (mechanical respirators and defibrillators; new techniques in organ transplantation) made it extremely difficult to determine the exact moment of total and irreversible loss of life. In this regard, "quite rapidly the questions of what constituted human death and how we could determine its occurrence had emerged as issues both philosophically rich and urgent" (DeGrazia). Changes in funerary regulations allowed for the introduction of *tanatorios* or funeral homes in the late 1960s when home vigils were the only accepted practice in the country, while pressing issues that led to new urban planning and public health policies slowly set in motion the social acceptance of cremation as a method of body disposal starting in the mid-1970s. Furthermore, Spanish writers and intellectuals of that time also shared the idea that the adoption of an American *way of life* would inevitably bring with it an American *way of death*, to use the title of Jessica Mitford's 1963 widely read critique of the American funeral industry. Interestingly, however, their concerns arose less from an aversion to a given culture's deliberate occultation of death, than to the market forces that exploit and pervert such cultural specificity. Philosopher Julián Marías, who had been banned by the Franco regime from teaching in the Spanish university system and spent several years in different teaching posts across the United States, said already in the mid-1950s that "la muerte tiene siempre aquí un aire de indeseable y, desde luego, no ha conseguido la ciudadanía americana" (death here always has an unpleasant appearance and, of course, it has not obtained American citizenship), blaming a business mindset of statistical calculation and economicist anticipation that American hospitals and funeral services used to their own benefit (47). A decade later, writer Miguel Delibes mockingly titled the last chapter of his travelogue *USA y yo* "La muerte disfrazada" (death in disguise), in which he went in length to describe what he sees as the average American citizen's "antipatía hacia la muerte" (150) (antipathy toward death) and how an entire industry emerged in the United States to make a profit from an event that had been artificially turned from a transformative moment in the social life of any individual (the management a loved one's passing) into an irritating nuisance: "Todo es cuestión de dólares. La fuerza del negocio es en Norteamérica una fuerza avasalladora y de nada han valido hasta ahora las protestas de la razón y la sensatez. El servicio fúnebre sigue en manos de especuladores, de vivos que medran a costa de los muertos" (153) (Everything is a matter of money. The power of business is in North America an overwhelming force, and reasonable, sensible protests have so far proved to be worthless. Funeral services continue to be in the hands of speculators, of the astute living who prosper at the cost of the dead). Back home in Spain, and in part due to the influence of an ominous censorship apparatus, the acute vision with which some of these intellectuals condemned the excesses of modern capitalism elsewhere turned, sadly, into a myopic unwillingness to see the profound transformations at work in the logics of *desarrollismo*.

On the other hand, 1959 in particular is crucial to understanding the political, social, and cultural debates that inform Spain in the twenty-first century. The inauguration of the Valley of the Fallen in April of that year embodied, in the nakedness and timeless character of stone, Franco's politics—or po*lithics*—of remembrance, one that has continued to divide Spanish society up to this day. The decree establishing the construction of the monument on April 1, 1940, stated unequivocally the dictator's grandiose desire to break with the modest character of the existing memorial landscape of the country, and his wish that "the stones that are to be erected have the grandeur of the monuments of Antiquity, that they defy time and forgetfulness" (Presidencia del Gobierno). Such language brings Jacques Lezra's words back to the forefront: death *then* was not what it is now, but Franco's disturbing willingness to collapse historical time and fuse his *now* with an archaic *then* ought to serve as a cautionary message against the safe distance that we too often take for granted between the now and then. When the pharaonic mausoleum was inaugurated, the flesh of the bodies of incarcerated men who had been forced to work in the construction as well as the remains of thousands of Republican victims who had not participated of "our glorious Crusade," and yet were buried in the basilica's crypt, had succumbed under the absolute erasure of a one-sided memory machine. Simultaneously, the calculated invention of ritual practices with the Valley at its core—exemplified by the *translatio* of the mortal remains of José Antonio Primo de Rivera from El Escorial to the Valley's Basilica the day before the monument's inauguration—provided Franco with a two-pronged political tool: the performative enactment of a structure of *sacratio* that, as William Viestenz has argued, "persists behind the façade of biopolitical inclusion" that the regime strategically adopted in the 1950s (100), and the domestication of a particular kind of fascist "emonationalism" that had broken loose with the initial parading of Primo de Rivera's remains from Alicante to El Escorial in 1939 (Varón González).

As Patty Keller points out regarding the Valley, "If there is one thing critics and historians agree on, it is that the monument cannot simply be ignored" ("Valley" 73). It represents the culmination of a process to "consecrate war, to glorify it and sanctify it within the visual and discursive logic of imperial Christian militarism" (75). It is also the maximum example of what Francisco Ferrándiz has called "funerary apartheid" to refer to the completely asymmetrical way in which the bodies of those killed during the war were treated in post-war legislation. While Franco rushed to create and enact a body of laws concerning the dead on the nationalist side, Ferrándiz notes, "the bodies of the defeated . . . continued to accumulate in mass graves and remained outside lawmaking," in what became "a cornerstone in the construction of dictatorial sovereign control of the country" ("Unburials" 65). More than fifty years after its inauguration, the Valley of the Fallen today embodies in a very localized fashion a myriad of unresolved social and political conflicts. In their introduction to *Death and Afterlife in the Early Modern Hispanic World*, John Beusterien and Constance Cortez speak of the ominous, almost unavoidable presence of the Cross that dominates the Valley of the Fallen in the center of the Iberian Peninsula: "[T]he visibility and materiality of the white cross represents a real issue that can *only* be spoken about in terms of invisibility and immateriality; ghosts still haunt a Spanish society that has not recovered from the trauma induced by Franco's politics of remembrance" (1; our emphasis). After all, as Jo Labanyi famously said, "modern Spanish culture can be read as a ghost story" (6). Spectrality provides a fundamental language to disarm the Valley's hostile memory and highlight the contours of the historical trauma of Francoism. But we also believe that the language of justice must accommodate the inevitable presence of matter in the relationship between death, politics, and the affects. Always oscillating between absence and presence, the visible and the invisible, as Patty Keller beautifully puts it, ghosts "indicate at once a deep unity as well as a deep wound within time—an object or feeling pertaining to one time now disturbingly appears in and injures another time, making it non-contemporaneous with itself" (*Ghostly* 6). The materiality of the cross serves the specific purpose of providing the material foundation for a perdurable myth, one based not on reconciliation, but on the erasure of the suffering and the death of those who were forced to work in the construction of the Valley. And to speak only in terms of immateriality both thwarts the possibility of concrete action and limits the actual, material effectiveness of a wide range of cultural interventions that participate in the ethos of spectrality precisely to subvert Franco's discursive and tangible attempts to instrumentalize the transcendent, immaterial, and mythical for his own personal benefit.

The Valley still stands as a memorial to the dictator's self-attributed providential role in the war and to National-Catholicism at large, despite repeated attempts at re-signifying the monument to stave off the threat of uncritically bequeathing Franco's legacy to future generations. In 2011, a government commission was tasked by then President José Luis Rodríguez Zapatero with providing an action plan for the monument, but the conservative majority that took power under Mariano Rajoy from late that year until 2018 killed every institutional platform and budget allocation related to the Law of Historical Memory, including the recommendations from the Valley commission. When the PSOE (Spanish Socialist Workers' Party) returned to power under Pedro Sánchez in 2018, a renewed impetus was given back to those initiatives, reaching a critical point on October 24, 2019, when the dictator's remains were exhumed from his grave in the middle of the Valley's underground Basilica and transferred to the Mingorrubio cemetery in Madrid's El Pardo. The heavy lifting of the tombstone—weighing almost two thousand kilos— that sealed Franco's resting place was symbolic of the larger set of herculean efforts (judicial, institutional, political, diplomatic, forensic, engineering, architectural, logistical) that were necessary to transfer the dictator's remains. And all of them are a reminder that Franco's is one of those dead bodies that are "heavy symbols," "the thing that is always more than a thing" (Verdery and Laqueur qtd. in Engelke 31), something that Spanish conservative discourse systematically ignores through a calculated maneuver that makes light of domestic and international calls for justice and reparation as mere "batallitas del abuelo" (García Longás) (grandpa's little war stories). Franco's exhumation provided us with a symbolic (albeit partial) closure of the arch opened in 1959 with the Valley's inauguration, but the COVID-19 pandemic (which, in spite of the chronological marker in its name, was the dominant event of the year 2020) forced us to reconsider our chronological framework toward the potential opening of a new chapter in the ways in which capitalist modernity handles death in Spain and elsewhere.

Although completed before the outset of the pandemic, the contributions in this volume establish a productive dialogue with visual and textual fictions that put the human species on the brink of extinction and understand death and transience within a post-apocalyptic framework. David Castillo and Brad Nelson's *Writing in the End Times: Apocalyptic Imagination in the Hispanic World* has explored the "massive outpouring of epochal anxiety" that exudes contemporary cultural production and media cultures, specifically in the form of an "obsession with military, epidemiological, and climate-related catastrophes" (2–3). Underneath this anxiety, there is a call to reevaluate the material conditions at the disposal of human beings to avert anthropological collapse. Part of the aesthetics germane to an end-of-times mentality escapes materiality-focused frameworks and threatens to invisibilize the disproportionate impact of mortality on specific population segments. As Judith Butler says

> Whose lives are cut short more easily? Whose lives are plunged into a greater sense of transience and early mortality? . . . [A] commitment to equality and justice would entail addressing at every institutional level the differential exposure to death and dying that currently characterizes the lives of subjugated peoples and the precarious, often as the result of systematic racism or forms of calculated abandonment. (47–48)

Silencing an investigation into "whose death?" under a desperate "we are all going to die!" the apocalyptic imagination becomes profitable entertainment and wastes the force of its specific vocabulary. In the twenty-first century, terms like emergency, rescue, or survival are reduced to a banal decoy for marketable simulacra of catastrophic experiences in the form of escape rooms and fitness-type survival races that trivialize the real plight of migrants and refugees escaping necropolitical horror.

This Volume

It may seem that what Claudio Lomnitz described as the cottage industry dedicated to the history of death, which started in the 1970s to engage in a critique of the Western denial of death, its disenchanting medicalization, and its invisibility, has ended, as we have already seen, in Thomas Laqueur's vindication of the new forms of re-enchantment and John Troyer's work on the ways in which technology makes the dead visible in distinctly modern ways. The academic devotion to death that starts in the field of anthropology around the same time, on the other hand, has produced powerful insights that still may help us today to understand the cultures of death in contemporary Spain. A number of foundational monographs and collections are useful here, including Maurice Bloch's *Placing the Dead: Tombs, Ancestral Villages, and Kinship Organization in Madagascar* (1971), Richard Huntington and Peter Metcalf's *Celebrations of Death: The Anthropology of Mortuary Ritual* (first version published in 1978), and *Death and the Regeneration of Life*, a volume edited by Maurice Bloch and Jonathan Parry in 1982. As Bloch and Parry explain in their introduction,

> with [Robert] Hertz we share a concern with the social implications of mortuary practices, though not his view of society as an entity acting for itself. If we can speak of a reassertion of the social order at the time of death, this social order is a product of rituals of the kind we consider rather than their cause. In other words, it is not so much a question of Hertz's reified "society" responding to the "sacrilege" of death, as of the mortuary rituals themselves being an occasion for creating that "society" as an apparently external force. (6)

It is not a matter of whether death has become invisible or not, secularized for better or worse, but of understanding the ways in which cultural, religious, and political work around death shapes society.

These projects largely build on Robert Hertz's essay "A Contribution to the Study of the Collective Representation of Death" (originally published in 1907), at the beginning of which he observes, "[t]he body of the deceased is not regarded like the carcass of some animal: specific care must be given to it and correct burial" (28). The fact that the flesh of the deceased is a corpse, that it demands care, and a kind of burial that fits predetermined patterns and satisfies a priori conditions, generates a constellation of material and symbolic practices that are crucial for any given society. As Maurice Bloch points out in *Placing the Dead*, "[b]urial in a tomb is the ultimate criterion of membership" (45). He is talking about the Merina people of Madagascar, but it is not difficult to see who gets buried where, and maybe more important, who is allowed to be buried where, is one important criterium for group-formation in many societies. The territories of the different Merina communities are defined by these tombs, and, once again, it is not hard to see the community- and nation-building role of all kinds of funerary constructions. Even more important, among the Merina, "the placing of the corpse in its ancestral tomb is the final act of atonement by at last transforming the social being into an actor in the imaginary society of the ancestors" (216). Inclusion of the dead in proper places of interment according to appropriate rites constantly reshapes the transhistorical community the dead and the living are part of, as the properly buried body of an individual endows them with the required cultural authority to become an actor (however minimal their actual importance might be) in a tradition that is reconfigured with each new addition.

Death is not the end, at least not for the living, but just the beginning of a very specific kind of cultural work. As Huntington and Metcalf remark, "Death is a transition. . . . Death relates to life: to the recent life of the deceased, and to the life he or she has procreated and now leaves behind. . . . Life continues generation after generation, and in many societies it is this continuity that is focused upon and enhanced during the rituals surrounding a death" (93). Death brings about a disruption with no possible solution for those who die, but the funerary practices of a given society may feed on that death precisely to foster a fantasy of continuity, impose a sense of stability, and overall work to maintain and extend the status quo.

If the analysis of funerals, burials, and other mortuary rites is still fruitful after the work of Bloch and Parry and Metcalf and Huntington, anthropological work on death has gone significantly beyond these points of interest, as Matthew Engelke has shown in a monumental overview of four decades of academic production on the topic (30). He finds the topic roughly framed by two main interests. First, how life persists: that is, funerals, mortuary rituals, grief and mourning, and other forms of conquering death and maintaining continuities (30). The second is what he calls "the brute stuff of death itself—above all . . . the corpse and its iconical and indexical forms (from statues, to organs, to shrunken heads)" (30). At the center of these works, Engelke finds out that "it is the body that matters," a trend that he traces back to Hertz (30). In general, as he shows, many fruitful anthropological studies based on Hertz are defined by "the centrality of a concern with materiality" (31). And, we may add, in this they follow Hertz's original insight when the French anthropologist points out, "The material on which the collective activity will act after the death, and which will be the object of the rites, is naturally the very body of the deceased" (83). Collective representations, feelings, anxieties, and cultural work about the dead begin, but not end, with the individual corpse. The matter of death includes not only dying and dead flesh, but the embodied symbolism of rituals (along with, of course, all kinds of material props, settings, and financial demands and obligations that those rituals imply), and all varieties of tangible remains of the passing of an individual (from their bones and other material remains in places of interment to all kinds of funerary commemorations, which may involve one individual or a whole class of people). The self may vanish into an unaccounted realm or just mere nothingness, but the materiality of death is very much with us, compelling us to ask the kind of questions that we try to answer here.

RITE

A stylized embodied performance of an idea, a behavior that gets supplemented and read along the lines of the transcendent, ritual is a notoriously difficult concept to pinpoint in precise terms. At the same time, once endowed with the very idea of ritual, an observer can identify/construct all kinds of social and individual practices as ritualistic, thus opening up the concept and thereby turning it both more present and abstract at the same time. As Lauren Ristvet puts it in regard to a context extremely far away from contemporary Spain, "ritual and politics are realized through the physical world, making an analysis of material culture necessary to understanding their operation" (3). The essays in this section consider the material realities in which death and ritual intersect in contemporary Spanish culture. As they perform cultural work around the departed, and therefore are built upon lives that now are only past, the ritual processes under examination here can be considered efficacious in more than one way. Sometimes, the productivity of these rituals consists precisely in its lack of an intended effect, in their failure. Sometimes, the way the collective imagines a new future for itself and a new fantasy of unity is precisely by ab-jecting the officiants of these death-related rituals. And sometimes, as with the beatifications and canonizations performed by the Catholic Church, the future imagined for oneself relies on the continuation of an authoritarian past that destroyed all futures that were not included in a very narrow script. In one way or another, by engaging with the past, those involved in these rituals open up possible futures for themselves and others thanks to the dead. In that sense, they seem to adjust to Marc Augé's insight that "ritual is focused on the future, and the emotion attached to its celebration is born of the feeling that it has succeeded in bringing something into being, that it has produced a beginning" (21). Encoded as an actual effect or as the hope for it, the future in the ritual is conjured up in and through the material conditions of its making.

In an essay published in the late 1950s, Albert Camus argued that the death sentence is a ritual act that does not cancel the disruption of the original crime, because "far from making amends for the harm done to the social body, adds a new blot to the first one" (132). State-sanctioned murder stands as a public performance of restoration of order while effectively extending the dissolution of the community. As a result, executioners are officiants of a complex ritual to which society may react in contradictory ways. In "Executioners and Cultures of Capital Punishment in Franco's Spain (1959–1975)," Ana Fernández-Cebrián explores how the Francoist cultures of the death penalty were constructed in José Luis Berlanga's film *El verdugo* (1963) and two nonfictional works: Daniel

Sueiro's book *Los verdugos españoles* (1971) and Basilio Martín Patino's documentary *Queridísimos verdugos* (1971–1977). The figure of the Spanish executioner is a sinister double of Francisco Franco, the head of state, and the essay explores the theological-political immunitary discourse upon which Franco the sovereign and state executioners become bound to one another. In the context of the *desarrollismo* project that starts in 1959, however, these works emphasize what Fernández-Cebrián describes as "the lumpenproletariat lives of the executioners." By looking into the material conditions of these ritualized performances of state power, Fernández-Cebrián shows how these executioners are abject figures shunned by a society that unites around the exclusion of these figures as much as around their unacknowledged inclusion as guarantors of the established political order through the ritualized death they dispense.

On the opposite side, the allure of tourism was instrumental in the dictatorship's multi-pronged effort to seek international legitimacy of its brutal regime, mainly through marketable forms of otherness and difference with deeply entrenched ideological foundations. As Luis Martín-Estudillo concisely puts it, "From romantic-era stereotypes about Spain's orientalist allure to dicta about its citizens' incapacity for achieving orderly self-governance, an array of notions emphasizing the country's eccentricity vis-à-vis Europe were used to validate National-Catholic authoritarianism" (75). In "State of Crucifixion: Tourism, Holy Week, and the Sacred Politics of the Cold War," Eugenia Afinoguénova explores how in the 1960s, the Francoist regime made of the rituals of the Holy Week precisely an example of this conjunction of self-othering and the capitalist logic of the tourist industry. Around the Passion of Jesus, the Ministry of Information and Tourism built a strategy to attract Northern European and American consumers of exciting and exotic images of Spanish Catholic belatedness. In her essay, Afinoguénova explores how Manuel Fraga Iribarne encouraged local authorities to get their Holy Week festivities certified as "Fiesta de Interés Turístico" (Celebration of Interest for Tourism), thereby fully entering the economic and political project of *desarrollismo* by making themselves eligible to receive State funding and advertising. In Afinoguénova's words, "the Holy Weeks were transformed into a very particular tourism product, tailored to facilitate Spain's coming out to the global political arena at the time of the Cold War." Local ritual celebrations of the most sacred of deaths, the death of Christ, were strategically recruited and re-signified to provide pleasant experiences to modern, sophisticated, and cosmopolitan tourist-consumers, as part of a program to infuse Franco's National-Catholic regime with a new life.

In "Carlos Saura: Death, Orphanhood, and the Commoners' Transition," Angel Loureiro looks at three films produced right before and after Franco's death. Through an analysis of the role of death in *La prima Angélica* (1974), *Cría cuervos* (1976), and *Elisa, vida mía* (1977), Loureiro explores what he calls "the commoners' Transition": that is, the ways in which individuals took stock of their past and came to envision a future that escaped the script of the Francoist regime. These films revolve around the ways in which a child deals with the literal or symbolic death of a parent and, as Loureiro argues, "end[s] up with a renewed determination to face their future." Rituals play a center role in these films. The plot of *La prima Angélica* revolves around the male protagonist's experience of transporting and reburying the remains of her mother, and *Cría cuervos* shows how the child protagonist uses ritual to take control over death and comes to accept her mother's passing precisely thanks to the failure of these rituals. In *Elisa, vida mía*, the titular character starts taking control over her own life by directing Calderón's *El gran teatro del mundo*, an *auto sacramental* that is centered on the deaths of the allegorical characters and the Catholic rite of the Eucharist. Escaping the authority of Calderón's ritual theater will lead Elisa to her unscripted future. In Loureiro's reading of these three films, death and complex encounters with specific rituals are what make it possible to critically engage with the past and the future.

As we, Andalusians, finalize the first draft of this introduction during the Holy Week of 2020, it is not hard to remember that at least 2,600 civilian victims of the Francoist regime lie unidentified in several mass graves in the cemetery of Andalusia's capital, Sevilla. Meanwhile, the remains of Gonzalo Queipo de Llano, the direct leader in the genocidal campaigns in Andalusia, are still buried in one of the most prominent churches in the city, the Basilica of La Macarena, and two brotherhoods of penance intimately connected to him, San Gonzalo and Santa Genoveva (named after his wife), still parade every year. These stark differences show the Spanish Catholic Church's lack of interest in addressing the state of "funerary apartheid" in Spain that Ferrándiz described above. In her essay "Martyrs and Saints of the Spanish Civil War Era: Enshrinement of the Right and Historical Memory," Elizabeth Scarlett explores the one-sidedness of the memorialization processes of the Catholic Church, which has deployed the ritualistic bureaucratic process of beatification and canonization to show its continuing allegiance to the National-Catholic side. In a classic study on the cultures of death, Maurice Bloch finds out something that can be extrapolated to another context: funerary rites of passage "act out the relation between the ideal unchanging society and the flux of the actual society" (138). Scarlett finds that a similar tension is at the heart of the strategies of the Church, which tries to intervene in a rapidly changing Spanish contemporary society by invoking the eternal values of a transcendental Catholic Spain. In her essay, Scarlett also shows how rituals such as the 2007 beatification mass to commemorate the deaths of the so-called Martyrs of the Spanish Civil War has material consequences beyond the bureaucratic dealings of the Church. The essay makes this tolerance for authoritarianism even more glaring through the contrast with the much more subdued public memorialization of the victims of the Francoist political violence.

For anyone familiar with the historical role of the Catholic Church in the political cartographies of nationalism in the Iberian Peninsula, it does not come as a complete surprise that its leaders in the Basque and Navarra regions made a public announcement days after the terrorist group ETA had completely disbanded on April 16, 2018. In their announcement, Catholic authorities including five bishops and one archbishop publicly admitted to "complicidades, ambigüedades, omisiones . . . por las que sinceramente pedimos perdón" (Bilboko) (acts of complicity, ambiguity, omission . . . for which we sincerely ask for forgiveness) (the ellipsis is in the original). In this complex landscape of death, forgiveness, and reconciliation, Annabel Martín's "The Future of the Dead: Reconciliation in Post-ETA Euskadi" introduces death as the third party in our relationships with our loved ones and wonders what laws are broken when "one sits at the vertex reserved for Death." Martín's essay focuses on the Nanclares de Oca prison project, which looks for civil reconciliation by sitting former members of the ETA and survivors of their victims in the presence of a mediator. Mutual listening and understanding are attempted by invoking the dead and offering them our memory. In Martín's analysis, these encounters between victimizer and victim in a highly codified space, under the eyes of an external officiant, represent a trip to the Underworld that would unlock an otherwise impossible future. The demands of the dead are met, and reparation is offered in the only possible way, by memory. In these carefully arranged and at the same time radically open dialogues, the past holds the key to the future. As Edurne Portela has written, "representar a la víctima y al perpetrador como entidades impermeables, inamovibles y dentro de un binomio claro y diferenciado no ayuda a reivindicar a la víctima sino, por el contrario, a mantenerla aislada en su diferencia radical" (124) (to represent victim and perpetrator as entities that are impervious to each other, unable to move and trapped in a clear and differentiated binary does not help to vindicate the victim, but to keep them isolated in its radical difference). By turning her eyes to the material conditions and intangible dimensions of the difficult encounters at Nanclares de Oca, Martín shows to what extent they offer an opportunity for reconciliation precisely by eliminating this stasis of victim and victimizer.

FLESH

According to Mayra Rivera, "Flesh is an ambivalent term that names a rather slippery materiality. Its propensity to change distinguishes 'flesh' from 'body.' . . . [F]lesh is conceived as formless and impermanent, crossing the boundaries between the individual body and the world. Flesh is always becoming" (2). Besides, in the Christian imagination, flesh inhabits the liminal space between belief and doubt, between truth and skepticism. Thomas the Apostle overcomes his zealous incredulity after he puts his fingers into the open wound in Christ's side, and the crucified body of Christ across centuries of Catholic art stands as a threshold between this and the other world. Seen in this light, the flesh of the dying body is the final hurdle before embracing truth and achieving salvation. There is both continuity and rupture in how Western modernity has inherited this theological mindset and secularized it into a larger political project that claims the inescapable truth of the flesh, flesh not as accessory but as necessity. As Jacques Rancière contends in *The Flesh of Words*, the meaning of God's incarnation in a mortal being and Jesus's inevitable death conjures up the act of writing, the Holy Scripture, as the salvific mechanism that fixates once and for all that sacrifice's meaning. The abstract power of the word overcomes the earthly limitations of the flesh, and the innate tendency to touch, to cling to, and to embrace the dead body is forbidden (*noli me tangere*, do not touch me). There is a moment, however, when the "entropy of interpretation," in Rancière's words, makes the sacred scripture stumble and, unable to keep the salvific power of its message intact, demands that a new sacrificial body be presented: "The truth of the suffering body of incarnation requires that there must always be a new body to sacrifice itself in order to attest to it" (84). In an inverse move from the original incarnation, the body now must go out into the world and be offered to the absurdity of self-sacrifice to become a testament to the truth of the written word.

Faced with postmodernity's endless proliferation of interpretation and the impossibility of language as a stable, closed system, flesh is again presented as a kind of antidote. "If truth in art is elusive," say the editors of *The Future of Flesh*, "truth in life and politics should not be so." And the flesh of the dead body is "the ultimate reality" that is summoned up: "The tortured, violated, victimized, racialized, or Orientalized flesh that haunts modern politics . . . is not a matter of fantasy or subjective evaluation" (Detsi-Diamanti et al. 2). The inescapable reality of the Other's dying flesh, its compelling us to act, neutralizes the yearning for an ethics beyond the flesh and the blood, and provides the dead body with a new sense of finality: "The dead body must be revered and valued, buried and kissed, because, after all, the dead body is never *only* a dead body" (2). The dead body, then, *does* do things: it reveals the vacuity behind modernity's universals (democracy, human rights, respect for life) and presents itself as truth-bearing evidence of the crimes committed in the former's name.

Flesh is the stage upon which death first performs, and this is an idea that runs throughout Patty Keller's essay "Capturing Death: Photography, Performance, and Bearing Witness." Here, the author takes the intersectionality of photography and the biopolitical to think about the radical materiality of death and notions of care in the context of contemporary culture surrounding the HIV/ AIDS epidemic. Keller's aim in her essay is twofold: to think through photography's material and conceptual relationship to death, across cultural contexts, and to parse the radical use of the medium—as documentation, as aesthetic regime, as encounter, event, performance, and action—as ever-increasingly bound up with life. After discussing the works of artist Hervé Guibert in conjunction with Jacques Derrida's *Athens, Still Remains*, and Roland Barthes's theorization of the nature of photographic medium regarding its materiality and tactility, the essay focuses on select works by Spanish artists Pepe Espaliú and Javier Codesal, in order to engage with questions about contact and the temporality of representation to explore common threads about the body, about not only the confrontation but also the signature of (and debt to) death, and the invitation to bear witness across these works.

Building on Martin Heidegger's and Jacques Lacan's concept of ex-sistence, Cristina Moreiras-Menor's essay "Death, Afterlife, and the Question of Autobiography (*Biutiful*, 2010)" is a much-needed intervention on the visual and symbolic journey that Alejandro González Iñárritu's proposes in his 2010 film *Biutiful*. Without relinquishing an urgent denunciation of the haunting effects of global capitalism in everyday urban reality, the Mexican director departs from conventional praxes of realism and forces the spectator through meticulous camerawork, composition, and photography to bear witness to, in Moreiras-Menor's words, "a revelatory perspective of being-for-death" through an enhanced material experience: an account of "ex-sistence" through "the act of walking, of traversing life, in preparation for death and accompanied by objects that help [the protagonist] prepare his transit, both in the sense of a departure as well as a survival." Some of these objects come in close contact with the characters' frail skin (the ring that Uxbal bequeaths to his daughter) and terminally diseased flesh (the syringe that slowly penetrates Uxbal's flaccid arm), creating a multi-layered experience of haptic visuality. *Biutiful*'s granularity immediately calls attention to the medium's texture, and the saturated sound in the opening and closing scenes of the film (the almost touching hiss of Uxbal and his daughter's whispers, and Uxbal's father's imitation of the whirling noise of the sea and the wind) unsettle interpretive paradigms centered on the optic dimension of cinema to represent arresting moments of passing and transit. Moreiras-Menor's analysis precisely moves beyond the all-too-visible readings of the film: the sociological critique, the spiritual journey, the historical situatedness, or the anthropological collapse of community "are already so clearly in sight for all to see." As interpretive frameworks that *Biutiful* wishes to relay almost explicitly, they risk turning the film into "a narrative-report on the end of a reality that is overwhelmingly present in our contemporary experience." For Moreiras, the film's radical political reason lies elsewhere, in the displaced locus of an after-image where transience and trace coexist.

The most uncanny moments in *Biutiful* happen almost without notice, when reflections in mirrors and glasses dissociate themselves from their carnal originals and acquire a life of their own. A gateway to the underworld, mirrors, turn Uxbal's reflection into a moving crystallization toward his own death while also translating in aesthetic terms the moral duty to accommodate the voices of the departed. Mirrors also play a key role in Daniel García-Donoso's analysis of Fernando León's cinematic language in his essay "What Do We Do with the Dead? The Posthumous in Fernando León's *Amador*." The film places at its very center the dead body of an elderly man who dies peacefully at home while being cared for by an immigrant domestic worker, putting a mirror up to a series of social issues in twenty-first-century Spain: the dependence of the elderly and the importance of their pensions, which indirectly subsidized unemployed families in the crisis; the country's aging population coupled with the European Union's lowest birth rate, and the indispensable need for immigrant labor. But mirrors in *Amador* are also liminal spaces, material surfaces where cinema and photography meet to recognize in each other, and portals where life and death communicate. Jean Cocteau, whose cinematic obsession with death and mirrors is arguably one of León de Aranoa's inspirations in his film, put it in the following terms through one of his characters: "I will reveal to you the secret of secrets. . . . Mirrors are the portals through which death comes and goes. Moreover, if you look at yourself in a mirror your entire life you will see death at work, like bees in a glass hive" (qtd. in Herbert 166). For Marcela, the work of care is indistinguishable from the work of mourning, which is experienced and portrayed as a posthumous life with the dead other, which is also the dead self. Beginning with a discussion of Marina Garcés's theory of *conditio posthuma*—that existential condition imposed by a cultural imagination that sentences the contemporary subject to wait passively for the human species to go extinct—García-Donoso explores how the posthumous in León de Aranoa yields a vibrant material world. Diametrically opposed to the spectacular Hollywood techniques that joyfully fixate the cinematic gaze in anthropological collapse, the director's craft of death leads ultimately to a commentary on the haptic experience of cinema, the foundational haunting of cinematic art by the photographic still.

Interestingly, the actor who plays Amador in León de Aranoa's film (Celso Bugallo) is also the one playing the elderly, Alzheimer's-ridden Kilian who dies at the end of *Palmeras en la nieve* (2015), one of the films N. Michelle Murray analyzes in her essay "On Dying Colonialisms and Postcolonial Phantasies in Recent Spanish Cinema." As the author herself states elsewhere, the well-frequented trope of the death of nationals in films dealing with colonial and postcolonial subject matters "invoke the regeneration of a diverse Spain" (48); and the political implications of the spaces where these deaths happen, as well as who dies and how, matter. In *Palmeras* and *1898: Los últimos de Filipinas* (2016), death takes place not in the decaying home of an elderly man in a Spanish working-class neighborhood, but in "the distanced realm of the colony as a death-space," a spatiotemporal configuration that "facilitates self-definition and transformation" when seen within the context of an identity crisis following the financial and political meltdown of the late 2000s–early 2010s. Murray's critique of the identity mechanisms deployed in two twenty-first-century high-budget films depicting Spain's colonial rule in the Philippines and Equatorial Guinea deconstructs the morphing attributes of the necropolitical and its uncritical commemoration in contemporary culture. Through a sustained commentary of Foucault's biopower and Mbembe's necropolitics, Murray's reading of the films' deeply problematic portrayal of the colonized's body and flesh sets the ground for an encompassing theorization of necropolitical representation in contemporary Spain. *Últimos* and *Palmeras* embody nationalistic clichés of the abandoned soldier and the rhetoric of good versus bad colonialism, and partake in the "spectacle of pain inflicted on the slave's body," making "slave life . . . a death-in-life" (Mbembe 21).

STONE

"Stone is primal matter, inhuman in its duration. Yet despite its incalculable temporality, the lithic is not some vast and alien outside. A limit-breaching intimacy persistently unfolds," muses Jeffrey J. Cohen in *Stone: An Ecology of the Inhuman* (2). The posthumous existence of the body is envisioned as the evacuation of the flesh and its transformation into ashes, or bones, or dust. The embrace of stone, either intimate (in the form of niche, monument, or carved surface) or grotesque (as a massive cross lording a former slave labor camp in the outskirts of Madrid) comes to stand for that vanishing of what was alive and has entered the incalculable temporality that Cohen describes. We are using stone here as a shorthand for the inhuman materiality that exists in a time of its own, as it shapes and is shaped by the cultures of death. It is in this general sense that the nonhuman temporality of stone comes to define a human necrogeography.

At first sight, the necrogeography of modernity is defined by the creation of the cemetery, and the move away from churchyard burying is a key historical process in modernity's attempt to effectively separate the dead body from the realm of the living. Establishing what Laqueur calls "the new regime of the dead," the consolidation of the modern cemetery in early nineteenth-century Europe was the most visible form of spatialization behind a complex set of legislative action seeking to remove from the hands of the Church its centuries-long sovereignty over the dead. With its "promise of liberty, landscaping, and cosmopolitanism" (161), the cemetery was a novel space that translated into architectural terms the secular gospel of modernity, whereby the dead body was stripped of its tradition-ally superstitious power over the living and "a newly configured idolatry of the dead served the interests less of the old God of religion than of the new gods of memory and history: secular gods" (212). But if that era largely starts with the new cemetery in New Haven, Connecticut, David Charles Sloane reminds us that, at the turn of the twenty-first century, "[w]e have seen the emergence of natural burying grounds that reject pesticides and embalming fluids, the development of the World Wide Cemetery and other virtual cemeteries, and the proliferation of everyday memorials for celebrities and ordinary people alike" (10). Society-sanctioned necrogeographies are constantly being negotiated and redefined by cultural shifts and material developments, the inhuman temporality of the silicon in semiconductors in online servers now embracing the dead as much as the marble and granite of conventional burial sites. But the territories of the dead go beyond the cemeteries and crematoria in which the bodies of private citizens are disposed of, and the state and community monuments in which the dead are put to work for political ends. In twentieth- and twenty-first-century Spain, along with other necrogeographies in which death is rendered a secret (such as the water border of the Mediterranean), we need to consider all the unmarked graves filled with the victims of the National-Catholic violence. In the context of battles over historical memory in contemporary Spain, Joan Ramon Resina reminds us that

the grave is not so much a transitional space to objectivize mourning and heal loss as a rupture that, under certain circumstances, reminds people of a discontinu-ity in the political order. A breach opens in the foundations of the polis when the state hinders the expression of the rupture that death brings about in the everyday and the familiar, when the state, that is, undermines the grave's function as a place of memory. (21)

In the following essays, the authors explore how the materiality of death fosters and thwarts memory in and through the lawfully regulated cemetery, and in and through the complete dissolution of the law in the mass graves left by the necropolitics of Francoism. In "A Stone that Makes Them Stumble: Mining the Lithic in Manuel Rivas's *O lapis do carpinteiro*," William Viestenz applies Jeffrey J. Cohen's ideas on stone, Bruno Latour's theories on nonhuman agency, and René Girard's understanding of the Christian concept of the *skandalon* to read Rivas's novel, published in 1998. Stone operates against and beyond the finitude of human flesh and its death; as Viestenz explains, "stone is a means of inscription and instigator of memory." Focusing not only on the stone of which the Falcona Prison and the Pórtico da Gloria façade of the Cathedral of Santiago de Compostela are made, but also on the graphite of the murdered carpenter's pencil that gives the title to the novel, Viestenz explores how stone works in the novel as a "lithic provocation" and therefore must be as agentive as human subjects. Stone and humans become entangled in reciprocal ways that go beyond humanist distinctions between human subject and lifeless object. In the context of death and memory, it also works as a *skandalon*, which must be read as a stumbling stone that at different moments in the novel prevents both an easy transition to a post-Francoist future and disrupts the smooth operation of the Francoist genocidal machine. As one of us has explained elsewhere, "[l]a imaginación religiosa que se invoca en *El lápiz del carpintero* se caracteriza por explotar una filosofía católica de la representación que enfatiza lo sensible y material como mecanismo de agitación del lector" (García-Donoso 222) (the religious imagination that is invoked in *O lapis do carpinteiro* exploits a Catholic philosophy of representation that puts emphasis on the sensible and the material as a mechanism to stir the reader). In Viestenz's lithic reading of the operations of death in this novel, Rivas's seemingly Catholic emphasis on materiality ends up precisely allowing the articulation of political alternatives to the Catholic Church–sponsored violence of the Francoist regime. Viestenz's reading of the stumbling stone in Rivas's novel offers parallels to the European project named *Stolpersteine*, or, literally, "stumbling stones": small brass plaques installed on the pavement in front of the last residence of victims of Nazi violence before they were forced into exile, killed, or taken to ghettos and concentration camps. As Alícia Hernàndez-Grande describes them in a fascinating essay, "*Stolpersteine* are generally unassuming. They can blend into the pavement yet also bring renewed focus and attention to past violence whose impact still exists today. When a pedestrian stops at a stone, they interrupt the daily motion of the street, and in that moment . . . create a memorializing performance that evokes the missing body of the concentration camp victim" and, as it was intended, "disrupts public space" (6). In the case of the "stumbling stones" installed in the Catalan town of Manresa to memorialize Spanish Republicans sent to Nazi camps, the performance of the pedestrian goes from memorializing the individual to a condemnation that "collapses a distinction between Nazism and Francoism" (6).

A cursory look at Spain's modern history of mortal remains reveals the continuities and discontinuities with respect to the master narrative that Laqueur delineates above. The passing in 1787 of Carlos III's royal ordinance banning traditional burial in churches and urging local authorities to build cemeteries outside municipal limits is often seen as a turning point in the nation's funeral history, and a decisive step toward the secularization of death and the commemoration of the deceased. The truth, however, is that the new law still took several decades to become a reality and, by the time it could be properly enforced, the Catholic Church had already gained the battle over who had legitimate control to manage public death within a new political, social, and economic scenario. The deep ties between ecclesiastical and state powers facilitated a hierarchical segregation of death, clearly separating the main Catholic burial ground from the civil cemetery, a second-class space often in abominable conditions or simply abandoned (Martorell Linares 662–63). In "Encounters between Memories and the Present: The Muslim Cemeteries in Contemporary Spain," Jordi Moreras and Sol Tarrés explore the history and present of Spanish Muslim cemeteries as a way to tackle the "funeral otherness" that was a part of the Spanish state-approved necrogeography for more than a century after the new burial regime was implemented. As they show, some of those Muslim cemeteries are a seemingly paradoxical heritage of the Civil War and National-Catholicism. However, as Eric Calderwood reminds us, during the Civil War and the dictatorship, there was "a vast propaganda effort to represent Franco and his government as allies of Islam, not only in Morocco but also throughout the Arab world" (143). As Moreras and Tarrés show in their analysis, the situation that Muslims experience in Spain in the present is defined by a complex set of historical traditions and what at first sight may seem remarkable contradictions.

As Susan Stewart has recently argued, "Anomalies in the landscape of the present, ruins are the architectural equivalent of the syntactical *anacoluthon*, or non sequitur. They do not follow or precede—they call for the supplement of further reading, further syntax" (2). If the ruin is the counterpart of the brand-new building, one may wonder to what extent mass graves are the unacknowledged counterpart of the State-built monument in the necrogeography of Spain, and to what extent mass graves are as much an invitation for a supplement as ruins. Digging in the ground and uncovering human remains demand and foster stories, testimonies, and memory practices that try to do justice to those victims of political violence and the Francoist and post-Francoist funerary apartheid. In "The Forensic Eulogy: Science and Invented Traditions in the Commemoration of Republican Dead from the Spanish Civil War," Layla Renshaw examines the ways in which communities represent the victims of National-Catholic violence during the collective ceremonies in which these remains are re-interred in local cemeteries. The encounter with the mass grave and the human remains produces what Renshaw calls "a representational vacuum" that sometimes is filled by what she conceptualizes as "the 'forensic eulogy,' in which the scientific analysis of the dead becomes a form of expressing post-mortem care for the dead." The materiality of the remains and the forensic instruments and practices used to recover them supplements and is supplemented by the memory practices the community engages in to remember its victims.

Finally, in Pedro Aguilera-Mellado's essay "De-Metaphorization of 'the Other' in the Wake of Modern Biopolitics: A Reading of Jesús Carrasco's *La tierra que pisamos*," Carrasco's novel exemplifies and goes beyond Francisco Ferrándiz's point that "mass graves can be understood as a sophisticated technology for the production of terror, with effects in the short, medium, and as we see now, long term" (*El pasado* 108). In the novel, the mass grave and the bodies, dead and alive, that burn in the pyre ignited by the army of the Empire offer the most forceful example of Carrasco's reflection on finitude and his denunciation of the theological-political systems that fuel and justify genocide and the secret, unacknowledged, denied necrogeography that genocidal regimes leave behind and found themselves upon. Aguilera-Mellado's essay ends with the assertion that "the highest risk of disappearance is the disappearance of death itself, in which the biopolitical and necropolitical controls over life unveil their own extremities and limits." In the end, in his reading of *La tierra que pisamos*, the materiality of death, the mass graves, and the human remains that stay unseen may provide the opening for the invention of the impossible.

Coda

To end at the beginning, let us ask ourselves once again, what was death like in 1600? Carlos Eire argues that in pre-Enlightenment Catholic Europe, death was the moment when salvation was decided and, as a result, "death was the unique moment, common to all, when the Church could make the ultimate claim over each individual and over society as a whole; it was arguably the consummate Catholic experience, the ultimate expression of a society's beliefs, and also the ultimate opportunity for shaping and controlling a society's behavior" (5). The material and symbolic monopoly of the Church over death was clear, and this monopoly was precisely a cornerstone of the power of the Church. As Matthew Engelke reminds us, scores of studies show that questions about who owns the dead and who gets to preside over funerals are intimately linked to questions of sovereignty, authority, and necropolitics (36). In the summer of 2020, when the first wave of the COVID-19 pandemic was declared over ("Hemos derrotado al virus" [We have defeated the virus], said President Pedro Sánchez in a public appearance), the Spanish Catholic Church tried to reclaim its former monopoly by scheduling a solemn mass for the dead. King Felipe VI accepted the invitation to preside over the strictly Catholic event and made sure that the mass was widely attended by all sorts of domestic institutional figures, which was seen by many as a form of boycott by the Church of the state ceremony scheduled for the following week (Bastante). The state *homenaje* (homage) to the tens of thousands of victims of the disease took place outside of the Royal Palace (a mere one hundred meters from the Almudena Cathedral, where the Catholic mass was hosted) and was also presided over by the royal family, but this event had a resolutely civil and nonconfessional character. Attendants sat in chairs placed in a circle at the same level around a fire in a cauldron on a round pedestal—an arrangement that conjured up images of eternal flames at unknown soldier monuments and the Olympic Games, all post-secular resignifications of sacred practices of remembrance and celebration. The government made very clear that this was not a funeral but "un homenaje," a ceremony to provide remembrance and company to the dead and those grieving their loss (González). And by securing the presence of some of the top representatives of the European Union, NATO, and the World Health Organization, the organizers conveyed a resounding endorsement of international cooperation and cohesion in the face of entrenched nationalism, isolationism, and science denialism.

At this self-consciously egalitarian, inclusive, nonreligious public commemoration of the dead, the extreme isolation of those dying during the first wave of the pandemic was emphasized by a frontline healthcare worker that was invited to speak. As Aroa López, a nurse at the Hospital Vall d'Hebron in Barcelona, speaking in representation of medical personnel and first respondents, put it: "Ha sido muy duro. Hemos cubierto las necesidades básicas y emocionales. Hemos sido mensajeros del último adiós para personas mayores que morían solas, escuchando la voz de sus hijos a través del teléfono. Hemos hecho videollamadas, hemos dado la mano. Y nos hemos tenido que tragar las lágrimas cuando alguien nos decía: 'no me dejes morir solo.'" (qtd. in ZML). (It has been very hard. We have attended to the basic needs of the patients and their emotional needs as well. We have been the messengers of the last farewell of old people that died alone, listening to the voices of their children on the phone. We have made videocalls, we have held people's hands. And we have had to hide our own tears when someone told us, 'Don't let me die alone.'"). The ways in which the living pass away and are remembered by those still alive have been radically altered by the material conditions in which these events take place in the midst of the devastation brought about by COVID-19.

In the Spain of the pandemic of 2020, individuals and communities fight death in isolation. Different public constituencies and institutions compete to define the handling of death and memory, putting the dead to work toward different political, cultural, and religious ends. Neoliberal governance is necropolitical governance, as it decides, in the name of an almost divine economic mandate, which lives should be protected and which ones are expendable: the elderly, and especially those living in nursing homes, manual workers in precarious jobs, and migrant communities falsely accused of spreading the virus while deliberately targeted for "selective lockdowns" (Minder). Regional governments in the hands of the so-called *constitucionalistas* parties quickly lift up lockdown measures to favor economic "recovery," thus ignoring Article 43 of the Spanish Constitution, which declares that the state must devote itself to protecting the health of the public. And all this struggle over who lives and who dies, defined by struggles in the field of modern biopolitics and the implementation and resistance to neoliberal economics, ends up in practices, uses, and protocols that combine many layers of remaining and reinvented forms of (re)enchantment and yearned-for connection, as we can hear in the account delivered by a nurse in front of a flickering flame. Death *now* is not what it was then, not indeed. But death is never simple.

NOTES

1.   Unless otherwise noted, translations are ours.

WORKS CITED

Alexander, Keith L., and Michelle Boorstein. "Covid-19 Has Forced Local Families, Funeral Directors to Rethink Final Goodbyes." *Washington Post*, 24 Mar. 2020.

Aragüete-Toribio, Zahira. *Producing History in Spanish Civil War Exhumations: From the Archive to the Grave*. Palgrave Macmillan, 2017.

Ariès, Philippe. *The Hour of Our Death*. Translated by Helen Weaver, Knopf, 1981.

———. *Western Attitudes toward Death: From the Middle Ages to the Present*. Translated by Patricia M. Ranum, Marion Boyars, 1976.

Augé, Marc. *The Future*. Verso, 2012.

Bastante, Jesús. "La intrahistoria del 'no funeral de Estado' de los obispos y los reyes." *elDiario.es*, 9 Jul. 2020.

Beilin, Katarzyna, and William Viestenz. "Introduction. Ethics of Life: Contemporary Iberian Debates." *Ethics of Life: Contemporary Iberian Debates*, edited by Katarzyna Beilin and William Viestenz, Vanderbilt University Press, 2016, pp. ix–xxxiv.

Beusterien, John, and Constance Cortez. "Introduction: The Politics of Remembrance." *Death and Afterlife in the Early Modern Hispanic World*, edited by John Beusterien and Constance Cortez, *Hispanic Issues On Line*, vol. 7, 2010, pp. 1–9.

Bilboko Elizbarrutia / Diócesis de Bilbao. "Los obispos de Navarra, el País Vasco y Bayona ante la declaración de ETA." *Bizkeliza.org*, 20 Apr. 2018.

Bloch, Maurice. *Placing the Dead: Tombs, Ancestral Villages, and Kinship Organization in Madagascar*. Seminar Press, 1971.

Bloch, Maurice, and Jonathan Parry. "Introduction: Death and the Regeneration of Life." *Death and the Regeneration of Life*, edited by Maurice Bloch and Jonathan Parry, Cambridge University Press, 1982, pp. 1–44.

Bloom, Clive. "Introduction to the Gothic Handbook Series: Welcome to Hell." *The Palgrave Handbook of Contemporary Gothic*, edited by Clive Bloom, Palgrave Macmillan, 2020, pp. 1–28.

Boret, Sébastien Penmellen, Susan Orpett Long, and Sergei Kan. "Introduction." *Death in the Early Twenty-First Century: Authority, Innovation, and Mortuary Rites*, edited by Sébastien Penmellen Boret, Susan Long, and Sergei Kan, Palgrave Macmillan, 2017, pp. 1–27.

Butler, Judith. *Notes toward a Performative Theory of Assembly*. Harvard University Press, 2015.

Calderwood, Eric. *Colonial Al-Andalus: Spain and the Making of Modern Moroccan Culture*. Harvard University Press, 2018.

Camus, Albert. "Reflections on the Guillotine." *Resistance, Rebellion, and Death*, translated by Justin O'Brien, Modern Library, 1963, pp. 132–79.

Castillo, David, and Brad Nelson. "The Poetics and Politics of Apocalyptic and Dystopian Discourses." *Writing in the End Times: Apocalyptic Imagination in the Hispanic World*, edited by David Castillo and Brad Nelson, *Hispanic Issues On Line*, vol. 23, 2019, pp. 1–15.

Cohen, Jeffrey J. *Stone: An Ecology of the Inhuman*. University of Minnesota Press, 2015.

Coleman, Jeffrey. *The Necropolitical Theater: Race and Immigration on the Contemporary Spanish Stage*. Northwestern University Press, 2020.

Congostrina, Alfonso L. "Empresas funerarias al límite: 'Ya no hay tiempo para fabricar ataúdes nobles.'" *El País*, 3 Apr. 2020.

DeGrazia, David. "The Definition of Death." *Stanford Encyclopedia of Philosophy*, 26 Oct. 2007, rev. ed. 9 Aug. 2016.

Delibes, Miguel. *USA y yo*. 1966. Odyssey Press, 1970.

Derrida, Jacques. *Aporias*. Translated by Thomas Dutoit, Stanford University Press, 1993.

Detsi-Diamanti, Zoe, Katerina Kitsi-Mitakou, and Effie Yiannopoulos. "Toward the Futures of Flesh: An Introduction." *The Future of Flesh: A Cultural Survey of the Body*, edited by Zoe Detsi-Diamanti, Katerina Kitsi-Mitakou, and Effie Yiannopoulos, Palgrave Macmillan, 2010, pp. 1–15.

Eire, Carlos. *From Madrid to Purgatory: The Art and Craft of Dying in Sixteenth-Century Spain*. Cambridge University Press, 1995.

Engelke, Matthew. "The Anthropology of Death Revisited." *Annual Review of Anthropology*, vol. 48, 2019, pp. 29–44.

Fernández de Alba, Francisco. *Sex, Drugs, and Fashion in 1970s Madrid*. University of Toronto Press, 2020.

Ferrándiz, Francisco. *El pasado bajo tierra: Exhumaciones contemporáneas de la Guerra Civil*. Anthropos, 2014.

_____. "Unburials, Generals, and Phantom Militarism: Engaging with the Spanish Civil War Legacy." *Current Anthropology*, vol. 60, no. 19, 2019, pp. S62–S76.

Fuente Lafuente, Ismael. "El movimiento del 'caballo.'" *El País*, 14 Apr. 1984.

García-Donoso, Daniel. *Escrituras postseculares: Sedimentos de la religión en la narrativa española (1950–2010)*. Biblioteca Nueva, 2018.

García Longás, José Ángel. "La batalla del abuelo." *Público*, 28 Aug. 2016.

García Lorca, Federico. "Teoría y juego del duende." *Prosa*, Alianza Editorial, 1969, pp. 169–89.

González, Miguel. "Esta ceremonia no es un funeral." *El País*, 16 Jul. 2020.

Herbert, James D. *Paris 1937: Worlds on Exhibition*. Cornell University Press, 1998.

Hernàndez-Grande, Alícia. "Stumbling over History: *Stolpersteine* and the Performance of Memory in Spain's Streets." *Theatre Research International*, vol. 45, no. 1, 2020, pp. 4–21.

Hertz, Robert. "A Contribution to the Study of the Collective Representation of Death." *Death and the Right Hand*, translated by Rodney Needham and Claudia Needham, Routledge, 2004, 27–86.

Hockey, Jenny, Carol Komaromy, and Kate Woodthorpe. "Introduction." *The Matter of Death: Space, Place, and Materiality*, edited by Jenny Hockey, Carol Komaromy, and Kate Woodthorpe, Palgrave Macmillan, 2010.

Huntington, Richard, and Peter Metcalf. *Celebrations of Death: The Anthropology of Mortuary Ritual*. Cambridge University Press, 1991.

Jiménez, Juan Ramón. *Diario de un poeta recién casado*. 1916. Edited by Michael Predmore, 2nd ed., Cátedra, 1998.

Josephs, Allen. "The Blood of a Genius." *New York Times*, 8 Oct. 1989.

Kellaher, Leonie, Jenny Hockey, and David Prendergast. "Wandering Lines and Cul-de-sacs: Trajectories of Ashes in the United Kingdom." *The Matter of Death: Space, Place, and Materiality*, edited by Jenny Hockey, Carol Komaromy, and Kate Woodthorpe, Palgrave Macmillan, 2010, pp. 133–47.

Keller, Patricia. *Ghostly Landscapes: Film, Photography, and the Aesthetics of Haunting in Contemporary Spanish Culture*. University of Toronto Press, 2016.

_____. "The Valley, the Monument, and the Tomb: Notes on the Place of Historical Memory." *Memory and Its Discontents: Spanish Culture in the Early Twenty-First*

Century, edited by Luis Martín-Estudillo and Nicholas Spadaccini, *Hispanic Issues On Line*, vol. 11, 2012, pp. 64–86.

Labanyi, Jo. "Introduction: Engaging with Ghosts; or, Theorizing Culture in Modern Spain." *Constructing Identity in Contemporary Spain: Theoretical Debates and Cultural Practice*, edited by Jo Labanyi, Oxford University Press, 2000, pp. 1–14.

Labrador Méndez, Germán. *Culpables por la literatura: Imaginación política y contracultura en la transición española (1968–1986)*. Akal, 2017.

Laqueur, Thomas W. *The Work of the Dead: A Cultural History of Mortal Remains*. Princeton University Press, 2015.

Lezra, Jacques. "Afterword: Hispanism—*disciplina moriendi*." *Death and Afterlife in the Early Modern Hispanic World*, edited by John Beusterien and Constance Cortez, *Hispanic Issues On Line*, vol. 7, 2010, pp. 187–93.

Lofland, Lyn. *The Craft of Dying: The Modern Face of Death*. 1978. MIT Press, 2019.

Lomnitz, Claudio. *Death and the Idea of Mexico*. Zone Books, 2005.

Marías, Julián. *Los Estados Unidos en escorzo*. Emecé, 1956.

Martín, Jessica. "Despedir a un ser querido sin velatorio ni funeral: 'Es inhumano no poder abrazarse en el dolor.'" *RTVE.com*, 20 Mar. 2020.

Martín-Estudillo, Luis. *The Rise of Euroskepticim: Europe and Its Critics in Spanish Culture*. Vanderbilt University Press, 2018.

Martorell Linares, Miguel. "'The Cruellest of All Forms of Coercion': The Catholic Church and Conflicts around Death and Burial in Spain during the Restoration (1874–1923)." *European History Quarterly*, vol. 47, no. 4, 2017, pp. 657–78.

Mbembe, Achille. "Necropolitics." Translated by Libby Meinties, *Public Culture*, vol. 15, no. 1, 2003, pp. 11–40.

Minder, Raphael. "In Madrid, Covid-19 Resurgence Divides Rich and Poor." *New York Times*, 30 Sep. 2020.

Mitford, Jessica. *The American Way of Death*. Simon & Schuster, 1963.

Murray, N. Michelle. *Home Away from Home: Immigrant Narratives, Domesticity, and Coloniality in Contemporary Spanish Culture*. University of North Carolina Press, 2018.

Poltergeist. Directed by Tobe Hooper, written by Steven Spielberg, Michael Grais, and Mark Victor, performance by Jobeth Williams and Craig T. Nelson, 1982, Warner Brothers, 2008.

Portela, Edurne. *El eco de los disparos: Cultura y memoria de la violencia*. Galaxia Gutenberg, 2016.

Presidencia del Gobierno. "Decreto de 1 de abril de 1940 disponiendo se alcen Basílica, Monasterio y Cuartel de Juventudes, en la finca situada en las vertientes de la Sierra del Guadarrama (El Escorial), conocida por Cuelga-muros, para perpetuar la memoria de los caídos en nuestra Gloriosa Cruzada." *Boletín Oficial del Estado*, vol. 93, 2 Apr. 1940, p. 2240.

Rancière, Jacques. *The Flesh of Words: The Politics of Writing*. Translated by Charlotte Mandell, Stanford University Press, 2004.

Resina, Joan Ramon. *The Ghosts in the Constitution: Historical Memory and Denial in Spanish Society*. Liverpool University Press, 2017.

Ristvet, Lauren. *Ritual Performance and Politics in the Ancient Near East.* Cambridge University Press, 2015.

Rivera, Mayra. *Poetics of the Flesh.* Duke University Press, 2015.

Sloane, David Charles. *Is the Cemetery Dead?* University of Chicago Press, 2018.

Stepputtat, Finn. "Introduction." *Governing the Dead: Sovereignty and the Politics of Dead Bodies*, edited by Finn Stepputtat, Manchester University Press, 2016, pp. 3–32.

Stewart, Susan. *The Ruins Lesson: Meaning and Material in Western Culture.* University of Chicago Press, 2020.

Taussig, Michael. *The Magic of the State.* Routledge, 1997.

Troyer, John. *Technologies of the Human Corpse.* MIT Press, 2020.

Varón González, Carlos. "Excepcional patetismo: Duelo y hegemonía emocional en la España de Franco." 11 Feb. 2019, unpublished manuscript.

Viestenz, William. "Living Off the Exception: Biopolitical Modernity and *Sacratio* in Francoist Spain." *The Sacred and Modernity in Urban Spain: Beyond the Secular City*, edited by Antonio Cordoba and Daniel García-Donoso, Palgrave Macmillan, 2016, pp. 99–118.

Vovelle, Michel. *Ideologies and Mentalities.* Translated by Eamon O'Flaherty, Polity Press, 1990.

_____. *La mort et l'occident de 1300 à nos jours.* Gallimard, 1983.

ZML. "Funeral de Estado: Unidos en el recuerdo a las víctimas del covid-19." *elPeriódico. com*, 16 Jul. 2020.

Part I: Rite

CHAPTER 1

Executioners and Cultures of Capital Punishment in Franco's Spain (1959–1975)

Ana Fernández-Cebrián

Before it was banned from Spanish movie theaters after four weeks of screenings, the film *El verdugo* (The Executioner) (García Berlanga, 1963) had undergone several changes suggested by the censors after its premier at the Venice Film Festival.[1] Berlanga's black comedy, which the ambassador of Spain in Italy Alfredo Sánchez Bella called "la película más antipatriótica y antiespañola que había visto jamás" (Gómez Rufo 254) (the most anti-patriotic and anti-Spanish film [he] had ever seen), was modified for the national public in two concrete ways: "cortaron todas las veces que el protagonista hablaba de irse a trabajar a Alemania y suprimieron el ruido que hacían los hierros del garrote dentro del maletín del verdugo" (Hernández Les et al. 97) (they cut every time the protagonist spoke of leaving [Spain] to work in Germany, and they silenced the sound of the iron parts of the garrote inside the executioner's briefcase). These two elements that made the censors uneasy—the emigration of workers and the executions—had also formed part of General Francisco Franco's End-of-Year Message. In his speech, the enthusiastic announcement of the first "Plan for Economic and Social Development, 1964–67" was accompanied by a patriotic and emotive shout-out to "los que, obligados por la necesidad, han buscado trabajo fuera de las fronteras" (5) (those who, forced by necessity, have sought work beyond our borders). At the same time, the Caudillo took advantage of the opportunity to scold those who had participated that year in "pequeñas conjuras urdidas por españoles resentidos, que prefieren desprestigiar el nombre de su país a cambio de pequeños éxitos personales o de apoyos intrascendentes para su trasnochado dogmatismo" (15) (small conspiracies concocted by resentful Spaniards who prefer to sully their country's name in exchange for small personal successes or inconsequential support for their antiquated dogmatism). With these references to the activities of the opposition to the regime, the dictator avoided speaking openly of the international campaigns against the assassination by firing squad of the communist Julián Grimau, in which the Caudillo had been portrayed as "verdugo" (executioner), "fabricante de cadáveres" (maker of cadavers), and "asesino" (murderer) (Carrillo 144). Nonetheless, he was always absent at the scenes of execution except to reinforce his power with the legal authority to interrupt the right that had been transferred to the executioner via a pardon.

General Franco considered Grimau's execution an "incidente . . . difundido ampliamente y tergiversado, con el exclusivo fin de poner en entredicho el buen nombre del pueblo español" (incident . . . widely spread and distorted, with the exclusive goal of calling into question the good name of the Spanish people). In his words, "afortunadamente, los millones de extranjeros que anualmente nos visitan permiten la más eficaz demostración de cuáles son las verdaderas condiciones que imperan en el interior de nuestra Nación" (15) (fortunately, the millions of foreigners who visit us every year allow for the most effective demonstration of the true conditions that reign in the interior of our Nation). Capital punishment crystallized at that historical juncture into a complex dialectic between the sovereign power as theologico-political power that "presents itself, represents itself as the right to decree and to execute a death penalty" (Derrida, *Death I* 22), and a biopolitical regime in which new modes of governance promoted and ordered emerging forms of life.[2] During 1962 and 1963, most Spaniards enjoyed a substantial rise in income, not only as a result of the consumer spending increase, but also as a consequence of the strikes in Asturias and Barcelona (Gallo 302–3). In this sense, the deterrent exemplarity of Grimau's death sentence was a violent reprisal intended to control the working-class demands and actions in the process of economic liberalization.

The aim of this essay is to examine the figure of the executioner as not only an embodiment of sovereign power, but also as abject and marginalized subjects in Franco's Spain. As I will argue, executioners became political emblems of the Franco regime that revealed the contradictions between the violent practices of the dictatorship and the social imaginaries of developmentalism in some cultural productions of the so-called Spanish economic miracle. The sacrificial nature of the theologico-political power in which capital punishment was inscribed in

Franco's Spain had already been questioned in Ramón J. Sender's political satire *El verdugo afable* (The Affable Hangman), published in Mexico in 1952. This novel had proposed a reflection on the complicity of the national community with the political and social structures that maintained the right to kill, turning every citizen into an "usufructuario del verdugo" (290) (usufructuary of the executioner). Following the counter-enlightenment philosopher Joseph de Maistre's reflections on the executioner as the "the horror and the bond of human association" (20), Sender creates a character who chooses this profession as a way to assume this complicity in a most fruitful way. Pursuing the teachings of Quietist mysticism, the "affable" executioner chooses the path of legal murder in order to achieve atonement by receiving "el desdén de toda la sociedad" (289) (the disdain of a whole society), and by assuming an abject function that confirms that the executioner and the sovereign are of a pair. In this unique space of moral autonomy, this character considers himself the sacred agent of a liturgical activity in which the infamy of the culprit victim is transferred to the executioner, and, by that fact, the sovereign and the assembled community experience both a restoration to purity, the expiation of a crime, and a communion of sovereignty.

In the context of the announcement of the First Development Plan, Spanish citizens could feel interpellated as beneficiaries of the newfound economic opportunities while also feeling protected by the illusion of "immunity" granted by the fact that the state executioners, such as the one portrayed in Sender's novel, embodied the sovereign right to kill. However, the situation of young Spaniards was entirely different. Following a direct order of General Franco, not only in the case of the killing of Grimau (Oliver Olmo 197) but also in other executions, all male citizens might be potentially involved as executioners since the role was exercised by men who were forced to be part of a firing squad while they carried out their compulsory military service.[3] According to Roberto Esposito, the notion of immunity (or, in Latin, *immunitas*) derives from its opposite *munus*, which refers to an office—a task, obligation, duty—and harkens back to the peculiarity of the situation of some members of the community defined by its release from a common condition:

> *Immunitas* is not just a dispensation from an office or an exemption from a tribute, it is something that interrupts the social circuit of reciprocal gift-giving, which is what the earliest and most binding meaning of the term *communitas* referred to. If the members of the community are bound by the obligation to give back the *munus* that defines them as such, whoever is immune, by releasing him- or herself from the obligation, places himself or herself outside the community. (6)

In Franco's Spain, the sense of *immunitas* provided by the fact of not being one of the state executioners prevailed over the little-known common duty that involved citizens in carrying out a death sentence under military jurisdiction. The acentric character of power in which sovereignty is exercised by a civil servant who keeps society and sovereignty free of the contagion of impure violence was extended in this way into the national community that became infected by the abjection derived from the power to dole out death.

As an example of "premeditated crime" (4), capital punishment can be considered one of the experiences of aversion and revulsion that Julia Kristeva described in her foundational conceptualization of the abject in *Powers of Horror*. In her words, "any crime, because it draws attention to the fragility of the law, is abject, but premeditated crime, cunning murder, hypocritical revenge are even more so because they heighten the display of such fragility" (4). Kristeva suggests that experiences of abjection, based on the expulsion or exclusion of the unclean, the improper, and the disorderly elements of corporeal existence, have a cathartic function for the individual subject as well as society as a whole. In this sense, as a "liminal state that hovers on the threshold of body and body politic" (McClintock 72), abjection gives expression to the need to secure the fantasy of a stable and whole self and society through the performative enactment of self/other distinctions, and regulatory operations of exclusion of the "alien within."

This essay proposes that the abject condition of both state executioners and ceremonies of capital punishment offers a privileged locus of enunciation to understand the complexity of the uneven development of the economic, political, and ideological instances of the Spanish social formation in the years of the so-called *desarrollismo* (developmentalism). Every social formation, according to Louis Althusser, is at some point unevenly developed, which means that the different levels of which it is comprised have to be in contradiction with each other in order to secure its "wholeness" (204–18). In the historical conjuncture of the Spanish *desarrollismo*, contradictions between economic development and ideological "backwardness" were restructured at the political level with the implementation of recurring technocratic policies that remained embedded in a neo-feudal ideological matrix. In this way, modern modes of governance, led by the technocrats of the Opus Dei within the state apparatuses, co-existed with the theological paradigm of sovereign power that was still visible in private execution ceremonies. By examining these ceremonies and the figure of the executioner as portrayed in cultural productions of this period, this work explores how abjection associated with capital punishment became a symptom of the displacement of the theologico-political ideological practices that had put state killing at their core toward the margins of the imaginaries of modernization and progress.

The first part of this essay discusses the virtualization of scenes of execution in cinema and other mass media, arguing that the imageries that represented state executioners as invisible figures or mere technicians did not allow viewers to assume the subject position of those civil servants. In the following section, I will take as a point of departure Roger Caillois's reflections on the executioner as a "sinister double" (239) of the head of state to analyze the new social *dispositifs* that instructed citizens in the disciplinary habits of consumer capitalism in *El verdugo*. In this film, the fictional experience of a novice executioner placed viewers directly in the position of a lumpen subject who staged the traumatic enforcement of the law in order to be incorporated into the new strategy of survival for the Francoist regime, based on the benefits of consumerism. Last, I will examine the public appearances of the state executioners in two projects that paid for their testimonies: Daniel Sueiro's book *Los verdugos españoles* (The Spanish Executioners) (1971) and Basilio Martín Patino's documentary *Queridísimos verdugos* (Beloved Executioners) (1971–1977).[4] Their parallel portraits of the lumpenproletariat lives of the executioners and the executed knitted together the dimensions of personal and collective poverty with the middle-class imaginary projected during the developmentalist years, which is revealed to be sustained by the sovereign violence that the executioners embodied as legal murderers. In this way, *Queridísimos verdugos* interpellated viewers as part of the national community that rejected those civil servants in practices of social abjection, understood as "a technique . . . which in effect binds together societies and states through 'including forms of exclusion'" (Tyler). As I will argue, Patino's film delved into these logics of social abjection by exploring the dialectical relationship between the stigmatized and marginalized status of executioners and the fantasies of progress of the same social body into which they were included as the most indispensable means of establishing political order.[5]

Virtual Scenes of Capital Punishment

El verdugo begins with the shot of a prison official eating breakfast while a prisoner is executed on the other side of the door. Amadeo, an executioner played by José Isbert, places beside his mug a briefcase, and the strident sound it makes as he does this erupts into the scene to take hold of the spectators, penetrating them on a real, immediate level. The censors were especially careful to avoid the sound of the garrote, no doubt aware of García Berlanga's intention in this scene to provoke that "sensación muy de tripa que ya nos relaciona con todo lo que tiene la película de siniestro y visceral" (Cañeque and Grau 46) (very much a gut feeling that already connects us with all the sinister and visceral elements of the film). Faced with the explicit prohibition of the images related to the moment of execution, the screenwriters decided to reinforce those audible details that can be analyzed using Slavoj Žižek's interpretation of Michel Chion's notion of *rendu*: "*Rendu* is opposed to the (imaginary) simulacrum and the (symbolic) code as a third way of rendering reality in cinema: neither by means of imaginary imitation nor by means of symbolically codified representation but by means of its immediate 'rendering'" (*Looking* 40). Žižek examines this concept in order to explain how the ambiguity of the Lacanian "Real" "is not merely a nonsymbolized kernel that makes a sudden appearance in the symbolic order, in the form of traumatic 'returns' and 'answers'" (39). Rather, it will be precisely the excessive presence of these types of sounds that will permit the suspension of diegetic reality through the reproduction of the Real contained within it.

This irruption of the Real in an everyday act like eating breakfast resonates with other images that populated the collective imaginary: the dictator revising death sentences in the domestic sphere. As historian Paul Preston has confirmed, during the Civil War, Francisco Franco did indeed read and sign the death sentences of the condemned "mientras comía" (while he ate), or "tomando café antes de la siesta" (drinking coffee before the siesta) (Cerdá). Spanish citizens never saw the dictator in these situations, just as they never had access to the images of three executioners on active duty before the publication of Daniel Sueiro's *Los verdugos españoles*. In contrast to the executioners, the photographs that allowed some of the most famous condemned men and women to be identified had filled the covers of sensationalist newspapers. *El caso: Semanario de sucesos* became, from its inception in 1952, one of the most widely circulated and read newspapers thanks to its inclusion of a *crónica de sucesos* or *crónica negra*—crime news limited to one bloody crime per week—that the rest of the media left out in their eagerness to transmit an image of peace and social order (Rodríguez Cárcela 220–25). *El caso* opened a space in the public sphere in which citizens could inform themselves about homicides, the development of legal and punitive processes, and news of the celebration of executions in a documentation that went further than the brief headline "Sentence carried out" or the appearance of a black flag hoisted in the windows of prisons after executions. As Roland Barthes argued, the *sucesos* (*fait-divers*) described in sensationalist newspapers preserve the notion of ambiguity and uncertainty in the construction of its political signification (194), thus permitting the circulation of publications such as *El caso* under censorship. However, as the executioner Antonio López recalled in 1970, he and his colleagues never appeared in this kind of news: "No solamente *El caso*, sino algunos periódicos más te hablan de todo lo ocurrido, de asunto de robos y atracos, de sucesos, de todo. Ahora con la televisión y con la radio, ya te dicen también otras cosas, ¿no? pero, claro, no las cosas estas nuestras" (Sueiro 319) (not only *El caso*, but also some other newspapers tell you about everything that happened having to do with robberies and hold-ups, crimes, everything. Now with TV and the radio, they tell you other things too, right? But, of course, not about this stuff—our stuff).

The spread of these *sucesos* in what Jürgen Habermas called the "plebeian public sphere" (425) generated new accounts of the justice rituals that were also incorporated into the genres of oral poetry in the tradition of the chapbooks (*pliegos sueltos*). These folk songs continued to be transmitted during the 1960s, as demonstrated by the recitation of the narrative poem or *aleluya* "Los crímenes del Jarabo" (The Crimes of Jarabo)—which has as its protagonist the spree killer José María Jarabo—in Carlos Saura's 1960 film *Los golfos* (The Delinquents). In this poem, the formulaic description of the execution projected the shadow of the death penalty over the actions of a gang of young men as "a type of itera-tion of what happens to the wrongdoer as he (and in rare cases, she) is brought to justice" (Sinclair 974–75), an inevitable punishment following the exemplary tradition of *pliegos sueltos*.

The plot of Saura's film was similar to that of *Los atracadores* (The Robbers) (1962), directed by Francisco Rovira Beleta as an adaptation of the 1955 novel of the same title by the Falangist writer Tomás Salvador.[6] In the final scene, one of those young criminals winds up being executed in the first images on the silver screen to show how the garrote worked. The zeal with which the censors wished to suppress the references to the garrote in *El verdugo* contrasts with the enthusi-asm with which *Los atracadores* was shown in Spanish theaters. In this case, the censorship of Rovira Beleta's film took place beyond Spain's borders: it was prohib-ited in France for six years and parts were cut in the Berlin Film Festival "por respeto a la hipersensibilidad del pueblo alemán después de la guerra" (Sánchez Barba 381) (out of respect for the hypersensibility of the German people after the war). The screenings of *Los atracadores* in France and Germany had pushed past the limits of decorum by shining a public light on that which was supposed to remain secret: the onscreen staging of a killing that subverted the state's preten-sions to act as the representative of individual interests, expressed in terms of the liberal idea of dignity and human suffering. According to the bureaucratic logic of modern death, hiding the carrying out of the punishment turned the execu-tion into a mere administrative procedure that was not meant to leave any cracks through which to exhibit publicly the body of the executed man, or any images that might confront the people-as-witness with the power that condemned (Pratt 25). In this sense, the vision of this staging was the sole property of government officials who, in their double condition as spectators and performers, embodied the ability of the state to perpetuate itself through the dramatization of its *necro-power* (Mbembe 161). However, as Derrida pointed out, by becoming virtual, the spectacle of punishment continues and one should speak not simply of invisibility but of a transformation of the field of the visible "toward another modality, another distribution of the visible . . . that can even . . . extend the virtual field of the spectacular and the theatrical" (Derrida and Roudinescu 12).

Spanish censors tolerated the thanatopolitical simulacrum in *Los atracadores* by interpreting the execution as the colophon of a moralizing tale. In his report addressed to the readers of the screenplay, Rovira Beleta expressed himself in these terms: "No vamos a argumentar nosotros, en imágenes, la legitimidad o la eficacia de su aplicación. Durante siglos nadie dudó de la justicia social de la pena de muerte" (qtd. in Sánchez Barba 582) (we ourselves are not going to argue, in images, the legitimacy or the efficacy of their application. For centuries no one was doubtful of the social justice of the death penalty). And he mentioned that the film, which deals with "sucesos verídicos vividos en nuestras calles" (truthful events lived in our streets) was directed at "los jóvenes de diez y seis a veintitantos años" (young people, sixteen-year-olds to twenty-somethings) and had as its goal "cubrir la apremiante necesidad de un film que muestre a los muchachos inadaptados socialmente el final inexorable de su conducta" (582) (to fill the urgent need for a film that shows young social misfits the inexorable outcome of their behavior). While prohibited from the proscenium of the execution, the film's audiences came to share, as witnesses, the simulacrum of its staging. Despite the use of extreme close-ups that provided the viewer with a privileged look at the condemned man in the moment of his death, Rovira Beleta's adaptation avoided the most sordid details of the reality of executions in which the death of the condemned was usually a long agony.[7] In contrast with the brutality displayed in strangulations by garrote, the executioner is portrayed in this film as a technician who manipulates his work tool effectively, and the death of the condemned person takes place instantaneously. In this way, by giving viewers a taste of the experience of witnessing an execution from shot angles that can only be the subjective ones of the field of vision of the condemned man, the film did not allow them to assume the subject position of the executioner, represented as a professional who masters the technology necessary to kill with a high level of detachment.

In the 1960s and 1970s, the circulation of visual representations of executions was not limited to film, gaining traction as well in the satirical magazines of the time. This was the case of the comic strips as well as short humorous stories in the magazine *La Codorniz*, in which scenes of execution always took place somewhere far away from contemporary Spain. As Ambassador Sánchez Bella affirmed after seeing *El verdugo*, for the regime it was imperative to maintain decorum in what was represented: "Que se hable de 'humor negro' o de lo que se quiera, pero evitando por todos los medios la referencia directa a la España actual" (117) (people can talk about "black humor" or whatever they like, but only if they avoid, in every possible way, a direct reference to Spain today). From the so-called *Burgos trial* in 1970 to the last executions of the Franco regime in 1975, scenes of execution became a recurrent theme in light of the increasing number of death sentences handed down by military tribunals.[8] Comedians Chumy Chúmez, El Perich, and Gila, among others, published comic strips and illustrations in magazines such as *Hermano Lobo* or *Triunfo* in which, except for the presence of the garrote, political satire was made using various forms of executions around the world. By turning the viewing experience into a moment of citizenship, these illustrations implicated audiences as complicit agents or potential victims of the state executioner. However, far from making viewers take a position of intersubjective connectivity with singular executioners, the replicable representations of these civil servants as technicians were only politically legible as a mere extension of their thanatopolitical tools. By doing so, this imagery did not offer audiences the possibility to identify themselves with the state executioners by means of inviting empathy or anxiety toward their role within the political and economic structures from which they emerged, revealed for the first time in Berlanga's film.

Sinister Capitalism in *El Verdugo* (Luis García Berlanga, 1963)

In the spring and summer of 1963, Spaniards could see images of the head of state enjoying his vacation in athletic attire, combining his free time with the possible commutation of death sentences. In Berlanga's film, José Luis, a novice executioner who faces his first execution in Palma de Mallorca, must interrupt an unexpected vacation on the island to carry out his job.[9] This parallel image of the executioner and the head of state as tourists can be explored considering Roger Caillois's reflections in his essay "Sociology of the Executioner" (1939), in which he lays out the relationship of affinity and complementarity between the executor of sentences—an accursed part of contemporary society—and the figure of the sovereign. This role of the executioner as an embodiment of the violence of sovereign power has been examined in contemporary theoretical discourses on the structures that modern sovereignty inherits from the archaic power of the throne and the scaffold. In this sense, philosophers such as Jacques Derrida and Michel Foucault often return to Caillois's reflections on the liminal figure of the executioner (mirrored in Ernst Kantorowitz's canonical analysis on the Christological theme of bi-corporeality in the king's two bodies) as a "sinister double" (239) of the head of state, who remains untainted by the purging trans-ference of guilt and abjection in the act of the execution. In this relationship of concordance, the executioner becomes an inverted figure that, in contrast to the sovereign who collects honor and respect, leaves the sovereign the prestigious part and "takes charge of the part that is infamous" and "every form of disgust and scorn" (244, 240) derived from the horror of the physical act of the execu-tion. Attempting to continue the work of Émile Durkheim and inspired by the death of a state executioner, Caillois's notions of purity and impurity and the double meaning of the sacred based on taboo and transgression are connected with contemporary media representations of the sovereign and the executioner. In these representations, both figures appear characterized in relation to "an average man," which brings them closer to an "homogeneous mass of citizens," identified with them at the same time that they are distanced from them, trapped "in a setting either frightful or seductive" (240). Because of this, in the public appearances of the sovereign and the executioner, the French press emphasized their "bourgeois habits" (240), like the flip side of symbolic identities marked by the ritual display by both of the power to take life.

In the case of General Franco and the protagonist in Berlanga's film, the every-day image of these "bourgeois customs" was shaped in 1962 using the figure of the tourist, the emblem of the new political scripts to instruct national subjects in the disciplinary habits of consumer capitalism. The dictator's new public appearance, with his informal attire substituted for his usual military uniform, was a reminder of the relationship of those who exercise the right to punish with "the sovereign's right to make war on his enemies" (Foucault, *Discipline* 48). Nevertheless, vio-lence in acts of war was a distant reality for the generations of young people who had not bloodied their hands through the experience of killing another person, an act that according to the former executioner, José Luis's father-in-law, "is the easiest thing in the world." Despite this, although José Luis did not participate in the military violence that had founded the political order of the Franco regime, if he wishes to form part of a "prototypical success-story of the early 1960s Spain" (Mira 115), governed by the commodities of the new consumption norms, he must become an official of the very same state that guarantees the "officially protected" flat where he sustains his family, the monthly payments on his new motorcycle, and even his holidays in Mallorca.

As the young executioner approaches the fantastical illusions of consumption, his hopes of being able to cancel the moment of carrying out an execution are dashed. In this way, the circle of consumption of José Luis and his family embod-ies the surplus enjoyment (*plus-de-jouir*) through which "power 'bribes' those it holds in its sway" (Žižek, *Living* 400). As Slavoj Žižek reminds us, Jacques Lacan took the Marxist conception of surplus-value, the cause that sets in motion the capitalist process of production, as the model for his idea of the surplus-enjoyment, the object-cause of desire or *objet petit a*. Therefore, in both cases, the surplus-enjoyment "has the same paradoxical power to convert things (pleasure objects) into their opposite" (*Looking* 12). By connecting the executioner's obligation to kill with his participation in the cycles of credit, Rafael Azcona and Berlanga were able to insert the abjection associated with the institutions that produce death into the heart of the imaginaries of domesticity and private consumption.[10]

Black humor is the mechanism that the screenwriters chose to codify or distort a reality that makes visible—if only for a moment—the traumatic dimension of the Real. In this sense, the superego's order operates not only as the mechanism that regulates external obedience to the Law as an injunction, which is experienced as traumatic and cannot be integrated into the symbolic order of the subject, but also as the trigger for black humor. As Freud pointed out, the contribution to humor is made through the point of view of a superego that maintains the distance with social reality where one would not expect it (432). In the film, this distance allows for the representation of the social inclusion of the executioner into the new forms of life promoted by capitalist biopolitics at the cost of a dead body: a corpse, to which paradoxically in the Kantian sense the *poena forensis* gives as a *noumenon* dignity and honor (Kant 105–8), that has to be fiercely sacrificed to be also incorporated into the political body of the nation. In this way, the objects of the desire for material well-being become in *El Verdugo* their traumatic and abject opposites, tainted by the state killings in which the lumpenproletariat and the working classes were forced to cooperate being executioners, either as civil servants or as forced recruits participating in firing squads.

When the moment of execution arrives, José Luis cannot identify himself with the law as categorical imperative. Spectators are confronted in this way with the irrational, traumatic figure of the executioner that stages the senseless acceptance of the commands of law, being able to inhabit other subject positions as a necessary locus to understand that if the enforcement of the law were not traumatic, its authority would not be unconditional. Unlike his father-in-law, who assumes his duty as an order of the current legal code, the conversion of the young man as a subject integrated into the developmentalist city is marked by a symbolic castration that creates an unsurmountable impasse between his moral autonomy and his subjection to a job that confers upon him both the status of civil servant and certain obligations.[11] The ceremony surrounding the execution is scaffolded in *El Verdugo* upon the logic of sacrifice, the very foundation of criminal law and justice. At the end of the film, José Luis is dragged to the place of execution along with the condemned man, who represents "the sovereign exception of one who has been able to defy and contest the monopolization of violence by law" (Derrida, *Death II* 46). Using black humor as a vehicle to showcase the "deviant" performance of the apprentice executioner, Berlanga and Azcona distorted the solemn ritual framework before the strangulation by garrote. Thus, prison authorities and a priest try to persuade José Luis to perform his duty in ceremonies of hospitality that mirror the script in which the prison staff shows an unusual attentiveness for the condemned person during the final countdown hours of the death-watch. In this sense, the respectively moral and physical sacrifice of each character turns them into scapegoats whose participation in the execution ceremony reconstitutes a sovereign power that does not allow itself to be contested. The violence of state killing that is veiled behind protocols of civility and the pretense of courtesy, the sordidness of jail spaces, and the lack of experience of the unwilling executioner allow viewers to imagine the gruesome reality of a scene of execution that remains invisible in this film.

For Berlanga, José Luis ends up being a victim who, "por obtener una mínima seguridad en su vida cae en una trampa mortífera" (Hernández Les et al. 98) (in order to obtain a minimum of security in his life, falls into a death trap). Meanwhile, his father-in-law "ha pasado de víctima a tecnócrata" (98) (has gone from victim to technocrat). Defending the efficacy of his methods, the old executioner helped to reproduce the sovereign violence in the country's transition toward an economic liberalization that José Luis, too, will benefit from in his new job. Law infinitely indebts José Luis who, from now on, will be subject to the payment of his financial debts in a social formation for which he will serve as executor of the power to eliminate other lives. Meanwhile, the rest of the society, the tourists who enjoy their vacations in Mallorca, and General Franco on his yacht were all protected by the privilege of being exempt from the duty of putting to death a citizen according to law and justice.

Underdevelopment and Terror in *Queridísimos verdugos* (Basilio Martín Patino, 1973–1977)

At the end of the documentary *Queridísimos verdugos*, a man wanders through the streets of Madrid, lit with the sparkle of Christmas lights. The man is Antonio López Sierra, the executioner of the Regional Court of Madrid (Audiencia Territorial de Madrid) from 1949 to 1975. Shots of the executioner alternate with images that capture signs in shop windows and movie posters. In this visual drifting toward spaces of leisure and consumption, Antonio appears at the margins of the circulation flows of images and merchandise. From this view of the city during the late Franco period, viewers can remember the stories that Antonio and his two professional colleagues, Vicente López and Bernardo Sánchez, have told at the beginning of the film about their respective lives, which are framed within the limits of the lumpenproletariat in twentieth-century Spain. Antonio's and Vicente's social trajectories are paradigmatic cases of this lumpen population in the post-war conjuncture: after serving in the Civil War as members of the Spanish Legion, they tried to survive alternating stays in prison with jobs as itinerant street vendors and by cooperating with the police as informants. This contact with the police facilitated their obtaining of information about the announcement of executioner positions offered in 1948. In the words of Antonio López, he accepted whatever profession to escape poverty "que lo mismo me da que sea verdugo, lo que sea, en tanto me dé de comer" (because it's all the same to me, to be an executioner, whatever, so long as it gives me something to eat). However, in the 1970s, the Spanish executioners not only sold their labor but also discovered a new way to increase their meager income by sharing the testimonies of their infamous lives with those who were willing to pay for it.[12]

In their works, Sueiro and Patino reproduced dozens of hours of conversation in which those civil servants provided all kinds of information about their lives and work. Voiceless and relegated to bureaucratic obscurity, the state executioners took advantage of the spaces where they were hired to articulate, in first person, the inalienable testimony of their lives. Through their voices, readers and viewers have access to their reflections on the stigma of their deteriorated identity, the legal claims about the precarious nature of their salaries, their frustrations and self-justifications about the compliance of their duty, and the complaints about the hypocrisy of a society that places upon their shoulders the responsibility to carry out a justice that, as they themselves recall, falls principally to those who make the laws. Along with these reflections on their profession, the Spanish executioners also placed for sale the details of the executions that up to that moment had remained hidden, the most intimate words and gestures that painted a picture of precisely that which excluded them and placed them at the height of social abjection. In this way, they were able to negotiate symbolically the meaning of their identity in the face of society. At the same time as the showing of the documentary in 1977, Antonio López once again sold his words and image to the magazine *Interviú* in an interview titled "I Executed Puig Antich." This time, the journalists tell how López had made a legal claim for financial recompense, arguing that "las gachís que enseñan todo también cobrarán" (qtd. in Siles 65) (chicks who show everything will charge, too). Just as the naked bodies of Spaniards were coming into the light of the public sphere, López began the "uncovering" of another type of new information that included the details of the last execution by garrote that took place in the country. Thus, López traded in democracy with that which the new media of the society of spectacle were willing to buy: a testimony that became public once the executioners had to cede their right to exercise sovereign violence in democratic Spain.

Antonio, Vicente, and Bernardo spoke before cameras in *Queridísimos verdugos*, which was filmed clandestinely in 1971. Facing the voice-over narrations about the glorification of violence, such as Maistre's quotations about the necessary existence of the executioners, their dialogues are part of a heteroglossia that combines testimonies of legal and scientific experts that display different ideological constructions of the delinquent and the criminal justice system. All these testimonies offer a dialogic framework to deconstruct, as Derrida suggested, "the logocentric, logonomocentric scaffolding in which the death penalty is inscribed or prescribed" (*Death I* 23). In Franco's Spain, this ideological scaffolding revolved around a notion of sovereignty that condemned a large part of Spanish society to death or to a life without dignity. In this sense, Patino considered his film a "radiography of underdevelopment and terror upon which the dictatorship was based" (Méndez 65).

Viewers of the film witness a chronicle of the request to General Franco for a pardon for Pedro Martínez Expósito, a soldier sentenced to death. The waiting period for this pardon alternates with images that show Madrid's citizens participating in the annual cycle of the renewal of merchandise on Christmas Eve. However, the apparent social access to consumption is belied by images of extreme poverty in the house of the condemned man, perpetrator of a double homicide committed during the course of a robbery. Within this pairing formed by underdevelopment and terror, audiences in 1977 had access to the experiences of those who were excluded from the economic growth in the Spain of the Development Plans, in which stories about the parallel lumpen lives of common criminals and executioners allowed them to see the dimensions of personal and collective poverty up close.[13] According to Patino, his purpose was to question in front of viewers the practices of social abjection that excluded the executioners by revealing and making visible the collective material conditions of existence that pushed them to accept their public offices:

> Después de conocer a fondo a los verdugos, me va a resultar muy difícil tolerar la hipocresía de que continúe haciéndole ascos la misma sociedad que los utiliza como coartada para lavar sus propias mierdas. Cuando a unos seres se les obliga a gastar todas sus energías en sobrevivir y defenderse, convertidos en cosas

indiferentes, lo de menos es que hasta acepten sumisamente el papel de ejecutar por orden superior a sus propios hermanos en la miseria, insensibles y atrofiados por todo lo que signifique amar la vida. (47)

(After thoroughly knowing the executioners, it will be very difficult for me to tolerate the hypocrisy of the society that rejects them and, at the same time, uses them as an alibi to clean up its shit. When some human beings are forced to spend all their energies in surviving and defending themselves, and turned into indifferent things, the least important thing is that they even submissively accept the assignment of killing their own brothers in misery following superior orders; insensitive and atrophied for everything that means to love life.)

Seen this way, it is important to recall how, months after the filming of the documentary, a journalist for ABC expressed his surprise at the fact that executioners still existed in the country, a discovery he had made because of a job offer that sought to replace the principal executioner of Seville: "Nosotros creíamos que ya no quedaban verdugos. Por lo menos aquí en España . . . ¿Habrá en estos tiempos nuestros quien solicite el cargo? ¿Quedarán por ahí individuos a los que les resulte grato y llevadero?" (80) (We thought there were no longer any executioners. At least here in Spain. . . . In our times, will there be anyone who applies for the position? Are there still, out there, individuals who find it pleasant and bearable?). All this exposed the erasure that had occurred in this supposed society of well-being surrounding the existence of those subjects who exercised what were considered anachronistic professions in late Franco Spain.

Faced with this homogenous and linear temporality of progress, the documentary shows a collage of heterogeneous and anachronistic images that combines representational forms of the death penalty. In these images, the historical continuity of the executioners as necessary civil servants is interrupted by their disappearance from the public scene as inferred from the pictures of the celebrations following the abolition of the death penalty during the Second Republic. Old engravings in chapbooks, photographs of the execution of Michele Angiolillo, who assassinated Spanish Prime Minister Antonio Cánovas in 1897, and pictures in magazines of the "freed" garrotes exhibited in the streets of Barcelona in 1932 come together as visible traces and remnants of what is impossible to fully see and what remains inaccessible as a whole in what Georges Didi-Huberman has called the archaeological work of montage (4). Each way of assembling and disassembling evokes encounters between disjointed temporalities and questions the conditions of possibility that enabled the historical mediation of those images. The montage becomes in this sense a theatrical device from which an analytical space for rendering visible the executions and the executioners that have remained in the shadows—just like the tacit, obscene rules upon which power was sustained—can be performed. The aesthetic and political archaeology of Patino's montage places side by side fragments of remnants of the cultures of the death penalty as a space open to political imagination where images can take position for a future time when the film can be shown. A future when a democratic community of viewers can contemplate itself in the mirror of the executioners and their victims, both icons of a regime of structural violence that, because of their abject, infamous condition, shaped those exclusions that had to be confronted to transform the social order.

At the beginning of the documentary, Antonio López mentions the Plaza de Oriente in Madrid, the place where General Franco addressed his followers from a balcony of the Royal Palace, as the location where "el Caudillo hace esas representaciones" (the Caudillo puts up those performances). This allusion to the public appearances of the head of state as "performances" is complemented in the film by another "performance" of the sovereign power: state executions. In this simulacrum of the ritual, they explain the mechanism of the garrote and show their command of this technology of death. Nevertheless, the executioners omitted in their performance the details of brutally botched executions that were revealed in the film in oral testimonies that exposed for the first time the cruel reality of these ceremonies. *Queridísimos verdugos* offered in this way the first multi-faceted account of real scenes of execution in Francoist Spain. As examined in these pages, while technical images of state killing were prohibited in mass media, executions had already been cinematically represented in fiction films during the 1960s. In *Los atracadores*, the first onscreen staging of strangulation by garrote, the execution was a controlled and bureaucratized ceremony. However, three years later, the role of an unwilling executioner portrayed as a victim in *El verdugo* made visible the violence of state killing in the private rituals and protocols before an execution that remained invisible. In this film, the representation of the abject condition of state executioners and executions became a nodal point where the unevenly developed effects of contradictions in the different levels of the *desarrollista* social formation were condensed.

Patino's documentary delved into these contradictions by revealing the historical conditions that enabled the displacement of capital punishment imaginaries in contemporary Spain. The film exposes how ideological practices displayed in Francoist execution ceremonies in which the theologico-political state dramatized its power to master an instant of death had been set aside in neo-capitalist society. At the end of the film, viewers are witnesses of the testimonies of a family facing the impending execution of their son. From this moment, Patino's historical account of capital punishment in Spain is punctuated with the rhythm of the final countdown to death. This new dimension of temporality in the film reveals a constellation of differential times in which the alleged "anachronism" of execution ceremonies and rituals always has co-existed and co-exists with the progressive time of *desarrollismo*. The dislocation of different temporalities in the social formation is articulated in *Queridísimos verdugos* around the lives of the real state executioners as historical subjects who face the contradictions of their own social role. In this way, executioners, who became an abject reverse of Francoist modernization, will no longer be invisible and anonymous civil servants that laid bare state violence at the nadir of the social hierarchy. As operators of the sovereignty's power to kill but also as marginalized citizens, the "beloved" state executioners embodied in hidden execution ceremonies the fundamental imbalance of power upon which other social and economic inequalities were founded during the so-called Spanish miracle period.

NOTES

Parts of this text have been translated from Spanish by Alexandra Vialla Méndez, Department of Latin American and Iberian Cultures, Columbia University. All translations from scholarly and journalistic texts originally in Spanish are ours. We have also rendered into English the dialogues from the films.

1. *El verdugo* is, at its core, a macabre farce and a love story about an undertaker, José (played by Italian actor Nino Manfredi), who marries an executioner's daughter, Carmen (Emma Penella), and reluctantly takes over the job of her father, a kindly old executioner named Amadeo (José Isbert), so the family can keep their government-allotted apartment. As reluctantly as possible, José goes along with the plan, but the very thought of taking another person's life makes him sick.

2. As *El verdugo* staged the performance of an execution in the resort city of Palma de Mallorca, in the first years of the 1960s, the integration of the Spanish government into the international political-military spaces and markets was characterized by the promotion of the emergent mass tourism (Vilarós 44). On the political dimensions of tourism as a "mode of governance," see Crumbaugh.

3. In his novel *Fusilamiento. Instrucciones de uso* (2005) (Firing Squad: Instructions for Use), Javier Maqua portrays the young recruits forced to be part of the firing squad in the execution of Pedro Martínez Expósito in 1972.

4. *Queridísimos verdugos* explores the personal stories of the three executioners still active in Spain in the early 1970s who were responsible for strangling prisoners sentenced to death. By paying the three men for their interviews, Basilio Martín Patino was able to show the practices of the dictatorship three years before the death of

Francisco Franco. The documentary was filmed in 1971 and its post-production was carried out between 1973 and 1977, the year it was released.

5. The abject status of executioners and their lumpen origins—understood in the Marxian sense of the term as "the lowest sediment of the relative surplus population," which "dwells in the sphere of pauperism" (659)—had been represented in nineteenth- and twentieth-century Spanish literary productions. In Espronceda's poem "El Verdugo" (1835), the executioner considers himself a victim of his accursed condition at the same time that he shows the *jouissance* obtained by inflicting pain. In the midst of contemporary debates over capital punishment, the executioners in Emilia Pardo Bazán's novel *La piedra angular* (1891) and Pío Baroja's *Aurora roja* (1904) also denounce their marginalization and justify the exercise of their profession as a legal resource to escape poverty.

6. *Los atracadores*, which ends with a gripping depiction of an execution by garrote vil, is based on a novel by Tomás Salvador, a former secret police agent. The film explains the motivations, evolution, and defeat of three young misfits from Barcelona who end up being robbers and murderers.

7. The cruelty of the executions prompted debates in the 1970s about the death penalty itself: "El movimiento abolicionista iría tomando cuerpo y cobrando fuerza en el tardofranquismo . . . desde el IV Congreso Nacional de la Abogacía Española celebrado en León en 1970 hasta las III Jornadas de Profesores de Derecho Penal . . . en 1975" (Gracia Ibáñez 128) (The movement to abolish the death penalty took shape and gained strength in the late stages of Franco's regime . . . from the fourth National Conference of the Legal Profession of Spain that took place in León in 1970, to the third Conference of Professors of Penal Law . . . in 1975).

8. Between 1960 and 1975, most executions were political. According to Almudena Portal González, eight people were executed for terrorism, five for killing members of the security forces, one for war crimes, and only two people on account of common crimes (16).

9. Tatjana Pavlovic describes this process using the Faustian imaginary: "José Luis regains a belief that he can benefit from the system without ever paying back. The promise of indefinite credit (Faustian motif) heightens his enjoyment" (172).

10. Annabel Martín analyzes this new masculine subject in relation to the genres of melodrama and comedy: "Si el melodrama no suele ocuparse del cuerpo contaminado del estado . . . Berlanga trastoca los presupuestos del género haciendo de ese 'cuerpo' el protagonista. Siempre en clave de humor negro, la película caracteriza al hombre de la España en desarrollo (tanto al reo como al nuevo verdugo) como un sujeto masculino en crisis, un sujeto débil, arrastrado y dominado por sus circunstancias" (280) (If melodrama does not tend to concern itself with the contaminated body of the State . . . Berlanga disrupts the presuppositions of the genre, fashioning that "body" into the protagonist. Always using dark humor, the film characterizes the man in developing Spain [both the prisoner and the new executioner] as a masculine subject in crisis, a weak subject, dragged and dominated by his circumstances).

11. Juan F. Egea examines the complexity of "the ethics of sympathy" (53), which articulates viewers' affective relationship with the characters through the uses of the camera

and space: "*El verdugo* is a filmic text with the capacity to turn affection into proximity and denunciations into detachment" (54).

12. I take this notion from Michel Foucault's essay "The Life of Infamous Men."

13. Patino explains his criteria: "A mí particularmente me impresiona mucho más la ejecución anónima, brutal, de un pobre ratero asustado, indefenso, cazado a lazo como un perro—que no logra enterarse nunca de por qué le matan y por qué ha malvivido—que las ejecuciones, que también me impresionaron mucho, por supuesto, llamadas políticas" (Méndez 65) (I personally am impacted more by the anonymous, brutal execution of some poor frightened, defenseless petty thief, hunted with a trap like a dog—who never finds out why they're going to kill him and why he has had to survive on so little—than by those executions, which also impact me greatly, of course, that are called political).

WORKS CITED

Althusser, Louis. *For Marx.* Translated by Ben Brewster, Verso, 2005.

Baroja, Pío. *Aurora roja.* Cátedra, 2010.

Barthes, Roland. *Critical Essays.* Translated by Richard Howard, Northwestern University Press, 1972.

Caillois, Roger. "The Sociology of the Executioner." *The College of Sociology (1937–39),* edited by Denis Hollier, translated by Betsy Wing, University of Minnesota Press, 1988, pp. 233–47.

Cañeque, Carlos, and Maite Grau. *¡Bienvenido Mr. Berlanga!* Destino, 1993.

Carrillo, Santiago. *Julián Grimau: el hombre, el crimen, la protesta.* Ediciones Venceremos, 1965.

Cerdá, Paco. "Preston: 'Franco firmaba penas de muerte tomando café.'" *El mercantil valenciano,* 10 Feb. 2010.

Crumbaugh, Justin. *Destination Dictatorship: The Spectacle of Spain's Tourist Boom and the Reinvention of Difference.* State University of New York Press, 2009.

De Maistre, Joseph. *St. Petersburg Dialogues, or, Conversations on the Temporal Government of Providence.* Translated and edited by Richard A. Lebrun, McGill-Queen's University Press, 1993.

Derrida, Jacques. *The Death Penalty: Volume 1.* Translated by Peggy Kamuf, University of Chicago Press, 2015.

_____. *The Death Penalty: Volume 2.* Translated by Elizabeth Rottenberg, University of Chicago Press, 2017.

Derrida, Jacques, and Elisabeth Roudinescu. *For What Tomorrow . . .: A Dialogue.* Translated by Jeff Fort, Stanford University Press, 2004.

Didi-Huberman, Georges. "Cuando las imágenes tocan lo real." *Macba,* 2008.

Egea, Juan F. *Dark Laughter: Spanish Film, Comedy, and the Nation.* University of Wisconsin Press, 2013.

Esposito, Roberto. *Immunitas: The Protection and Negation of Life*. Translated by Zakiya Hanafi, Polity Press, 2011.

Espronceda, José de. "El verdugo." *Antología poética*, edited by Gabriela Pozzi, Akal, 1999, pp. 80–83.

Foucault, Michel. *Discipline and Punish: The Birth of the Prison*. Translated by Alan Sheridan, Vintage Books, 1995.

_____. "The Life of Infamous Men." *Power, Truth, Strategy*, translated by Paul Foss and Meaghan Morris, Feral Publications, 1979, pp. 76–91.

Franco, Francisco. *Pensamiento político de Franco: Antología*. Servicio Informativo Español, 1964.

Freud, Sigmund. "Humour." *The Pelican Freud Library Volume 14: Art and Literature*, Penguin, 1985.

Gallo, Max. *Spain under Franco: A History*. Allen & Unwin, 1973.

García Berlanga, Luis, director. *El verdugo*. 1963. Buena Vista Home Entertainment, 2002.

Gómez Rufo, Antonio. *Luis G. Berlanga: La biografía*. Instituto Alicantino de Cultura Juan Gil-Albert, 2009.

Gracia Ibáñez, Jorge. "Dos espejos enfrentados: *El Verdugo* y *Queridísimos Verdugos*. Franquismo y pena de muerte a través del cine." *Intersexiones*, vol. 4, 2012, pp. 123–44.

Habermas, Jürgen. "Further Reflections on the Public Sphere." *Habermas and the Public Sphere*, edited by Craig Calhoun, The MIT Press, 1996, pp. 421–61.

Hernández Les, Juan, Manuel Hidalgo, and Luis García Berlanga. *El último austro-húngaro: Conversaciones con Berlanga*. Anagrama, 1981.

Kant, Immanuel. *The Metaphysics of Morals*. Translated and edited by Mary Gregor, Cambridge University Press, 2003.

Kantorowitz, Ernst. *The King's Two Bodies: A Study in Medieval Political Theology*. Princeton, 1957.

Kristeva, Julia. *Powers of Horror*. Translated by Leon S. Roudiez, Columbia University Press, 1982.

Maqua, Javier. *Fusilamiento: Instrucciones de uso*. Algaida Editores, 2005.

Martín, Annabel. "Familia, turismo y garrote vil: *El verdugo* de Luis García Berlanga (1963)." *Hispanismo y cine*, edited by Javier Herrera and Cristina Martínez-Carazo, Iberoamericana; Vervuert, 2007, pp. 269–92.

Martín Patino, Basilio. "Así fue el rodaje de 'Queridísimos verdugos.'" *Cuadernos para el Diálogo*, vol. 206, 1977, p. 47.

_____, director. *Queridísimos verdugos*. Produced by Turner Films, 1973.

Marx, Karl. *Capital: A Critical Analysis of Capitalist Production*. Translated by Edward Aveling and Samuel Moore, Swan Sonnenschein, 1906.

Mbembe, Achille. "Necropolitics." Translated by Libby Meintjes, *Biopolitics: A Reader*, edited by Timothy Campbell and Adam Sitze, Duke University Press, 2013, pp. 161–92.

McClintock, Anne. *Imperial Leather: Race, Gender and Sexuality in the Colonial Contest*. Routledge, 1995.

Méndez, José. "Radiografía del subdesarrollo." *Ajoblanco*, vol. 29, 1978, pp. 62–66.

Mira, Alberto. *The Cinema of Spain and Portugal*. Wallflower Press, 2005.

"Noticia de un verdugo." *ABC*, 30 Jun. 1972, p. 80.

Oliver Olmo, Pedro. *La pena de muerte en España*. Síntesis, 2008.

Pardo Bazán, Emilia. *La piedra angular*. Cátedra, 2013.

Pavlovic, Tatjana. *The Mobile Nation: España cambia de piel (1954–1964)*. Intellect, 2011.

Portal González, Almudena. "Los muertos del régimen de Franco entre 1952 y 1975." *Aportes*, vol. 85, 2014, pp. 7–50.

Pratt, John. *Punishment and Civilization: Penal Tolerance and Intolerance in Modern Society*. SAGE, 2002.

Rodríguez Cárcela, Rosa. "*El caso*. Aproximación histórico-periodística del semanario español de sucesos." *Correspondencias & Análisis*, vol. 2, 2012, pp. 219–35.

Rovira Beleta, Francisco, director. *Los atracadores*. PEFSA, 1962.

Sánchez, Bernardo. *Rafael Azcona, hablar el guion*. Cátedra, 2006.

Sánchez Barba, Francesc. *Brumas del franquismo: El auge del cine negro español (1950–1965)*. Universitat de Barcelona, 2007.

Saura, Carlos, director. *Los golfos*. 1960. Instituto Cervantes, 2010.

Sender, Ramón J. *El verdugo afable*. Nascimento, 1952.

Siles, José M. "Yo ejecuté a Puig Antich." *Interviú*, no. 53, May 25, 1977, pp. 65–66.

Sinclair, Alison. "The Ambiguities of Retribution." *Bulletin of Spanish Studies*, vol. 94, no. 6, 2017, pp. 955–75.

Sueiro, Daniel. *Los verdugos españoles: Historia y actualidad del garrote vil*. Alfaguara, 1971.

Tyler, Imogen. "What Is 'Social Abjection.'" *Social Abjection*, n.d. Accessed 7 Apr. 2020.

Vilarós, Teresa. "Banalidad y biopolítica: La Transición española y el nuevo orden del mundo." *Desacuerdos 2. Sobre arte, políticas y esfera pública en el estado español*, MACBA, Arteleku, 2005, pp. 29–56.

Žižek, Slavoj. *Living in the End Times*. Verso, 2010.

———. *Looking Awry: An Introduction to Jacques Lacan through Popular Culture*. MIT Press, 1992.

CHAPTER 2

State of Crucifixion

Tourism, Holy Week, and the Sacred Politics of the Cold War

Eugenia Afinoguénova

In 2017, Spain's Holy Week was declared a "Representative Manifestation of Intangible Cultural Heritage" (Ministerio de Educación, Cultura y Deporte). Not only do these celebrations trigger more domestic travel than Christmas and long weekends, but they also continue to structure the nation's public life at a time when politics and economy are making Spain less and less "different" (Olmos Juárez and García Cebrián 264). Spain's tourism authorities no longer collect separate economic impact statistics on foreign and domestic travelers. Still, it is significant that, in 2016, 12.4 percent of all tourists visiting Andalucía cited Holy Week celebrations as the reason for their journey, and that more than 17.4 percent of those coming to Andalucía for the Holy Week were specifically attracted to "popular celebrations/folklore" (Consejería de Turismo y Deporte, 2016, 6). Only the beach (28.6 percent) and the climate (24.8 percent) were cited as more appealing reasons to visit or travel within Spain. (In 2017, for reasons yet unknown, the interest in folklore and celebrations plunged to 5.1 percent while "prices" became 5 percent more attractive [Consejería de Turismo y Deporte, 2017, 6]). Facilitating interaction between locals and visitors and confirming the locals' sense of belonging, Spain's locally and regionally diversified Holy Weeks appear to be as important for the making of place brands as they are for circulating them on domestic and international markets.

What kind of brand is it, however, that relies on remembrance and celebration of death, the exposure of mortified flesh to the public eye, and, sometimes, the parading of an image of an already dead Jesus? While we usually identify these religious festivities with the Catholic Church, in the diverse components comprising Spain's present-day celebrations, its institutional power is deeply intertwined with popular religion. It was not until 1964 when local elites, who had been using the Holy Weeks for place identity-making since the turn of the twentieth century, began to work with the State and, in some instances, with Church officials on transforming these and other festivities into localized heritage products embedded into the centralized program of tourism development. That year, under the leadership of the innovative Manuel Fraga Iribarne, the Ministry of Information and Tourism gave every locality a chance to have its most cherished festivals certified as a "Fiesta de Interés Turístico" (Celebration of Interest for Tourism) (Ministerio de Información y Turismo). Together with the festivals' enthusiasts, local authorities put together dossiers that a special qualifying commission of the Ministerio evaluated, thereby determining which festivals to mention in the official calendar of Spain's tourism celebrations. Only the places with certified festivities could opt for funding from the Ministerio and be included in the national advertising of all festivals.

Surviving the end of Franco's regime, the view of the Holy Week as a tourist attraction has successfully adapted to the leisure-centered economy. Even when the responsibility for tourism planning was entrusted to autonomous governments and the previous orders were repealed in 1987, the state continued to regulate the certification of festivities (Ministerio de Transportes, Turismo y Comunicaciones). Only in 2006 did regional tourism authorities finally receive a role: a five-year record of having been declared "a celebration of interest for regional tourism" was now required to apply for a national or international certification (Ministerio de Industria, Turismo y Comercio), and these are the regulations currently in place. For autonomous governments, Holy Week festivities are now providing precious opportunities for discussing regional identities. This is not, of course, what Franco's officials had in mind. Still, following the 1960s turn that this essay will examine, tourism and the Holy Week celebrations have become inseparable in Spain. Regions such as Andalucía even developed a special tourism product called "The Ways of Passion" (Junta de Andalucía). Though, on the surface, the Partido Socialista Obrero Español—that autonomous community's ruling party until the December 2018 elections—had no interest in empowering the Catholic Church, tourism-inducing popular religiosity was reinforced and became a pillar of socialist-led identity-making.

Just as with other festivities included in the hospitality business, a blend of historical and anthropological approaches is required for understanding how tourism-based economy, State-guided identity politics, and the symbolic reenactments of Christ's suffering and death came to empower each other. Mobilized to support transnational consumption, Holy Weeks are heritage products as well as modern rituals developing in contact with tourism. Yet, as will be argued here, a historical perspective reveals that, in the 1960s, the Holy Weeks were transformed into a very particular tourism product, tailored to facilitate Spain's coming out to the global political arena at the time of the Cold War.[1] On the surface, tourism-based modernization that Fraga championed in the 1960s addressed the disastrous effects of the economic autarky of the 1940s–1950s. In reality, however, as Sasha D. Pack argues, Fraga's Ministry was offering to national and international audiences a vision of Franco's regime that could suit Spain's becoming a global neocapitalist economy (107–9).

According to Tatjana Gajic, in a Spain seeking ways to become a European nation, considerable intellectual effort was focused on recasting Franco's power, not as some anti-liberal regime, but rather as an innovative take on core liberal values, "such as freedom, rule of law, sovereignty and authority" (161). As the Cold War polarized the world's nations along the liberal and anticommunist versus anti-liberal and communist axes, Franco's self-styling as a "Caudillo" blending *auctoritas* and *potestas* (the sacred and the political power) deserved special attention, argued Jesús Fueyo, a political theoretician affiliated with the Falange (128, qtd. in Gajic 164). Carl Schmitt—the German conservative political philosopher who corresponded with Fueyo—wrote extensively on sacred sovereignty and the importance of Franco's form of it in the Cold War context. Fraga's political thinking was also deeply influenced by Schmitt. In 1962, as the President of the Instituto de Estudios Políticos (Institute for the Study of Politics), Fraga awarded Schmitt a Medal of Honor (Fraga). Published in the same year, Fraga's homage to Schmitt and the response by the German philosopher introduced the political vocabulary that explained a new vision for Spain. Insisting that the Cold War was still a war between communist and capitalist states, Schmitt argued that the 1960s would be the time when the world split in two by World War II would be replaced by a multi-centered map of nations drifting toward either side of the communist-anticommunist divide. To quote from his 1962 speech in Spanish at the Instituto de Estudios Políticos, Spain would loom high on this new map as "la primera nación que se reafirmó por sus propias fuerzas, de tal forma que, ahora, todas las naciones no comunistas tienen que acreditarse en este aspecto frente a España" (19) (the first nation to reaffirm itself by its own force, so that, now, all non-communist nations would have to present to Spain their credentials). What this meant was that if Spain's former foes—the Western liberal democracies—were to become her friends, the time was ripe to resuscitate the communist enemy and Franco's heroic victory over it. The problem was, however, that for a regime that had just begun to legitimate itself as a guarantor of peace and well-being, reenactment of the Civil War in the new Cold War climate would have to be symbolic.

How this symbolic war was waged in Spain's fiction and on the streets of its cities is the subject of fascinating recent scholarship, including William Viestenz's *By the Grace of God* (2014), Daniel García-Donoso's *Escrituras postseculares* (2018), and *The Sacred and Modernity in Urban Spain,* edited by Antonio Cordoba and García-Donoso (2016). In his chapter on *sacratio* in that volume, Viestenz fruitfully connected Giorgio Agamben's understanding of sacralization as ritualized exclusion from the rule of law with Michel Foucault's "biopolitical modernity" to demonstrate how the two processes of ontological inclusion and exclusion complemented each other in Francoist Spain. The advent of the body-centered consumer society in the 1960s made this double logic even more apparent. The beach became, of course, the main location for staging what Teresa Vilarós has eloquently termed "la progresiva y celebrada autoconversión del sujeto nacional en sujeto turista, y por tanto consumidor" (52) (the unstoppable and celebrated self-conversion of the national subject into one that was a tourist and therefore a consumer). Yet farther away from the beach, the political production of "bare life" (a notion that Agamben developed in his 1995 *Homo Sacer*) through sacralized stagings of the state of exception was also ongoing. The Orwellian cunning of Fraga's vision can be appreciated in the ability of his 1964 campaign celebrating "twenty-five years of peace" to channel the Civil War into a modern war-within-peace-and-consumption. Elsewhere, I dated the first attempt to transform the Civil War into historical heritage and an object of tourism consumption in 1959, when the giant cross of the Valley of the Fallen was unveiled (420).

Against such a turbulent political background, the renovation of Spain's festivals may seem like a minor event. Yet following Agamben's insight in *State of Exception* that archaic-styled modern festivities should not be traced back to the agrarian cycle, but should be rather "related . . . to the state of suspended law" (71), we must distinguish in Fraga's modernized Holy Weeks an attempt to channel the debates concerning Franco's authority and a need for a new legitimating vision of it. In Agamben's words, these feasts

> point to the real state of exception as the threshold of indifference between anomie and law. In showing the mournful character of every feast and the festive character of all mourning, law and anomie show their distance and, at the same time, their secret solidarity. . . . They celebrate and parodically replicate the anomie through

which the law applies itself to chaos and to life only on the condition of making itself, in the state of exception, life and living chaos. (*State of Exception* 72–73)[2]

If religious celebrations such as Holy Week had emerged in the Christian world to modernize the spring rites and other agrarian festivities, under Fraga's auspices, they were turning into modern anomies exemplifying Spain's state of exception. An examination of the correspondence between local and central authorities that accompanied the declaration of the first Holy Weeks as tourism attractions in the 1960s demonstrates that Holy Week's "sacralized" time and space offered a unique opportunity to channel the questions of sovereignty in order to ensure the regime's domestic and international viability. In what follows, I will analyze this correspondence, focusing on the techniques of capitalist consecration (to use Agamben's terms) of rituals of the Holy Week that belonged to the realm of popular religion to uncover the processes inherent in Fraga's *desarrollismo*, thanks to which not only were the local festivities, but also the religiosity of Spain's inhabitants and Jesus's death brought out to the global leisure market and mobilized for secular purposes.

"Sacralizing" the Holy Week

Tourism and Heritage Studies approaches allow us to see Holy Week celebrations as modern rituals collapsing the distinction between participation and spectatorship, and between religious and civil authority. The Church had reason to worry, as Fraga's mobility-centered policies were seeking to trigger social and cultural modernization, a process that, if unguided, would threaten to make Spain a secular nation. In the background of the debates concerning the morality of intersex mingling and tolerance of the bikini, the question of diminishing religious authority was looming high. Since it was really the state that, through the Opus Dei lineage of its technocratic ministers, was incorporating the functions traditionally reserved to the Church, religion became a part of every government program. Fraga was not from the Opus Dei, but *España*—a 1962 compendium publicizing the national idea that his Ministry consolidated and projected—named "profundo sentido religioso" (deep religious sense) among the "constantes de la sociedad española" (Spanish society's constant traits) (Anonymous 43). Transforming Catholicism into an ethnic marker was Fraga's alternative to Church power, and, under Fraga's leadership, the heritage industry was launched to preserve the values associated with the Church while empowering the government to become the driving force of religious renovation. When considering all of this, one must remember that, as argued by Laurajane Smith, "there is, really, no such thing as heritage," but rather what she terms Authorized Heritage Discourse (AHD) (11).

As we shall see, the exchange between the Ministerio de Información y Turismo and religious authorities exemplifies the State's push to establish itself as the arbiter in deciding which Holy Week to "sacralize" for tourism consumption using the secularized criterion of beauty. In his foundational book *The Tourist: A New Theory of a Leisure Class*, Dean MacCannell explains that a process of "sacralization" is required for transforming any site into a tourist attraction. Its different phases involve marking the object "off from similar objects as worthy of preservation," officially recognizing it as meriting protection, and using copies and print media to circulate its images. At the final stage, an object becomes a productive force behind new identities, when places and businesses assume its name (42–45). Although MacCannell refers to sites, my sources point at a similar process at work with temporal, as opposed to spatial, attractions such as the Holy Week celebrations.

Neither spatial, nor temporal commoditized destinations are to be confused with those that communities use for their own needs. The diverse popular rituals of the Holy Week, for instance, were, for most part, products of nineteenth-century regionalist elites that used or "invented" (to use Eric Hobsbawm's famous coinage) their traditions to reinforce communal spirit. Not until the 1960s, however, did these local or regional touchstones become an object of State-driven global consumption. Theatrical metaphors that Erving Goffman, the Chicago School sociologist, famously used for dividing collective performances of identity into socially normalized "frontstage," the elusive "backstage," and the secret "outside," have allowed early tourism scholars to map the process by which consumption by tourists moves everything local to the forefront of social interaction via consumption by outsiders (105–40). "Sacralization" is what propels the pre-global sites and performances to the tourism market. Both MacCannell and Nelson Graburn, another pioneer of tourism studies, thus assert that the tourist's quest for authenticity defeats its own purpose producing "sacralized" sites instead of the sacred (read: authentic, non-commoditized) ones that the tourists desire (MacCannell, *Tourist* 42–45; Graburn, 24–31). For MacCannell, the dynamic of postmodernity fueled by and fueling the need to travel makes the journey itself impossible, because, in lieu of pre-modern "others," the tourist is doomed to find either professionals performing Otherness in exchange for money or modernized "ex-primitives" whom the tourist would not even care to meet (*Empty* 26).

As the State was taking over the local nationalist celebrations, it was also seeking support from the Church, making it appear that these "sacralized" performances would only reinforce the power of Church-governed rites over popular religious manifestations of a pre-global age while also facilitating the connection between National Catholicism, Church constructions of the Passion, and market-conscious local elites. This process was not without its tensions, as the exchange with Church authorities reveals considerable misunderstanding—or even discord—between the local brotherhoods and the Church, between local elites and national ones, between the Church's universal message and the actual experience of participants in specific manifestations of popular religiosity.

Archbishops were routinely consulted prior to certifying a specific location's Holy Week, yet the tourism authorities' requests for consultation often sounded either dutiful or hypocritical. For example, having received the dossier for certifying the Holy Week of Granada, the members of the qualifying commission asked the Archbishop of Granada to weigh in on its comparative importance vis-à-vis other regional Holy Weeks: "sobre su calidad y valor, y si la misma es merecedora, con preferencia a las que se celebran en la provincia de Granada, al título de la celebración de interés turístico" (AGA (3)49.12 Box 4489, 5 Feb. 1968) (on its quality and value, and whether it deserves the title of a Celebration of Interest for Tourism above all other Holy Weeks celebrated in the province of Granada). The Archbishop could only find the most favorable terms to describe the celebration: "La Semana Santa de esta capital se hace más notable de año en año por la piedad, esplendor y brillantez de sus Cofradías de Penitencia" (AGA (3)49.12 Box 4489, 8 Feb. 1968) (The Holy Week in this capital is becoming every year more and more distinguished due to piety, splendor, and the shine of its Penitence Confraternities). Whether the prelate understood that the question was not about the qualities of the celebration, but rather about its deserving a preferential treatment for tourism funding, the committee interpreted the Archbishop's response as a permission to give such preference, and in February 1968, the Holy Week of Granada became a Celebration of Interest for Tourism.

Conversely, in the Diocese of Murcia, the Archbishop Ramón Sanjurjo y Marcé doubted whether including the Holy Week into the repertoire of tourism attractions would reap spiritual benefits. Having received, in early 1965, a petition signed by the Mayor of Cartagena, the qualifying commission wanted to know specifically "si existía alguna razón aparte de la estrictamente religiosa que aconsejara la declaración de interés turístico" (AGA (3)49.12 Box 44891, Feb. 1968) (whether there was any reason beyond the strictly religious one that suggested that it should be declared a Celebration of Interest for Tourism). Since the Holy Weeks of the nearby Murcia and Lorca were also in the queue to be certified, the commission needed reasons to also certify Cartagena's Holy Week. The certification process went slow and, in 1967, under some high-level internal pressure and with the two other celebrations already certified, the Ministerio de Información y Turismo resumed the process.[3] Dispatched to Cartagena during Holy Week, the Delegado Provincial de Turismo found enough aesthetic appeal to support the proposal on grounds that were not merely religious, concluding that,

> [j]unto a las características estrictamente religiosas, las procesiones de Cartagena son una explosión de luz y de color que las hacen realmente objeto de interés turístico. Y en este aspecto se puede afirmar que la realidad se ha adelantado a la declaración oficial, ya que en estas épocas Cartagena y la zona del Mar Menor se ve invadida [sic] por miles de personas atraídas por el renombre obtenido por sus procesiones. (3, original underlined by hand)

> (Next to its strictly religious characteristics, the processions in Cartagena are an explosion of light and color truly making it an object of interest for tourism. And in this respect, it is possible to state that practice has gone ahead of official action, since during these seasons Cartagena and the zone of Mar Menor are invaded by thousands of people attracted by the fame of its processions.)

The Archbishop, however, was of the opinion that, with the government's support, these seasonal "invasions" might further exacerbate the threat to the Holy Week's real purpose already challenged by the excesses of popular religion. Unlike his peer in Granada, while exalting the beauty and the spirit of the holiday, he also warned the officials that commercialization could jeopardize religious fervor and the Confraternities' spirit: "Con todo queremos advertir de la posibilidad [de que] se desvirtuarían del espíritu religioso en actos que habiendo surgido única e exclusivamente con dicho carácter [religioso], pueden ser utilizados con otros fines, especialmente de orden económico, comercial etc., ajenos a los mismos" (AGA (3)49.12 Box 44891, 16 Feb. 1968) (Despite all the above we wish to warn about the possibility that [the processions'] religious spirit would [be] thwarted in acts that, having emerged uniquely and exclusively with the aforementioned [religious] character, could be used for other purposes, especially of an economic or commercial nature, that are foreign to them). Still, two weeks later, on February 29, 1968, the Holy Week of Cartagena was certified as a Celebration of Interest for Tourism.

While at present the Holy Weeks may allow Spain's localities to develop productive internal and external identities, the discourses that brought these festivals to life reveal a peculiar hope that the renovated, commoditized rituals would also somehow codify Holy Week as a token of the Church's distributed power that local elites performed in front of central authorities. Writing to the Ministerio de Información y Turismo, some authors argued that the certification would help preserve Spain's National-Catholic idea and even open new evangelizing opportu-nities by including the citizens of liberal democracies—Spain's former enemies—as new friends. In the dossier filed for the Holy Week in Granada in September 1967, Antonio Rivas Arias, President of the Comisión de Propaganda de la Federación de Cofradías de la Semana Santa (Propaganda Commission of the Federation of Holy Week Confraternities of Granada) went as far as stating that the Holy Week Confraternities "perpetúan e identifican al pueblo soberano, con la más sugestiva y representativa imaginación de los conceptos y vida pública del Mundo Cristiano" (AGA (3)49. 12 Box 44891) (14) (preserve the sovereign nation and identify it with the most suggestive and representative imagination of the concepts and public life of the Christian World). During these collective remembrances, people inhabit-ing Spain's towns—alongside their domestic and foreign guests—could become, not only symbolic witnesses, but also symbolic imitators and even perpetrators of Christ's death, thus clearing the foundational moments of Christianity for their entry into a modern Spain and certifying the links between religious and laical communities epitomized in the confraternities. Or at least this was the message that local authorities articulated in an effort to convince the central government that the regime's foundational moment was alive in the Holy Week rituals.

One might speculate that, in the example of Cartagena mentioned above, the city's well-known resistance to the Nationalist army during the Civil War also fueled local authorities' interest in reasserting the victory of the Nationalists by invigorating local Holy Week. And in fact, the dossier from Cartagena revealed an effort, on behalf of local civil powers, to present the work of confraternities and the processions that they organized as a step toward a revival of the local community predicated on the revival of the Church:

> Está en el ánimo de todos esta procesión del Viernes de Dolores, el día grande cartagenero, esos encapuchados, esos cirios, ese Santocristo con cuatro grandes velas; esos rezos, son, contienen, proclaman, una afirmación. Que Él ha vuelto allí arriba. Y que unos hombres de buena voluntad están dispuestos a lograr, con la simiente de su ejemplo, que surja la cosecha de un nuevo templo en esas ruinas . . . maravillosas, vivas, dolientes u majestuosa [sic] . . . de la que fue la primera Iglesia de España. (AGA (3)49.12 Box 44891) (3–4, original underline)

> (This procession of the Friday of Mourning, a great day for Cartagena, these hooded figures, these candles, this [figure of] Holy Christ between four enor-mous candles are on everyone's mind; these prayers are, convey, proclaim one affirmative truth. That He has returned from there above. And that some men of good will are determined to achieve, using his example as a seed, that a harvest

of a new temple grows on these marvelous, living, hurting, and majestic ruins <u>of what was once</u> Spain's First Church.)

The petitioners' metaphors may have been mixed, but the message was clear: thanks to the believers' effort, a new triumphant Church would rise from the Holy Week rituals, and the tourism authorities' certification was expected to bring this future to fruition.

Nothing summarizes better the connection between what local authorities believed to be Franco's legitimizing discourse and their attempts at governing through tourism (Crumbaugh 45–48), than the following passage written by the Mayor of Híjar, an Aragonese town in the Province of Teruel whose male inhabitants are known to earn self-inflicted wounds through continuous drumming between the night of Holy Thursday and the evening of Holy Saturday. Arguing that the tourists' emerging interest in the celebration required investment in hotels and infrastructure, the Mayor reminded the authorities that by helping his town preserve the rituals they would honor Franco's victory over the Second Republic, whose government had banned religious manifestations in public places: "Nuestros propios esfuerzos y sacrificios hicieron posible el 'milagro' de este espléndido resurgir de 'aquella' Semana Santa que manos sacrílegas conviertieron totalmente en escombros y cenizas. . . . Pero nosotros seguiremos teniendo fe en Dios que sigue estando con nosotros" (AGA (3)49.12 Box 44873, 27 Jun. 1965) (15) (Our own efforts and sacrifices made possible the "miracle" of this splendid recovery of "that" Holy Week that sacrilegious hands had completely transformed into rubble and ash. But we will keep believing in God that is still in our midst). The Mayor's clear interest in strengthening "us"—a community united by faith and blessed with a Godly presence that had preserved Holy Week— contradicted his manifest purpose of making the celebration more inclusive. It was, however, a productive contradiction that did not require resolution since both local and central authorities had an interest in promoting allegiance to their own side, against a God-hating and sacrilegious "other"—an "other" the memory of which tourism-induced renovation never wanted to dissolve.

The Mayor's effort to ascribe to his community a ritual identity maintained the locals' distinction from the strangers, but these strangers could be included by showing an appreciation of the festivities:

Por tratarse de la fiesta la más religiosa de todas, como es la Semana Mayor de la Cristiandad, en la que se conmemoran los más grandes y sublimes misterios de Redención por Jesucristo, el Hijo de Dios Crucificado, es muy natural que Híjar tan católica, la celebre cada año con más amor y fervor religioso, entregándose a ella con una fe y un ardor, y una posesión, imposibles de describir y sí solo de comprender viviendo mezclado con los Hijareños y su propia semana santa. (7)

(Since this is the Most Important Week of Christianity, the most religious of all celebrations in which the greatest and most sublime mysteries of Redemption through Jesus Christ, the Crucified Son of God, are remembered, it is only natural that such a devout town as Híjar celebrates it every year with increasing love and religious fervor, and with a possession that is impossible to describe and that can only be understood mixing with the people of Híjar [during] their very special Holy Week.)

The Mayor claimed that "gentes llegadas, acaso, de todos los puntos de España, también algunas del extranjero" (13–14) (people coming, perhaps, from all parts of Spain and some even from abroad) were already joining in and that many foreigners were also demanding a tunic and a drum.

La Tamborrada—the drumming celebration of Holy Thursday common in Low Aragón but branded in 1966 as a Celebration of Interest for Tourism taking place in Híjar—codified a community brought together by its shared "possession" of, and by, religious spirit yet was maintained thanks to periodic participation of strangers in its rituals. The bondage between "us" and "them" was sealed by blood from the wounds inflicted after long hours of drumming. According to the petition, the Mayor saw a clear connection between an invigorated Holy Week and the reversal of the town's decline. Without help from tourism authorities, he suggested, there was no remedy against the

problema de hospedaje que cundirá al desaliento de los que llegan sin poder ser atendidos debidamente, y la Semana Santa de Híjar, diferente a todas las demás de España, con toda su gigantesca fuerza y belleza, con todo su sagrado y tradicional ritual, irá a menos reducida a las limitadísimas posibilidades de su cada día más "limitadísima" población. Esto es lo que, por muchas cosas, ha comenzado a preocuparnos. (14–15)

(lodging problem that would discourage those who come yet cannot be properly served, and the Holy Week of Híjar, different from all other ones in Spain, with all its giant force and beauty, with all its sacred and traditional ritual, will decline, reduced to the very limited possibilities of her increasingly "limited" population.)

The dossier of this tamborrada, currently a part of the tourism product known as "Ruta del tambor y bombo" and a "celebration of international tourism interest," illustrated the tensions implicit in all religious holidays reinvented in the 1960s.

For local authorities, exalting the regime's National-Catholic foundations through Holy Week was one way to ensure the continuing importance of the Church at a time when local and regional territory planning were rising on the central government's agenda. Yet despite the belief, needed from all parties involved, that a seamless transition between religious rituals and tourism events was possible, the ideas of community, agency, and beauty undergirding the two types of celebrations were marked by so many contradictions that conflicts were bound to emerge. This is what happened in the capital of the province of Murcia, where Holy Week was certified in 1967 as "Fiestas de Primavera." That was a blanket label for rites encapsulating everything from the pagan Burial of the Sardine to the Catholic Easter. Given the capital's proximity to the coast, it didn't take long for the Carnivalesque, body-centered, beach culture aesthetic to clash with Holy Week's spiritual message. In Spring 1970, a frivolous poster advertising the Fiestas caused protests in the local press, which stated: "Nos parece demasiado pretencioso querer reflejar, en una como orgía infernal de conchas marinas con señoritas dentro, una celebración tan importante, seria y grandiosa como es la Semana Santa murciana" (AGA (3)49.12 Box 44888, complaint on 21 Mar. 1970, with a cut-out article from *La verdad*, Murcia, of 17 Mar. 1970, 3) (We consider it too pretentious to try representing a celebration as important, serious, and grandiose as the Holy Week in Murcia, as some kind of an infernal orgy of seashells with young ladies inside). In 1969, Fraga was fired from his position, and in the lead-up to the first post-Fraga season, Holy Week enthusiasts were signaling through the local press that they had not yet surrendered their celebrations to the state.

Cold War Under the Sun

Since tourism authorities' involvement opened infinite opportunities for "sacralizing" even those places, times, and forms of celebration that were splintering from National Catholicism, the renovation of Holy Week far surpassed the simple dichotomy of Church versus State. In order to understand why renewed Holy Weeks became part of the core of Spain's identity, we need to remember what the tourism-triggered development known as *desarrollismo* was first intended to be: an all-encompassing program designed to ensure the viability of Francoism. It is therefore not surprising that the most successful, conflict-free festivities of the 1960s were not seeking to preserve any tradition but rather to jump onto the modernization wagon to create something crowd-pleasing and technologically enhanced. Whether it was a coincidence or not, this happened most in the areas close to the beach, where more day-trip destinations were needed to satisfy tourist masses: in Esparreguera, 50 km from Barcelona; in Ulldecona, 100 km from Tarragona and not far from the Costa de Azahar; and in Moncada, 7 km from Valencia. In contrast to the rituals in which participants imprinted on their own bodies their sympathy with Christ's suffering, in these towns, the scenes of Christ's suffering were performed on stage.

In Catalonia, the tradition of the sacred drama representing the last hours in the life of Jesus, known as "La Passió" (The Passion), has existed since at least the seventeenth century. In April 1966, the Patronage Board of one of the most famous of these performances—La Passió d'Esparreguera—applied for Catalonia's La Passió to be recognized as a Celebration of Interest for Tourism. It is unclear whether, like in other parts of Catalonia, the citizens were using the tourism boom to advance regionalist and nationalist causes. The dossier reminded the central authorities that La Passió, whose texts used to be "pasados de padres a hijos" (AGA (3)49. 12 Box 44886, Apr. 1966) (passed on from fathers to sons), was an important identity-maker for the community. There was no mention of whether La Passió was performed in Spanish or Catalan at that time. Yet the fact that the document blended Catholicism and the exaltation of local spirit in ways reflective of the position of the Catalan Church suggests that tourism-centered renovation of traditions could satisfy a whole array of claims whose discrepancies, for the time being, did not have to be addressed.

The explicit reason for demanding the certification, according to the authors, was the effect that the performance had on spectators, especially foreigners. The description, quoted below at length, typified tourists as agnostic city-dwellers whose spiritual life would be forever transformed thanks to the show:

> En la semi-oscuridad se admira la persistente atención con que el espectador sigue el desarrollo de La Passió, se emociona con sus escenas y con lágrimas abundantes supera ya los momentos culminantes, y su aplauso unánime al final de cada cuadro, siendo lo más admirable, ver el rostro emocionado de los indiferentes, de los que han asistido al espectáculo "porque sí", porque la fama de La Passió valía el viaje, aunque "ellos no están por estas cosas". Sin embargo, su emoción es el mejor tributo a La Passió y el recuerdo de la vida de Jesús irá unido a su visita a Esparraguera [sic] y ya por siempre más aquellas personas, en el bullicio de la ciudad, no pocas veces pensarán que "vieron" al que murió por la salvación de todos. Se comprenderá ante esos detalles [la] función social y edificativa que representa La Passió. (AGA (3)49. 12 Box 44886, Apr. 1966)

(In the semi-darkness one can admire the persistent attention with which a spectator follows the development of La Passió, feels touched by its scenes and by abundant tears overcomes the culminating moments, and his/her unanimous applause at the end of each scene. What is most admirable are the deeply moved faces of the indifferent, of those who had attended the performance "just because," because La Passió's fame justified the trip, although "they are not concerned with these things." Their emotion is, however, the best tribute to La Passió, and the memory of the life of Jesus would become a part of their visit to Esparraguera, and from then on, amidst the tumult of the big cities, these people would keep thinking that they had "seen" the One who had died to save us all. These details explain the social and educative function that La Passió fulfills.)

Essentially, those wishing to bring more visitors to Esparreguera by putting its traditional performances on the central government's radar suggested that certification would somehow allow sacred drama to fulfill its original function: the strengthening of the spectators' faith. Only now, it was also foreigners and not just locals who were receiving the light of faith. In 1967, La Passió de Esparreguera received the certification, and in 1969, a new Teatro de la Passió was inaugurated. At present, this five-hour-long show is reported to employ a thousand people (about 5 percent of the town's population) and attract around fifteen thousand spectators (Generalitat de Catalunya).

Not far from Esparreguera, in the town of Ulldecona in the province of Tarragona, performances dedicated to the suffering, death, and resurrection of Christ started very recently. In 1955, the rector of the local church found in the parochial library archive a seventeenth- or eighteenth-century manuscript containing a short text in Catalan. A director of medieval theater productions from Barcelona was called in and determined that it was a copy of a sixteenth-century play (Murillo 11). The president of the local cultural and recreational center then decided to stage a version of the text in Spanish, called "Pasión de Nuestro Señor Jesucristo" (The Passion of Our Lord Jesus Christ) and, seeing its success, decided to repeat the performance the next year. In 1967, journalist Enrique Murillo reported that these productions were drawing ten thousand people to a town of only six thousand (13). Still, with 80 percent of its spectators coming from nearby Castellón and Valencia, this Pasión was experiencing "tremendous" competition from the "grand Catalan Passiós" like the one from Esparreguera (13). The text has changed several times, but since 1965, the definitive version has been one by José María Junyent Quintana, a local art critic. In 1965, arguably with the purpose of showing support for a new tradition, Fraga visited Ulldecona in the company of Vicesecretario General del Movimiento and other government officials, and a year later, the Mayor submitted the application to have the performance certified as a Celebration of Interest for Tourism. Though it is easy to see how, given the town's proximity to the beach, the involvement of the Ministerio de Información y Turismo could improve the local economy, the Mayor appealed to the memories of the Civil War to insert this event in the regime's sacred chronology. Blurring the timelines, the dossier implied that the Civil War (which ended in 1939) had something to do with the first performance, which the document dated "en la época moderna, tras la Guerra de Liberación [Guerra Civil], en la primavera de 1955" (AGA (3)49.12 Box 44888, 13 Jun. 1966) (in modern times, after the Liberation War [Civil War], in spring 1955).

Just like their peers from Esparreguera, the organizers insisted that the performance was helping to strengthen the community and evangelize strangers. The promotional leaflet published in 1965 by the Patronage Board of the Pasión de Ulldecona contained a text by "L.V.A." (presumably a Board member) suggesting that the play had already become an identity ritual for the locals and a spiritual act for visitors: "los vecinos se sienten identificados con la obra, actúen o no, en ella. Nuestros espectadores la ven y la vuelven a ver, pero viviéndola, sacándole provecho espiritual, aprenden deleitándose y la propagan y de ella hablan a sus próximos y a sus alejados, como sintiendo y lamentando que ellos no la hayan presenciado" (1) (The locals identify with the play, whether they are acting or not. Our spectators see it and come back to see it again, but living it through, reaping spiritual benefits, they learn while also enjoying themselves, and they advertise it and speak about it to their close and remote ones, as if they were sorry that [other people] had not witnessed it). This was an official communiqué for the locals—not a text written to persuade the officials—and yet its logic was identical to one permeating the dossier for festivity certification. These similarities suggest that not only the government officials but also the local elites were looking for ways to use anomie performances—the state of suspension of law and order epitomized in the Holy Week celebrations—to maintain their power in ways that would no longer be supported by force but rather by a quest for pleasure (*deleite*) attracting an audience of strangers.

In 1965, the play already employed two hundred actors and required a set so big that a new stage had to be built. Still, when asked to give an opinion, the Delegado Provincial described the performance as an old, religious, and folkloric tradition: "los intérpretes y el montaje escénico del drama sacro constituyen una actividad que bien puede calificarse de extensa e intensa cultura artística popular" (The actors and the staging of the sacred drama constitute an activity that may well be qualified as a manifestation of the wide and deep [extensive and intensive] popular artistic culture). The fluctuating meaning of "popular culture" allowed the authorities to codify new traditions like this one as consumable heritage relevant for the building of communities. And indeed, in January

1967, "Drama Sacro de la Pasión" of Ulldecona was certified as a Celebration of Interest for Tourism. Having overcome its earlier economic challenges, the performances continue until today. Between 1993 and 2014, the Pasión of Ulldecona was staged in Spanish and Catalan, and since 2014, it has been performed only in Catalan (Patronato de la Passió d'Ulldecona).

If lack of historical patina had no negative effect on the government's decision in Ulldecona, the certification of another Pasión—the "Misterio de la Pasión" (Mystery of the Passion) in Moncada near Valencia—demonstrates what was needed for the officials to overcome their doubts when dealing with newer traditions. Initiated as recently as 1960, Moncada's performance was designed for the masses. At that time, between Holy Tuesday and Thursday, the productions employing two hundred actors and a seventy-voice choir were held in the local sports arena, at one extreme of which there was a one-hundred-meter wide stage with thirty high-power microphones and a fifty-thousand-watt lighting system (AGA (3)49.12, Box 44889). The authors of the dossier made a special effort to describe the event as a communal effort involving every aspect of the town's life. Even the fabric for the costumes was locally produced. Most important, not only did the entire local economy depend on the celebration of the Misterio, but the show was expanding, incorporating new scenes, adding more days, and already taking over the town's landscape:

El Viernes, último día de la representación, se inicia en [sic] juicio ante Pilatos, sigue a continuación la calle de la Amargura, por el camino que va del campo de deportes a la colina de Santa Bárbara, montículo natural de inmejorables condiciones para la representación, donde se celebran las impresionantes escenas de la Crucifixión. En la misma colina existe una ermita, desde la cual, una vez terminada la representación, se organiza la procesión con el Cristo yacente hasta la iglesia del pueblo. Se tiene proyectado celebrar el año que viene la Resurrección del Señor, con lo que quedaría completa la representación del Misterio.

(Friday, the last day, begins with the trial before Pilate, then continues along The Bitter Pathway [of Christ's procession to Calvary], then follows the road from the stadium to St. Barbara's Hill—a small natural hill offering perfect conditions for the representation, on which impressive scenes of the Crucifixion are celebrated. On the same hill there is a hermitage from which, once the performance ends, there starts a procession carrying Christ in the Tomb [a figure of Cristo Yacente] toward the town church. Next year, we are planning to represent the Resurrection of Our Lord. With this, the performance of the Mystery will be complete.)

One is left to imagine Moncada transformed into a "sacralized" land, with its inhabitants always either performing or preparing to perform the rites of Christ's suffering, death, and resurrection.

Though this megalomaniac vision resembled Franco's own efforts to place Spain's landscape and social life under the shadow of the gigantic cross of the Valley of the Fallen, having in 1965 received the first petition from the Mayor's office to certify the event, the officials of Ministerio de Información y Turismo must have had their doubts. In 1967, after a second petition, a Delegado Provincial was dispatched to witness the Mystery himself and judge whether it was worthy of certification and, if so, to decide which part of the long performances would make the best tourism attraction. Praising the costumes, the characters, and especially the "realismo verdaderamente impresionante" (really impressive realism) of the Via Dolorosa, he recommended for certification the Holy Thursday performance and the ensuing procession of Holy Friday. The official's report suggests that, while he was specifically looking for the marks of beauty and good taste that were usual reasons to certify celebrations, it was the realism of the procession through the town and the Crucifixion—the two parts of the performance taking place in real urban space—that left the biggest impression on him. These were the parts of the Misterio certified in 1967. Currently, however, both acts take place on an "enormous permanent stage" and thus no longer pretend to sacralize the landscape (Misterio de la Pasión de Moncada).

It is not yet understood what the national and transnational sacralization of time and space of local festivals does to people and communities. This should be the theme of another study. However, given the longevity of this and other anomie celebrations, we can appreciate how, in an effort to support both tourism and local economies, the State succeeded in making the daily lives of residents in Spain's towns and cities compatible with annual, collective exposure to the acts of death repurposed to fuel its centralized and regionally diversified tourism-driven economy without breaking local allegiances. Understanding now that the ritualized reenactments of Jesus's death were meant to make local economies viable while also allowing their members to remember their foreign and internal enemies and draw in new sun-loving friends, we can begin untangling the symbolic web of meanings still supporting the popularity of Holy Week.

For Goffman, "audience segregation" is what allows individuals and groups to develop credible personae by establishing relations of trust with different social collectives. There was no audience segregation, however, in 1960s Spain, where the government created special "contact zones" for citizens to develop national, regional, local, and personal identities imitating foreigners' habits. Invigorated thanks to the state's assistance, the Holy Week celebrations of that age of mobility made irrelevant the distinction between "authentic" rituals and ones that Mac-Cannell would term "sacralized." Well-rooted locals, domestic visitors, labor migrants, recent transplants, tourists—everyone was welcome to become participant *and* spectator in the anomie events that maintained, on a transnational local scale, the authority of the clergy, confraternal associations, and festivities' organizers, thereby preserving their male dominance. Keeping no performance off-stage as long as local elites, the Church, and the state could negotiate their terms, rejecting audience segregation, the tourism-guided renewal of Holy Week celebrations thus threatened to impoverish the repertoire of identities available to the inhabitants of Spain's towns and cities in ways that also displaced the allegiances that these rituals could not accommodate. Long lists of dark drama and action plots of film and fiction set against the background of the Spanish Holy Week make it evident that symbolic violence still persists in this normalized union of the Church, popular religion, and modernization with hospitality business.[4] The victims may be local or foreign, but we are yet to explain the mechanisms of inclusion and exclusion set in motion by the consumerist *sacratio* of the 1960s to understand, not only these fictional deaths, but also the lives of real people inhabiting the spaces of these celebrations or coming to witness them.

While the convergence of performative and participatory rituals that the local authorities and central government officials were seeking to achieve together reversed the split between a ritual and a show that tourism is normally thought to induce, my story of how Holy Week celebrations stopped being merely sacred in the religious sense to become instead a vehicle of *sacratio*, suggests that the messages of peace, political aperture, and consumption of Spain's tourism boom also conjured a godless "enemy" that tourists and Spaniards now had to contain together. The somber days of the Holy Week, with their scenes of the suffering and death of Christ, channeled the Cold War passions that Spain's proverbial sun was unable to sooth.

NOTES

The author wishes to thank Sally Anna Boyle for her editorial work on this piece, and the editors of this volume for their useful suggestions for revision and, especially, for their notes, some of which she appropriated into her text. The research was developed for the project *La modernidad paradójica: experiencia artística y turística en la España desarrollista (1959–1975)*—an interdisciplinary research initiative funded by the Ministry of Science and Innovation of Spain #PGC2018-093422-b-i00, codirected by José Díaz Cuyás (ULL) and Vicente Benet (UJI).

1. Not only did Franco remain the head of state and commander-in-chief at that time, but he was also his own prime minister (Carr 166). (He was, however, forced to establish the position of vice-president in 1962, following an injury in a hunting accident at the end of the previous year.) In 1962, in an effort to suppress the coal miners' strike that paralyzed Asturias and was spreading to other regions and sectors of industry, the government declared a state of emergency, giving Franco even more power. Earlier in the same year, Spain put itself forward for admission into the European Economic Community (EEC, a predecessor of the European Union), and in June, a group of former and current Spanish politicians representing a political spectrum ranging from exiled republicans to Falangistas met in Munich to discuss a proposal that urged European powers to demand substantial changes from Franco. The reaction of Franco's government, which denounced the meeting as "el contubernio de Munich" (the Munich conspiracy) and imprisoned its Spain-based participants, as well as the human rights violations in Asturias were some of the reasons cited by the EEC in its rejection of Spain's petition for acceptance. In the next few years, the government kept seeking ways to reopen the talks with the EEC (Powell 22–25).

2. Émile Durkheim coined *anomie* to denote "normlessness."

3. The documents carry a handwritten note from Luis Fernández Fúster inquiring about the status of the application. Better known as the author of the first theory of tourism in Spain (*Teoría y Técnica del Turismo*) among many other even better-known compendia, Fúster was at the time Jefe del Servicio de Información Turística de la Subsecretaría de Turismo.

4. Among many others, Juan Bonilla's *Nadie conoce a nadie* (1996), and the 1999 film based on that novel, directed by Mateo Gil; Fernando Carrasco's *El hombre que esculpió a Dios* (2008); more recently, *Caníbal* (2013) directed by Manuel Martín Cuenca; and *7LR (Siete Lágrimas Rojas)* by Juan Miguel de los Ríos (2016).

WORKS CITED

Afinoguénova, Eugenia. "'Unity, Stability, Continuity': Heritage and the Renovation of Franco's Dictatorship in Spain, 1957–1969." *International Journal of Heritage Studies*, vol. 16, no. 6, 2010, pp. 417–33.

Agamben, Giorgio. *Homo Sacer: Sovereign Power and Bare Life*. 1995. Translated by Daniel Heller-Roazen, Stanford University Press, 1998.

———. *State of Exception*. 2003. Translated by Kevin Attell, University of Chicago Press, 2005.

Anonymous. *España*. Editora Nacional, 1962.

Archivo General de la Administración (AGA). (3)49.12 Box 44873, 27 Jun. 1965.

———. (3)49. 12 Box 44886, Apr. 1966.

_____. (3)49.12 Box 44888, complaint on 21 Mar. 1970, with a cut-out article from *La verdad*, Murcia, of 17 Mar. 1970, 3; 13 Jun. 1966.

_____. (3)49.12 Box 4489, 5 Feb. 1968; 8 Feb. 1968.

_____. (3)49.12 Box 44891, Feb. 1968; 16 Feb. 1968.

Carr, Raymond. *Modern Spain, 1875–1980*. Oxford University Press, 1980.

Consejería de Turismo y Deporte. *Seguimiento de la demanda turística en Semana Santa 2016*. Junta de Andalucía, 2016.

_____. *Seguimiento de la demanda turística en Semana Santa 2017*. Junta de Andalucía, 2017.

Cordoba, Antonio, and Daniel García-Donoso, editors. *The Sacred and Modernity in Urban Spain: Beyond the Secular City*. Palgrave Macmillan, 2016.

Crumbaugh, Justin. *Destination Dictatorship: The Spectacle of Spain's Tourist Boom and the Reinvention of Difference*. State University of New York Press, 2009.

Fernández Fúster, Luis. *Teoría y Técnica del Turismo*, vols. 1 and 2, Editora Nacional, 1967.

Fraga Iribarne, Manuel. "Carl Schmitt: El hombre y la obra." *Revista de estudios políticos*, vol. 122, 1962, pp. 5–18.

Fueyo Álvarez, Jesús. *La época insegura*. Ediciones Europa, 1962.

Gajic, Tatjana. "Francoist Legality: On the Crisis of Authority and the Limits of Liberalism in Jesús Fueyo and José Ortega y Gasset." *European Legacy*, vol. 13, no. 2, 2008, pp. 161–74.

García-Donoso, Daniel. *Escrituras postseculares. Sedimentos de la religión en la narrativa española (1950–2010)*. Biblioteca Nueva, 2018.

Generalitat de Catalunya. "Passió d'Esparraguera: A Great Performance with More Than 50 Years of History." *Patrimoni Cultural*, n.d. Accessed 7 Apr. 2020.

Goffman, Erving. *The Presentation of Self in Everyday Life*. Doubleday, 1959.

Graburn, Nelson H. H. "Tourism: The Sacred Journey." *Hosts and Guests: The Anthropology of Tourism*, edited by Valene L. Smith, University of Pennsylvania Press, 1977, pp. 21–36.

Hobsbawm, Eric. "Introduction: Inventing Traditions." *The Invention of Tradition*. Cambridge University Press, 1983, pp. 1–14.

Junta de Andalucía. *The Ways of Passion*, 2011.

L.V.A. n.t. In *Pasión de Ulldecona, Hoja del Excelentísimo Sr. Gobernador Civil y Jefe Provincial del Movimiento y de la Excelentísima Diputación Provincial de Tarragona. Temporada 1965*. Ulldecona, 1965, pp. 1.

MacCannell, Dean. *Empty Meeting Grounds: The Tourist Papers*. Routledge, 1992.

_____. *The Tourist: A New Theory of the Leisure Class*. University of California Press, 1976.

Ministerio de Educación, Cultura y Deporte. "Real Decreto 384/2017, de 8 de abril, por el que se declara la Semana Santa como Manifestación Representativa del Patrimonio Cultural Inmaterial." *Boletín Oficial del Estado*, vol. 86, 11 Apr. 2017, pp. 28899–900.

Ministerio de Industria, Turismo y Comercio. "Orden ITC/1763/2006, de 3 de mayo, por la que se regula la declaración de fiestas de interés turístico nacional e internacional." *Boletín Oficial del Estado*, vol. 135, 7 Jun. 2006, pp. 21642–43.

Ministerio de Información y Turismo. "Orden de 30 de septiembre de 1964 por la que se crea la denominación honorífica de 'Fiesta de Interés Turístico.'" *Boletín Oficial del Estado*, vol. 251, 19 Oct. 1964, p. 13624.

Ministerio de Transportes, Turismo y Comunicaciones. "Orden de 29 de septiembre de 1987 por la que se regulan las declaraciones de interés turístico nacional e internacional." *Boletín Oficial del Estado*, vol. 257, 27 Oct. 1987, pp. 31990–91.

Misterio de la Pasión de Moncada, 7 Apr. 2020.

Murillo, Enrique. "La Pasión de Ulldecona." *ABC* (Madrid), 23 Mar. 1967, pp. 11–13.

Olmos Juárez, Lourdes, and Rafael García Cebrián. *Estructura del mercado turístico*, 2nd ed., Ediciones Paraninfo, S.A., 2016.

Pack, Sasha D. *Tourism and Dictatorship: Europe's Peaceful Invasion of Franco's Spain*. Palgrave Macmillan, 2006.

Patronato de la Passió d'Ulldecona. "La Passió d'Ulldecona." 7 Apr. 2020.

Powell, Charles T. "Spain's External Relations, 1898–1975." *Democratic Spain: Reshaping External Relations in a Changing World*, edited by Richard Gillespie, Fernando Rodrigo, and Jonathan Story, Routledge, 1995, pp. 11–28.

Schmitt, Carl. "El orden del mundo después de la segunda guerra mundial." *Revista de estudios políticos*, vol. 122, 1962, pp. 19–38.

Smith, Laurajane. *The Uses of Heritage*. Routledge, 2006.

Viestenz, William. *By the Grace of God: Francoist Spain and the Sacred Roots of Political Imagination*. University of Toronto Press, 2014.

Vilarós, Teresa. "Banalidad y biopolítica: La Transición española y el nuevo orden del mundo." *Desacuerdos 2. Sobre arte, políticas y esfera pública en el estado español*, MACBA, Arteleku, 2005, pp. 29–56.

CHAPTER 3

Carlos Saura

Death, Orphanhood, and the Commoners' Transitions

Angel Loureiro

Narratives, and critiques, of the Spanish transition to democracy have usually centered on the institutional process that took Spain from a dictatorship to a democracy in a short period of time. Early interpretations of the transition to democracy celebrated it as an unabashed political success; however, that narrative, which for a long time became hegemonic, has been replaced in recent times in many quarters by a view of the transition as a missed opportunity to come to terms with the Francoist legacy as well as a failure to set up a more proper political and constitutional framework. Both views/narratives are highly questionable, each of them for specific reasons that are not pertinent here, being more relevant for the purposes of this essay to point out the shortcomings they share, besides their common simplification of very complex and messy social, economic, and political changes. The centrality of the political-institutional process in the transition is undeniable. However, by focusing exclusively on that process, and on the narrow time frame in which it took place, both views sideline or simply ignore many other developments and activities that took place in a vibrant, complex, and multifarious period that started before Franco's death in 1975 and didn't stop with the 1979 elections that included all political parties.

Some cultural critics—prominently among them Germán Labrador Méndez—have rightly proposed narratives of those years that attend to the richness of its cultural production and alternative political formations. While this essay focuses on some films released shortly before, or in the years of, the political transition, its aim is not to examine them just for the sake of an analysis in itself, nor to rescue from oblivion neglected cultural-political communities and accursed figures. Instead, the focus will be on the vicissitudes of the films' ordinary protagonists.

Between the political factions and their leaders, on the one hand, and the alternative communities that flourished at the time, on the other, there is a vast middle ground of common citizens, whose problems and political participation paint a very different picture of the 1970s. The transition had common people at its core, not merely elites and politicians, as featured in the most widespread, triumphalist narratives of the transition, as well as in the most critical ones. Through multiple ways of action and resistance, the incipient Spanish civil society kept the political establishment on its toes and forced the country's democratization, an "other" transition—here called the commoner's transition—that will be examined in more detail at the end of this essay.

Simultaneous to the political process, and irrespective of whether they were having an active political involvement or not, many people took stock of their lives' narratives. In the autobiographical boom that took place after Franco's death, many former collaborators of the regime rushed to retouch their past to make it look more democratic, or assumed a late repentance for their connivance with Francoism; some other people—mainly privileged upper-middle-class liberals—effected drastic changes in their mores and personal lives; still others— the generations that already had well-established lives in the 1970s—had to assume the inevitable, that their lives were set, that it was too late to change anything; and countless others—and this was perhaps the most tragic consequence of Francoism, and one that still waits to be explored—had to live with the memory of a might-have-been (to use Faulkner's words) that Francoism made impossible: a memory of what might have happened had they lived under democratic conditions, a memory that overlapped, and in many cases possibly overwhelmed, the memory of what actually had occurred in their lives.

More than any other artistic form, Spanish cinema of the 1970s focused extensively on the ways this middle ground of common citizens lived the transition, and no other director did it with such unremitting and affecting intensity as Carlos Saura did in the films he directed in the mid-1970s, *La prima Angélica* (Cousin Angelica) (1974), *Cría cuervos* (Raise Ravens) (1976), and *Elisa, vida mía* (Elisa, My Life) (1977). Examined as a unit, the three films give shape to a narrative that could be expanded to include other films of the period, such as *El espíritu de la colmena* (The Spirit of the Beehive) (Víctor Erice, 1973), *El desencanto* (Disenchantment) (Jaime Chávarri, 1976), and *Asignatura pendiente* (Pending Exam) (José Luis Garci, 1977), as well as other films by Saura released in the early and late 1970s.

It is not by chance that Saura's three films revolve obsessively around death, memory, personal refashioning, and the uncertainty of the future; still more remarkably, despite their close chronological proximity and their many similarities, each of them deals with those issues in strikingly different ways. The three films have at their core the death of a progenitor and the ways a son—in the first film—or a daughter—in the last two—deals with its demise and aftermath. In the three films death is very real: bones, agony, labored breathing, physical collapse, none of the three films spares the spectators the materiality of the body's physical labors, trials, and ultimate dissolution.

Filmed with an impassioned immediacy to the social and political turbulence of the 1970s, but without any explicit reference to them, the three films place death at the center of generational conflicts or complicities. The protagonists' precarious situation could be captured with the idea of orphanhood, be it figurative or real: a son reburies his mother's remains and has to come to grips with his traumatic remembrances of the Civil War (*La prima Angélica*); a mother's death and an unacceptable father haunt a young girl (*Cría cuervos*); a father leaves his family and, years later, a daughter meets him again and examines her tribulations in the light of her father's (*Elisa, vida mía*). In the three films, the protagonists—members of a younger generation—are enmeshed in disorientation and paralysis but end up with a renewed determination to face their future. Tellingly, with each new film, Saura progressively endows its protagonist with increasing agency and purposefulness.

La prima Angélica: Revisiting the Past

The first Spanish film in Spain in which the Civil War is seen from the point of view of the defeated (Sánchez Vidal 86), *La prima Angélica* "opened a road toward the unmaking of the Francoism imaginary" of the Civil War (Quintana 96). The story narrated in *La prima Angélica* is bracketed between two heart-rending childhood memories of the Spanish Civil War. It begins with the frozen frame of the just bombed-out dining room of the male protagonist's childhood school, a reference to the stasis of Luis's traumatic remembrances of many of his experiences in the war years. Gradually, the pupils and priests in the frame come back to life and, in an abrupt cut, the next scene takes us to Barcelona's Montjuïc cemetery in the early 1970s, where Luis and his father are witnessing the exhumation of the remains of Luis's mother, which he will take to Segovia for reinternment in the family vault. In its final sequence, the film goes back to the war years: after Luis and Angélica attempt vainly to bicycle to Madrid, they are returned home by Francoist soldiers and Luis receives a vicious belting by Angélica's father. The film closes with a lingering, fixed shot—again a hint to a long-enduring pain—of Angélica shedding a tear while her mother slowly combs her hair, with a song associated with Luis's and Angélica's childhoods—the *copla* "Rocío"—playing wistfully in the background.[1]

La prima Angélica develops around various forms of memory, which point to different ways in which the past and the present are connected. The most salient type of memory foregrounded is Luis's remembrances of the Civil War, which he is forced to relive when he returns to his aunt's house in Segovia—where he spent an unspecified amount of time during the Civil War—to reinter his mother's bones, twenty years after her death. While in the first part of the film, Luis has difficulty remembering episodes from his childhood's time in Segovia, in the second part, he returns to the city determined to confront his traumatic remembrances of 1936.

As soon as he steps into his aunt's home, Luis's conflictive remembrances begin to assail and overwhelm him, to the point that he conflates Angélica's father with her husband Anselmo, a confusion that points to the ideological continuity between the past and the present in Luis's mind. His desire to portray this continuity led Saura to discard using flashbacks (Brasó, "New Interview" 18), opting instead for employing the same actors to represent different characters—Angélicas's father and husband; Angélica as a child in 1936 and her daughter in the present—or, as is the case with Luis, to use the same actor to represent the same character in two different times, the present and 1936. In this way, Saura wants to emphasize the persistence of Luis's traumatic memories as well as his need to relive them, to be again the child he was in 1936, in order to overcome his painful past. As Marvin D'Lugo argues, in Luis's remembrances, "the past is not merely evoked, but reenacted" (119).

In his stay in Segovia, Luis's traumatic memories come to the surface but end up being restored to their rightful place in the flow of time, leading him to broaden the rift with his Segovian conservative relatives. "Han pasado treinta años y todavía hay quien se acuerda de la guerra. Pregúntale a mi hija lo que sabe de la guerra. Nada. Absolutamente nada. Y es lógico, el tiempo lo borra todo. Arreglados estaríamos si no fuera así" (After thirty years, there are people who still remember the Civil War. Ask my daughter what she knows about the War. Nothing. Absolutely nothing. It's logical, time erases everything. We would be in a good mess if it were otherwise), states Angélica's husband Anselmo, attempting to deflect Luis's interest in remembering his traumatic experiences in his aunt's house during the Civil War. Against Anselmo's interest in forgetting the memories of the war, ultimately both sides of the family are painfully aware of the impossibility of forgetfulness or reconciliation. "Hay que irse. ¿Qué tengo yo que hacer aquí?" (Time to go. What do I do here?) monologues Luis at the end, hammering home the unbridgeable fracture that still exists in the 1970s between the opposing factions of the Civil War, his recollection of the hatred his family displayed toward his Republican father being the reminder that the memory of the war is still painfully alive.[2] However, as Saura emphasizes through the two distressing scenes that frame *La prima Angélica*'s narrative, there is no such thing as a completely sutured trauma, because even if the traumatic memories are put "in their place," the pain suffered endures in the present. There can be palliatives for an injurious past, but not truly a cure.

In a literary portrait of the filmmaker, Juan Marsé wrote that Saura's physical traits "expresan un deseo único, una exclusiva obsesión: recuperar la memoria perdida del país, la memoria que fue manipulada, camuflada y adulterada. . . . La frente apacible luce este tema: Sin memoria no somos nada" (46) (express only one wish: to recover the lost memory of the country, the memory that was manipulated, hidden, adulterated. . . . His placid forehead exhibits this motto: Without memory we are nothing). Marsé didn't write this description in the context of the collective call to remember the traumatic past of the Civil War that was so reiterated in the early years of this century. They were published in the magazine *Por favor* in the mid-1970s, and expressed the urgent need, felt by the opponents to Franco's regime, to keep alive a memory that had been hidden or manipulated in the years of the dictatorship, when all the books on the Civil War published in Spain, without a single exception, were written from a Francoist point of view. So much for the memory of the Civil War being swept under a rug in the years of the transition to democracy.[3] There is in *La prima Angélica* a complex sense of memory that makes sound irredeemably naive the reduction of the memory of the Civil War to a simple choice between memory or forgetfulness, in which memory is furthermore conceived as a willful exercise of restoration of the past, in contrast with the supposed willful forgetfulness that supposedly afflicted Spaniards in the years of the transition. Without pretending that *La prima Angélica* "represents" a view of the historical past shared by all Spaniards in the early 1970s (in fact, Saura has stated that it is based on his remembrances of the Civil War), it still offers compelling evidence that the memory of the Civil War was far from simple in the early 1970s, a point that is further illustrated by the attempts by *ultra* groups at the time to prevent the film from being shown on Spanish screens—stealing part of roll in a theater in Madrid; throwing a bomb in a movie theatre in Barcelona (Sánchez Vidal 87)—which ultimately led to its withdrawal from all screens.

Up to a point, Luis overcomes his traumatic past—or at least has the courage to face it in an attempt to restore the flow of time—but his pain endures even after he, somehow successfully, resolves to confront his disturbing memories. One will not find in this film the facile rhetoric of remembrance and restoration that has been the norm in the calls made in recent years about the curative, reconciliatory ends of the compulsion to remember.

Cría cuervos: The Power of Death

Saura's next film, Cría cuervos (1976), returns to the interplay between death, memory, and the self. This time, the protagonist is a melancholy girl, Ana, who is discomfited by a recent, distressing past. Confronted with her mother's demise at an age at which she is still incapable of understanding death, Ana will undergo a process over a few summer weeks from the unremitting sorrow about her mother's disappearance to an acceptance of her irrevocable departure. Memory in this film works as a form of consolation and a strategy of resistance; it also serves as a reservoir of strength and an inducement to revenge. Although a number of experiences and rituals help Ana process and finally accept her mother's death, it can be argued that her passing never passes, that her death transcends the physical dissolution of an individual's body to linger in the end as a figure of irrevocable loss, as testimony of a collective "might-have-been that is more true than truth," to express it in Faulkner's words in Absalom, Absalom! (115).

Cría—as the film is known in English—intersperses two complementary narratives. Mixing fantasy and remembrance, in the first storyline, Ana, searching for consolation for her loss, wills her mother to reappear or recollects memories of times spent together.[4] This plot of restoration and remembrance consists of a series of memories and fantasies that allow Ana to assuage her pain and to recall grievous situations that ultimately induced her to inflict revenge on her father, who she believes is responsible for her mother's sorrows and demise. In the final sequence of this chronicle of recall and restoration, Ana closes her eyes tightly in bed wishing for her dead mother to visit her. Her mother dutifully materializes at her bedroom door, but Ana's fantasy soon dissolves and reality sets in.[5] Ana, realizing her mother is gone forever, repeatedly cries out in desperation, a final vain attempt to conjure back her mother: she will not invoke her mother again in the film's remaining thirty minutes, a disappearing act that signals that after that night, Ana—the work of mourning done—lets go of her wishful self-delusion of being able to bring back the dead through fantasy or memory, and recognizes the finality of death.

This narrative of remembrance and wishful recollection—which ends two-thirds into the film—is weaved with a storyline about Ana's conviction that she has real and symbolic power over death, a narrative that, in contrast with the former, extends almost to the end of the film. In the first episode of this storyline—the film's first sequence—Ana's father dies of a heart attack while having sex with his lover, an accident that will lead Ana to believe she has killed him, as was her intention, by lacing milk with a white powder her mother had ordered her to throw away, with the jesting warning, lost on Ana, that it was a powerful poison—it turns out to be calcium carbonate and other harmless ingredients.[6] This narrative continues in several episodes: in one, Ana jumps (in her imagination) from the roof of a building, but instead of crashing to earth she is able to fly. In another episode, she plays hide-and-seek with her sisters, and when she uncovers their hideouts she commands them to die, so that she can resurrect them by praying to her Guardian Angel.[7] In the next scene of this narrative of death, Ana tells her mute, wheel-chair-bound and death-wishing grandmother she can help her die, only to be rebuffed by the old woman when she realizes Ana's powder is just a harmless stomach medicine.

The two final events in this storyline show that Ana finally comes to terms with death, instead of refusing to accept it or trying to dispense it. When, near the film's end her guinea pig Roni dies, she takes his death as a natural event and buries him in the garden. This narrative about death ends a little later, when Ana attempts to murder her disciplinarian aunt Paulina—a replacement for her dead sister, Paulina has failed miserably to win the children's hearts—lacing milk with the white powder as she had done to "kill" her father, only to see with astonishment her aunt alive and restful the morning after. Ana's fantasy opposite to bringing back the dead—her presumed power to inflict death upon the living—will also dissolve and, cleansed of delusion, she will be ready for rebirth.

Positioned between the hide-and-seek scene and Ana's offer to help her grandmother die, there is a revealing sequence about mothering and rebirth. While Rosa performs kitchen chores, Ana plays with a doll pretending it is her daughter and asks Rosa whether babies are born with hair. After replying to Ana's question with examples from her personal experiences, Rosa segues into issues of mothering and childbirth, talking about her offspring, teaching Ana how to hold a baby, and then going into detail about Ana's birth: her father's disappointment (he wanted a son); her seeming refusal to come out of the womb; the use of forceps to deliver her; the incapacity of her delicate mother to breastfeed her, which leads Rosa to tell Ana that she was really the one who nursed her; and, finally, to expose her big breasts, after Ana's insistent request.

In this scene about fertility and mothering, Ana is born again through a narrative (Rosas's) that replicates her previous, material birth. When she soon learns that she has no power over death—the rebirth sequence is followed by the grandmother's rejection of Ana's powder and her failed attempt to kill her aunt—Ana will be ready to resume life, an idea illustrated by the film's final sequence, in which the three sisters get out of the house for the first time in the film and march to school, leaving behind an oppressive house and haunting death. However, while pointing to life resumed and a semblance of normality, this ending does not imply that Ana's past and its injurious memories are left behind for good. As the adult Ana illustrates in one of her explanatory scenes—the film's true ending, but not its final word—pain endures, and so do the mysteries of memory and time uncertain: Ana will have to lead her life burdened with the memory of loss and a still obscure past full of fears.[8]

Faced with films like *Cría cuervos* and the others examined in this essay, critics are inevitably tempted to take the easy, allegorical route out. The charged political context of the year the film was made (1975); the somber, claustrophobic atmosphere of the house; the disciplinarian aunt; the military father, who not only fought in the Civil War but was also a volunteer with the *División Azul*; and the father's military friend, whose loaded gun is central in a late episode in the film: all of these features would seem to inevitably entice some critics to make an allegorical interpretation of the film—a perennial trap with films produced during the dictatorship—simplifying its rich content and, above all, missing its temporal dynamics, which, as in *La prima Angélica*, are so central to the film. In this regard, it is paramount to distinguish between causes and merely contextual information. Ana's father is a military man, but that does not automatically imply that Ana's predicaments stem from that fact. For Ana, her father's unfaithfulness and cruelty to her mother are much more important than his military affiliation, a fact the adult Ana, in her reflections on her childhood that are interspersed throughout the film, does not refer to at all when taking stock of her early years.[9]

In the companion booklet to the Criterion DVD edition of the film, Paul Julian Smith offers very valuable information, but also falls on facile allegorical interpretations: the father's gun is a "sign of the legacy of violence that is bequeathed from one generation to another, from guilty or forgetful adults to uncomprehending children"; the house, "claustrophobic in spite of its ample size and extensive garden, is a transparent metaphor for the regime"; the swimming pool would be "a symbol of sensual pleasures lost or unfulfilled"; the noise that comes from the street suggests that the repressed memories return as ghosts. This type of linear, allegorical interpretation immobilizes films in the present in which they were filmed, in this case not only simplifying—and rendering dated—a film that is very open-ended and self-questioning, but also missing the dimension of futurity—and therefore the impossibility of closure—that is embedded in it. As in

La prima Angélica, Saura uses in *Cría cuervos* some distancing devices that serve two purposes: to prevent the spectators from resorting to sentimental, identificatory interpretations, and to provide a self-reflective narrative that disrupts all easy interpretations. In *Cría cuervos*, this double role is fulfilled by the three short scenes in which the adult Ana breaks up the narrative flow by injecting reflections about the events narrated in the film. In the most significant of the three interventions, she curtails the temptation to make her military father into an allegory of the regime when she wonders why she was intent on killing him, stating that the answers she can come up with twenty years later "are too simple, they don't convince me. The only thing I remember very clearly is that at the time I was convinced my father was responsible for all the sadness that embittered the last years of my mother's life. I was convinced that it was him and him alone who brought about her illness and death." Complicating matters still more, she adds that her mother could have been a good pianist, but she stopped giving concerts to take care of her daughters and seemingly regretted "giving up a profession that could have brought her freedom . . . I also think that deep down she feared she might not be the prodigy her friends had foretold and she preferred a quiet and well-ordered life."[10]

No matter the cause of the mother's suffering—her husband's insensitivity, her timorous renunciation to a professional career, or both—in her professional unfulfillment and premature death, she is a figure of the heartbreaking sense of loss that pervades the film. Thus, the undeniable evidence contained in the film is the reality of loss and the need to reorient one's life as a result of it. As in *La prima Angélica*, in *Cría cuervos*, the main character overcomes the immediate obstacles, but there is no intimation of closure of a wounded past, no miraculous cure for a sense of profound loss. As it happens with Luis, Ana will have to face an open-ended future with the haunting memory of loss, burdened with a past that will never pass.

Elisa, vida mía: Life as Representation

While a very distant car riding on a desolate landscape gradually and silently begins to approach the static camera, a male's voice-over narrates a visit, which seems to be related to the approaching car:

Hacía años que no veía a mi padre, y la verdad es que en todo ese tiempo no lo había echado de menos. Creo que no pasarían de los dedos de la mano las veces que le había escrito. . . . La enfermedad de mi padre coincidió con la crisis de mi matrimonio, bueno, con una de las crisis. Cuando recibí el inquietante telegrama de mi hermana *María* anunciándome la enfermedad de papá y después de una angustiosa conversación telefónica con mi familia en donde me di cuenta de la gravedad de la situación y de la necesidad de mi urgente presencia en Madrid . . . encontré al fin un pretexto para alejarme de casa unos días y poder así recapacitar tranquilamente sobre mi situación. Conforme me iba alejando de casa y de Antonio se iba afirmando en mí la idea de no volver nunca más junto al hombre con quien habían transcurrido siete años de mi vida. *Me marché, y ahora lo veo claro, para no volver más* (My emphasis)

(I hadn't seen my father in many years, and I truly didn't miss him in all that time. I think one could count with the fingers on one hand the number of times I had written to him. . . . My father's sickness coincided with my matrimonial crisis, well, with one of its many crises. When I received a distressing telegram from my sister *María* informing me about dad's sickness, and after an anguished phone conversation with my family let me see the gravity of the situation and the need of my urgent presence in Madrid . . . I finally found an excuse to leave my house for a few days to think serenely about my situation. As I was getting farther away from home and from Antonio, the idea of not returning to the man with whom I had lived for seven years was becoming firmer. *I left, and now I see it clearly, never to return again.*)[11]

Soon after the car, carrying a young woman and her husband (Isabel and Julián), their two daughters, and Isabel's sister Elisa, arrives at an isolated house, some parallelisms between the actual visit and the one narrated in the voice-over account begin to emerge: two daughters visit their father (Luis); one of them (Elisa), who has not seen him in years and has rarely been in touch with him, has agreed to visit him in part to reflect on her marital problems. However, a number of significant discrepancies become also evident: although at the end of the film he dies, apparently of a heart problem, at no moment in the film is there any mention of Luis having had surgery; Isabel is called María in the voice-over narrative; and finally—and strikingly—the protagonist of the narrated and the real visits is a woman, but the narrator's voice is Luis's—Elisa's father.

It will turn out that Luis is writing what seems to be a proleptic chronicle of his daughters' visit, a narrative that, in its usurpation of a voice and in its anticipation of the events it describes, raises suspicions about its potential motivations. The events that follow and the knowledge we gather from them will provide the keys to unveil the mystery. Luis, who, fed up with rules and conventions had left his wife and two daughters (Elisa was then nine) and, renouncing property and propriety, started a new life living in isolation in the countryside, is concerned about the memories and views Elisa might have of him (although not stated, Isabel seems to have been in touch with him more often than Elisa), molded as they were by the wife he abandoned. Luis happens to be a prolific writer whose imagination is easily triggered by almost anything he sees or hears around him, and especially by stories about the past that have an enigma at their core. His almost instant connection with Elisa, his desire to guide her thoughts and decisions out of her marital dilemmas, and the particularly strong effect she has on his imagination will end up leading him into unsuspecting territories, as he continues throughout the film the narrative whose initial sentences are heard at the beginning.

The connection between Luis and Elisa—wished for by him before she has even arrived—will find an almost instantaneous accomplice in his daughter. As soon as she sets foot inside the house, Elisa begins to roam around full of curiosity, ending in Luis's office while in the background we hear Satie's *Gnossienne n° 3*, a musical theme associated throughout the film with Luis's imagination at work, be it engaged in actual writing or in thinking about a potential narrative. After scanning the room, she takes notice of some handwritten pages left by Luis on his desk and, curious about her father's life, she picks them up and starts to read them. Shortly, she turns her head away from the page, freezes in reflection while her voice-over continues, and then lowers her head toward a picture—Isabel and herself as little girls—that Luis keeps on his desk. Like a drowned corpse emerging from the depths, Elisa's face begins to appear on the picture's glass, until her blurry figure ends up superimposed on her early, cheerful image, a ghostly face laden with affliction upon the smiling specter of happy childhood gone: Luis's autobiographical ruminations about being directionless in life have struck home with his daughter who, as her father's narrative had already anticipated, is as lost as he is. However, in contrast with her father's decision to leave his family, she is mired in passivity and indecision, and lacks the courage to break up with her husband.

The stakes are set for the film's particular dynamics: moved by Elisa's vicissitudes and confessions, Luis will attempt to script Elisa's life in advance of the facts, and his anticipatory chronicle will work as a wished-for mirror for his daughter. His narrative is also a trap that will almost end up snaring his creator, a new Pygmalion who becomes infatuated with the work he has created.

Elisa: her mind as blurry and baffled as her face in the mirror of her early picture's glass; her life: a mess without direction; her will: as puzzled as a rover at a forked path. The mirror will work its magic; the toll: Luis's life. Otherwise, unlike Galatea's rejection of her maker, the tale could end up with the carnal coupling—at least on paper—between a father and his daughter, creator and created. A simultaneous benefit: Luis's demise—a costly substitution for Galatea's rejection of her maker—will release Elisa from the role her father had created for her in the theater of the world. Because it will turn out that the seventeenth-century Spanish playwright Pedro Calderón de la Barca will also wield a mirror, but one to be mocked and rejected. Luis provides the example and the incitement, but Elisa will gain freedom and agency by her own effort and decisions. Near the film's end, after her father dies, she will take his place directing Calderón's *El gran teatro del mundo* (The Great Theater of the World), a play about a Sovereign Author who creates a world in which all human beings have pre-assigned roles they are forced to perform—all resistance being in vain—in that great representation that is life. Elisa's direction of the play will be a first step in her path to becoming the maker and mover of her life: no longer the passive pawn who has hewed to the roles handed down to her, but a woman endowed with agency and resolve, ready to make decisions about her future.

The parallels between Calderón's plot and Luis's and Elisa's stories are obvious; the differences, revealing. Luis decided years ago to break with the role he had been socially assigned, and now, seeing that Elisa feels as trapped as he was, he wants her to emulate him, driven by a desire that, for all its benevolence, still makes of him a microcosmic sovereign. Elisa will follow the role prefigured for her by her father's life and writings, two mirrors—one facing the past, the other showing the future—that will help her take control of her life.

No longer mired in passivity and self-pity, Elisa's subtle change in attitude is drastically affirmed shortly thereafter when, after reading a letter she has received from Antonio, discards it with irritation, her first gesture of rebellion, her first step toward self-fashioning. What follows next she also does with an impetuous fury: after placing a blank piece of paper between two pages of a women's magazine, she frantically does the partial tracing of that page's back, resulting in a woman's smeared face, its right side mostly missing, a mesh veil covering her face, hair to mouth. Unlike the previous, passive overlapping of her blurry, aching face with the image of the child she was, she now contemplates herself in the smeared figures of her tracings: from blur to blotch, from minute six to sixty-six, by the middle of the film, Elisa has begun to take steps toward her own self-affirmation.

Writing another person's life can have unexpected consequences for the biographer, and much more when the writer impersonates his daughter. Luis wants to fashion Elisa's future life, but surreptitiously, another story has been developing in his imagination: Pygmalion seems to have fallen in love with Galatea, or at least his fantasy seems to toy with that idea, as it happens in the scene in which he imagines himself and his daughter in a startling amorous embrace. Of course, it is a fantasy, and Saura left in the film an intriguing ambiguity about whose imagination is fashioning this scene of potential incest (Brasó, "Interview" 50–51). Rejecting the idea of incest, his narrative spoiled, Luis starts a new version of the whole story: "Hacía años que no veía a mi padre, y la verdad es que en todo ese tiempo no lo había echado mucho de menos. Creo que no pasarían de los dedos de la mano las veces que le había escrito" (I hadn't seen my father in many years, and I truly didn't miss him in all that time. I think one could count with a hand's fingers the number of times I had written to him), but now with a very significant difference: the story really happens in Madrid, and the focus falls now squarely on a very sick Luis, no longer on Elisa's trip and tribulations.[12]

In the early morning of the following day while taking a walk, Luis's imagination cannot cease to work. "Escribí toda la noche y me siento bien" (I wrote all night long and I feel good), he says in a monologue, before immediately transposing his experience to his daughter: "Ha pasado toda la noche en vela . . . pero no le importa, le gusta permanecer despierta en la oscuridad . . . dejando volar su imaginación, esperando que lleguen los recuerdos . . . ¿qué recuerdos?" (She has stayed up all night long . . . but she doesn't mind, she likes to stay awake in the darkness . . . letting her imagination fly, waiting for memories to surface . . . what memories?). Here, a baffled Luis stops, unable to continue impersonating Elisa, void of content for his new story about her. Appropriately, when he reaches this dead end in his role as the script-writer of his daughter's future, a sudden pain in the chest makes him fall to the ground. Confined to bed by his doctor, Elisa replaces him directing the rehearsal of *El gran teatro del mundo*, and she and the girls have a ball doing it, their ever louder laughs sounding as a dissonant counterpoint to the stern harmony of Calderón's rigid script. At the end of this sequence, the girl that acts as the Great Sovereign proclaims, barely able to contain her laugh: "Ya sé que si el hombre pudiera elegir, nadie elegiría hacer el papel de sentir y de padecer, todos querrían hacer el papel de mandar y dirigir, sin mirar, sin advertir, que eso es también representar, aunque ellos piensen que es vivir . . . En este gran teatro del mundo, toda la vida representación es" (I know that if men could pick their role, nobody would choose to feel and suffer, everyone would pick the power to order and direct, without realizing that playing such a role is still a representation, even if they think that it is living. . . . In this great theatre of the world, life is only a representation).[13]

After Calderón's authority has been dismissed, the time has come to also do away with Luis's. When Elisa returns home after having taken up his directing role in the rehearsal, she finds him dead on the same path where he had previously fallen writhing in pain. At this point, Pygmalion's aria begins to sound—for the last time in the film—opening a new sequence in which the camera slowly pans the interior of the house, repeating a movement that had previously been associated with Luis's imagination, while we hear Elisa's voice-over, beginning the third and final version of her visit's narrative: "Hacía años que no veía a mi padre" (I hadn't seen my father for many years). This version differs from the first one in that now we hear her own voice, not her father's, and her sister has her real name—Isabel, not María—as in the first version. While Elisa writes these words, a very distant car riding on a desolate landscape gradually and silently begins to approach the static camera, bringing the film to an end with a loop to the film's first take, but signaling also a new beginning to Elisa's life.[14]

From her initial confusion, passivity, and indecision, Elisa evolves throughout the film, bringing it to a close with a gesture of agential affirmation that combines an acceptance of her father's legacy of rebellion against an immobile social world, as well as an appropriation of his pen, a sign of independence by which she transforms herself from a character in someone else's narrative into an author of her own story, an act of rebellion against pre-assigned social roles that opens her life to a new, although uncertain future.[15]

The Commoners' Transitions

In an exemplary book, Germán Labrador Méndez writes about the Spanish process of democratization as a "bifid transition," to indicate that at the time, eschewing institutional politics, communities of young people created "new types of lives" linking inextricably culture and life, in an alternative, high-risk politics that in many cases cost the lives of their agents. Labrador is undeniably right, and his study has injected new life, and new protagonists, into the stale view of the transition. However, there are still many unanswered questions. What happened in the transitional years with generations and groups of citizens other than young people? What did they do with their lives and their bodies? Where have been registered their dilemmas, their views about their lives, their pasts, and their (im)possible new futures?

An essential assumption of this essay is that the processes and changes that took place in Spain in the 1970s—and not only the political and institutional changes— were accompanied by many individuals' reflections about their pasts and about the possibility of scripts for their futures that no longer hewed to the traditional values fostered by Francoism. This transition followed a different *tempo* and temporality than the institutional one. In many cases, these other transitions—the transitions of the commoners—took place only as wishful thinking in the silence of the mind, but even if they were never registered, some cultural artifacts, and especially several films, attempted to approximate and inscribe them. In contrast with historical writings, by focusing on affects and daily dilemmas documentary and fiction film—and perhaps the latter even more—can get much closer to the truth than written history or autobiographical works.

Filmed between 1974—two years before Franco's death—and 1977—date of the first democratic elections—the films examined in this essay revolve obsessively around the legacy and burden of the past. Taken as an ensemble, they can be seen as forming an extended narrative with some continuous threads: the past as a troubled time; the interplay between generations; the absence or death of a progenitor; the dilemmas faced by characters who dare to come to grips with their heritages and troubles, which leads them to find a newfound determination to take an active role in shaping their (uncertain) future.

There are several other films that could fit in this ensemble, and primarily among them *El desencanto* (1976) and *Asignatura pendiente* (1977). The latter focuses on some issues that can help shed new light on an understanding of the films explored here. Referring to life under Franco, its protagonist, a thirty-five-year-old labor lawyer tells a former girlfriend, who is now a dissatisfied wife: "They have stolen so many things from us. . . . The times you and I could have made love and didn't. The books we should have read. The things we should have thought but didn't. . . . . It is for those reasons that I cannot forgive them."

This late lamentation refers to a fundamental cost of the dictatorship that has barely received any attention: Francoism as a theft of potentialities, of (other) pasts and futures. Together with the memory of their past, the generations that paid that price had to live with the ghostly memory of a might-have-been that has not been registered anywhere but still has shaped lives and attitudes: invisible but indelible, the memory of what could not happen, but might have happened, can be more lasting than the memory of what actually took place. *Asignatura pendiente* narrates the failure of its male protagonist's effort to recover the lost time of Francoism through his resumption of a romance from his teenager years, an attempt to solve in an amorous key a problem for which politics has no remedy because change has come too late for people of that generation. By resorting to that substitute solution, *Asignatura* becomes inevitably a nostalgic narrative, its protagonist resigning himself to his loss but yearning for a past that could not be. However, despite its double failure—the protagonist's in his vain attempt to compensate for his loss through the resumption of a love story; the film for its ultimate nostalgia and resignation—*Asignatura* points to a deficient past, to an emptiness or deficit of experience whose consideration is vital to fully understand the noxious biopolitical consequences of Francoism. Of course, a might-have-been is part and parcel of anyone's experience of time, but it becomes paramount and profoundly affecting in precarious, long-lasting, life-crushing periods like a dictatorship.

The excess of trauma resists all efforts to narrativize it, and melancholy can only reiterate its senseless ruin, but deficits are prone to prompting narratives of reinvention. In this contest, deficit in good measure also means orphanhood, another form of deficiency that could allude to an inacceptable father, to the interruption of a tradition, to the lack of appropriate models and "maestros," or to the nonexistence of a civil society in which to grow and be nurtured: all the above are types of deficits that afflicted several generations of Spaniards under Franco, those who discovered, in most cases too late, the spurious or deficient nature of lives lived under a dictatorship.

It is thus understandable that the characters in the three Saura films feel the pressing need to revise their lives, to search for new filiations, to start anew. In contrast with *Asignatura*'s literalness, which inevitably dates the film, and to the sentimentally compensatory dedication that closes it—"To us, who have arrived late to everything: to childhood, to adolescence, to sex, to love, to politics. . . . To us, who were robbed, year after year, of the meaning of everything around us, even of the smallest things, of the least important ones"—Saura's films, with their scarcity of direct references to the historical moment, do not take the easy way out of nostalgia and sentimentality, but plomb instead the depths of disorientation and uncertainty, allowing their protagonists to actively rebuild their lives despite being burdened with a traumatic or distressing past. With an emphasis on agency and the future that seems to increase chronologically with each of the three films examined, these stories avoid easy solutions and point to arduous futures. Luis finds the determination to confront his childhood's traumatic memories at the price of reopening the ideological fracture with his family; in the three times the adult Ana appears in *Cría cuervos*, she underscores the obscurity of her past's feelings and actions, admitting that her confusion continues in the present; and while Elisa takes the pen to write her story, it is clear from the disorientation she shows throughout the film that her future will be as difficult and tentative as her past was.

In these three films, Saura wrote the script for a possible transition of the commoners in which some Spaniards recognized their plea in the 1970s, even if for some of them the future was already set. Filmed in the intense turmoil of the transition's years, Saura's three films do not attempt to *represent*, but strive to give shape and create meaning out of the chaos and confusion that dominates the lives of their protagonists. The dead body of a progenitor serves as the starting point for the first two films, and her father's death is the event that releases Elisa from the grip of any predetermined script for her life. In their heart-rending affect and their enactment of transient meaning, Saura's three films fulfilled also a performative role, being akin to cathartic ceremonies that brought to light, in the darkness of the movie theaters, a hitherto invisible community, one that was amalgamated by the shared affects foregrounded in the films—the sense of loss, the deeply scarred memory of a might-have-been, the bewilderment of the present, the uncertainty of the future—that gripped many Spaniards in the course of a transition of the commoners that has not been sufficiently acknowledged and much less analyzed.

NOTES

1. Haunted by that image, Saura decided at the last minute to end the movie with it, explaining that Angélica's tear expresses the adults' inability to understand the impact a punishment can have on a child, as well as the isolation a child can feel surrounded by adults that only remind him of cruel absences (of his parents, in Luis's case) and total indifference (Brasó, "New Interview" 21). Saura included in this film several of his childhood memories of the Civil War (Willem, ix; Géal 101–2).

2. Luis's father—who is seen only briefly in a couple of scenes—will be a leitmotif in a narrative in which the family will deplore his Republican sympathies to Luis's face. Most of the references to Luis's father and the Civil War in general attracted the attention of the censors (Sánchez Vidal 87). For the censorship of *La prima Angélica*, see also D'Lugo 116–18; Sánchez-Biosca 219. The translations into English of all films' dialogues quoted in this essay are taken from their respective DVDs, with occasional corrections.

3. There is a crucial difference between the need to reconstruct the memory of the Civil War in the years of the transition and in recent times: in the 1970s, there was the urgent need to know the history of the War from the Republican point of view, which was still an *epic, heroic* vision of an ideological war; in recent times, when there are already thousands of books on the war, the need to remember comes not from lack of knowledge, but from a completely different *sensibility*, a quasi-religious need of remembrance that manifests itself in most Western countries at the end of the twentieth century, and has the *victim* at its core. The memory of the historical past has a history, changes with new needs and sensibilities of each generation. The same body buried in a collective grave has a different meaning with each passing decade, the issue therefore being not forgetfulness but different forms of remembrances according to the needs of each generation: the memory of history has itself a history. See Loureiro, "Inconsolable Memory" and "Crisis de la historia."

4. Ana's grief suggests her mother has died recently. Late in the film, the maid Rosa mentions that Ana's mother was alive a year earlier. Saura's opinion that children do not see death as dissolution but as disappearance fits with Ana's belief she can will her mother to reappear (Brasó, "Interview" 44).

5. Usually, Saura indicates that a scene of remembrance is coming up with a close-up shot of Ana's face, her eyes lost in thought.

6. This episode is followed immediately by the first scene of the resurrection narrative, in which Ana's mother suddenly appears while Ana is washing the glass she used for the "poisonous" milk.

7. Spread throughout the film, several rituals and games—playing hide-and-seek; playing house with her sisters, mimicking their parents fights, with Ana playing the mother's role; listening to the song "Porque te vas"; burying Roni; playing with her doll—will help Ana master distressing events she witnessed or had to endure.

8. A grown-up Ana—she must be around twenty-seven, and the date is probably 1995, as the film's main action takes place twenty years earlier—appears three times in the film to provide explanations that shed light on the past, while simultaneously working as an estrangement mechanism that curtails the spectator's emotional involvement in the film.

9. The censors themselves saw the military father as a secondary character, and not an intent on Saura's part to make a generalization about the military class (D'Lugo 137). See also Sánchez Vidal for some protests made by military people about the portrayal of the character (98).

10. This self-reflective estrangement is reinforced thematically in the film by having Ana "doubling" herself in her doll, criticizing it for actions committed by herself. In her second interruption of the narrative, the adult Ana declares she does not share the common opinion of childhood as the happiest of times, averring that she remembers her own childhood as a long, sad period filled with fear; at his point, the film cuts to her memory of her bed-ridden, dying mother crying out in pain. This idea of a tortured childhood, which is shared also by Luis in *La prima Angélica*, reflects Saura's own experience (Brasó, "New Interview" 18). To counterbalance this grim view, in her third intervention, Ana explains that not all her childhood memories are sad, offering as an example the family's excursion to the countryside property of Amelia, who will turn out to be her father's lover.

11. All translations into English of dialogues from *Elisa, vida mía* are mine.

12. Another, significant difference is that, in this new version, Luis's wife returns to take care of him.

13. These words, which bring the rehearsal to an end, are accompanied by *Schiarazula Marazula*, a piece by the sixteenth-century Italian composer Giorgio Mainerio that serves as a leitmotif for the theme of life as representation at the center of *El gran teatro del mundo*. Besides sounding simultaneously with the rehearsal of Calderón's *auto sacramental*, this music also has the very significant function of sounding as background to the film's opening and closing credits, stressing the prominence of

preordained roles in a conservative society, and therefore emphasizing the value of rebellion—first Luis's, later Elisa's—against such an allotted fate.

14. Originally, the script ended when Elisa found her dead father outside the house (Sánchez Vidal 125). For obvious reasons, the addition of the scene in which Elisa's voice-over begins to narrate her story was a wise decision.

15. As Saura has stated, "the death of Luis . . . represents her own birth. . . . Elisa comes into being out of an experience that predates her, that of her father, and through it she organizes and solidifies her identity" (Brasó, "Interview" 45).

WORKS CITED

Brasó, Enrique. "Interview with Carlos Saura on *Cría Cuervos* and *Elisa, vida mía*." 1977. *Carlos Saura: Interviews*, edited by Linda M. Willem, University Press of Mississippi, 2003, pp. 42–51.

_____. "New Interview with Carlos Saura on *La prima Angélica*." 1974. *Carlos Saura: Interviews*, edited by Linda M. Willem, University Press of Mississippi, 2003, pp. 17–21.

Chávarri, Jaime, director. *El desencanto*. 1976. Video Mercurio Films, 2005.

D'Lugo, Marvin. *The Films of Carlos Saura: The Practice of Seeing*. Princeton University Press, 1991.

Erice, Víctor, director. *El espíritu de la colmena*. 1973. The Criterion Collection, 2013.

Faulkner, William. *Absalom Absalom!* Vintage International, 1990.

Garci, José Luis, director. *Asignatura pendiente*. 1977. Vertice Cine, 2009.

Géal, François. *Onze films de Carlos Saura, cinéaste de la mémoire*. Aléas, 2006.

Labrador Méndez, Germán. *Culpables por la literatura. Imaginación política y contracultura en la transición española (1968–1986)*. Akal, 2017.

Loureiro, Angel G. "Crisis de la historia e historicidad de los muertos." Unpublished manuscript.

_____. "Inconsolable Memory." *Hispanic Issues On Line*, vol. 10, 2012, pp. 100–22, retrieved from the University of Minnesota Digital Conservancy, http://hdl.handle.net/11299/184320.

Marsé, Juan. *Señoras y señores*. Planeta, 1977.

Quintana, Ángel. "A Poetics of Splitting: Memory and Identity in *La prima Angélica* (Carlos Saura, 1974)." *Burning Darkness: A Half Century of Spanish Cinema*, edited by Joan Ramon Resina, State University of New York Press, 2008, pp. 83–96.

Sánchez Vidal, Agustín. *El cine de Carlos Saura*. Caja de Ahorros de la Inmaculada de Aragón, 1988.

Sánchez-Biosca, Vicente. *Cine y Guerra Civil Española. Del mito a la memoria*. Alianza, 2006.

Saura, Carlos, director. *Cría cuervos*. 1976. Criterion Collection, 2007.

_____. director. *Elisa, vida mía*. 1977. Manga Films, 2009.

_____. director. *La prima Angélica*. 1974. Manga Films, 2004.

Smith, Paul Julian. "The Past is not Past." *Cría Cuervos*, directed by Carlos Saura, Criterion Collection, 2007. DVD.

Willem, Linda M. "Introduction." *Carlos Saura: Interviews*, edited by Linda M. Willem, University Press of Mississippi, 2003, pp. vii–xv.

CHAPTER 4

Martyrs and Saints of the Spanish Civil War Era

Enshrinement of the Right and Historical Memory

Elizabeth Scarlett

The enshrinement of Civil War-era victims is one of the most asymmetrical areas that confront anyone who contemplates the legacy of this war, its prelude, and its aftermath into the twenty-first century. The Valley of the Fallen still stands despite the toppling of most statues of Francisco Franco, a physical emblem of how religious memorialization has withstood efforts at democratic revision-ism.[1] Sacred monuments with a political purpose are one of the forms of transfer between power and glory, or between the Government and the Kingdom, of the kind theorized by Giorgio Agamben in *The Kingdom and the Glory*. The Catho-lic Church enacts a "sacralization" of deceased persons through the processes of beatification and canonization, and is prone to use canonization protocols to intervene in the public sphere when it feels under threat. Although several other religions recognize sainthood and partake to some degree in a cult of the saints (Lutheranism, Anglicanism, Russian Orthodoxy), only Roman Catholi-cism maintains a formal bureaucratized system for the production of new saints (Woodward 16). As a bureaucratized process involving a hierarchy of functionar-ies, canonization lends itself to extension into the political zone, where it mirrors the working of a government machine. Admission to the pantheon of sainthood grants the memory of the deceased person a material presence in society as long as this faith endures. Saints become eligible for a place (shrine, church, or chapel), a spot on the calendar of saints, and pages in reference works that propagate their veneration and emulation, and promote pleas for divine intercession addressed to them. Increasingly, digitized media provide further platforms for attaching glory to this special kind of deceased person.

Where Spanish Civil War-era victims are concerned, only those religious people killed in Revolutionary (the Asturian miners' revolt of October 1934) and Republican-held territories have to this day been considered valid candidates for beatification and canonization. Regarding the connection between these two processes, recognition as a martyr grants the first step, that of beatification, and thereby facilitates the passage into sainthood. The definition of martyrdom is a subject of political manipulation that equates the clerical or religious social identity of victims of Republican violence with automatic status as a martyr for the faith. The adoption of a single side of the Civil War to memorialize, sanctify, and canonize is one of the many ways in which the formerly official state religion of Catholicism continues its intrusive influence upon life in contemporary Spain. As Agamben notes, "[o]nly in the mirror of glory . . . do being and economy, Kingdom and Government appear to coincide for an instant" (209). The transfers between politics and theology afforded by glory are not limited to one form of government or even one political party; they continue to operate in the age of "consensual democracy," in which social communication enhances the effects of glory and harks back to the earlier age of acclamation, liturgy, and ceremonies (258).

Sacralization applied to only one side, even regarding non-Francoist clergy killed during the war by Nationalist forces, supports the political injustice committed by post-Francoist Spanish governments in refusing to open mass graves of Republican victims for identification and appropriate burial for decades, and leaving Francoist monuments and memorials standing untouched until the twenty-first century. Examination of a few key wartime statistics contributes to a perspective on the magnitude of this injustice. Although exact figures may never be determined, reliable estimates of those killed in noncombat situations by Spanish Loyalists or Republicans (the Left, for practical purposes) hover around 38,000, while noncombat killings due to the policy of systematic elimination of political enemies at the hands of the Nationalists (the Right) during the war and its aftermath are over five times greater, close to 200,000 (Beevor 87, 94). The systematic elimination of political enemies was integral to Nationalist policy during the war and the postwar period. On the Republican side, political killings were characteristic mainly of the initial chaos, and ran counter to Republican authority (Preston xiv). Of course, the numbers and explicit policies of the warring sides are only part of the story; there is a political theology that runs deeper and seeks vindication in the massive campaign on the part of the Vatican and the Spanish Catholic hierarchy to cast the religion itself as a victim of the Spanish Civil War, despite its emergence on the winning side and entrenchment as the official state religion for over thirty-five years afterward.

Using martyrdom and sainthood as political tools for attaching glory to an *oikonomia*, or government of men, infuses the governmental machine with divinity, while keeping alive the goal of redemption to be achieved by both politics and theology. The new martyrs and saints are exemplary subjects of their three-person divine monarchy (the Holy Trinity), the entrenched Spanish monarchy, and its democratic state (even Socialist ministers have attended the acclamatory ceremonies). Agamben elaborates that modernity has erased God from the equation only in appearance; secularization is more of a signature than a wholly separate phase in Western political history. His work holds that divinity infuses the government of men (*oikonomia*) into the present, with attendant supports of acclamation, providentiality, and glory. The ultimate goal of salvation is implemented to overshadow the institutionalized tolerance for authoritarianism entailed in this one-sided glorification. He notes that the modern state, in a way similar to theological constructs, fosters notions of both Providence and fate operating at different levels; Providence corresponds to the order of transcendent primary causes (the government's concern for its people, exemplified by the president or ruler who visits the citizens or subjects), while fate corresponds to the effects or immanent secondary causes that we might identify with bureaucracy and the executive branch (126). The Roman Catholic vindication of the Nationalist victory and ensuing dictatorship has resulted in 1,875 beatifications of religious people. Eleven of these cases have reached the final goal of sainthood at this writing. This glorification not only reinforces the transference of power between theological and political structures, but raises questions about the motivations and timing behind the highly visible acclamations that accompany the en masse beatifications and clerical canonizations.

The timing suggests certain possibilities that no doubt combine in larger or smaller measures: accentuating the "heroic" to combat the growing historical realization of Vatican complicity in the Holocaust, European fascism, and other forms of totalitarianism; combatting the perceived secularization of formerly officially Catholic states such as Spain, which legalized divorce and same-sex marriage and began breaking down the barriers to reproductive freedom for women; distracting attention from the explosion of clerical sex abuse cases, many of which involve children as victims; answering calls for the removal of special privileges for the Catholic Church that still exist in the Spanish education, medical, and taxation systems; countering the Spanish Historical Memory movement, which promises to accord recognition to forgotten Republican victims while reminding the public of Catholicism's primary role as supporter of the Nationalists. Catholic privileges found heightened protection in the twenty-first-century Spanish public sphere because of the conservative policies of the Partido Popular, so this party would stand to benefit from the acclamations, ceremonies, and pomp associated with sacralization of victims on the Right. This in turn blurs the theoretical distinction between strictly religious concerns and political ones and aggravates the inequality of enshrinement practices.

Figures of the Left from the Civil War era become subjects of a less pervasive secular memorialization. Some remnants of sacralization move into the secular sphere. However, when Leftist icons are memorialized, it must take place outside of the sacred spaces of Catholicism, and with neither the acclamations of glory that only an established religion can provide nor the symbolism shared among ecclesiastical and governing bodies: insignia, flags, crowns, logos, and other building blocks of iconography. Regarding the formation of the Western state, Agamben reminds that these insignia are not "merely the formal apparatus and pomp of power [but] the original juridical core of an essential transformation of Roman public law" (183). Furthermore, the Spanish Episcopal Conference, one of the most conservative in the Catholic world, has spoken out against recognition for Civil War dead by first blocking the Ley de la Memoria Histórica, and then seeking to choke funding for it once the law had passed (Bedoya). Regarding the Civil War dead who are buried anonymously in mass graves as an explicit tactic of the Nationalists to prevent their commemoration, the head of the Episcopal Conference stated in 2008 that it is best to learn to forget ("Rouco sobre la Memoria Histórica").

Even without the intervention into political discussions of ecclesiastic actors, it would not be necessary according to Bourdieusian theory for religious indoctrination and prescribed ritual to perpetuate traces of the sacred in Spanish life; these structures, as they are embedded in the habitus, will continue to proliferate and inform cultural dispositions on their own (78). Pierre Bourdieu's metaphor of the orchestra that keeps on playing without a conductor, with endless variations on a theme known to the musicians, is an apt one for the persistence of religious structures beyond official links between church and state, though to be sure these relationships have not completely disappeared in twenty-first-century Spain, and are held to be on the rise.[2] The habitus also impregnates the context in which martyrs for the Left arise, carrying over into a nominally atheistic discourse from which God has been erased, though theology has not (Agamben would answer that all these structures—whether economic, political, or theological—are evolving signatures of a paradigm that emerged from the Judeo-Christian tradition) (65). The progressive mode of canonization must relinquish the more tangible, acclamative, and lasting forms of monumental and liturgical practices available to the Right. If for no other reason than Spanish monarchism, power needs glory as a buttress. As Agamben delineates, this glory entails ceremonial and liturgical regality; the canonization of certain dead people constitutes a site of collusion but also contradictions "between power as government and effective management, and power as ceremonial and liturgical regality" (xii). Or, in other words, glory is the uncertain zone affording collusion and contradiction between the bureaucratic protocols that determine whether someone meets the requirements to become a saint, and the political agenda of a Vatican that wants to use canonization as a way to intervene in an age defined by the memory boom, the centrality of the Holocaust in debates about historical memory, and post-secularist understandings of political discourse and the public sphere.

Catholic beatification and sanctification provide a conceptual and symbolic framework of immortality, divinity, and privilege that informs how glory can be understood and experienced in the Spanish habitus. Religion and modern media become entangled in their support of power in a modern democracy: it is the media, according to Agamben, that "enable the control and government of public opinion, but also and above all [because] they manage and dispense glory, the acclamative and doxological aspect of power that seemed to have disappeared in modernity" (xii). With perceptions and opinions manipulated by inflationary media, even in modern democracy rulers are not so much elected but proclaimed, for their associations with glory. Along with the ruler, ministers or secretaries and cabinet members are proclaimed, or anointed by the ruler, and arranged into hierarchies that mirror the orders of angels and saints busily working to administer God's Kingdom.

Glory and sainthood are inextricably combined. For theologian Peter Brown, saints are dead human beings who have a role in "the joining of Heaven and Earth" (1). The cult of the saints emerged in late antiquity and became central to Roman Catholicism, surviving the Counter Reformation and adapting to the modern world, in which the otherworldly position of the saint gives way to an accent on celebrity status. The saint brings together embodiment and enshrinement, since the saint's body is believed to possess supernatural power and to signal his or her presence in this world after death. Ethnicity, geography, and gender are of supreme importance in the selection and veneration of saints because the link to divinity needs to be articulated for each group or clan, location, and personal identity. Saints of the Right partake fully of the special status afforded by a shrine, relics, and presence on a calendar. They can be said to truly mark space and time for the believers. Adherents of icons on the Left may have special days and sites for their heroes as well, but their calendar is not marked on a daily basis, and there is less of a notion of pilgrimage to special sites for worship. They tend not to explicitly project their heroes into an afterlife, and are not constantly reminded of their role in connecting them to a higher power. In some sense, this is because they have liberated themselves intentionally from these structures and paradigms. Yet, as Agamben argues, secularization only displaces sacral energy from one point on the spectrum to another; it does not neutralize it. Heroes of the Left are sometimes accorded civic presence through a monument, as a semblance of a shrine, but without an explicit invocation of a higher power, since that would defy the church/state barrier and militate against freedom of belief. In effect, shrine-like monuments devoted to the Left are often of secondary importance. It is quite possible to visit Washington, D.C., without seeing or learning of the Martin Luther King Monument, but the Washington Monument is visible from all points on the Mall. The Thirteen Roses are commemorated in Madrid by a fountain, a thoroughfare, and a plaque, but these sites are in out-of-the-way areas that do not mark a touristic destination like the Valley of the Fallen. Meanwhile, the Basilica of the Valley of the Fallen was built to entomb a spectrum of wartime victims, including José Antonio Primo de Rivera, who is widely considered both a political martyr and a candidate for beatification in conservative circles, and Francisco Franco, the only non-casualty of war. These two have the only named crypts; the other 34,000 remains were massed together without identification, mirroring the de-individuation of fascism. Both the Nationalist and Republican dead were disinterred and reburied at the monument without the consent of their families, imposing a hegemonic sacralization of the Civil War as sacrifice and redemption on a national level (Jones). Agamben characterizes Christianity as a "historical religion" with a historical personage (Jesus) and a specified time line (44). Francoist sacralization of the dead, extending into the current century with the combined efforts of native Spanish ecclesiastic authorities and the Vatican to produce martyrs and saints, synchronizes the Christian chronology with the recent Spanish past in an even more intrinsic way than the well-known application of the term "Crusade" to the military coup by Nationalist and Catholic official culture.

A continuum from classical heroes through Christian saints can be traced, but what differentiates the latter is the closeness to God and capacity to intercede for the living that is attributed to them (Brown 6). Not only is their attachment to physical places and objects redeeming for the living, but they are also accessible at all times to the consciousness of the believer as "invisible companions" (50). As privileged dead, all saints made belief in the afterlife tangible and death less dreadful; the martyrs in particular had chosen death, and "died in a special way"

(70). Martyrs persevere unto death, and both select their fate and are selected by it, refuting the ordinariness of death. If the traditional martyr represents a triumph over death, the progressive hero provides a testimonial to injustice that might save future mortals if heeded. There is still a healing quality to be experienced for followers of progressive icons like John Lennon or Martin Luther King, but it is not experienced directly through the body or its shrine as with the Christian saint or beatified person.

Influences work both ways, and the habitus of modernity begins to inform the machinery of Roman Catholicism around the middle of the nineteenth century. Modernization means accomplishing tasks quickly and efficiently, and this would go on to foster an assembly line for beatification and canonization, processes that used to take centuries or many decades. Seepage of modernity in the habitus into religion affects the transmission of belief, which now has to reach the faithful in the most advanced technological manner possible. At first, it is the means that are modernized, but not the dogma. In fact, as scholars have demonstrated regarding the apparitions at Lourdes and Fátima, and the Immaculate Conception, the dogma may accentuate orthodoxy and resistance to change as the modes of transmission are modernized.[3] In the twentieth century, turning points in canonization history include: the 1983 approval of a new Apostolic Constitution (*Divinus Perfectionibus Magister*) that streamlined the processes and allowed for accelerated canonization/beatification; John Paul II's series of apologies, beginning in 1992, for the Church's complicity or association with major crimes against humanity going back two thousand years, sparking the need for saintly heroism as counterbalance; the culmination of accelerated beatification and politically instrumental implementation of it in the 2007 beatification mass celebrated by the Vatican for the 498 Spanish martyrs killed between 1934 and 1939, with both Partido Popular and Socialist Party attendance, three days before the Spanish congress passed the Law of Historical Memory. Another noted case of acceleration and politicization of Spanish sainthood is Josemaría Escrivá de Balaguer, whose views and projects were consonant with the Franco regime; he characterized the Caudillo as a "good Christian" and cooperated with him, speaking by invitation and sending him correspondence to let him know of his availability. Escrivá was canonized in 2002, twenty-seven years after his death. The quickened time line foreshadows the swiftness of canonization that would affect later Catholic celebrities such as Mother Teresa of Calcutta and the creator of accelerated sainthood himself, John Paul II.[4]

Escrivá masqueraded as a mental patient to escape the wrath of Madrid Republicans during the Civil War and eventually passed into the Nationalist zone with help from friends. Other clergy who lacked his wiles, connections, or resources were not so fortunate and became victims of the violent unrest that was unleashed in Republican zones when the Nationalist coup began. Being murdered for their social identity was elevated to the classification of martyrdom in beatification and canonization processes of the recent past, adding fuel to the fire of the historical memory movement, which assails the unequal memorialization of victims on the Right with respect to those on the Left. To have been killed during the Red Terror is synonymous in pontifical discourse with being a victim of religious hatred in cases of clergy and religious people. However, the priesthood and the Church had declared themselves the political enemy of the Republican state, calling into question the application of religious martyrdom.[5] The so-named 498 Martyrs of the Spanish Civil War (not all were of Spanish nationality) were beatified en masse by Pope Benedict XVI in 2007. His predecessor John Paul II had beatified five hundred such Republican zone victims at different ceremonies, and canonized eleven of them. In 1962, Paul VI had called a moratorium on all proceedings for beatifying Spanish Civil War era victims precisely in order not to show sympathy for the Franco dictatorship. This was also in solidarity with the more liberal Spanish clergy of the time (Woodward 132–33). The present pope, though seen as more progressive than most past pontiffs going back to John XXIII and Paul VI, is still placing additional Civil War victims of anticlerical violence on the path to canonization, with scant regard for the usual additional proofs of sainthood, such as investigated miracles. After an initial beatification of 522 such victims in 2013, he has approved more groups annually, for a lifetime total thus far of close to one thousand. The proofs of sainthood work out to be elastic according to political affiliation, for being designated a martyr relieves the caseworkers of validating the two miracles required for beatification, and "remains to this day the surest route to canonization" (85, 52).

The contradictions between power as the bureaucratic process of canonization, which creates saints along modernized protocols, and power as ceremony and regality, as well as the creation and reproduction of sacrality in the times of the "memory boom," become clear upon examination of the aborted beatification of Jesuit priest Fernando Huidobro Polanco. As a chaplain moving with Falangist militia, he counseled the legionnaires against extermination of the enemy, particularly of those wounded in battle. Since he was killed on the outskirts of Madrid, and showed all the signs of a virtuous and exemplary life, his order began to assemble the case for his beatification in 1947. However, "when it was discovered that Huidobro had been killed by the Francoists [for his pacifism] and not by the reds, the Vatican shelved the case" (Preston 340). In Father Polanco's case, the Church was caught cheating at its own canonization game. In the case of sixteen pro-Republican Basque priests who were executed by Nationalists in

1936, the absence of any effort to memorialize, let alone canonize, them contrasts with the treatment of official Nationalist martyrs; the glorification of the latter makes the former's oblivion more conspicuous (Montero).

Pope Francis's strategy appears to be that of proceeding with the beatification and canonization of Civil War martyrs and preserving overall the definition of martyr as anyone who was killed "in hatred of the faith," while appealing to more liberal Catholics with a show of equilibrium, by canonizing a liberal Spanish reformer (who worked mainly in the nineteenth century) and beatifying a high-profile victim of an authoritarian Latin American regime.[6] At the same time as he recognized these two leftward leaning holy people, he placed an additional one hundred Republican zone victims (out of his total to date of one thousand) on the path toward beatification, joining the hundreds who are still in the pipe-line created by the two previous popes. The liberal reformer he used to counter-balance this further aggravation of the Spanish Historical Memory movement was the case of a priest who pursued progressive social aims by founding schools for girls, Faustino Míguez (1831–1925). Specifically, Francis furthered Míguez's canonization by authorizing a miraculous cure performed by the latter through expertise in botany. This concession to the Krausist reform movement of the late nineteenth century is almost certainly meant to soften the blow for liberal Spaniards of seeing another hundred Civil War martyrs recognized despite the greater numbers of Republican losses, and the anonymity, oblivion, and neglect still suffered by victims on the Left and their families.[7]

Despite these small concessions to the more liberal Spanish-speaking circles, the application of the term "martyr" to the victims of anticlerical violence dur-ing the Spanish Civil War era remains divisive and problematic. As Paul Preston clarifies, "[t]he popular hatred of the Church was the consequence both of its traditional association with the Right and of the ecclesiastical hierarchy's open legitimation of the military rebellion" (235). Hence, these killings, as tragic as all loss of life in the conflict, stemmed more from the social identity and per-ceived political affiliations of the clergy.[8] Clergy were the self-declared political enemies of Spanish Republicans, cooperating fully with the Nationalist take-over, sermonizing on its behalf, providing confessions to Republican prisoners of war at the site of their execution, and even militating directly. In politically motivated killings, the religious faith of the victim was usually not the focus.[9] It is true, as Preston notes, that in some Aragonese villages, the parish priest "was murdered after being forced to watch parodies of the Mass and offered life if he renounced God" (249). However, dying purposefully for faith was not the case for the majority of anticlerical victims, who were assassinated in the early part of the war by anarchist or unionist crowds on the basis of social identity alone:

in Barcelona, it was sufficient to walk the street wearing a cassock to be gunned down. No matter how brutal and horrendous their deaths, these still are not the equivalent of martyrdom for a cause, especially in an overall context in which their faith is mainstream and aligned with the ideology of the ruling classes.[10]

The large majority of those already canonized after being proclaimed martyrs of the alleged religious hatred espoused by the Spanish Left are the nine Martyrs of Turón, who were shot during the two-week-long Asturian miners' revolt in October 1934. This group includes the first Argentine ever to be canonized, Héctor Valdivielso Sáez (St. Benito de Jesús). The eight friars in this group had been working as schoolteachers, and the priest was the confessor in their religious school. The Spanish Republic had outlawed religious operation of schools, and had mandated secular education. This group was arrested for having broken a law enacted by a democratic government. The motive for their subsequent execution was the far greater number of casualties that were resulting from the brutal repression of the miners' revolt in surrounding areas. The army killed sixty-one noncombatant civilians as order was re-established, and summarily executed twenty-five to fifty prisoners (Shubert 132). More than martyrs of religious hatred, the nine members of this group were victims of a tragic atmosphere of retaliation and panic.

Several shortcuts and easements in the pathway to sainthood speed clerical victims from Republican and Revolutionary-held territories toward the highest form of glory. The Church views clergy as natural prey to religious hatred of certain affiliations on the Left, including anarchists and communists. The only definition of martyrdom is the classic one put forward by the early Church: "an innocent victim who dies for the faith at the hands of a tyrant who is opposed to the faith" (Woodward 129). Eventually, this evolved into a criterion of provocation of a tyrant through profession of faith. Without a dogmatic definition for martyrdom, modern popes have found it sufficient for a person's murder to be interpreted as caused by religious hatred, and for the victim to die willingly for the faith rather than renounce it, in order to define the deceased as a martyr. In this matter, doctrine holds that the pope exercises infallibility. The religious hatred test began to be implemented more broadly by John Paul II in 1983 in his attempt to canonize Edith Stein, a Jewish convert to Catholicism who perished in a Nazi concentration camp. There is evidence that Stein was murdered primarily because of her Jewishness rather than her Catholic faith (142). Hence to assert that she was a martyr for Catholicism not only displayed the Vatican's bias toward accentuating the suffering of Catholic religious at the hands of the Third Reich and proclaiming its own heroism despite not taking direct action against the Holocaust, it also minimized the magnitude of anti-Semitism. As canonization took on more

political overtones throughout the 1980s, John Paul II would extend the definition of martyrdom in order to condemn not only Nazism but also Communism
by glorifying victims of anticlerical violence in Spain. This was in keeping with
the Polish pope's profoundly anti-Communist feelings (Appleby 17). The attainment of martyr status means that the miracle normally required for beatification
is waived. Thereafter, only one miracle is needed for canonization (Woodward
139). Since the investigation and confirmation of two miracles on the pathway to
sainthood (one for beatification and another for canonization) is a sticking point
for many cases, the reduction by half is a significant advantage.

For the single miracle required of martyrs and two miracles required of non-
martyrs, including "confessors" (those who suffer from opposition to their faith
but not to the point of death), the close working relationship between the Spanish
Catholic Church and the health care system is another definite advantage. Almost
all miracles that are investigated and confirmed by the Vatican are inexplicable
cures.[11] The cure must be miraculous in nature, and the divine intercession of the
proposed saint must have been sought (Duffin 41). The pervasive involvement of
Catholicism in the Spanish healthcare system is bound to have facilitated invocation of the Civil War-era blessed and venerable persons; one can only pray to
a person if one has been informed about them. The religious presence in hospitals and clinics has also widened the gamut for prospective medical personnel
willing to testify to miraculous healings. Unfortunately, detailed confirmation
is difficult because the copious records surrounding each miracle in the Vatican
Secret Archives are sealed for six papacies.[12]

The fast track to beatification and canonization of Spanish Civil War-era clergy
also responds to the destabilization of dogma; Bourdieu stresses that, in times
of social upheaval, the line separating the "givens" or doxa from the arbitrary is
subject to a push and pull (169). Catholicism has responded in situations like this
by creating new dogma to secure its central position, as in 1864 with the doctrine
of the Immaculate Conception. In historiography on clerical victims of the Civil
War era, there was a destabilized space created by a spectrum of approaches and
assessments and general social upheaval. The church beatified and canonized
to pin down the shifting perspectives and emerge as the persecuted rather than
the oppressor in a war that nonetheless resulted in its entrenchment as official
religion for over thirty-five years. How did this come to pass, and what were the
underlying causes both within Spain and for the Vatican?

In 1987, John Paul II beatified the first of the Civil War victims, three nuns
from Guadalajara. The ceremonies became increasingly spectacular as 122 clerical victims were proclaimed by him in St. Peter's in 1992 before an audience of
twenty thousand mass attendees, most of whom traveled from Spain (Serrano

Moreno 78). The overall motivations that scholars and analysts have identified behind the John Paul II papacy must have had much to do with his initiation of this wave of Spanish Civil War-era beatifications and canonizations. These include his view that the unregulated capitalism of the West propagated a self-absorbed consumerism that was weakening the traditional family structure through divorce, alcoholism, abortion, euthanasia, crime, and other social ills and departures from Catholic dogma. Though the number of Catholics worldwide was on the rise, the number of priests and nuns fell sharply in Europe and North America between 1965 and 1995 (Appleby 15). Attaching the glory of heroic martyrdom to fallen clergy could thus shore up the flagging tide of interest in clerical vocations, while upholding the sacrifice of the victims could be used to counter the perceived self-centeredness and material obsession in Western Catholic communities. This also assigned villain status to Civil War-era revolutionaries, whose struggle for secular education had been renewed by the Spanish Socialist Party, making it the target for proponents of mandatory religious education in Spanish schools (Stuart).

In 2007, the Spanish Episcopal Conference, in tandem with the Vatican Office for the Causes of the Saints, organized a *fiesta de beatificación*, calling upon worshippers to make a pilgrimage to the Holy See for the ceremony. This was calculated to place Spain at the center of global Catholicism and spark a religious activism within Spain that could reshape many aspects of the state (Serrano Moreno 79). The fiesta was brought home to Spanish soil in 2013 with Francis's beatification of 522 martyrs before a crowd of 25,000 pilgrims. Motivations that can be attributed to the Spanish Episcopal Conference for these spectacles include distracting from and combatting the Historical Memory movement, attempting to recover lost ground in the educational and healthcare spheres, and defending against threats to the tax-free status of the church, all burgeoning under the consolidation of the Spanish Socialist Workers Party from 1982 to 1996 and from 2004 to 2011. Since the triumph of the Partido Popular in the 2011 general elections, the religious sector has been in political ascendancy, but the more neutral progressivism of the Socialist Party has splintered into vocal groups like Podemos that openly oppose the Monarchy (though in the case of Podemos, the transversal aim means openness to a grassroots Christian base). As more twenty-first-century Spanish Republicans have emerged and demanded an end to the Monarchy, the Church stands to lose a political figurehead intimately entwined with divinity: the king. The administration of the heavenly house finds its theological-political parallel in the royal family and its functionaries (Agamben 42); the feast day of Christ the King was instituted in 1925 soon after the rise of Mussolini (192). Common to both the leadership of the church in Spain and in Rome is a reaction against what Benedict XVI called the "aggressive laicism" of Spain under the Socialist Party, with greater rights for women and gay people seen as threatening the traditional family (Serrano Moreno 72).

Previously, Paul VI had made a conscious decision as a point of diplomacy not to memorialize the Asturias revolution and Spanish Civil War victims of the Red Terror, in order not to antagonize the opposing side with its greater and unrecognized losses, and risk calling attention to the role of Catholicism in European fascist movements that led to World War II. The Spanish episcopate during the democratic transition included leaders who were critical of Francoism and in favor of reconciliation with its former foes (Serrano Moreno 76). John Paul's determination to throw this caution to the wind shows that other priorities had begun to supplant the thinking behind the Vatican's avoidance. The Church began assuming blame and asking forgiveness for sins of the distant past (such as the persecution of Galileo, the genocide of New World indigenous peoples, and the Inquisition). These grievances were safely remote from the modern era. As for the twentieth century, the Church would only admit the fault of some of its "sons and daughters," but not its own stand vis-à-vis Italian-German fascism and the Holocaust, or the Nationalist takeover of Spain (Appleby 20). Besides eliding its guilt for having acquiesced to the Holocaust (Agamben denounces the "conniving silence" of Pius XII when a thousand Roman Jews were deported to extermination camps in 1943 [16]) and supported totalitarianism in Spain, the Church would cast itself solely as a victim of religious hatred by Spanish Republicans. For John Paul II, the situation of Spanish clergy during the civil war era paralleled Poland under communist rule as a site of anticlerical persecution.

In addition, new saints and blessed persons/martyrs could distract from the allegations of clerical pedophilia and sexual abuse that were on the rise as John Paul II magnified his campaign of recognizing those killed by Republicans and revolutionaries in Spain in the 1930s for their association with the Catholic religion. Nearly every country with a large Catholic community has seen the tide of abuse allegations and convictions rise, as incidents of previously hidden harassment, molestation, illicit affairs, and rape have become known. The first wave of these scandals hit in the last decade of the twentieth century, with the high-profile cases of Bruce Ritter and John Geoghan in the United States. By 2004, this corruption had reached international notoriety, when Pedro Almodóvar directed *La mala educación* (Bad Education) based on abuse he claimed to have witnessed in his religious school. The heroism of martyrs and saints, while not intended at first as a direct drowning out of this scandal, did provide an option for good press that might deflect attention away from it in some measure. The positive energy of these new heroes and celebrations could also relieve the burden of Catholic association with the rise of Right-wing agendas in Europe, taking the form of ethnocentric and xenophobic political parties and the return of anti-Semitism.

Colluding to insert Catholic victimhood into the struggles of mid-twentieth century Europe are the post-1978 papacies and their Vatican bureaucracies, Spanish bishops, and officials of the conservative Partido Popular. The latter acclaimed the beatification in St. Peter's Square alongside other pilgrims in 2001, for the most massive ceremony up to that date ("El Papa"). Even the Socialist foreign affairs minister Miguel Ángel Moratinos attended the 2007 mass beatification in Rome that was held within a week of the passing of the Law of Historical Memory. The PSOE official line was that he attended in order to de-politicize the ceremony, but the gesture looks the exact opposite (Cué and Aizpeolea). Partido Popular officials are also visible when beatification ceremonies are held locally in the home communities of the slain, as in Tarragona in 2013 (Cañas). Conservative historiography also continues to support these strategies. A 1998 article in the *Journal of Contemporary History* by Julio de la Cueva Merino exemplifies this current by enumerating clerical victims in isolation from the context of far greater numbers of Republican dead. However, less high-ranking clergy and the Spanish lay populace often criticize the one-sidedness of this memorialization (Nash 24). The Historical Memory movement has gained momentum since the late 1990s. For the first time, modern technology was used to recover remains from mass graves in 2000. Spanish bishops qualify the effort at recovering remains, revising history, punishing the guilty and making amends to the aggrieved, and memorializing the Republican dead as destructive to social reconciliation (Serrano Moreno 80).

A newer form of material presence for the saint, beyond chapels, shrines, churches, namesake schools, portraits, medals, and reliquaries, is the digital platform. Digital/electronic media extend the reach of sanctification that has been instrumentalized to support the notion that Catholicism was persecuted more than it persecuted others in the Civil War era. Insofar as the canonized and beatified are acclaimed through these media, the latter augment the drowning out of memorialization of those killed by the Nationalists. These outlets range from the semi-scholarly encyclopedias that are uploaded almost verbatim from books and other print media, to the popular websites and apps that have sprung up to capitalize on sainthood as a celebrity culture within Catholicism. Although these websites and apps are often kitschy and lacking in impact, they are presences with a stability that is elusive to victims that have not been sanctified. The so-named Thirteen Roses or Thirteen Red Roses (young women who were not militants in the Civil War but who were executed en masse after the war ended in 1939, in retaliation for the murders of a Guardia Civil officer, his daughter, and their chauffeur) were meant to be recognized by a foundation in their name. However, at this writing, the Fundación Las Trece Rosas website comes up as "expired," taken over by domain name aggregators.[13] Fortunately, in real life, the Centro Cultural Trece Rosas hosts vital community events.

Pope Benedict XVI favored Internet outreach, unlike his predecessor John Paul II, who excelled at touring the globe in person. Working in tandem, Benedict's accent on new media furthers John Paul's proliferation of saints and the blessed, particularly those who lived in contemporary times. Internet glory and acclamations are another feature of the asymmetrical memorialization of political victims on the Right. As more worship and fundraising activities take to the digital realm, this unevenness grows in significance, accentuated by a diminishing number of parish churches and an aging devout population. The calendar of saints' feast days is known in Spanish by a single word—the *santoral*—signaling its centrality to Hispanic cultures in temporal demarcation. The *santoral* is a potential daily reminder of prior human models and namesakes for the living upheld as ideals and acclaimed for their glory, which resides in their assumed closeness to God. The saint is assumed to have gone directly to Heaven, and the canonization process only serves to identify that person's recognition by God as a mortal who was without sin. In early church history, spontaneous and local acclamation by the vox populi was sufficient to establish saintliness. For this reason, many early saints have been lost to history. In the early Middle Ages, bishops regulated the process, and by the late middle ages, the Pope was in charge. This led to a bureaucratization whereby a Congregation for the Causes of the Saints was charged with a more formalized canonization process that continues at this writing, as the only form of continuous and ongoing system for recognizing the sanctity of specific dead people in any world religion. The cult of the saints has taken to the Internet in many forms, with the *santoral* occupying a privileged place for its function of constant remembrance. There are hundreds of these websites in Spanish alone. They include: Santopedia, which aspires to be a Wikipedia for the canonized and the beatified; the Spanish-language branch of the EWTN Catholic cable television network; the Archdiocese of Madrid website; the Spanish edition of the online communication service Aleteia, based in France; the hardline Catholic news and opinion site ForumLibertas, in operation since 2004.[14] The latter, though lacking a *santoral*, covers recent subjects of canonization and beatification, especially from the Civil War era, in some detail. It provides links to sale platforms of extreme Right author Santiago Mata's chronicle of anticlerical violence *Holocausto católico: Los mártires de la guerra civil* (2013).

Sainthood and alignment with Catholicism afford conspicuous Internet video exposure as well. The organization Rome Reports maintains a YouTube channel that chronicles matters of the faith and promotes Catholic causes. When Óscar Parra de Carrizosa directed a film entitled *Bajo un manto de estrellas* (Under a Mantle of Stars) (2014) about the massacre of Dominican friars in Almagro, Rome Reports posted an interview and trailer. While Rome Reports in Spanish has not been active on YouTube since 2015, Rome Reports in English posts at least one video per day. Rome Reports continues to produce Spanish-language videos for its own website. Gloria.tv, based in Switzerland and run mainly by Catholic lay people, offers the film in full on its website, a major outlet for religious videos. YouTube also provides a platform for the feature-length *Un Dios prohibido* (A Forbidden God) (2012) and the trailer for *Poveda* (2016), both directed by Pablo Moreno for the production company Contracorriente and focusing on clergy killed during the Civil War. The biopic *Poveda* is also promoted on the bilingual website pedropoveda.org. This extensive website deals with the life of St. Pedro Poveda, an Andalusian priest killed in Madrid, and the eleventh Civil War-era martyr to be canonized. Like the Turón friars, he was targeted for teaching.

Perhaps the most tangible inequality of enshrinement is the non-recovery of remains of vast numbers of victims of the Nationalists, which still affects thousands of people in their families.[15] The mortal remains of eight of the nine Martyrs of Turón executed in the October 1934 Revolt are now buried under the main altar of a twelfth-century monastery outside of Burgos, Santa María de Bujedo de Candepajares (only the remains of the Passionist priest now known as St. Inocencio were lost). St. Jaime Hilario Barbal, a Catalan friar killed in Tarragona and canonized at the same time as the Turón group, is commemorated with portraits in schools and monasteries run by De La Salle Brothers, and a school named for him in the Philippines. St. Pedro Poveda also has a school named after him in the Philippines. Not only have martyrs consecrated by Catholicism generally received more visible and accessible resting places and sites of veneration and memorialization, their very remains are regarded as sacred, and must be treated with care. This contrasts starkly with the anonymous mass graves that awaited Republican victims, often after receiving rites from priests working with the Nationalists who were about to execute them. The Vatican has articulated more exacting guidelines for the handling and preservation of relics and the remains of saints to ensure their preservation. The guidelines are regulated by the same officials who consider beatification and canonization cases ("Vatican Directive"). The gulf between the anonymous and forgotten mass grave that awaited the victims of fascism, of the sort in which Lorca's body probably still lies, and the opulent reliquary for a saint's remains that accompanies processions or occupies a central spot in a cathedral, cannot be more pronounced. Furthermore, the overall effect of the Episcopal Conference, with its link to the politics of the Partido Popular, is to squash the efforts at an equitable social memorialization. From the criticism of the project as being divisive, to the limitations placed on public budgets for a modern recovery process, the beatification and canonization contrasts increasingly with the insistence upon oblivion for those not sanctified by the campaign to place Catholicism as a victim of religious persecution rather than as a problematic political agent in the twentieth century.

In closing, it may not be far afield to note that two important forms of Spanish cultural capital in the current millennium are the byproducts of death and materiality. Saints with their relics and (in some cases) incorruptibility, and their relevance to the living beyond family members and descendants, linger after death as special deceased persons who can infuse the governmental machine of a modern nation with a sense of glory and immortality. Relics were once a key part of saintly culture, but have grown less central since the time when Franco's theft of a relic of St. Teresa of Ávila exemplified the relic as symbolic capital directly linked to glory in an *oikonomia* or government of men. With democracy came an appropriation of St. Teresa by the Left, including feminism and designer culture, in biopics directed by Josefina Molina and Ray Loriga, respectively. The contemporary strategy behind canonization de-emphasizes the magical properties of the relic to concentrate on persecution and victimization. The other special dead person emerging from Spain in our century, especially as a media export, is the zombie of popular horror cinema (the *[•REC]* franchise and many individual films by Spanish directors). The zombie's materiality beyond death would seem the polar opposite of the saint. This walking corpse that cannibalizes and contaminates everything in its path repulses the living and causes them to fight back or take flight. Yet in economic terms, the zombie is a lucrative item for Spanish cinema on the global market. The Spanish state and religious institutions obtain no glory from the immortality of the zombie body the way they can with the legacy of martyrs and saints. The zombie makes an abject remnant of the immortal body, in a grotesque reversal of saintliness. The subversive popular appeal of the zombie both lampoons and upholds blended religious and political traditions surrounding holiness and death. Films and other products and texts of the "undead" bring in profits but no glory or high cultural capital, although cultural studies scholarship has started to study the phenomenon. The symbolic capital of martyrdom and sainthood, however, are political instruments in pursuit of which the conservative sectors are willing to glorify their institutions and thereby further alienate the descendants of and sympathizers with the far more numerous victims of twentieth-century fascism. To honor the dead, it should not be necessary to rub salt in the wounds of the living.

NOTES

1. Patricia Keller considers the cultural resonance of the Valley of the Fallen from many standpoints, finding that it was designed "to consecrate war, to glorify and sanctify it within the visual and discursive logic of imperial Christian-militarism" (75).

2. Jorge Pérez asserts that the prescriptions and indoctrinations of the sacred have remained ongoing in and through the Partido Popular: José María Aznar's neo-liberalism approximated a "religion of the market"; he attached new ceremonial significance to the flag and national anthem, and promoted a clause designating Christian heritage in the Constitution of the European Union in 2003.

3. Ruth Harris studies this nineteenth-century modernization, or Catholic renewal (220–23, and throughout).

4. Escrivá counseled his followers not to throw in their lot with the political Left, lest they become vulnerable scapegoats like the alleged Civil War martyrs (Allen 60–61). Although his beatification and canonization occurred through the Vatican in Rome, the case was championed by clergy and officials (including Supreme Court justice Rafael Mendizábal de Allende) based in his home country, and points to the continuation of Francoism in the political culture of Spain. In conversation, Escrivá was known to downplay the Holocaust and defend Hitler. Even within Catholic circles, testimony of Escrivá's objectionable behavior involving rages and verbal abuse and reports published in 1992 of his virtual abduction of Venezuelan numerary María del Carmen Tapia were not sufficient to slow the process (48–51).

5. The complicity of clergy with the Nationalist coup is well documented, including being present at noncombat executions to hear confession, blessing Nationalist troops before combat, denouncing and revealing the whereabouts of Republican parishioners, and taking an active role in the killings (Preston 330, 467, 455).

6. Archbishop Óscar Romero was assassinated in 1980 for criticizing the corrupt military government of El Salvador. He opposed the clergy on the Right who supported this regime, but was not affiliated with the liberation theology movement. Francis beatified, then swiftly canonized him as well. However, the less elite, more grassroots-based and liberation-affiliated Father Rutilio Grande has not been beatified yet, though he was massacred by government agents three years before Romero, and he had been instrumental in turning the latter against the political status quo in his country (Gibson).

7. Preston and his source, Monsignor Antonio Montero Moreno, set the number of clergy killed in the Republican zone at 6,832 (235). This should be taken in context with the 200,000 people killed in battles (with the Republicans suffering higher losses leading to their ultimate defeat); 120,000 to 180,000 assassinations in the Nationalist zone, 38,000 to 50,000 assassinations in the Republican zone (including the aforementioned clergy), and the 20,000 executed by the Nationalists in the years after their victory. For seeking justice regarding the latter and other Francoist atrocities, judge Baltasar Garzón was banned from the bench for eleven years in 2012 in a retaliatory measure

based on his recording of attorneys for the opposition. This had the effect of ending his legal career.

8. Catholic clergy were known as enemies of Spanish Republicanism not only for the misgivings they began expressing as soon as the Republic was proclaimed in 1931, but also for their rejoicing at the coup of Miguel Primo de Rivera in 1923. Their sympathy for autocratic government was already established well before the outbreak of war (Lannon 37).

9. Notwithstanding, these victims may have gone to their deaths with an attitude befitting a religious martyr, as laboriously documented by Catholic apologist research (Ramón Solans 5). This still does not make them apolitical as targets, a thesis convincingly sustained by Serrano Moreno.

10. Preston cites examples of anticlerical violence balanced by protection of the clergy in the Republican zones of Andalucía that quickly fell to Queipo de Llano (148, 157).

11. Urban VIII (1568–1644) established beatification and canonization as two distinct processes, each requiring proof (Duffin 13). Paul VI concentrated the ceremonial aspects of both in the office of the pope, either while traveling or in Rome, sparking pilgrimages by communities to attend a ceremony (14). The Counter Reformation tightened control of scientific authentication of miracles. By the late nineteenth century, professional medical testimony supporting inexplicable cures became routine, and in 1949 the Medical Council was created to investigate proposed miracles. Members are mainly male academics from Rome and environs; they receive an honorarium for their service. They must be "distinguished physicians who are practicing Catholics" (34).

12. Speaking of the mid-twentieth century, Woodward notes that Southern Italy was more fertile terrain for producing medical miracles than Communist Eastern Europe because of the difference in cooperation from medical personnel (193).

13. What memorialization exists for the Trece Rosas takes the form of written texts such as the historical essays of Carlos Fonseca and Jesús Ferrero, accounts of female Republican prisoners in the aftermath of the Civil War, a stretch of Salvador Allende Avenue in Getafe that has been renamed in their honor, a fountain with spouts grouped around thirteen truncated figures in the same suburban/industrial town on the outskirts of Madrid, and a plaque in the Madrid Almudena cemetery. These women also constitute a powerful backdrop to Dulce Chacón's novel *La voz dormida (2002)*, and the film of the same name(dir. Benito Zambrano, 2011), as well as a film devoted solely to them (*Las 13 rosas*, dir. Emilio Martínez-Lázaro, 2007)

14. Santopedia spotlights one (often Spanish or Hispanic) saint per day, providing a clickable biography. Each date also contains additional saints and blessed persons whose clickable biographies range from paragraphs to a line or two. In terms of social media, Santopedia offers a Facebook page and a phone app. The Facebook page is rudimentary and seldom updated. The app promises to identify the saint's day of one's social media friends, but this is not achieved automatically. Instead, the user enters the name manually to search for the highlighted saint for that day. A reminder function offers to contact the user as the saint's day approaches. Both the website and the phone app

are highly monetized, with advertisements and a donation box. Outside entities (fast food, etc.) as well as Catholic organizations (papal missions) use the website and app to tap into revenue streams. A Twitter account, updated daily from Barcelona, links the app to the website's highlighted saint of the day. The accuracy of the site has been called into question; it does not always concord with the more authoritative *Catholic Encyclopedia*. The latter is a branch of the New Advent website, one of the oldest religious websites, with more elaborate subsidiaries on Facebook and Twitter and no non-religious advertisers, but it lacks a Spanish language version and does not offer a calendar of saints. The EWTN Catholic cable television network provides only the spotlighted saint of the day, so there are far fewer entries than Santopedia. Consequently, none of the controversial Civil War–era saints or beatified appear, with the exception of Josemaría Escrivá de Balaguer. Saints and a few blessed persons are also searchable alphabetically by name. While not as reader-friendly as Santopedia, EWTN is less relentlessly commercialized and cites its sources. The Spanish commercial website Calcuworld offers a saint's day calculator with search boxes by date and by name, but connects to random advertisers such as dating websites. Under "Oración y liturgia," the Archdiocese of Madrid posts its own calendar of saints' days and holy days, bereft of biographical information (a principal saint is the headline, followed by a list of the others). Aleteia is another go-to site for the *santoral* of the month in progress, in its spirituality section. Aleteia began in 2012 as an effort to utilize the Internet more fully for proselytizing globally and inexpensively. It contains both original and aggregated content in eight languages. Aleteia is intensively monetized, with localized corporate banner ads and pop-up requests to send regular alerts to the user.

15.   The impact of exhumations of anonymous mass graves from the Civil War upon 21st-century Spanish society and culture is examined in Jerez Farrán and Amago, eds., *Unearthing Franco's Legacy*.

WORKS CITED

Agamben, Giorgio. *The Kingdom and the Glory: For a Theological Genealogy of Economy and Government (Homo Sacer II, 2)*. 2007. Translated by Lorenzo Chiesa, Stanford University Press, 2011.

Allen, John L., Jr. *Opus Dei: An Objective Look behind the Myths and Reality of the Most Controversial Force in the Catholic Church*. Doubleday, 2006.

Appleby, Scott. "Pope John Paul II." *Foreign Policy*, vol. 119, Summer 2000, pp. 12–25.

Beevor, Antony. *The Battle for Spain: The Spanish Civil War 1936–1939*. Penguin, 2006.

Bedoya, Juan G. "Los obispos apelan al perdón por beatificar a 500 mártires de la Guardia Civil." *El País*, 19 Apr. 2013.

Bourdieu, Pierre. *Outline of a Theory of Practice*. 1972. Translated by Richard Nice, Cambridge University Press, 1977.

Brown, Peter. *The Cult of the Saints: Its Rise and Function in Latin Christianity*. University of Chicago Press, 1981.

Cañas, Gabriela. "Entre fosas y homenajes." *El País*, 20 Oct. 2013.

Chacón, Dulce. *La voz dormida*. Punto de Lectura, 2002.

Cué, Carlos E., and Luis R. Aizpeolea. "Moratinos y Montilla irán a Roma a la beatificación de 498 mártires." *El País*, 30 Oct. 2007.

De la Cueva Merino, Julio. "Religious Persecution, Anticlerical Tradition and Revolution: On Atrocities against the Clergy during the Spanish Civil War." *Journal of Contemporary History*, vol. 33, no. 3, 1998, pp. 355–69.

Duffin, Jacalyn. *Medical Miracles: Doctors, Saints, and Healing in the Modern World*. Oxford University Press, 2009.

"El Papa beatifica a 233 'mártires' de la guerra civil española." *El País*, 10 Mar. 2001.

Gibson, David. "John Paul II, Oscar Romero, and the Politics of Making Saints." *Huffington Post*, 1 May 2013.

Harris, Ruth. *Lourdes: Body and Spirit in the Secular Age*. Viking, 1999.

Jerez Farrán, Carlos, and Samuel Amago, editors. *Unearthing Franco's Legacy: Mass Graves and the Recovery of Historical Memory in Spain*. University of Notre Dame Press, 2010.

Jones, Sam. "Spain to Begin Civil War Exhumations at Valley of the Fallen." *Guardian*, 23 Apr. 2018.

Keller, Patricia. "The Valley, the Monument, and the Tomb: Notes on the Place of Historical Memory." *Memory and Its Discontents: Spanish Culture in the Early Twenty-First Century*, edited by Luis Martín-Estudillo and Nicholas Spadaccini, *Hispanic Issues On Line*, vol. 11, 2012, pp. 64–86.

Lannon, Frances. "The Church's Crusade against the Republic." *Revolution and War in Spain 1931–1939*, edited by Paul Preston, Methuen, 1984, pp. 35–58.

Martínez-Lázaro, Emilio, director. *Las 13 rosas*. Enrique Cerezo Producciones, 2007.

Montero, Manuel. "Sociedad: Otros 'mártires' de la Guerra Civil." *El País*, 6 May 2007.

Nash, Elizabeth. "Spanish Plea for 'Martyrs' Opens Civil War Wounds." *Independent on Sunday*, 5 Mar. 2000, p. 24.

Parra de Carrizosa, Óscar, director. *Bajo un manto de estrellas*. Mystical Films, 2013.

Pérez, Jorge. "De la España Sagrada a 'España va bien': Religión y economía en el período post-franquista." Modern Language Association Convention, 8 Jan. 2017, Marriott Hotel, Philadelphia, Pennsylvania, Session 790: "Traces of the Sacred." Conference Presentation

Preston, Paul. *The Spanish Holocaust: Inquisition and Extermination in Twentieth-Century Spain*. Norton, 2013.

Ramón Solans, Francisco Javier. "They Walked Toward Their Death as if to a Party: Martyrdom, Agency, and Performativity in the Spanish Civil War." *Politics, Religion & Ideology*, vol. 17, no. 2–3, 2016, pp. 210–26.

"Rouco sobre la memoria histórica: 'A veces es necesario saber olvidar.'" *El País*, 24 Nov. 2008.

Serrano Moreno, Juan E. "De la cruzada a la persecución: Las canonizaciones de los mártires de la guerra civil." *Intersticios: Revista Sociológica de Pensamiento Crítico*, vol.

10, no. 2, 2016, pp. 71–87.

Shubert, Adrian. "The Epic Failure: The Asturian Revolution of October 1934." *Revolution and War in Spain 1931–1939*, edited by Paul Preston, Methuen, 1984, pp. 113–36.

Stuart, Paul. "Catholic Church Steps Up Campaign to Oust Spanish Government." *World Socialist Web Site*, 19 Sept. 2005.

"Vatican Directive: Saints' Relics Require Special Care." *National Catholic Register*, 19 Dec. 2017.

Woodward, Kenneth L. *Making Saints: How the Catholic Church Determines Who Becomes a Saint, Who Doesn't, and Why*. Simon & Schuster, 1990.

Zambrano, Benito, director. *La voz dormida*. Warner Bros., 2011. Film.

CHAPTER 5

The Future of the Dead

Reconciliation in Post-ETA Euskadi

Annabel Martín

> "Buscas gasolina en el odio. Te da fuerza para andar.
> El odio es un alimento muy fuerte, mientras
> tú, por dentro, estás podrido."
> (Hate fuels you. It gives you strength to not give up.
> Hatred is very strong nourishment, while you,
> on the other hand, are dead on the inside.)
> IÑAKI REKARTE (ex-ETA member, Nanclares de Oca Project)[1]

We walk through life with varying degrees of ignorance, immersed in processes of discovery that beg to undo the blunders that stem from inexperience, immaturity, and from the many inapprehensible realities that surround us and go unnoticed until it is too late. Sometimes it seems that only the most sensitive or traumatized take notice that secret laws are relentlessly at work, rules that quietly govern in the background. One of these is the law of friendship (Derrida, *Politics*), a dictum that crudely states that one must go before the other. We live our relationships with our loved ones unknowingly as a secret threesome: death being the uninvited third party. And because "one must go before the other," loss bonds love with mourning forever. It is never an easy task to accept the law of friendship but when death comes "naturally," despite its brutal randomness, mourning turns death into a painful process of life: an affair of memory and of future. However, not all departures happen "organically" and this makes us wonder. If the cruelty of natural life already divides humanity into victims and survivors, into those who will depart first, leaving the other to mourn and remember so that there may be a future, what happens to this natural triangulation when the death of a loved one happens at the hands of another? What fundamental laws are transgressed when, in the name of political ideology, national independence, state unity, police brutality, ethnic superiority, or sheer hatred, one sits at the vertex reserved for Death?

As we think about political violence in the Basque context, as we try to understand the moral death of societies that find wars of terror justifiable, as we look at the road to radical militancy, as we ponder the illegality of state-sponsored counter-terrorism efforts, we can't avoid considering the burden of responsibility that sits on the shoulders of those who have survived the brush of Death. On the one hand, we find those who will be marked forever, individuals who will always mourn not having been able to live the law of friendship to its fullest, brutally forced to acknowledge how fragile and unfair the dance of life can be. Responsibility here gets entangled with mourning and claims of reparation. Collectively, however, societies face a different kind of burden, a responsibility that demands justice and memory, if there is to be hope for a different kind of future. The Basque context has only recently acknowledged the erosion and degrading of its social fabric in the case of ETA (Euskadi Ta Askatasuna) violence. Even the institutional recognition of the rights and needs of victims, the 2016 "Ley de reconocimiento y reparación de víctimas," was an extremely contentious piece of Basque legislation in its attempt to address human rights violations suffered by both ETA and Spanish counter-terrorist victims. Collective life in this society can no longer look the other way or write off the past deaths of civilians or members of Spanish and Basque security forces, as the collateral damage of a blind political war. Likewise, in today's post-ETA environment, we have happily reached a moment when the claims for a comprehensive history that includes reparation for crimes authored by state-sponsored violence can finally be heard. In all cases, the law of friendship was shamelessly violated by someone who intercepted Death's exclusive right to take life. This essay will focus on the triangle, reckon with the processes that lead to violent political action, inquire about the effects of poisonous contexts on the perpetrator, and ask how a victimizer can return to the world of the human, of community, after having embodied Death. Is there a road back to the mundane, to the everyday, after having experienced necropolitical power—the right to kill—at its height? Can the law of friendship, the knowledge of futility and precariousness, bring the dead back from the grave in ways that allow for mourning and for a better future?

We live with the dead; they are "with us" only insofar as they are "in us" (Brault and Naas 2). The expected departure of a loved one—death by natural triangulation—allows for the departed to be "in me" for I hold an "image" and a name. This "face" (in Levinasian terms) serves as condolence and comfort for the living given how the dead are no longer accessible in their state of being "inaccessible to this appellation" (Derrida, *Mourning* 46). Nevertheless, they are present and interiorized by "exceeding, fracturing, wounding, injuring, traumatizing the interiority that it inhabits or that welcomes it through hospitality, love or friendship"

(166). The dead hurt for they occupy a wounded interiority that they themselves have caused. This "inside" of sorts is always a space too small to contain the departed, for they now encompass the incommensurability of the entanglement of itself and that part of me that owes itself to this relationship. I now not only hold myself but the missing you. And the space for us both is too small. It aches.

He who holds a gun to the head of another, he who tortures to the point of murder, dispossesses Death's right in the law of friendship. The murderous individual intercepts and interrupts the triangle, the recognition of the I-you bond, and legitimizes his actions to himself through negation: that is, by not recognizing in the Other his own history, his own humanity. Blinded by political ideals, immersed in a twisted version of political struggle, fueled by a need for collective justice in the form of vengeance, and embodying a toxic model of the masculine I (the warrior), the terrorist subject deprives himself of his humanity and becomes an instrument of war. Armed conflict unbinds the social contract, eliminates the law of friendship, and erases the material messiness of day to day life, its irregularities, inconsistencies, and unpredictability. Necropolitical power turns life into a clean and straight road toward self-negation and self-aggrandizement to the tune of war. Nevertheless, one must remember that the warrior not only intercepts and kills the Other in his/her triangle of life; the warrior is also a "casualty" of that same logic. The death of the Other is, in actuality, the beginning of a new murderous triangle between the deceased and the assassin, both of them forever linked in a necropolitical bond, one that underscores, interestingly enough, the supreme loneliness of the assassin.[2] The murdered never die alone for there existed a part of themselves irreducibly tied to another, an interior space in the living for the I-you. They will be mourned, albeit in tragic terms, but a future lies ahead, for the dead "live in us" even if they inhabit a space beyond us.

However, in the case of the one who kills, who will mourn that part of himself gone forever? There is no space in the interior life of the warrior for the "Other in me" given how, in order to kill, that connection needs to be severed. There can be no Face for that would imply an entanglement with humanity, with our own core precariousness and vulnerability, and recognize those same qualities in the Other. He who kills, or tortures, cannot embrace our collective responsibility to question hegemonic belief systems and to embrace uncertainty as an integral part of our individual and social identities. The warrior proves that we "have" ideas but that we "live" our beliefs, the former being susceptible to amendment and contestation, the later becoming a fixed modus vivendi.[3] He who murders in the name of beliefs is able to blunt his moral imagination for he is drunk with a moral superiority that his activism fools him into believing. He taps into the social logic of emotions, into a collective density of feeling that requires convincing oneself of a moral fallacy: that belief systems (national identity, independence, national unity, ethnic superiority) trump humanity, the "you-in-me," the law of friendship.

This would be the starting point for a reflection on the kind of socially responsible work that is needed within societies that have endured "scoundrel times" (Hellman), where death has outplayed life. In the case of Spain and Euskadi, radical nationalist ideologies of Basque independence together with repressive and regressively defined models of Spanish statehood have carefully whittled away at core human rights issues in the name of questionable and anachronistic definitions of national and political identity. This has been a long and painful process that has been scoundrel and indecent in its permissiveness toward violence and indifference to victims, reprehensively causing a numbing and souring of the public sphere.

This essay will focus on victims of ETA terrorism but not in the usual way: that is, by focusing on those murdered at the hands of ETA and the dire personal and collective outcomes of such acts of violence. Instead, following the leads of philosophers Judith Butler and Reyes Mate, we will look at the extraordinary work in civil reconciliation that the Nanclares de Oca prison project withholds for both Basque and Spanish society, a project whereby former ETA members sit face to face with survivors, both brought together in their shared wish to search for the "Face" of the Other. In the testimonies of these meetings, one finds that the quest for mutual listening and understanding offers both sides the priceless gifts of life and reconciliation. These interior gifts are achieved, however, thanks to a journey to the Underworld, a visit with the dead, that they separately take and where each return with a greater sense of peace, with hopes for a personal and collective future, with space for "the-Other-in-me."

Naturally, victims of violence demand adequate legal formulations to bring justice and reparation to those aggrieved; however, this justice takes a different turn when addressing the demands of the dead for the only route toward reparation, in this case, is through memory, through that risky trip Margaret Atwood describes in her *Negotiating with the Dead*, as the visit the writer (in her case) makes to the Underworld "to bring something or someone back" (157). In that same spirit of public good, Margaret Atwood argues that the goal of the writer is to revert to the past in the guise of a thief, for the task at hand is to "[c]ommit acts of larceny, or else of reclamation, depending on how you look at it. The dead may guard the treasure, but it is useless treasure unless it can be brought back into the land of the living and allowed to enter time once more—which means to enter the realm of the audience, the realm of readers, the realm of change" (178).

Is this not what victims and victimizers of the Nanclares de Oca project (restorative justice encounters between ETA militants and victims, see below) were invited to pursue as each made that journey to the Underworld to find a piece of themselves? Can the warrior leave behind armed conflict and become a custodian of the dead? Why do victims offer the law of friendship to those who mercilessly killed a loved one? These are some of the questions this essay wishes to explore as it ponders on the implications of making the dead core interlocutors in processes of collective reconciliation and, therefore, of the deepening of democracy in those communities. Processes of reconciliation are never short, easy, or without discomfort, but when the tenets of restorative justice guide the road, a deeper level of justice and internal peace is attained for survivors, victimizers, and, possibly, even the dead. For, if memory is all that we have left of the violently departed (Derrida, *Mourning* 32–33), no other process of reconciliation allows for wounded societies to better "negotiate with the dead" so that they remain in and between us. There are life-changing secrets hidden in the Underworld that will surface and offer a future for those no longer here and for those who mourn.

Density of Feeling

In a remarkable 2015 interview with Spanish investigative journalist Jordi Évole, former ETA militant Iñaki Rekarte provides numerous examples of what ETA victim and former Socialist MP Eduardo Madina refers to as ETA's "deber de uniformidad" (Madina) (loyalty to uniformity). Quoting María Dolores Katarain, "Yoyes," (the former ETA leader killed by the organization in 1986), Madina uses Katarain's critique to undermine the notion of Basque identity that permeated the organization as one that erased (literally, in many tragic instances) the logical complexities and differences of thought, feeling, and life experiences that exist in all societies. I will use Rekarte's interview to help highlight these moves toward simplicity and distortion, but first it might help to try to understand these self-proclaimed representatives of Basque life in the broader context of Spanish national politics and the different revolutionary moments that were at work in the 1960s and early 1970s worldwide. ETA gets its theoretical inspiration from the many decolonization struggles in Africa, the Latin American Marxist and indigenous movements, the anti-capitalist militarized formations in Europe, and the fight for black empowerment in the United States.

The Basque conflict (1959–2011) was Western Europe's last site of internal political armed conflict until the recent rise of ISIS. This was a situation stemming from the outcome of World War II and the special socio-historical circumstances that governed the later years of the Franco regime in Spain (1939–1975). The end of the dictatorship was a contradictory ethical period of Spanish history.

Many of those pushing for democracy looked the other way when political vio-lence was deemed a legitimate avenue of action given the longevity and brutality of the dictatorship.[4] This triggered a complex renegotiation of national identity for Spaniards and Basques alike during the country's subsequent transition to democracy after Franco's death in 1975. At the time, most progressives both in and out of the Basque Country joined in the Basque nationalist sentiment and equated *Spanish* national identity (the adjective) with the legacy of the dictator-ship. In the Basque context, regionalism, whether nationalist or not, promised to correct the democratic deficit for which an excessively strong centralist Span-ish state was held responsible. Victims of terrorism, both at the hands of ETA and the Spanish state, were the ugly price placed on the political demands of the separatists and the political stability of Spain, respectively.[5] A toxic fire was camouflaged as a circle of love toward the homeland. Both hid the dirtiness of nationalist violence under the powerful emotional ties the communal space elicits. In Euskadi, this hermeneutical and moral confusion generated an incomprehen-sible tolerance and apathy toward the victims of ETA terrorism, an acceptance grounded, in part, on the resentment provoked by the excesses of the Span-ish state in its anti-terrorist efforts and the weak exercise of democracy in that region: an eye-for-an-eye deadly indifference, an unhealthy legacy of the Franco dictatorship. The invisibility of the victims, their "inevitability" given the larger political goals, marks one of the lowest ethical moments of Basque and Spanish societies. It highlights a mean-spiritedness or "souring of social conscience and compassion" (Rich 157) that will take years to overcome even as a new climate of reconciliation begins to take root.

Basque writer Bernardo Atxaga has eloquently written about the attraction toward this fire in his 1993 novel *Gizona bere bakardadean* (The Lone Man).[6] There he focuses on what Sara Ahmed terms a "thickness of sociality" (28) that confers ETA militants, in this case, with an airtight belief system that, while inspired in the insufficiencies within the outcomes of democracy in the Basque Country, is better understood as being fueled by a particular model of heroic masculinity. Following Sedgwick's analysis of gender, militancy in ETA demands toxic "homosocial bonding" (1), an identity that is imbued with necropolitical "rights": that is, with a license to kill driven by overdetermined feelings of hatred directed toward those elements of Basque society that have *injured* the collective romanticized nationalist I in a figurative and/or literal sense. Hatred toward tor-turers, disgust toward "outsiders" (maketos), repulsion toward non-nationalists, animosity toward all ideological dissenters, heroic love for land and country, all driven by the urge to rid that society from elements that pollute this illusory social space. Atxaga's characters embody the "noble" warrior (166) who risks his life for a collective cause and enters a space reserved for the "chosen." In the main character's words, they were not

> los que agachaban la cabeza en sus fábricas y oficinas; los que desde los veinte años vivían con la única aspiración de convertirse en funcionarios; los que aguardaban el invierno para tener un pretexto para refugiarse en casa, todos ellos y muchos más, eran cobardes, mezquinos, serviles. Por eso se había incorporado él a una organización armada siendo todavía un adolescente, por no querer entrar a formar parte de aquella masa vulgar. . . . La convicción de que eran diferentes ponía alas en sus pies y en sus corazones. (167)

> (those who sat with bowed heads in their factories and offices, those whose one ambition from the age of twenty was to become a civil servant, those who looked forward to the winter so as to have an excuse to stay at home, all of those people and many more like them were cowardly, mean-spirited, servile. That was why he had joined an armed organization when he was still an adolescent, because he did not want to form part of that commonplace mass. . . . The belief that they were different lent wings to their feet and to their hearts.) (138)

Iñaki Rekarte, who was sentenced in 1999 to 203 years in prison for killing three people and injuring two dozen more after making a car bomb explode in the city of Santander, was part of this toxicity. He joined ETA in the 1980s, during the "Años de Plomo" (Lead Years), a terribly tragic moment for Basque and Spanish societies, a time when, in 1980 alone, ninety-eight people died at the mercy of ETA. In his words, he joined because it was "in the air" and because he saw how the Spanish police had detained and tortured his father on false pretenses (Rekarte interview). These were the days of widespread *preventative* raids amongst nationalist communities and organizations suspicious of supporting ETA in any fashion, police operations geared toward instilling fear and that inevitably added unnecessary logs to the already toxic fire of hatred and self-proclaimed necrological rights. This biopolitics of Basques versus Spaniards was at its zenith during the time of the illegal paramilitary activities of the GAL, or Grupos Antiterroristas de Liberación (1983–1987), counterterrorist organizations that operated under the Socialist party-led government and that were responsible for the deaths of twenty-seven people, several of whom with no links to ETA.[7]

In the Évole interview, Rekarte explains that he and others in ETA thought of themselves as members of an army, at war with a faceless Other, even ridiculing those militants who were more sophisticated in political terms, those who questioned and tried to better understand the battle they were fighting. He recalls, no one wanted to be known as "el politiquillo" (the little politician), and "¡Déjate de chorradas! Estabas en un ejército" (Rekarte interview) (No talking drivel! We were in an army!). The former ETA member shatters the myth or aura of the well-informed, militant-intellectual, the warrior who fights with a deep knowledge of the wrongs his struggle will remedy. On the contrary, "Éramos unos críos . . . y ser de ETA era ser un héroe" (Rekarte interview) (We were kids and being a part of ETA made us heroes). They were fueled by hatred, justifying killing the enemy, Spanish security forces, for example, because they torture, or drug push-ers because they were ruining Basque youth. But like Iñaki Gabilondo writes in the prologue to Javier Elzo's indispensable *Tras la losa de ETA* (2014): "Tu cri-men no borra el mío, se suma" (7) (Your crime doesn't cancel mine; they add up). These young men were easy prey for the toxic fire that was driving Basque youth to armed political activism in times when powerful global forces of neo-liberal erasure of identity, self-worth, and of the demos itself gave new meaning to fighting with blood, sweat, and tears. Nothing else felt "real," as Baudrillard would write of the period on the global scale.

In sociological terms, a good portion of Basque society understood this war and supported the struggle either in direct or indirect fashion. The Univer-sity of the Basque Country's research group, Euskobarómetro, offers referential statistical information on Basque society's attitudes toward a wide number of socio-political issues, one of them being, of course, its stance toward ETA and victims of violence.[8] The numbers in an October 2017 survey are telling. Today, 76 percent of Basques consider ETA to have been either an extremely negative or quite negative presence for the Basque Country, up nine points from 2014 (61 percent of nationalist voters, 40 percent of Euskal Herria Bildu [EHB] voters, 100 percent of Partido Popular [PP] voters). Only 7 percent believe ETA has been a positive force in Euskadi (17 percent EHB).[9] In the most recent statistical data offered in the 2017 report by the Basque Government's Centro Memorial de las Víctimas del Terrorismo, it is startling to note that while ETA was still operative (until October 2011), only 42 percent of Basques felt favorably toward the family members of ETA victims, while 18 percent felt indifferent, and 27 percent felt unfavorably. On the other hand, 34 percent see ETA prisoners in a positive light, while 30 percent are indifferent, and 22 percent see them negatively. Perhaps the most striking statistic is in regard to the appreciation of Spanish security forces by Basque society: only 14 percent of Basques approve of the Spanish Guardia Civil and/or state police; 11 percent are indifferent; and 65 percent disapprove equally amongst nationalist (67 percent) and non-nationalist (65 percent) voters (Centro Memorial de las Víctimas del Terrorismo 19). From these numbers it is not difficult to see that there was and still is a long road toward reconciliation if less than half of Basque society felt only a few years ago little or no empathy toward victims of ETA terror, and two-thirds of Basque society felt during that same period that Spanish security forces (and what they represent) are harmful for the public sphere. It is inevitable that the many instances of anti-democratic and repressive logic of the Spanish state be on the table for reconciliatory measures to take root.

Before going into detail on the core issues at stake in processes of reconciliation, it would be helpful to try to understand why the power of the warrior has had until very recently such a stronghold on Basque society. Some would point to the abuses and shortcomings of democracy stemming from the unhappy and insufficient transition to democracy after the end of the Franco regime. This is, without a doubt, one of the logs on the lethal fire of political violence in that context. However, it is also true that, due to the insufficiencies of the transition to democracy, Basque and Spanish society are amnesiac communities in regard to the debt owed to those who died at the hands of political and human rights abuses stemming from the Civil War and more recently from ETA and counter-terrorist efforts by the Spanish state. The power of the terrorist (of any shade) resides not so much in his gun but rather in the collective push to forget, in that often-reprehensible urge to "turn the page" and go on living and pretending that we live *normal* lives despite the dead (Mate 27). We speak here not of the individual processes of recovery for victims, those that will always entail specific routes of healing that will certainly include some sort of "turning of the page" as the embers of pain cool, but rather of societal amnesia, of a rewriting of our collective history.

Reyes Mate has written extensively on the role that memory should play in the move toward freer and more just societies in contemporary Europe. His writings on the Holocaust, the Spanish Civil War, or on ETA violence and victims of terrorism are inspirational in that he maps a way for rethinking modernity through the responsibility we inexorably bear with the suffering and inequities of the past. This is a responsibility based not so much on the importance of remembering the atrocities Europe has committed on those deemed its Others both inside and outside its borders, but rather more importantly, on making the memory of that experience a lived part of our rethinking of today, whether it be in social pedagogies toward peace, in rethinking the nationalist state, or incorporating the experience of the victim into our collective understanding of the social sphere. In Mate's words, "La memoria es una exigencia moral con carga política" (37) (Memory is a moral obligation with political demands). Just how delicate and attentive a society becomes to these dictates will invoke the degree to which it strives for a civic culture of reparation, one of the stepping-stones of democracy.

There is a growing awareness in Basque society of just how sour the collective social conscious became during the years of ETA violence. The statistical data referenced earlier unquestionably points to this transformation. The nationalist normativity that guides much of the political architecture is being questioned today as the new emphasis is no longer on a Basque utopia but rather on the effects of ideas on people.[10] We cannot bring the dead back from the grave but surely this new political context without ETA favors memory's coming of age here. The loss of life is an irreparable and tragically irreversible temporal moment, one where time stands still. However, today's political situation allows for the reparation of something possibly far worse and sinister (at least in moral terms), what Mate describes as making the victim "hermenéuticamente irrelevante" (hermeneutically irrelevant), the elimination of meaning, the belittlement of that death (27–28). In this context, memory acts as a remedy against this "second death" of the victims, a buffer that ameliorates the abyss that leads to the irreversibility of forgetting.

Memory facilitates a trip to the Underworld (a temporal movement back to the dead) while also enabling a route toward the future. Memory has a double-edged "temporal core" (Adorno xvii), deeply rooted in death but firmly engaged in life in each and every historical moment. Today, we live in a time where "the need to enable suffering to speak . . . [has become] the precondition of truth" (xvii–xviii). However, this "outing" of pain, this making of irreversibility (what can never be the same or undone) the center of a social theory of reconciliation, needs to avoid grounding this push toward truth (democracy) in a recurrent loop of despair or meaninglessness (Arendt 236). The faculty to make and keep promises—in our case here, the renunciation of violence—dispels the unpredictability and chaotic uncertainty of the future (237), the dead-end of irreversibility. It is because of the faculty of making and keeping promises that a door opens toward reconciliation, possibly through the discrete and personal act of forgiveness.

Acts of Reconciliation, Acts of Transformation, Acts of Forgiveness

The Nanclares de Oca prison project was an unfortunately short restorative justice initiative that took place between 2011 and 2012 under the Socialist government of José Luis Rodríguez Zapatero and was later discontinued under the PP government of Mariano Rajoy (Terradillos 168). Directed and coordinated by Esther López Rodríguez, a labor attorney, in conjunction with Juan Antonio Zárate, the director of the Nanclares de Oca prison, ETA inmates met with victims in the presence of a mediator. These were men who were driven by the will to face the Other they had denied for so long. All of the participants were serving sentences of nearly thirty years and none would improve or shorten their time in prison in exchange for their participation in the program. Dialogue and tears were not to become instrumentalized in a barter of recognition or in requests for forgiveness. Having fully separated themselves from ETA and from the ETA collective of incarcerated militants, thirty inmates who were struggling with their past came to the initial meeting. In their words, it was irresolvable for them to merely "turn the page" ("El final de ETA"). Only fourteen, however, were to actually face their victims. The road to reconciliation starts from within and not everyone can take that journey, especially if it entails a trip to the Underworld to search for the dead.

The first encounter took place on May 26, 2011, between the director of the Basque Government's Office for Victims of Terrorism, Maixabel Lasa, and former ETA member Luis María Carrasco Asenguinolaza at the Nanclares de Oca prison. Lasa had been the director of that regional government office for ten years at the time (2001–2012), but professional matters had not driven her to Nanclares de Oca, despite her being an exemplary advocate for peace and reconciliation in the Basque context. Her motivation was of a personal nature: she herself was a survivor of ETA violence: her husband, Juan María Jauregi, former civil governor of Gipuzkoa, had been gunned down by Carrasco in July 2000. She had come as a participant in the reconciliation project. In a 2014 interview on Basque public television (EITB), Lasa explains that there is no simple explanation that guides her willingness to meet with her husband's assassin. On a sociopolitical level, she is a firm believer in the potential of these conversations in encouraging a culture and climate of peaceful coexistence in post-ETA times. Pragmatically speaking, all former ETA militants will eventually return to civil society, so she asks herself if it is not in society's interest to smooth out the wrinkles in their reinsertion process by offering them a second chance, by supporting their road back from necropolitical power. Had they not made the first move, according to Lasa, by requesting to meet the families, expressing the need to ask for forgiveness, having gone through a process of self-critique, and reflecting upon the innocent and society? (*EITB Hoy*).

But all was not altruistic in Lasa's motivations. There was a hermeneutical crisis that she needed to clarify, something about the reality of the warrior that she needed to understand. It was crucial for Lasa to ask Carrasco some basic questions in order to "make sense" of her husband's death. Did he understand who Juan Mari was? Did he know that her husband had also been an early member of ETA in his youth? Did he realize that Juan Mari had shut down the infamous Zumalakarregi prison (San Sebastián) in the hands of the Civil Guard? Was he aware that Jauregi investigated all cases of torture to the end? Did he not appreciate that her husband had been an expert witness in the Lasa and Zabala case (*EITB Hoy*)?[11] Lasa was attempting to find a logic to the violation of the Law of Friendship, some ghastly justification for her husband's death. The answers to her questions are mindboggling to anyone unfamiliar with the processes of othering and dehumanization. Carrasco replied that he killed her husband unknowingly. He received the order to execute him and obeyed.

Similarly, when asked about the identity of his victims, Iñaki Rekarte, another Nanclares de Oca participant, surprisingly explains that it is customary for all militants to learn the names of their victims many years later, in prison or during the trials, as was his case. Death comes anonymously for these warriors and names are meaningless, for the Other has been dehumanized and reduced to "un objetivo" (a target). In his own words, "Has matado a uno. ¿De qué te sirve saber su nombre?" (Rekarte interview) (You've killed someone. What good is it to know his name?). Even at the time of the Évole interview, Rekarte finds it very difficult to name his victims. He painfully tries, clearly holding back tears, but he cannot or will not conjure their names, referring to them as "the couple" or the "young guy," for the name contains the Other. It might be counterproductive and threatening to the warrior to know the name of his target, that is, acknowledging and being attuned to what is precarious in another life (Butler 134), but it is indispensable in finding the road back to the living. For the name, the "Face," is not only what we see or make of the Other; it is also an idea: Thou shalt not kill. Keep in mind that the Face makes various utterances at once: "it bespeaks an agony, an injurability, at the same time that it bespeaks a divine prohibition against killing" without the need to precisely speak it (132–35). The self-proclaimed warrior needs to deafen his ears to this call, in order to fulfill his necropolitical duty. But by doing so, by embodying his self-proclaimed right to kill, by taking the place of Death, he also compromises and violates another instance of the prohibition to kill, the Law of Friendship, and with it, his own humanity and interior life.

The Nanclares de Oca conversations bring these socio-ethical premises to life. Those encounters facilitated a literal coming to terms with the "Face" of the Other: victims and victimizers actually recognizing the complexity and incommensurability of each other for the very first time, as we read in their testimonies. One must recall that the "Face" is not a true and complete representation of what lies within the Other; quite the opposite. It is, in fact, the recognition of a disjunction between the hope to understand and the impossibility of total access to that experience. The road to reconciliation requires making that disjunction visible and honorable, a part of each other's incommensurability. And with that in mind, it is imperative that this process recognize that part of that incommensurability lies in an affective reservoir hidden in the Underworld.

The Nanclares interlocutors were able to see the humanity in each other because they separately embarked on a painful journey to Hades to meet and mourn the dead that they share. This was a process that demanded reconfiguring the "triangle" that the terrorist had single-handedly redrawn, becoming cognizant that they had no necrological right to take Death's place in the triangulation with a loved one. Reconciliation does not transpire at a societal level, although there are, undoubtedly, momentous core implications for the wider body politic.[12] Appeasement, atonement, and sometimes forgiveness can only transpire between individuals, after that harrowing and bitter trip to the underworld. This requires an *outbound* journey that implies traumatic movement and approximation to death, remorse, and grief, and an *inbound* movement where each traveler reappears with the secret of the dead: acknowledging the grievable condition of our shared humanity, the key for a personal and collective future. The noxious fire of violence put into question the immutable Law of Friendship, but this premise has not always been the social currency of Basque society. For too long victims were held by many as deserving of their lot; terrorist actions turned into defensible means of collective contestation. But times have changed when what was once deemed a justified war against an enemy becomes an internal war within the psyche and moral imagination of the messengers of death themselves.

Fortunately, a slow but profound, bottom-up transformation is at work in the Basque context, one based on reconciliation practices that demand a process of intellection, a "real communication with the offender and a real transfiguration of the offended person" (Jankélévitch 68). From the testimonies of those who participated in the Nanclares project, these transfigurations materialized as powerful moments of change that affected both victims and victimizers on their road back to life. For the terrorists, the process that culminated in the encounter with victims began as a long and painful journey for breaking the demands of the Law of Friendship dispossessed them of their place in community, a social concept that would take them years to (re)discover. He who has killed in the name of country or hatred returns from that territory by virtue of acknowledging that "each of us is constituted politically in part by virtue of the social vulnerability of our bodies," that "loss and vulnerability seem to follow from our being socially constituted bodies, attached to others, at risk of losing those attachments, exposed to others, at risk of violence by virtue of that exposure" (Butler 20).

The victim knows this all too well, for her loss begins with the violation of the command not to kill, on the day when someone tragically interfered with the dance of life and severed ties that were designed to remain beyond the reach of the assassin. For his part, in order to kill, the warrior must not ask himself "to what are we tied?" (Butler 21), for one cannot claim necropolitical rights if one is undone by the Other, dispossessed by the Other, in an interdependence that claims uneven and messy social bonds, connections that assert rights to autonomy through acknowledged interdependence. The killer is antisocial, for he exploits a "primary tie, that primary way in which we are, as bodies, outside ourselves and for one another" (27). However, a return path to the living begins for him once there is acknowledgment of loss: that there was something *in* the dead for which he will forever be responsible. Understanding the weight of this burden will bring about for him a profound understanding of this wounded "I," one that will allow the former terrorist to "not only become a friend of [humanity] but to become a friend of oneself" (Jankélévitch 69) again. How does one re-establish that primal bond after having violated the basic laws of humanity? How does one forgive oneself for the unforgiveable? For in Rekarte's words, "Si no te perdonas a ti mismo, no puedes seguir viviendo" (Rekarte interview) (if you don't forgive yourself, you can't go on living). The magic occurs when the victimizer acknowledges a desire for transformation (Kristeva 286), for introspection, and accepts his responsibility (Butler 129) in the severing of the I-you entanglement. And asks to be pardoned.

Luis María Carrasco Asenguinolaza, the assassin of Juan María Jauregi, attempts to explain in a chapter of *Los ojos del otro* (2013) his need to ask for forgiveness. After acknowledging "una cruel injusticia, de un inmerecido sufrimiento" (277) (the cruel injustice, of undeserved suffering imposed on his victims), he deeply thanks the victims for meeting with him: "Para mí era vital escucharlas" (277) (it was vital that I listened to them). He had undergone a long and agonizing process that "instaló en mi fuero interno el sentimiento de culpa, de arrepentimiento, la necesidad de pedir perdón" (279) (instilled in me the feeling of guilt, of remorse, the need to ask for forgiveness). And recalls the day of his face to face encounter as one where he had to

> afrontar su presencia desde mi vergüenza y mi arrepentimiento, y consciente de la trágica posición en que me había situado el devenir de mi propia trayectoria personal, empeñada muchos años atrás en un desatinado transitar hacia ninguna parte, consagrada al servicio de un terco y necio delirio de sinsentidos que, mientras duró, solo consiguió sembrar odio y dolor. Aquella mañana me disponía a pedir perdón por un crimen imperdonable. (280)

> (accept her presence from the position of my shame and remorse, aware that the tragic position that I was in was of my own doing, one that began many years ago and that was ridiculously racing toward a dead end, devoted to enabling a stubborn and foolish delirium of meaningless acts, that only achieved sowing hatred

and pain while it all lasted. That morning I was ready to ask to be forgiven for an unforgiveable crime.)

His victim, Maixabel Lasa remembers it differently:

Personalmente, pensaba que el encuentro no me aportaría gran cosa, pero no fue así. Cuando él apareció en la salita donde nos encontramos y, después de las presentaciones, nos miramos a los ojos, me di cuenta de lo mal que lo estaba pasando. Creo que estaba como avergonzado. . . . Estuvimos hablando y preguntándonos durante casi tres horas. No quiero entrar en detalles, pero lo que más me impresionó durante la conversación fue lo que repetía una y otra vez; tenía la autoestima por los suelos, no veía nada bueno en él y decía: "Todo en mí es malo", "No hay nada bueno en mí". Le respondí que eso no era cierto: "Si lo fuera, no estaríamos aquí ninguno de los dos". Y añadí: "Creo que has sido muy valiente en reconocer todo el daño causado, has sabido comprender que todo lo que hiciste en el pasado fue un gravísimo error y has pedido perdón por ello; pero, lo más importante, has recuperado tu libertad y el derecho a ser un ciudadano." (14)

(Personally, I didn't think the meeting would offer me much, but I was wrong. After he walked into the room where we met, and after the introductions, after looking into each other's eyes, I realized how difficult this was for him. I think he felt ashamed. We spoke and asked each other questions for almost three hours. I don't want to go into details but what affected me the most during the conversation were the words that he repeated over and over again; he had very low self-esteem; he saw nothing good in himself. He would say, "Everything in me is evil"; "there is nothing good in me." I replied that wasn't true: "If that were the case, neither of us would be here today." And I added, "I believe you've been very brave by acknowledging all the hurt caused; you've understood that all the things you did in the past were a grave error and you've asked for forgiveness; but, the most important thing is that you've recovered your freedom and the right to be a citizen.")

Quite astonishingly, Lasa offers Carrasco a priceless gift as she looks outward, toward the executioner, and allows the miracle of grace to occur: she "abstains from denying her essential similarity with the guilty person; [s]he does not exploit the advantageous position that [her] innocence confirms upon [her]" (Jankélévitch 161–62). Does she forgive? Her offender asks for pardon but she withholds a simple answer: she offered him a second chance and that "says a lot and says it all" (EITB Hoy). Lasa teaches us that there is a way to turn private pain and intimate dialogue into a politics and pedagogy of collective good. To forgive is:

[n]either to change one's mind on the score of the guilty person, nor to rally around the thesis of innocence . . . Quite the contrary! The supernaturality of forgiveness consists in this, that my opinion on the subject of the guilty person precisely has not changed; but . . . it is . . . my relations with the guilty person that [are] modified, it is the whole orientation of our relations that finds itself inverted, overturned, and overwhelmed! The judgment of condemnation has stayed the same, but an arbitrary and gratuitous change has intervened, a diametrical and radical inversion, *peristrophē*, which transforms hatred into love. (Jankélévitch 152)

To conclude, the restorative justice project that took place under the direction of Esther Pascual Rodríguez refuses to allow us to dehumanize the dead as the "eliminated" (Berger 4) as much as it opens a door for those already "dead" (the killers) to return to life. If peace is to return, we must reimagine the lost as the grand collective that we, the living, victims and victimizers, already belong to (4). The scale of restorative justice is small but the goals are far reaching given how societies tormented by political violence can only renew themselves if they aspire to redefine the core values of the community, those that govern the space allotted to the Other, which in this particular case, means burying the dead outside of the logic of vengeance and hatred. To mourn requires that the living walk together with the dead, acknowledging their place in the collective future, living on in new pedagogies of memory, care, and recognition. Change will come about when the law of friendship is reinstated, when the natural triangle and not necropolitical power governs the already cruelly short passage of life. An intense beauty lies in making the incommensurability of the Other the core value of our shared humanity. The Nanclares prison project is one step in this direction as it attempts to design a road map toward reconciliation based on this principle. The face to face encounters of victims and victimizers bring to light just how fragile, profound, and generous the human soul can be. In Esther Pascual's words, "No es un camino ancho, no puede ni debe transitarlo todo el mundo, aunque esté abierto a cualquiera; es un sendero pequeño y estrecho, pero bellísimo, cuya existencia renueva nuestra fe en las personas y nuestras esperanzas de verdad, justicia y memoria" (16–17) (This is not a wide road; it is not, nor should it be, for everyone, although all are invited. It is a small and narrow path but a most beautiful one. Its existence renews our faith in humanity and our hopes for truth, justice, and memory). This is the path Basque society is beginning to travel and imagine for itself.[13]

NOTES

1. Unless otherwise indicated, all translations from sources not published in English are my own.
2. For a literary rendition of this theme, see Bernardo Atxaga's *Gizona bere bakardadean* (1993), translated into Spanish as *El hombre solo* (1998) and English as *The Lone Man* (1996).
3. I am following the lead of Spanish philosopher Victoria Camps who in her *Elogio de la duda* (2016) makes a case for uncertainty and doubt as political tools in times of ideological security. In this particular case, she references Ortega y Gasset's maxim "las ideas se tienen, en las creencias se está" (90) (one possesses ideas but lives with beliefs).
4. For more on this political mindset in the Basque context, see Gurutz Jáuregui's *Entre la tragedia y la esperanza* (1997) or Juan Aranzadi's *El escudo de Arquíloco* (2002). On this understanding of Basque society, Txetxu Aguado writes

   > ETA contó con un fuerte apoyo social desde sus comienzos. La mezcla de nacionalismo de raíz sabiniana, para liberar al pueblo vasco de la opresión franquista, junto con su izquierdismo, para lograr una sociedad vasca más justa, ha formado parte de su ideario desde sus orígenes. A ello se añade la idea religiosa de sacrificio, incluida la muerte, del militante de ETA para que su pueblo sea y siga existiendo. La violencia funcionaría como ritual de unión entre el militante con su comunidad, a la que purifica, protege y salva del mal. (87)

   > (ETA had widespread social support from its inception. The combination of a Sabinian version of nationalism, which intended to liberate the Basque people from Francoist oppression, together with its left-wing ideology, geared toward a more equitable Basque society, has been part of its ideological framework from its origins. To this one must add religious notions of sacrifice, even the death of the ETA militant in order to preserve his people. Violence functions as a ritual of brotherhood between the militant and his community, a collective that he purifies, protects, and saves from evil.)

5. The Grupos Antiterroristas de Liberación, better known as the GAL, operated in Spain and France during the Socialist government of Prime Minister Felipe González (1983–1987), targeting ETA members, nationalist activists, and several others who had no links to political activism. This was a time when ETA killings had reached their peak. Several police officers and high-ranking government officials from the Ministry of the Interior, including the Cabinet Secretary, José Barrionuevo, and Security Secretary of the State, Rafael Vera, were convicted of kidnapping, briberies, and embezzlement of government funds. For an excellent study of the context and the illegal activities, see Paddy Woodworth's *Dirty War, Clean Hands: ETA, the Gal, and Spanish Democracy* (2001). A filmic rendition of the brutality of the illegal operations of the GAL is Pablo Malo's tough and incisive film *Lasa eta Zabala* (2014).

6.   See my "La gramática de la duda: Opacidad y transparencia terrorista en *El hombre solo,* de Bernardo Atxaga" (2018). For a first-hand account of the context and internal transformation, see former ETA member Iñaki Rekarte's *Lo difícil es perdonarse a uno mismo* (2015). I refer readers to Teresa Brennan's *The Transmission of Affect* (2004) for an understanding of the social underpinnings of affect.

7.   In its latest report, El Foro Social Permanente, a human rights platform working to consolidate peace in Euskadi (www.forosocialpaz.org), affirms that there are still 484 cases of fatal terrorist acts that have not been clarified in 2018. Of these open cases, 61.4 percent are killings committed by the GAL (37 percent) or by the Batallón Vasco Español (24.4 percent), while 23.2 percent of those murders were committed by ETA (Albin "Terrorismo").

8.   Basque sociologist Javier Elzo offers very useful longitudinal statistical information on these issues. For example, in 1974, 50 percent of Basque society was either extremely afraid or quite afraid to discuss political affairs; in 2006, that percentage had dropped to 24 percent. In regard to ETA, the figures indicate that there has been a steady decline in the number of Basques who unquestionably supported ETA: from 8 percent in 1981 to 1 percent in 2010. Basque society has evolved from 23 percent of its citizens fully rejecting ETA in 1981 to 60 percent opposing the organization in 1997. However, as Elzo points out, there is one important distinction to be made. Despite Basque society's extremely low categorical support for ETA, approximately 30 percent of Basque society has supported ETA from a distance. This includes those who differentiate between supporting ETA's goals but not its methods ("fines sí, medios no") or those who affirm they were supporters in the past but not today ("antes sí, ahora no") (107–8). In terms of national identity, Elzo points out that over the course of thirty-three years (1981–2014), there has been a consistent breakdown in how Basques envision their identity: about one-third consider themselves as much Spanish as Basque; roughly 10 percent only Spanish or more Spanish than Basque; and 45–50 percent of Basques consider themselves only Basque or more Basque than Spanish (110).

9.   When asked about the name Basque citizens believe best describes ETA members, 31 percent felt that "terrorists" was the most suiting; 6 percent agreed with the term "assassins"; 15 percent with "fanatics"; 10 percent with "patriots" (up 6 percent); and 28 percent with "misguided idealists" (up 9 percent). The latter is the most common choice for Partido Nacionalista Vasco (PNV) and EHB voters: 55 percent and 69 percent, respectively (Euskobarómetro 58). Roughly half of Basque society votes either party.

10.   One sees a significant sociological shift in Basque society with the rise of the Podemos party in that context. The new 15M-inspired party (against independence but in favor of an independence referendum) was the most voted party in Euskadi in the national parliamentary elections of 2016 and third most voted party (behind the PNV and EHB) in the elections to the Basque Parliament of 2016. It is also significant that this party's candidate for the presidency of the Basque Government would be peace activist Pilar Zabala, the sister of GAL torture victim, Joxi Zabala.

11. The brutal torture and killing of Josean Lasa and Joxi Zabala in October of 1983 is considered to be the first terrorist act committed by the GAL. The alleged eighteen-year-old ETA sympathizers were kidnapped in Bayonne, France, and mercilessly tortured in the Intxaorrondo barracks of the Civil Guard in San Sebastián-Donostia and in the basement of the official residence of the civil governor of the time, the socialist Julen Elgorriaga, as recent government documents have revealed (Albin "Lasa y Zabala"). They were then taken to Busot, Alicante, where they were each shot several times in the head and buried covered in lime. They had been "disappeared" but their bodies were fortuitously discovered in March 1995.

12. Maixabel Lasa unequivocally laments the fact that the PP government stopped these encounters:

> Esta es una experiencia que comenzó con el gobierno socialista. Ahora mismo esa experiencia que se llevó a cabo, esos encuentros restaurativos, están rotos. ¿Por qué? Porque el gobierno del PP los ha roto. No le gustan, no están de acuerdo con ellos. Es una pena porque estas personas que están en esa disposición, me refiero a los presos de la vía Nanclares, podrían hacer mucho trabajo no solamente dentro de la cárcel con los demás presos, que puedan compartir debate, hablar del tema, incluso cuando salen fuera de prisión, cuando salen con permisos a sus pueblos, a sus ciudades, que puedan debatir con jóvenes, especialmente de la izquierda abertzale, que pueden explicar su trayectoria de cómo han hecho ese cambio de actitud personal ante el uso de la violencia y que ahora mismo su posición es la deslegitimación total del empleo de la violencia. (*EITB Hoy*)

> (This project started under the Socialist government. That experience, the restorative meetings, are no more. Why? Because the PP government has stopped them. They don't like them; they disagree with them. It's a real shame because these people who have changed, I mean the inmates of the Nanclares project, could do a lot of good work not only in prison with other inmates by debating, sharing experiences, but also when they leave the jail, on furloughs, in their towns and cities. They can speak to Basque youth, especially those within the radical Basque left [*izquierda abertzale*], and explain their personal story, their shift and rejection of violence. And that today their position entails its complete de-legitimatization.)

13. In today's society, with ETA having declared a permanent cessation of all military actions in October of 2011 and disbanded in April 2018, the numbers are a bit more optimistic in regard to recognizing the deep harm done to Basque society in general. To wit, in 2017, 80 percent of Basque society believed that ETA victims were deserving of public recognition and remembrance, 61 percent felt that victims of the extreme Right or paramilitary terrorism are deserving, 42 percent believed ETA members killed in showdowns with the police should be remembered, and 33 percent approved of the public display of recognition for ETA members who served their prison sentences

(71 percent of EHB voters, 32 percent of Podemos voters, 23 percent of PNV voters) (Centro Memorial 21). When a growing 45 percent of Basques believe that terrorists who show remorse and wish to abandon armed conflict should benefit from social reinsertion programs, change is on the horizon (Euskobarómetro 58).

WORKS CITED

Adorno, Theodor W. *Can One Live After Auschwitz? A Philosophical Reader.* Edited by Rolf Tiedemann, Stanford University Press, 2003.

Aguado, Txetxu. "*Lasa eta Zabala* (2014) de Pablo Malo, el GAL, y el terrorismo de estado." *Imágenes de la memoria. Víctimas del dolor y de la violencia terrorista,* edited by Pilar Rodríguez, Biblioteca Nueva, 2015, pp. 79–100.

Ahmed, Sara. "Collective Feelings or, The Impressions Left by Others." *Theory, Culture & Society,* vol. 21, no. 2, 2004, pp. 25–42.

Albin, Danilo. "Lasa y Zabala fueron torturados en la residencia oficial del Gobernador Civil." *Público,* 6 Apr. 2018.

————. "Terrorismo en el País Vasco: Más del 60% de los crímenes de la guerra sucia contra ETA siguen impunes." *Público,* 17 Mar. 2018.

Aranzadi, Juan. *El escudo de Arquíloco. Sobre mesías, mártires y terroristas.* Machado Libros, 2002.

Arendt, Hannah. *The Human Condition.* 1958. University of Chicago Press, 1989.

Atwood, Margaret. *Negotiating with the Dead.* Cambridge University Press, 2002.

Atxaga, Bernardo. *El hombre solo.* Translated by Arantza Sabán and Bernardo Atxaga, Ediciones B, 1995.

————. *The Lone Man.* Translated by Margaret Jull Costa, Harvill Press, 1996.

Baudrillard, Jean. *The Transparency of Evil: Essays on Extreme Phenomena.* Translated by James Benedict, Verso, 1993.

Berger, John. *Hold Everything Dear: Dispatches on Survival and Resistance.* Pantheon, 2007.

Brault, Pascale, and Michael Naas, editors. "To Reckon with the Dead: Jacques Derrida's Politics of Mourning." Introduction. *The Work of Mourning,* by Jacques Derrida, University of Chicago Press, 2001, pp. 1–30.

Brennan, Teresa. *The Transmission of Affect.* Cornell University Press, 2004.

Butler, Judith. *Precarious Life: The Powers of Mourning and Violence.* Verso, 2004.

Camps, Victoria. *Elogio de la duda.* Arpa y Alfil Editores, 2016.

Carrasco Asenguinolaza, Luis María. "'Aquella mañana me disponía a pedir perdón por un crimen imperdonable.' Mi experiencia personal como ex miembro de ETA ante los encuentros restaurativos." *Los ojos del otro. Encuentros restaurativos entre víctimas y ex miembros de ETA,* coordinated by Esther Pascual Rodríguez, Sal Terrae, 2013, pp. 277–80.

Centro Memorial de las Víctimas del Terrorismo. *Informe del Centro Memorial de las Víctimas del Terrorismo: La sociedad vasca ante la memoria de las víctimas y el final del terrorismo.* July 2017.

Derrida, Jacques. *The Politics of Friendship*. Translated by George Collins, Verso, 1997.

_____. *The Work of Mourning*, edited by Pascale-Anne Brault and Michael Naas, The University of Chicago Press, 2001.

"El final de ETA: La historia de 14 encuentros restaurativos." *El País*, 24 Oct. 2013.

Elzo, Javier. *Tras la losa de ETA: Por una sociedad vasca justa y reconciliada*. PPC, 2014.

Euskobarómetro. Oct. 2017.

Gabilondo, Iñaki. Prologue. "Con ilusión, pero sin hacerse ilusiones." *Tras la losa de ETA: Por una sociedad vasca justa y reconciliada*, by Javier Elzo, PPC, 2014, pp. 5–9.

Hellman, Lillian. *Scoundrel Time*. Little, Brown, 1976.

Jankélévitch, Vladimir. *Forgiveness*. Translated by Andrew Kelley, The University of Chicago Press, 2005

Jáuregui, Gurutz. *Entre la tragedia y la esperanza. Vasconia ante el nuevo milenio*. Ariel, 1997.

Kristeva, Julia. "Forgiveness: An Interview." *PMLA*, vol. 117, no. 2, 2001, pp. 278–95.

Lasa, Maixabel. *EITB Hoy*. Interview. Aired 10 Feb. 2014.

_____. "Prologue." *Los ojos del otro. Encuentros restaurativos entre víctimas y ex miembros de ETA*, coordinated by Esther Pascual Rodríguez, Sal Terrae, 2013, pp. 13–14.

Levinas, Emmanuel. *Totality and Infinity: An Essay on Exteriority*. Translated by Alphonso Lingis, Dusquene University Press, 1969.

Madina, Eduardo. "Memoria y convivencia en Euskadi." *El País*, 10 Mar. 2018.

Malo, Pablo, director. *Lasa eta Zabala*, produced by Joxe Portela, Alberto Gerrikabeitia, and Joan Antoni González, ETB, 2014. Film.

Martín, Annabel. "La gramática de la duda: Opacidad y transparencia terrorista en *El hombre solo*, de Bernardo Atxaga." *El mundo está en todas partes. La creación literaria de Bernardo Atxaga*, edited by Iker González-Allende and José Ángel Ascunce Arrieta, Anthropos, 2018, pp. 109–26.

Mate, Reyes. *A contraluz: De las ideas políticamente correctas*. Anthropos, 2005.

Pascual Rodríguez, Esther. "La preparación del encuentro entre las personas que han sufrido la violencia de ETA y quienes la causaron." *Los ojos del otro. Encuentros restaurativos entre víctimas y ex miembros de ETA*, coordinated by Esther Pascual Rodríguez, Sal Terrae, 2013, pp. 111–41.

Rekarte, Iñaki. Interviewed by Jordi Évole. *Salvados*. Aired 12 May 2015.

_____. *Lo difícil es perdonarse a uno mismo*. Península, 2015.

Rich, Adrienne. *Arts of the Possible: Essays and Conversations*. W. W. Norton, 2001.

Sedgwick, Eve Kosofsky. *Between Men: English Literature and Male Homosocial Desire*. Columbia University Press, 1985.

Terradillos, Ana. *Vivir después de matar: Los terroristas de ETA que dejaron las armas cuentan por primera vez su historia*. La Esfera de los Libros, 2016.

Woodworth, Paddy. *Dirty War, Clean Hands: ETA, the Gal, and Spanish Democracy*. Cork University Press, 2001.

Part II: Flesh

◆　　CHAPTER 6

Capturing Death

Photography, Performance, and Bearing Witness

Patty Keller

For Julian. In memory of Ross.

The Photograph's Demand: "As Close to Death as Possible"

What is photography if not the capturing of death? And how do we understand—and grasp—the exigency that comes with every photograph? Its powerful but fragile demand? Hervé Guibert, throughout his work, likens the photograph to an experience "as close to death as possible" ("au plus près de la mort").[1] In the two texts that bracket the last ten years of Guibert's life—*L'image fantôme* (*Ghost Image*, 1981) and *La pudeur ou l'impudeur* (*Modesty and Shame*, 1990–1991)—the link between photography and death is inextricable, poetic, and elaborate. Indeed, the two texts bridge two angles (two views) on a certain desire to touch death—the first, motivated by the persistent fantasy of coming into close proximity with death, a fantasy that emanates from a deep fascination with looking at photographic images; the second, rooted in the reality of confronting one's own death and the necessity to bear witness to that reality by representing—specifically, by *capturing*—photographically the life of the artist/author (Guibert himself) in the daily process of dying. Whereas the earlier 1981 written essays imagine various encounters with death, the later 1990–1991 video essay functions as a survival strategy that hinges on the death of the author, but also, importantly,

on the author's ability to "face death." [2] As such, the text presents itself as neither "memoir" nor "thanatographical writing" but instead "establishes itself as a
form of *life writing*" (Meyers 79). That is, a form of "living on in order to write"
(death) and a form of "writing *toward* the dying body" that literalizes a "way of
'writing to the end'" (Chambers 117; Orban qtd. in Meyers, 78–79). This "writing
to the end"—both an address *to* the author's mortality and a temporal frame *of*
that address's duration, demarcated *by* mortality—constitutes the condition of
survival, and thus also conditions life. Here, the condition is doubled and refers
to both the life of the artist whose death has been recorded visually *and* the life of
the reader whose encounter with the text, and thus whose experience of reading
(or viewing) the author's death permits his/her "successful recruitment," in the
words of Ross Chambers, "as an appropriate agent of the continued witness" that
the author's "own interrupted testimonial demands" (32).

   "Living on in order to write"; writing (and writing one's death) as a condition
of survival (Chambers 117). But Chambers reminds us that "survival . . . whether
in the form of living to tell the tale or of dying to tell it, is synonymous with *deferral*, and that acts of witness are necessarily acts of deferred (not 'immediate' or
'direct') communication" (117). Witnessing is central to my readings here, and
arguably central to what constitutes photography and what we might call the
"photographic act." This is not so much about what photographs *are* (although
that interests me too since they are ubiquitous material objects originating from
and circulating in the world, touching it, and us, endlessly). Rather, I take the
connection with witnessing as a way into thinking about what photographs *do*,
which is to say how they operate, perform, act, and call us to act too. Of particular interest here is thinking about the ways that photographs not only help us
to see, by giving us things to "look at," but—and here much more demanding a
task—how they challenge our thinking by blinding us from seeing what is *already*
there, what might, in fact, be standing right in front of us but that nevertheless
escapes our sight. Allow me to table briefly the importance of bearing witness
to something unbearable, atrocious, unspeakable, or untranslatable, in order to
take up another key term introduced by Chambers (and one that runs throughout Guibert's work, beginning with *Ghost Image*): deferral.

   Like witnessing, the concept of deferral is indeed crucial—a key component for
understanding how the photograph acts, enacts, and re-enacts the moment, both
belatedly and repeatedly. Etymologically, "deferral" means to "bring (or carry)
apart," from the Latin *dis* (apart) and *ferre* (to bring, to carry). For reasons that,
I hope, will become clear later on, I am partial to thinking of deferral in terms
of a "carrying apart" or "carrying at a certain distance," or better still, a "carrying separated by a [specified] distance." Deferral, distance, carrying. But how do

these concepts connect to the material substance of photography, the actuality of images that make their way into the world after being captured? How might delay, separation, and bearing witness relate to this sense of capture—being seized, then held and fixed, framed and printed, duplicated and sent back out into the world?

Lurking in the background of the intimate, melancholic ruminations that comprise *Ghost Image* are the voices of photography theory's most cherished if usual suspects—Bazin, Benjamin, Barthes, to name but a few. Though Guibert, having died from AIDS in 1991, could not have read Jacques Derrida's 1996 essay on photography, *Demeure, Athènes* (*Athens, Still Remains*), one cannot help but wonder if Derrida was perhaps the influenced reader of Guibert, especially when he writes, at the beginning of *Athens*, "we owe ourselves to death" ("nous nous devons à la mort") (4). Although throughout the essay's twenty "stills" (textual vignettes), Derrida, unsurprisingly, offers many interpretations of this phrase ("this oracular thing," as he calls it [4]), the immediate context, at the outset, is a discussion about the time of desire as the time of delay in the photographic act (4, 1, 13–15). About halfway through the text, Derrida offers a more compact, detailed, and poetic (though no less enigmatic) reading of "nous nous devons à la mort," suggesting that embedded within the phrase is a twin-logic of deferral and indebtedness that can also be found in the medium of photography. He writes: "An acknowledgment of a debt or an IOU with regard to death is signed by everything that *reflects* in the photographic act as well as in the structure of the photogram" (47).

Before this "signature" of debt/death, which is reflected in the act and object of photography, in the opening paragraphs of *Athens*, Derrida describes the photograph as a "funerary inscription." He writes: "for the entire series of photographs collected in this book . . . each of them remains in its turn what it becomes: a funerary inscription with a proper name. Having to keep what it loses, namely the *departed*, does not every photograph act in effect *through* the bereaved experience of such a proper name, through the irresistible singularity of its referent, its here-now, its date?" (2–3).

Photographs—presumably *all* photographs—will "remain" what they "become." Future; future conditional. And this becoming is inscription itself—a form of writing ("light writing" is the etymology of photography) that names, gives a *proper* name, and is linked to loss, departure, and debt, but also to a deferral. The debt, according to Derrida, comes from death, is *tied to* death, and in many ways *is* death itself. The deferral is the delay that comes with exposure, the time lag connected to appearance, and the action (the *becoming*, then the *remaining*, the language of which is laced with a certain degree of latency) that occurs through the experience of mourning.

Figure 6.1. "Autoportrait au papillon, 1986," Hervé Guibert, self-portrait, courtesy christine guibert © hervé guibert

Consider the following, fuller passage from the first photograph ("Still I") of *Athens*, worth quoting here at length:

> This acknowledgment of debt, this IOU, was like a thing, a simple thing lost in the world, but a thing already owed, already due, and I had to keep it without taking it. To hold on to it as if holding it in trust, as if on consignment, consigned to a photoengraved safekeeping. What does this obligation, this first indebting, have to do with the verb of this declaration that can never be appropriated, "we *owe* [*devons*] ourselves to death?" What does the obligation have to do with what the declaration seemed to mean? Not "we owe ourselves to the death," not "we owe ourselves death," but "we owe ourselves *to* death." / But just who is death? (Where is it—or she—to be found? One says, curiously, in French, *trouver la mort*, to "find death," "to meet with death"—and that means to die.) (5)

When we link Derrida back to Guibert, then, "one meets death," before dying, *in* the photograph. One stands *before* death, in both a spatial and temporal relation of proximity. And this encounter with death occurs in the space-time—however confined, however expansive, however fleeting or enduring—of the photographic image itself. That mirror that isn't *really* a mirror. A fact articulated throughout Guibert's photographic works, not least of which is echoed in the numerous self-portraits he made that play with mirrors, window panes, and door frames that texture and illuminate his own image as reflective, refractive, and almost always obscured by shadow. (Fig. 6.1) The passage from *Athens* elaborates what is meant by "debt"—the IOU, the obligation—but equally striking is the language of capture that Derrida employs, a language that, here, intermingles with desire, rapture, and loss. "I had to keep it without taking it," he writes. To keep without "taking," to hold without "having," without possession. "To hold on to it *as if* holding it in trust" (5; my emphasis). The verbs—all related to the logic of capture—are noteworthy. Capture denotes the action of holding and containing (from the Latin noun *captura*, and verb *capere*, meaning "seized" or "taken") and thus implies seizure, ownership, and possession. "Keeping," "taking," "holding." These are terms that activate the image of death, but they also bring us into photography's vernacular. Following this triad, Derrida introduces another: "in trust," "on consignment," "safekeeping." Just as the author is indebted to the image, the photographic image is indebted to safekeeping death, to holding *it* still.

Later on, Derrida will invoke a similar contradiction underlying his desire. "My original impulse, of inscribing it in stone," he writes, "right there, right away, the idea of fixing it or focusing on it precisely like an idea, *eidos* or *idea*, a form, a figure, in this element of eternity" (7). Interestingly, the desire for inscription is coupled with the "idea of fixing it or focusing on it precisely"—two actions that bring to mind photographic processes. "Fixing" the image on paper through chemical solution, in traditional darkroom processing of gelatin silver prints, for example, this is commonly known as "fixer," an elixir or "bath" of thiosulfate salts that stabilize the image, allowing it to be "held" in place. "Focus," of course, indicates bringing the image into sharper view, or balancing a certain perspective in the image with different degrees of sharpness. British photographer Paul Graham likens the focal component of photography to consciousness—whereas aperture refers to light and shutter speed to time, focus refers to sight, but also significantly to perception and insight, knowledge, and vision.

The idea of taking, fixing, focusing, and holding (the holding *on* and *in*) that occurs in and through the photograph—the very idea underlying the logic of capture, as I have been suggesting up until now—resonates with the previously (but only briefly) mentioned idea of witnessing, and of bearing witness. We would do well to think about what this connection means—how it shifts and unsettles—when dealing not with just any photographs, but specifically with photographs of death. Photographs which themselves might be classified as unsettled, unsettling, or obscene because they frame loss in an explicit, even confrontational way—perhaps graphic, gruesome, grotesque, and therefore deemed "unfit" for viewing.[3]

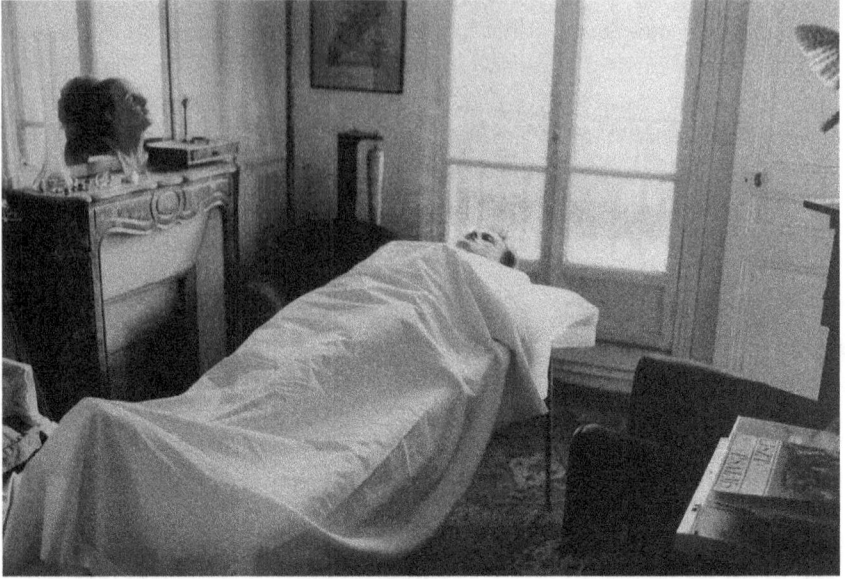

Figure 6.2. "Autoportrait, rue du Moulin-vert, 1986," Hervé Guibert, self-portrait, courtesy christine guibert © hervé guibert

That is, because they "show" death or because, rather than "showing," they overtly anticipate it. There are, no doubt, countless photographs that might fall under this category, but I am thinking particularly of photographic images that display, with varying degrees of intensity, diseased or ailing bodies, wounds, punctures, bruises, scars, sites of infection and illness, or, in some cases, photographs not of the dying but of death itself, such as in the case of port-mortem portraits, images of corpses.[4] (Fig. 6.2) Between capturing the process of dying and "focusing on" and "fixing" the moment of death, we might situate that difficult-to-categorize class of photographs that represent people with HIV/AIDS (PWAs). Often, these are images that bring to the surface, in a palpable way, the frailty of the human body, its proximity to death, its becoming remains.

Photography's Touch: Material Objects, Dead Facts, like
All Metals of Alchemy—Alive!

In a famous passage from *Camera lucida*, Roland Barthes writes "what matters to me is not the photograph's 'life' . . . but the certainty that the photographed body touches me with its own rays and not with a superadded light" (80).[5] Integral to

Barthes's analysis of photography as a process of mourning and a form of bearing witness is that the image operates as a kind of "evidentiary force," one that fills the viewer's sight.[6] But equally essential to his understanding of photography is its haptic quality—the fact that it touches us, our bodies, our sight: "From a real body, which was there, proceed radiations which ultimately touch me, who am here" (80). This is precisely why Barthes feels his mother's touch from looking at the (now legendary though never visually reproduced) "Winter Garden Photograph," which he describes in the following way: "however pale, is . . . the treasury of rays which emanated from my mother as a child, from her hair, her skin, her dress, her gaze" (82). The mother, the loss of whom Barthes so desperately mourns throughout *Camera lucida*, is "the loved body" that becomes "immortalized . . . [and] like all metals of Alchemy, is alive" (81).

The "thing of the past" is made known to Barthes, the distant future observer, through a kind of luminance—"the immediate radiances . . . really touched the surface which in turn my [Barthes's] gaze will touch" (81). These "delayed rays of a star" extend from the past, through "a sort of umbilical cord" to touch two surfaces—on the one hand, the surface of the photograph itself, which preserves the thing photographed as a kind of skin, a "light" transfixed in "a carnal medium"; on the other hand, the surface of the son's gaze, recipient of this body-light/light-writing (81). Light becomes the marker (and thus the wound) but importantly also the measure, the *index* of this connection—the cord between the past and the future.

The indexical is key for Barthes not only because it gives proof of a once-was (the well-known "*there-has-been*" in his writing), but because in pointing and saying "here," it "scatters well," it radiates, reaching across time to touch a viewer far removed in time and space from the object captured. And in this way, the image (but also the body—the thing captured *in* the photograph—the mother) remains what it becomes: immortalized and thus alive. In other words, it *survives*. And its survival (its afterlife) happens by passing it on, as if in a kind of relay. Recalling Derrida's desire, when gazing at Bonhomme's photographs of Athens, it is *kept* without having been *taken*.

I would like to pause for a moment on this notion of life—indeed, this *extension* of life that persists through the umbilical cord linking, but also *nourishing*, the light (the radiance) between two separate surfaces. For Barthes, there is an "aliveness" to photographs, a trait that notably recurs throughout his writings, and one that distinguishes him from his contemporaries. For example, Allan Sekula's idea that the photograph is a kind of dead letter and that photographs thus constitute "repositories of dead facts" (56). Or one might conjure up any number of associations from earlier theorists especially (though not exclusively) with regards to the photographic image as "stuck," "frozen," "fixed," "dead," or "embalmed." The idea that photographs are imbued with an "aliveness"—that they might, in fact, *be* living things, and therefore have *life* (or *lives*)—is a particularly attractive idea for our purposes because it gets us back to questions of survival and witnessing. But the double-implication (to say nothing of the potential problems) of equating photographs with "life forms," is that they are tangible, but also perishable. Survival, in this regard, is not linked to the object—the photograph—but to the viewer, the one who chooses to look, the one who makes a decision not to look away.

"Aliveness" also calls to mind Kate Steinman's insistence that "the photograph is mutable" or Derrida's idea that "the photograph is untranslatable"—that is, that the image remains what it becomes, but is always at the same time becoming something different, something else, something *other*. (There is a queerness at play here.) Perhaps most fundamentally, at the heart of such "aliveness" is the materiality of photography. Paul Christopher Johnson, echoing Barthes, articulates this best when he writes:

> Photographs are visual artifacts but also, at least prior to digital photography, material objects endowed with all the qualities of things: *edges, shape, texture, solidity, and varying durability over time.* . . . As both an image and a thing, a photograph at once mediates something occurring elsewhere and else-when—a scene or person in a place and time different from the one in which the photograph is being viewed—and in the here-and-now, as an object that *attracts my gaze, has weight in my hand, occupies space in a file*, or *pulls downward on the nail that secures it to the wall.* The hybrid nature *of being at once an image and a thing* is important because it means that photographs have *plural lives across multiple dimensions.* (25; my emphasis)

Plurality, as a condition of the photograph's "hybrid nature," means that images once "taken" and "captured" do not only connect objects and observers across time, but themselves occupy various positions at different points in time, in "multiple dimensions"—they are both objects viewed and viewing objects. What I find particularly useful—and particularly striking—about Johnson's description is how he so beautifully moves from the material qualities of photographs (all the physical attributes that make them "artifacts") to their temporal and ontological qualities as forms of active mediation. And this mediation (this *action*, in fact) has a number of key elements: it has the ability to reach across time and "attract" the gaze, but it also has *weight*, takes up space, and pulls downward on something that we normally consider "secure."

Several theorists in recent years have taken up the idea that photographs "act," that they are "active," "reciprocal," or "participatory," and that the medium constitutes an activity and thus functions as a *form of action*. In *What Photography Is*, art critic James Elkins defines photography as action over substance. For Elkins, "photography is essentially not about art, society, or representation," but rather is an "emblem" of the "essentially solitary" act of seeing (viii). This solitary act does not negate (indeed, to the contrary, it finds common ground with) a form of seeing that is *in solidarity*. That is, in alliance with death. Such complicity with death also demands a commitment to testimony—to touching the past with our gaze—and, by extension, a commitment to bearing witness. In the case of photography and other visual media that represents the HIV/AIDS epidemic, which I will turn to in the next section, this kind of commitment stands as a form witnessing (here, with Nan Goldin's words in mind) against our inevitable vanishing.[7]

What Photography Is is a curious book of critique and creativity. The work involves "writing into and through Barthes's book [*Camera Lucida*], . . . inhabiting the book" (xi). Elkins, reacting against Barthes, links photography to death in the following extraordinary passage:

> Photography is not only about light and loss and the passing of time. It is about something harder. I agree with Barthes that at one of its own limits, ordinary photography of people has something to do with the viewer's unfocused ideas about her own death. *But I also think that photography has given us a more continuous, duller, less personal kind of pain.* Again and again photographs have compelled people to see the world as they had not needed or wanted to see it. *Photographs have forced something on us: not only a blurred glimpse of our own deaths, a sense of memory as photographic grain, a dim look at the passage of time, or a poignant prick of mortality, but something about the world's own deadness, its inert resistance to whatever it is we may hope or want. Photography fills our eyes with all the dead and deadening stuff of the world, material we don't want to see or to name.* I am after a certain lack of feeling, a coldness I miss in Barthes. (xi–xii; my emphasis)

Photographs are objects that we hold usually in our hands, but with our eyes too—with the gaze, that powerful, enigmatic, inescapable, and at times, intractable thing. That "thing" that brings us "as close to death as possible," to the surface, to the "dead and deadening stuff of the world," as Elkins puts it. But this process—*this relation*—is a reciprocal one. For, photographs hold us too. In—and out—of balance. Indeed, in the midst of Elkins's poignant critique of Barthes, I believe *this*—this undesired reciprocity where we see death beyond our will—is what he means when he writes "[b]ut for me the famous punctum is just a pinprick. I think the wound is much larger" (xii).

In the following sections, my aim will be to show how photography, in relation to performance and video art, can and does work in "alliance with death"—as close to it as possible—and that this alliance indeed involves a certain degree of mutability and transference, of reaching and touching, of extension and tact. Moving across various art works, my hope is to show how the work of PWAs operates in complicity, which is to say, in proximity and solidarity, with death. How proximity and solidarity lead us inevitably back to witnessing, itself a form of counter-denial, resistance against oblivion, and an experience that occurs through closeness to but also survival after having come into contact with death. In this regard, bearing witness is about shifting and shaping and unsettling too. It is precisely *not* about allowing the object witnessed to remain what it becomes but, on the contrary, allowing that object (the thing "close to death") to both endure in *and* move through time, to fill the present.

Ultimately, at stake is the unsettledness of witnessing—the uneasy weight that comes with bearing witness, that comes from letting something *survive* in its death. To leave it without losing it (after Derrida). How is such survival related to but also perhaps conditioned by the inscription of a debt? I am interested in thinking about how such a debt relates to viewer responsibility—specifically, in the context of the materiality of the photographic image, its "objectness," what is held by its frame. Some of the aforementioned terms will continue to circulate and permeate my readings of Pepe Espaliú's and Javier Codesal's work, which draws on photography but is also located in other corners of visuality, namely, performance and video: deferral, endurance, duration, relay, reach, touch, the palpable, desire, debt, and inscription. Inscription could be likened to the practice of owning, of calling something one's own and thus of claiming it. But inscription can also act as a form of naming oneself *as* other, as a form of othering and otherness. This otherness is crucial for opening up a space where one (in concert with others) might bear witness to an experience—with a person, situation, or object—as close to death as possible.

Bearing It: The Photograph as Temporal Monument

Photographs capture death, they make demands, they reach across time, they touch us. In the previous sections, I made the case for photography's vitality—its "life" force—and a certain quality of "aliveness" that emanates from within the photographic image, allowing it to multiply, taking up occupancy in many places and bodies at once. In this section, I connect the idea of "photography's touch"—its tactility, the fact that we can hold photographs in our hands (most of the time, anyhow), and the ways in which photographs touch our bodies, our gaze—to two central concepts: care and carrying. This is a way of thinking about tact as a strategy for maneuvering in the world, as a way of seeing, gaining sight and insight into what Elkins calls the "dead stuff of the world."

On September 26th, 1992, Spanish sculptor and AIDS activist Pepe Espaliú's "Carrying" project was organized and performed in San Sebastián and then performed again, a few months later, in Madrid. The Madrid "action" coincided with a piece Espaliú wrote titled "Retrato del artista desahuciado," which was published in *El País* on December 1, the same day as the "Carrying" action took place in the capital and also the day recognized internationally as "World AIDS Day." A literal translation of the *El País* article would be "Portrait of the artist declared incurable" (or "Portrait of the terminally ill artist"). An equally literal version might read something like "Portrait of the artist evicted." Eviction, in English as in Spanish, has the connotation of being "homeless," a point echoed in Pepe Espaliú's comments on the carrying project: "los enfermos estamos en una paradoja, seguir en el mundo sin tocar el mundo, seguir caminando sin tocar la tierra" (as sick individuals [PWAs] we're caught in a paradox, we're in the world but cannot touch the world, we're supposed to keep walking without touching the ground).[8] But "desahuciado" has the additional meaning, in connection with the "Carrying" project, of "being out on the streets," which is typically expressed colloquially, through the phrase "echar a la calle" ("to be thrown out on the streets"). Espaliú answers this condition of "thrownness" (a condition based on positive diagnosis, and thus having to live with AIDS) with a response of collective action based on the principles of care and solidarity—that is, by carrying *with* and being carried *by* others. Indeed, the idea of solidarity is fundamental to Espaliú's work, and most specifically to his "Carrying" project, the heart of which was the traversing of public urban space in a collaborative effort to weave together a network of people who would both receive and transport his body. This display of solidarity relates in some intriguing ways to the plurality of the photographic image, an idea to which I will return after a brief description of the work itself.

"Carrying" was, we could say, an extension of the sculptural work and drawings that Espaliú was most known for—a body of work primarily anchored in metaphors for illness, disease, containment, and concealment. Images of cages, crutches, nests, and death masks were repeated throughout Espaliú's corpus in striking and tender ways, oftentimes dealing with the concept of negation through forms of domesticated enclosure, or conversely, the rupture of enclosed spaces.[9] "Carrying" was an action, a performance, and a video testimonial—a kind of AIDS diary—but it was also what we might call a "living sculpture" involving

Figure 6.3. "The Carrying Society, 1991," Pepe Espaliú, still from *Carrying*, Diputación Foral de Gipuzkoa

an intimate but public display of collective confrontation with AIDS, and the burden of carrying the weight of the disease together, trafficking it, so to speak, through the city's streets. As choreographed action, and coordinated display of activism, it embraced love as the other side of rage. But it also fully embraced the other side of fear with its insistence on *tact* and *contact*.

At the heart of the project is a confrontation with both the materiality of the diseased body and the circulation of the body's decay. For approximately one kilometer, the artist, barefoot, would be passed from one pair of "carriers" to another. With arms interlaced, each pair would bridge themselves to form a *palanquín*, a chair or covered seat traditionally used to carry royalty, which is also, and perhaps not coincidentally, related to the Spanish word *palanca*, meaning originally "a pole to carry a burden"—a metaphor that Espaliú felt especially drawn to because of its ability to figure as both container and transporter, and to bring into equivalence the idea of the sovereign body with the sick one. Barefoot, in a seated embrace, and passed from one human *palanquín* to the next, his feet never touching the ground, the artist was then carried along a determined route through the city—a kind of living funerary inscription, collectively written. (Fig. 6.3)

Figure 6.4. "Carrying, 1991," Pepe Espaliú, Pepe Espaliú, still from *Carrying*, image courtesy of pepe cobo y cía

There are many other ways we could classify "Carrying." Indeed, the genre is difficult to nail down—being situated between sculpture and activism, between ephemeral installation, roving monument, and protest, between radical cartography and personal testimony. It is also a performance that hinges on affirming life while anticipating death, wherein the body of the artist as contagion becomes a kind of tomb, marked but unsealed, that announces the collective debt we owe to death, and thus the shared burden that befalls us all. In a time when Silence = Death, like so many incredible works that take up the difficult task of representing the HIV/AIDS epidemic, "Carrying" chose visibility and thus chose life, even and *especially* as the artist confronted his own death. The project, in this way, *touched* death. *Televised* death. *Carried* death. But all for the purpose of *witnessing*, for the purpose of allowing something otherwise invisible to be seen, and thus to *survive* despite its vanishing.

With extraordinary power in its ephemerality, the "living sculpture" of "Carrying" carved out a visible path of love and resistance, sewing those affects into the urban fabric of two major Spanish cities, if only fleetingly. The point was to *be there*, to come into contact with AIDS: the comingling of bodies in a unique support system that testified not only to the presence but also crucially to the passage and transmission of the disease among us. Interestingly, the operative logic of the piece hinged on disappearance—"Carrying," with all its emphasis on creating a public zone of contact to bring the epidemic into plain view, obviously worked against disappearance, silence, shame, and invisibility. It did this not as an agent of epidemiological change or cure, but as a symbolic chain of gestures that brought the problem of confrontation into the fold of the social and intertwined it with awareness and knowledge through haptic experience. But the work also deeply depended on the *endurance* of such a zone in the social and cultural imaginary once the performance had ended, which for as profound as it was at the time, was still, all things considered, relatively brief. The after-effects of the project's impact (whether affective shock-waves, residual emotions, or the persistent after-image of a bethroned but frail and dying Pepe Espaliú—for the artist would soon die thereafter) are, in part, undeniably linked to its brevity.

Privileging the body in its very contingency and transience without monumentalizing it is one remarkable way that "Carrying" attends to the materiality of the body and shifts its locus of power, meaning, and agency to the very site of its impermanence. Here, the body is literalized as an object whose movement depends on a set of spatial practices that are themselves temporary, leaving no trace, save the images documenting the event. The body becomes a temporary site of connection and contact, but it also takes on the form of a static object, the movement of which between carriers depended on the latter's constant ambulation. This chain of signification, in turn, re-frames the project's action *as* a temporal monument, where neither being nor meaning are fixed in any one place or time. (Fig. 6.4) Instead, the visual and material economy of the work (the *palanquins*, the body's temporary im/mobility, the bare feet) poignantly evokes an itinerant grave where the artist's visibility as becoming-corpse is presented by and mediated through the peripatetic action of others.

Nicholas Muellner, commenting on the inherent strangeness of traditional monuments, writes

> the monument is never itself. . . . [T]he monument can assert its physical self only when it fails to transmit its idea. . . . The monument is inextricably caught between its meaning and its being—the one defying the other. . . . Its value as an idea-receptacle is not, ultimately, based on any conceptual or linguistic communiqué, but on its fundamentally blunt materializing assertion: the battle was here, the poet lived here, the victims were shot here. (iv)

For Muellner, the insistence that "meaning adheres in fixed physical spaces and determinate objects" is precisely what lends monuments their uncanny quality. There is a certain degree of discomfort, in his reading, with the idea that meaning would be "fixed" in place, rendered immobile, static. But there is also a reaction against the idea of the monument as "an attempt to place meaning . . . back in the earth of its inception: to insert the idea back into the physical." Muellner continues:

> As if the event and what it has come to mean cannot be ripped free from the patch of ground, like the chemical-laden sheet that is torn off a Polaroid print when the thirty seconds of development are up. . . . The problem is, the meaning never lived there. And thus, the monument, for all its granite or basalt or bronze, is never itself. In this, the monument is like a photograph. (iv)

The link from monuments to photographs here is both curious and compelling. According to Muellner's analysis, both objects (or structures, if we keep Derrida and Barthes in mind) are capable of lodging—or "fixing"—meaning to a physical location or thing, but this production of meaning is, in reality, a projection, since "meaning never lived there," in the patch of ground or Polaroid print. Actions, gestures, and performances, by virtue of their ephemerality, sidestep the predicament of "fixedness" precisely by dislodging meaning from any synchronic conception of place and time.

But what happens when we consider Espaliú's project from the vantage point of film and photography? The videos of "Carrying" are as moving as they are haunting, to be sure. This is perhaps, in part, due to the fact not that Espaliú has already died when we view the footage today, but that the video replays for us the perpetual fact that he is going to die, imminently. In capturing the time before his death—a time when illness was already becoming visible for the artist, through the typical external symptoms associated with AIDS such as extreme thinness, skeletal facial structure, and accelerated aging—and then projecting that time into the present moment of viewing, we are confronted with what Barthes calls the "horror [of] an anterior future of which death is the stake" (96). In the same passage, he will link this horror to the fact that in every photograph there exists a "defeat of Time . . .: *that* is dead and *that* is going to die" (96). Such a time-out-of-joint is marked by a double temporality. It is, at once, our understanding that death has arrived for the subject of the image and our realization that, in the moment of the subject's capture, death has not yet arrived, or in Barthes's idiom "the photograph tells me of death in the future" but what *pricks* "is the discovery of this equivalence," "*a catastrophe which has already occurred*" (96). This dual temporality underlying film and photography, and overtly detectable in the "Carrying" footage, similarly surfaces in other works whose aim is to give visibility to AIDS through the capture, relay, and replay of fragments of daily life for those living with the disease. On this point, we might recall Guibert's aforementioned video diary *La pudeur ou l'impudeur* or Nicholas and Bebe Nixon's collection of photo essays *People with AIDS*, both from 1991. In all of these works, there is a poignant anticipation of death that fuses with the stark reality that death has, in fact, already knocked at the door for these individuals.

If the material substance of photographs constitutes what I have called a temporal monument, then we would do well to think of the function of these images not as documents or memorials, but *as momentary inscriptions*, living *impressions*, the traces of which continue to *carry* on the force of facing death, and thus continue to touch us, as contemporary viewers of these images, through the relay effect that I mentioned earlier. As photographs, the images work against disappearance insofar as they are objects that capture death, coming "as close to death as possible," and in doing so they bring us, viewers and survivors, into relation with death's unknowability, not to master but rather to recognize it as a part of our lives despite its fundamental foreign-ness. These images seem to have the unique ability to synthesize two seemingly antithetical facts: that death is inherent to our being in the world, and that the reality of its appearance is always "other" than, and thus removed from, distant, or outside of ourselves. That the photographs and video footage of "Carrying" technologically perform the reproduction of death (a reproduction intimately linked to the constitutive impermanence underlining all beings and things—a being-toward-death) is vital to understanding the material and affective power that these images have in the present. As objects that continually displace, relocate, and reconfigure meaning, they also instigate our contact with death through the gaze. They bear witness not only to the significance of the "once-was"—the event, a day in the life of the artist—but also to the potential for reinvention of meaning each time we look at these images, each time we choose not to look away.

DÍAS de SIDA, Exposing Time and the Wound

Images, according to Hans Belting, "once served as vessels of embodiment, replacing the lost bodies of the dead" (84). But what happens exactly when the body—the dying or diseased body, the body marked by death, or the corpse—becomes an image? What takes place when the body undergoes this kind of ontological transfer? The answer is at once simple and not easy: the image gains a new kind of authority. In the cases of Hervé Guibert's self-portraits and footage from Pepe Espaliú's ensemble performance, such authority endows the image with both a debt and a duty—to present death through images that capture the dying body, and to represent through practices of inscription the body's death as immanent and intractable; to make death's inevitability visible, overt, and extreme. I am speaking here of the obligation and responsibility to bear witness, and the ways in which these works, by extending the conditions of witnessing through their technologies of representation, move between foreshadowing death and embracing it as a tactic of survival.

From the carried body, inscribed in public space, transported in plain view, and reproduced through technological representation intrinsic to the medium of film and photography, we turn now to the photography and video work of Javier Codesal, whose approach to representing HIV/AIDS is notable for its emphasis on the marks, scars, and inscriptions *on* the surface of ailing bodies. Such visible traces of disease and symptoms of infection, often rendered unsuitable or inappropriate for viewing, or conversely ones exploited to the point of equating the illness with abjection and fear, become the focal point of Codesal's images, where their centrality is illuminated and aestheticized. For the purposes of this essay, I will propose a close reading that takes up this treatment of the infected body as a triptych, the trajectory of which moves from isolation, to symptomatic expression, and finally ends with the open wound. This tripartite movement articulates a new exposure *of* but also *to* the epidemic, just as reading the three images in tandem brings into view, through a kind of prismatic effect, different angles on the body—as media interface, as text and texture.

Much of Codesal's work is oriented around questions of the human body in relation to the social body, and his images often portray the body's fragility and vulnerability. Aside from the obvious connections with Espaliú—both are Spanish artists, working from the margins of a cultural context during the 1980s and 1990s where institutional support for and recognition of projects related to HIV/AIDS were largely absent—Codesal's work also emerges from within the conceptual and theoretical space of *accionismo* and public intervention to bring the themes of solidarity and temporality into dialogue with the space and circulation of artistic production. To be certain, this production served not only as response to the crisis but as a mechanism of survival for many artists themselves.[10]

In *Fábula a destiempo* (*Fable Out of Time*, 1993) Codesal frames the difficulty in representing the necessity and necessary conditions of nourishing the body, while alluding to a certain atemporality of both. *Fable Out of Time* consists of a

Figure 6.5. Javier Codesal, still from *Fábula a destiempo*, 1996. Video installation, 2-channel.

two-channel color video installation that pairs two subjects into a synchronous one. The video on the left-hand channel displays a man sitting at a table, feeding someone who is absent, because out of frame; the right-hand channel similarly features a man eating by himself. Each man appears to be isolated, sitting alone in a hospital room, but are brought into a kind of false contact, the illusion of which is broken by the frame of the television monitors which screen each subject individually. Given the positioning of each, such that they appear to share a common space (the room, the table) and common practice (breaking bread, meal time), the perspective is such that the subject in the right-hand channel stands in for the missing figure on the left, and vice versa. This is indeed a work about illness and about the common space of caring for others. But it is equally about synthesis, substitution, and a kind of solidarity that transpires through images, here moving in, out, and, as we will see, *against* time.

Of course, the coupling of the two scenes (visitor on the left, with in-patient on the right) is illusory—an illusion which, to be sure, depends on the "aliveness" of each video in creating a mutual exposure in the fictional but simulated experience of eating together that transpires through the effect of the double screen. The allusions are simple but effective. The two men sit opposite but facing one another at what appears to be one table as they share a meal and each other's company, proximity, and fate. Being separated in *real* time and space they are denied access to one another, such that the creation of solidarity, community, interconnectedness, contact, and care can only be constituted, mediated, and framed via the technological apparatus. This occurs first with the camera, then the projector, and finally the dual screens, which in their dexterity, appear to dialogue while also mimicking or mirroring one another. (Fig. 6.5)

The mirroring effect of *Fábula* created through a sense of continuity established by the alignment of screens also reinforces the temporality of each individual's isolation. This kind of false alignment further underscores the impossibility of their encounter, the fact that it can *only* occur "out of time," as the English translation might suggest, or conversely, that their coming together can only happen "at the wrong time," a point echoed in the title's inclusion of the peculiar word "destiempo," which could imply latency or an "after-the-fact-ness" to the whole scene, but seems to much more strongly connote an *undoing* of time, in which one might enter into the world of myth and "fables." Rut Martín Hernández's reading of *Fábula* suggests that actual separation of the two bodies in space and time is crucial to understanding the whole piece as "una metáfora sobre el aislamiento" (a metaphor for isolation) and an exploration of the loneliness of those who "habitan asépticos espacios sanitarios" (inhabit aseptic medical spaces), in which the healthy and the sick are segregated (*Cuerpo* 447). Of course, what the video achieves is the spatio-temporal synchronization of these bodies, placing them in union through a gesture of synthesizing a commonality or mutual bond rather than emphasizing their "real-time" estrangement.

Thus, this shared time, artificially produced through the technologies of representation specific to the medium of film, rematerializes two bodies otherwise distant and unknown to one another, and places them in the same frame, in contact. But whether "out of time," "under," or "after" it, the title in its entirety—*Fábula a destiempo*—encapsulates the bidirectional movement of the work, both forward *and* against time. This bi-directionality, the pull and push of time we might say, is duplicated in the mirror positioning of each figure in relation to the other, the simulation of their gazes, which "meet" across the space of the double frame, and in the gestures each performs: one giving food, the other taking it.

Transitioning from the body displayed as interface of communication—spliced and re-edited—to the body exhibited as symptomatic, the next work I will discuss also alludes to an indefinite sense of time through its title, which is indeterminate though not totally unambiguous: *DÍAS de SIDA*. In fact, the title alone establishes the poetics at play in the project—a certain symmetry detectable in the anagram that comprises the two key words "días" and "sida," further emphasized by the use

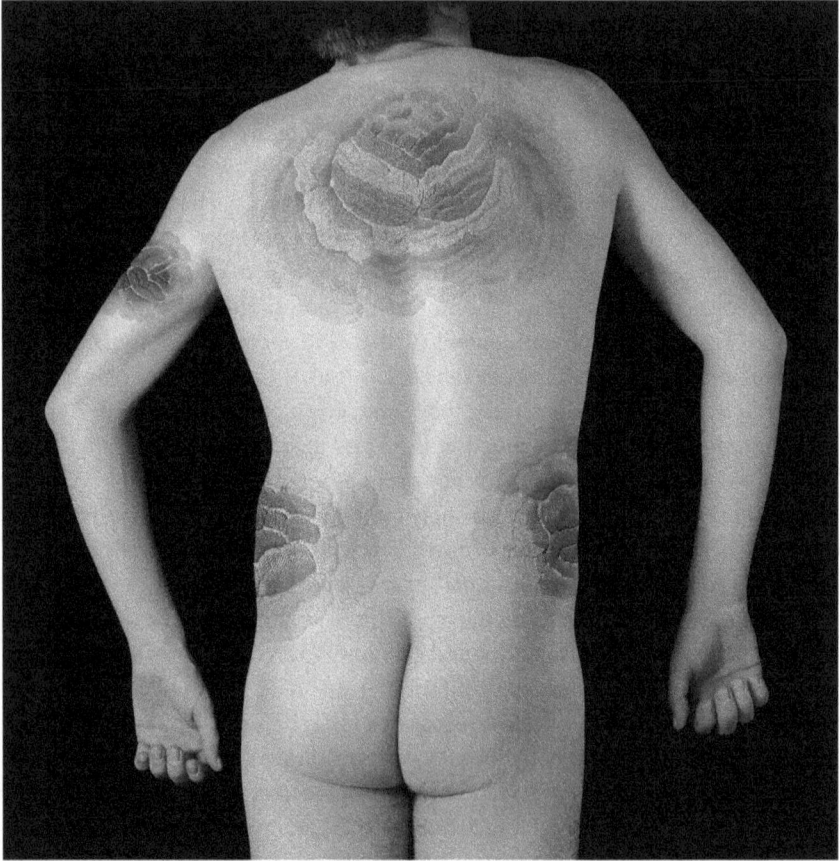

Figure 6.5. Javier Codesal, *DÍAS de SIDA*, 1989. Photograph and poster.

of uppercase lettering, and a certain allusion to the mirroring effect or inverse reflection produced when time and illness coalesce in the same space. At stake in this body of work is a driving question about the measure and, we could say, measurability, of the epidemic in—and out of—time.

DÍAS de SIDA (1989–1996) is a multi-part, mixed genre body of work consisting of various smaller works created over the course of approximately seven years, including a number of staged photographs of male bodies. Central to *DÍAS* are, once again, the themes of isolation, solidarity, anonymity, and temporality, in addition to the suspension, arrest, and plurality of the human form. Indeed, one could argue that the images in *DÍAS* are much more abstract than the portraits we see in Espaliú's and Guibert's oeuvres, a detail evidenced across the numerous photographs that Codesal makes of bodies without a face or without a head altogether. From the "quarantined" body in *Fábula*—segregated and simultaneously brought into face-to-face contact with another body (the "caretaker" who feeds and nourishes)—we now move to the scarred body featured in Figure 6.

The giant roses mark the skin in an overt allusion to Kaposi sarcoma lesions, one of the most recognizable symptoms of AIDS surfacing on the body. The conversion of the lesion, an unmistakable sign of disease, occurs through its transformation into a simulacrum of beauty; the symbol of abjection and disfigurement turned into a positive, powerful stamp of the natural world, the "bloom" that re-signifies the body, in its positive status, as alive, fertile, and productive (flowers are, after all, the reproductive organs of plants).

Overt exposure of corporeal signs of positive status, here enlarged and refashioned, are most striking perhaps in their visual analogy to wounds. But in Codesal's rewriting of the body as a map that charts the externalization of death's symptoms, this image is willfully devoid of any associations with shame and fear. Indeed, the attention to wounds stands at the forefront of another image made in relation to *DÍAS de SIDA*, from 1995, titled *Tras la piel*. Of the myriad possible translations of the title—literal and metaphoric—are once again another set of temporal allusions, which while not mutually exclusive, are also not necessarily compatible. Like the previous image, it is clear that this photograph is concerned with the skin of the body as surface of inscription and infection. *Tras*, however, is somewhat more difficult to pinpoint since it could mean "through" (as in *through the skin*), though more conventionally would be understood either temporally as "after" or relationally as "behind" the skin.

Four photographs in a grid feature a naked man, squatting in a frog-like position, with his back facing the camera. Read left to right, the first image shows only the faint trace of a mark on the man's back. In the second and third images the mark morphs into a visible gash, the skin torn along a large section of the spinal column. And in the fourth and final frame, the open wound becomes the aperture through which we see the body; it is the centerpiece of both body and image. Wounds are places where the interior and exterior coincide and clash. They are also metaphors for thinking about social and political spaces of invisibility that become exteriorized, exposed, made visible and remain open through cultural production and works of art. In *Cultura herida*, Cristina Moreiras calls these spaces "zonas de conflicto" (zones of conflict)—moments of rupture, fissure, breach—importantly *not* the scar, but the *open wound*, the site of injury in culture where the residue of the past lingers and dwells, and *demands* our attention (22). The crucial question before us, then, is how to *theorize* wounds—the mark of loss, lack, absence, and injury, but notably also the mark of *radical openness*—in relation to photography; to ask, that is, how the wound might function as a critical response to the perpetual and perpetuated invisibility of HIV/AIDS in an age largely characterized by image saturation and over-exposure.

Photography's Lament: *Courage, Bread, and Roses*

At the end of her diary, *Walking Through Clear Water in a Pool Painted Black* (1989), Cookie Mueller laments the loss of so many artists and friends to AIDS—the "extraordinary ones," she writes, "who lifted the quality of all our lives" and whose "war against ignorance, the bankruptcy of beauty, and the truancy of culture" fought the intolerance, bigotry, and "blindness that makes life hollow." These victims to the virus were the very ones, she notes, who "tried to make us see" (148–49). The final text included in Mueller's memoir is the last letter, dated 1982, from her filmmaker friend Gordon Stevenson, then quite sick, in which he writes that when he gets to the "somewhere far away" that he knows is paradise, he will be sure to send her a postcard with "a complete description of, and map for locating . . . Courage, bread, and roses" (150). The day Cookie Mueller received Gordon's letter was the day he died. And although the edges of that handwritten letter are "all frayed," she tells us, "the message is crisp" (148).

The key, it seems, is to keep the message crisp—relevant and readable. And to keep reading and looking. To return to these texts with the idea of attending to their fray while holding on to what they communicate, what lingers and remains. David Caron, in his introduction to Hervé Guibert's *Cytomegalovirus: A Hospitalization Diary*, argues that it is not simply the passage of time that causes a collective loss of interest in the HIV/AIDS epidemic—or any epidemic, for that matter—but the fact of the virus's removal from contemporary discourse, its disappearance from the public eye at the hands of larger cultural and political forces (19). "If we, as a culture, don't think about AIDS so much anymore—that is, if we don't think about it other than negatively, as a cause for rejection or psychological trauma rather than as a call to action—it is very likely that we've been induced not to by certain public discourses" (20). And so the task also involves a gesture of returning—going back to these texts, photographs, videos from another time in the not-so-distant past, in an effort not only to remember but, more important, to *activate* our lines of sight within the thresholds of the invisible so that we may participate in the shared burden and responsibility of looking at—*and seeing*—something difficult, something impossible even. In the preface to *Facing*

It, Ross Chambers writes "when it is not possible to fight disease, save lives, or escape pain, it is still important to bear witness to that impossibility" (vii). This is, after all, what the work of art, criticism, and theory can do—it gives us the tools for seeing and understanding.

My readings throughout this essay have attempted to understand photography as a demand, as a form of testimony and a call to bear witness, and ultimately as a kind of encounter that activates the past in the present moment of viewing. This reading necessarily involves dislodging the medium from the idea that it belongs squarely in either the category of the material or the category of the spectral and calls for our allowing it to occupy and perform in both. Photographs are, of course, objects in the world—material things that come from a chemical process of transference, transfixation, and translation, all of which is the result of time and light. But they are something else too—events, sites of affect, the immaterial residue of which transcends the specific coordinates of a given space-time, the "here and now," the "there," and the "once was." Always linked to the materiality of the photograph, its transcendent qualities are what allow for a kind of afterlife or survival. Giorgio Agamben writes of survival in terms of a "mute apostrophe" that takes place in the photographic image and has to do with a "certain exigency" that "*demands* something from us" (25). He goes on to say: "the concept of exigency is particularly important and must not be confused with *factual necessity*. Even if the person photographed is completely forgotten today, even if his or her name has been erased forever from human memory—or, indeed, *precisely* because of this—that person and that face *demand* their name; they demand *not* to be forgotten" (25). In its refusal to be silenced or ignored, in its demand to be looked at and named, "the photograph is always *more* than an image" (26). It is the breach and the bridge between life and death.

NOTES

1. "Au plus près de la mort," is a phrase that comes from Hervé Guibert's *Ghost Image* (137–40). Guibert concludes the section titled "The Photograph, As Close to Death as Possible" with the following provocation, in parenthetical: "(But in a painting, it is the wound we look at, the red opening in Christ's side, and in the street, the excrement left by a dog. So why shouldn't photography's two biggest attractions also be blood and waste?)" (140).

2. Here the phrase is borrowed from Ross Chambers's 1998 book *Facing It*: "The crazy, delirious hope is that 'facing it' by means of representation, capturing 'it''s image'—the image of death—in the mirror of writing will make it possible both, heroically, to decapitate

the Gorgon and to survive, like Theseus, the fate of petrifaction. . . . But . . . the cure of the author is not only a function of the mirror held up Theseus-like to AIDS in his writing but also of the 'indoctrination' of readership that is required to be so engaged, so *totally* committed to the author's cause, that the Gorgon will prove powerless" (120).

3. For a detailed discussion of the obscene in relation to photography and witnessing, see Keller and Snyder.

4. This image has strong resonances with other photographs that feature the living but AIDS-infected body as corpse, such as those in William Yang's *Sadness* and David Wojnarowicz's now iconographic portrait of his lover Peter Hujar on his deathbed. In both Yang's and Wojnarowicz's work, each includes images of the living person "as close to death as possible" as well as post-mortem portraits.

5. The subtitle to this section comes directly from three distinct positions on what constitutes the photograph, respectively, from Paul Christopher Johnson, Allan Sekula, and Roland Barthes.

6. See Keller and Snyder's Introduction for a close reading of Barthes's concept of "force" and how photographs "fill our sight with force."

7. Slightly reworded version of the title to the exhibit "Witnesses: Against Our Vanishing" curated by Nan Goldin at the Artists Space in New York City, November 16, 1989–January 6, 1990.

8. My translation. All translations are my own unless otherwise noted.

9. Examples of this include crutches rendered un-useable by being tethered to other crutches or surfaces, fixing them so that they would be immobile. For an in-depth overview and critical discussion of Espaliú's work, see Juan Aliaga's essays in the exhibition catalogue *Pepe Espaliú*.

10. Martín Hernández ("Within") discusses in detail the institutional support (and lack thereof) in Spain during the outbreak of the HIV/AIDS epidemics.

WORKS CITED

Agamben, Giorgio. *Profanations*. Translated by Jeff Fort, Zone Books, 2007.

Aliaga, Juan Vicente, and José Miguel G. Cortés. *De amor y rabia: Acerca del arte y el SIDA*. Universidad Politécnica de Valencia, 1993.

Barthes, Roland. *Camera Lucida: Reflections on Photography*. Translated by Richard Howard, Hill and Wang, 2010.

Belting, Hans. *An Anthropology of Images: Picture, Medium, Body*. Translated by Thomas Dunlap, Princeton University Press, 2011.

Caron, David. "Respect, One Dessert Spoon at a Time." Introduction. *Cytomegalovirus: A Hospitalization Diary*, by Hervé Guibert, translated by Clara Orban, Fordham University Press, 2016, pp. 1–26.

Chambers, Ross. *Facing It: AIDS Diaries and the Death of the Author*. University of Michigan Press, 1998.

Codesal, Javier. "DÍAS de SIDA." Photograph (color). 1993.

———. "Fábula a destiempo." Video installation (two channels, color). 1996.

———. "Tras la piel." Photographs (black and white). 1995.

Derrida, Jacques. *Athens, Still Remains: The Photographs of Jean-François Bonhomme*. Translated by Pascale-Anne Brault and Michael Naas, Fordham University Press, 2010.

Elkins, James. *What Photography Is*. Routledge, 2011.

Espaliú, Pepe et al. *Pepe Espaliú*. Exhibition catalogue. Museo Nacional Centro de Arte Reina Sofía y Centro Andaluz de Arte Contemporáneo. Documenta, Artes y Ciencias Visuales, 2003.

Espaliú, Pepe. "Carrying" Action/Performance/Video footage. San Sebastian, 1992.

———. "Retrato del artista desahuciado." *El País*, 1 Dec. 1992.

Goldin, Nan et al. *Witnesses: Against Our Vanishing: November 16, 1989 to January 6, 1990*. Exhibition catalogue. Artists Space, 1989.

Graham, Paul. *The Whiteness of the Whale*. Lecture notes from CCA, San Francisco, California, Sept. 2015.

Guibert, Hervé. *Ghost Image*. Translated by Robert Bononno, The University of Chicago Press, 1996.

———. *The Mausoleum of Lovers: Journals 1976–1991*. Translated by Nathanaël, Nightboat Books, 2014.

———. *To the Friend Who Did Not Save My Life*. Translated by Linda Coverdale, High Risk Books/Serpent's Tail, 1994.

Guibert, Hervé, and Jean Baptiste del Amo. *Hervé Guibert: Photographe*. Éditions Gallimard, 2011.

Johnson, Paul Christopher. "Objects of Possession: Photography, Spirits, and the Entangled Arts of Appearance." *Sensational Religion: Sensory Cultures in Material Practice*, edited by Sally M. Promey, Yale University Press, 2014, pp. 25–46.

Keller, Patricia, and Jonathan Snyder. "Encounters with the Unsightly: Reading (AIDS) History, Photography, and the Obscene." *On Photography, History, and Memory in Spain*, edited by María Nilsson, *Hispanic Issues On Line*, vol. 3, Spring 2011, pp. 91–115.

Martín Hernández, Rut. *El cuerpo enfermo: arte y VIH/SIDA en España*. 2010. Universidad Complutense de Madrid, PhD dissertation.

———. "Within the Limits of the Body: Artistic Images of HIV/AIDS in Spain and its Relation with the Cultural Industry." *HIV in World Cultures: Three Decades of Representations*, edited by Gustavo Subero, Ashgate, 2013, pp. 121–38.

Meyers, Todd. "Remainders." Afterword. *Cytomegalovirus: A Hospitalization Diary*, by Hervé Guibert, translated by Clara Orban, Fordham University Press, 2016, pp. 75–82.

Moreiras Menor, Cristina. *Cultura herida: Literatura y cine en la España democrática*. Libertarias, 2002.

Mueller, Cookie. *Walking through Clear Water in a Pool Painted Black*. Semiotext(e), 1990.

Muellner, Nicholas. *The Photograph Commands Indifference*. A-Jump Books, 2009.

Nixon, Nicholas, and Bebe Nixon. *People with AIDS*. D. R. Godine, 1991.

Pepe Espaliú. Museo Nacional Centro de Arte Reina Sofía y Centro Andaluz de Arte Contemporáneo, edited by Juan Vicente Aliaga, Adrian Searle, and Marie-Laure Bernadac, Documenta, Artes y Ciencias Visuales, 2003.

Sekula, Allan. *Photography against the Grain: Essays and Photo Works 1973–1983*. Press of Nova Scotia College of Art and Design, 1984.

Steinmann, Kate. "Apparatus, Capture, Trace: Photography and Biopolitics." *Fillip*, vol. 15, Fall 2011.

Wojnarowicz, David. *Close to the Knives*. Vintage Books, 1991.

Yang, William. *Sadness*. Allen & Unwin, 1996.

CHAPTER 7

Death, Afterlife, and the Question of Autobiography (*Biutiful*, 2010)

Cristina Moreiras-Menor

Materiality of death will always be metaphorical, referential or otherwise symbolic. Materialities of passing, on the other hand, refer to actual handling of decaying matter and the vanishing of life through which the passage of time can be observed; with things passed on prior to dying, with the anticipation of death, and with the material forms with which people attempt to transcend or interact with the ultimate nothingness of those who have—or that which has—passed.   (Bjerregaard et al. 6)

The gravest and most painful testimony of the modern world, the one that possibly involves all other testimonies to which this epoch must answer (by virtue of some unknown decree or necessity, for we bear witness also to the exhaustion of thinking through History), is the testimony of the dissolution, the dislocation, or the conflagration of community.   (Nancy 1)

It is with this statement that Jean-Luc Nancy's *The Inoperative Community* opens. The statement is of interest to me here because it invokes certain aspects that I would like to take up in relation to a beautiful film that speaks of death, extinction, and restoration, while at the same time proposing, through the film's intense mnemonic images, a manner of thinking about political and historical potentiality. I am referring here to Alejandro González Iñárritu's *Biutiful* (2010), a film that testifies, via the suffering of the protagonist Uxbal, to the presence of an essential uncertainty: life as transition. I am, in reality, interested in thinking through the way the film, disturbing in its violence and in its accumulation of dispossessed and un-rooted subjects, addresses the recuperation of experience under the framework of an historicity that, in history's exhaustion and in the dissolution of community to which Nancy makes reference, has been wiped out. *Biutiful*, in an intimate perspective achieved via a camera that follows Uxbal's constant itinerary in a desolate city—a perspective that I will call "autobiographical" —the viewer becomes aware of the way the film emphasizes the experiences of life and death. And it does this in such a way as to recuperate a thinking of death as a transformative power; as a political intervention on contemporaneity and its avatars.

My reading of the film will center, then, not so much on the current history of a wildly global and capitalistic Barcelona portrayed in the film as a kind of favela by means of dark and dreary images of various (predominantly African and Chinese) immigrant communities surviving in the underbelly of a desolated global city dominated by the omnipresent ghost of Gaudí's unfinished *Sagrada Família*, a constant reminder of an unfinished modernity that has presided over Barcelona's history since the twentieth century while also highlighting the model of the traditional family that has been so central to consolidating the dominant ideology of a homogenous nation enclosed within its well-established limits. Neither will my reading center on the exhaustion of community, which is represented in the film as an irrefutable reality. Nor will I focus on the radical isolation and violence that governs cohabitation between those various nationalities and ethnicities upon which the film's narrative revolves, and where Uxbal moves about as the world's prime mediator and communicator. Finally, neither will I pay attention to Uxbal's spiritual journey, nor to the possibility that Uxbal—the best of the worst of characters (whose motto might be "I must feed my family, so anything goes")—might be redeemed upon confronting his own death.

I will not focus on any of these aspects nor on the political and social messages that, like its critical content, the film wishes to relay. And I won't do that precisely because these attributes are already so clearly in sight for all to see: *Biutiful* has been read sociologically as a story of immigration, and will continue to be read as a film that treats the global, capitalistic, and postmodern city in negative terms by employing the fantastic cinematographic conversion of a luminous, modern, and European Barcelona (a Barcelona that dominates the international imagination, turning it into one of the world's largest tourist destinations) into a dark, intensely violent city absent of hospitality toward those destitute migrant families who arrive. These readings are perfectly sound and accurate, and comprise what we could call *Biutiful*'s sociological realism, where its narrative strategy is molded on a likeness of the real, on the idea of mimesis, on old models of representation that are destined to tell stories of the present from an absolutely recognizable place (the family, the social collective, terminal illness, the reality of immigrants, and so on). This is a socio-anthropological reading in which perhaps the most we can hope to gain is a representational appreciation of how community, family, and history live in our modern imaginaries. All of this is fundamental fodder for the film: it is the message that the film wishes to relay, a representation that wishes to be credible, a chronicle of a present marked by violence and isolation, as well as solidarity. This is *Biutiful*, a narrative-report on the end of a reality that is overwhelmingly present in our contemporary experience.

However, *Biutiful* is also the story of a coming and a going, of a departure and an arrival pertaining to the moment in which the character takes notice of his own finality and essence, and sees himself "thrown towards his destiny." The film presents this transition, this thrown-ness, within the cinematographic interval that occurs between the opening scene (Uxbal and his daughter in bed, discussing a ring) and the closing scene (the same as the opening but now with Uxbal himself observing his daughter from outside, and seeing his own body as a corpse on the bed). My analysis will home in on this inter-scene and in how the transition (which narrates Uxbal's lived existence, his actual presence between the period spanning the opening and closing scenes) is constituted, because, as I will try to show, it is through this transition between the opening and closing scene that one can glimpse a political reason through a realism that surpasses all testimonies of a diminishing community or of a collective narrative, moving them instead toward their radicalness of a revelatory perspective of being-for-death.

The realist characteristics I have just enumerated are all found on screen by means of a violent and pensive image (following Jacques Rancière) that will unfold in the form of an after-image. I will develop this concept further below, during the analysis of the film. Suffice it to say for now that, according to Rancière, "pensiveness thus refers to a condition that is indeterminately between the active and the passive" (107). This is to say that when constructing a narrative of a life, or of a lived existence, the story is not built out of an apparently realist image represented with exactitude, but rather out of the effect that remains suspended and persistent once the image is no longer there. Or in what amounts to the same thing, it is built out of what is glimpsed within the image in its moment of transit. The glare of the image, in its moment of evanescence, eludes any temporal marking but keeps enclosed within itself that persistent trace—a transient time that opens up toward historical reason. In other words, it opens itself up to that dangerous moment that Walter Benjamin terms *awakening*, a moment of dialectical rupture that gives place to true knowledge, and to what Jacques Derrida calls the non-contemporaneity of the self.[1] In that moment of danger, where knowing appears in all its radicalness (in the instance of being conscious of death, of being "thrown toward destiny"), the glare of the non-contemporaneity of the self clings to the after-image (the moment of temporal dislocation), or to what remains after its apparition, revealing a temporality that is constituted by the simultaneity of the multiple and heterogeneous—of life and of death—the transformative potentiality of which will equate to a moment of subjective opening, to a moment constitutive in its relation to what is *essentially* human, and to what gives its historicity: its being-toward-death.

In his introductory chapter to the volume *After-Images of the City*, Joan Ramon Resina has already brought us close to this image and to this concept that hides subjective, or essential, power. He states:

> Detached from the presumed transcendence implied by "post-," the hyphenated term "after-image" retains the full sense of its constituents as well as the meaning of the non-hyphenated form. It denotes a visual sensation that lingers after the stimulus that provoked it has disappeared, and opens the idea of "image" to a cluster of theoretical possibilities based on temporal displacement, sequentiality, supersession, and engagement. Unlike "post-image," however, the concept of after- image does not suggest that one transcends and leaves behind the imaginary. The image is fully retained, but is now a temporalized, unstable, complex image brimming with the history of its production. (1)

An image that retains a shadow or a light, indicating thus another image contained within itself (but as a remnant, sensation, or unfamiliar impression—now as an after-image), is temporalized due to its condition of trace, giving presence therefore to another history unveiled in that shadow or sensation that persists vaguely.[2]

I will attempt in the following pages to pursue and trace this *other* story, no longer the sociological one of migrants, or the one that gives life to a wildly capitalistic and global Barcelona, but that *other* story, which unveils itself in the wake of the after-image because, in my opinion, it is this story that instigates all the rest. This is the story of an individual, Uxbal, confronting his own mortality and, as such, tracing the intimate experience and annals of communal everydayness changing them into something that reveals the interstices that both separate and unite the private and the public, the personal and the collective. Desperately transiting a devastated city, a life at the brink of appearance, and a beyond that brings him ever closer to both the memories of his late father and to those long since dead, whom he has helped "die better," Uxbal registers his own essence as a subject for death. "No one can take the Other's dying away from him," Heidegger's famous line from *Being and Time* tells us (284). In Uxbal's incessant wanderings, he takes charge of this reality, or of this essential truth, and faces his own finitude.

The film is indeed conceived as a journey toward death (the protagonist is diagnosed with terminal cancer at the start of the film) and toward Uxbal's confrontation with, or his awakening to, his own mortality. In passing through the underworlds of Barcelona, he is able to recover a sense of humanity by way of recuperating memories of certain stories long abandoned to oblivion: The story of his father, of his exile in Mexico and the arrival of a dictatorship as a result of the war, the encounter with his corpse and with his burial. The story of the community of Chinese workers and their abject lives, the story that ends with all of them dead in the basement of a factory where they lived as though they were animals or, perhaps, as Jews in concentration camps awaiting the crematoria. The story of the Africans and their precarious labor conditions. The story of his family, which includes, due to mental illness, a violent, manic-depressive wife and two kids exposed to this maternal violence and the criminal life of his brother. The story of his own utter exhaustion, and his family's social precariousness. And finally, the stories of the dead with whom Uxbal tries to communicate and ease their transition in order to earn a few euros for his children for after his death. Through these stories, all of which are interconnected via Uxbal's itinerancy as he prepares his death and his legacy, the film is able to establish a temporal reason in order to show a subject-[made]-for-death making room for the possibility of relaying another story, which contains within it its more intimate self: the subject as ex-sistence.

I would like to propose that the account of ex-sistence that Iñárritu presents for us in *Biutiful* is what we could call the materiality of death: the act of walking, of traversing life, in preparation for death and accompanied by objects that help Uxbal prepare his transit, both in the sense of a departure as well as a survival (his legacy). In this way, his trajectory through Barcelona is accompanied by the objects that will allow him to die at ease: the engagement ring he gives to his daughter at the moment that precedes his death; the owl that accompanies the memory of his father and anticipates his presence; the forest that reproduces the "re-encounter" that lay beyond life and the money that Uxbal obsessively accumulates for his children. Robert Harrison, in *The Dominion of the Dead*, states that within the subject, what is human "is a way of being mortal and relating to the dead. To be human means above all to bury" (xi). These are the objects that will be present during his death, at his funeral. With them, Uxbal finds that "they" happen to him when, for the funeral, after his father's corpse has been returned from Mexico where he was living in exile, the possibility arises (and of which he makes use) to accept that his family's legacy is the same legacy as that of his own story. It is only when Uxbal sees and accepts this legacy as his ultimate responsibility, as that which guides him toward that life after life, that his subject can then be represented in its full humanity, that is, in its being-for-death—its ultimate and radical recognition. This is, then, what emerges from *Biutiful* as the ultimate condition of possibility for Uxbal, a possibility that gives him his only chance at restitution.[3]

The figure of the after-image, or of what remains as a trace after the image is no longer there, and the figure of the afterlife—of a life after life[4]—in Uxbal's figure of continuous transit, allows me to reflect on the promise of a new politics of memory wherein a singular narrative of the present (realism) opens itself up toward temporal dislocation, offering not a closure for the past but a promise of an openness for the future. "Historical 'understanding' is to be grasped," states Benjamin, "as an afterlife of that which is understood; and what has been recognized in the analysis of the 'afterlife of works' . . . is therefore to be considered the foundation of history in general" (460). Or what Benjamin calls true historical knowledge.[5]

Biutiful leaves open this possibility of historical understanding, which includes the active relationship between three historical temporalities, in order to leave space for its very rupture, its breaking open, or what Benjamin calls "the actualization of the present." A counterpoint to a realist account that re-presents the lives of communities in poverty is established with different, yet similar, forms of destitution: solitude, illness, abject poverty, workplace violence, forced removal, mental illness, and with that *other* that is born out of the intimate recognition of one's own mortality as a form of transit, not as an end. In other words, these competing accounts emerge from their realist interstices—in the after-image's unveilings—revealing an intimate and symbolic story that dilutes and washes away all possibility of assigning a chronological temporality to the events the film portrays. For this reason, we encounter, at beginning and end, a forest that carries us beyond the thresholds of reality and myth. Indeed, this is also the place of encounter with Uxbal's ominous though familiar father; a spiritual space where Uxbal speaks to the recently departed as a way of accompanying them in their journey and helping to ease their way in the name of hospitality.

Both registers, the realist (immigrants, the chronicling of Uxbal's everyday life, Barcelona, and so on) and the symbolic (the forest, Uxbal's clairvoyance, and so on) are in dialogue through images of memory and of objects that distort both the realism and the symbolism that are contained within each memory and object. These are objects that materialize the journey, facilitating a language and a narrative: the ring, the owl, the dead whales, the industrial chimneys, or the forest as the image of a life after life. In the forest, one finds written the index of the *other* film: the non-historical temporality that allows for all the other stories to be seen like a suspension of a realist chronology of the afterlife, thereby dissolving all certainties regarding what life and death are. It is this that allows for a confrontation with one's own finality, and, as such, brings reason to its knees before the true, the only, question of auto-bio-graphy.

The film, let us not forget, ends with the image of Uxbal smiling hospitably at his father right at the moment of his death, which is where the inscription is produced of an "awakening" to the radicality of time's in-finity. This can also be said of the ring with which the film's realist account both begins and ends: a dying father passing on to his daughter his own memories as well as those of her mother. The after-image and the afterlife are figures that feed the story of Uxbal's death, as the moment in which the spectator witnesses the awakening of a "knowledge-not-yet-conscious of what it has been" (Benjamin 458). As we know, in the space of history, "mythological" existence dissolves. This dissolution is the moment in which the story's most radical intimacy (one's own death) is revealed as the moment in which history meets its historical index, its radical reason for being.

As is well known, for Benjamin, the work of awakening historical understanding is intimately related to the text and to the work of editing, which is something that continues to have significance in the film we are discussing. With this in mind, I want to analyze *Biutiful* as an unconventional autobiography since it breaks with the primary logic of being told in the first person. This is the auto-biography of a subject, Uxbal, who in the moment of his death (his transit toward death), imagines and, in imagining, inscribes in an instant his familial biography (the uninterrupted flashback that organizes *Biutiful*'s narrative arch from the first image of the forest, in the beginning, to the last image of the forest, at the end). This flashback is the story of his father and the inheritance he receives (material-ized and symbolized in the ring he gives to his daughter at the time of his death); his relationship with a criminal and deceptive brother; his marriage to a manic-depressive woman; his own fatherhood; his work life; his spiritual life (his capacity to mediate between the living and the dead); as well as his own death. From this perspective, *Biutiful* can be read as *the text* of Uxbal's life—a text written by him-self (it is the editing of the film that allows for an autobiographical reading since, for Uxbal, his life appears as a flashback at the moment of his death)—in which mourning the one who is going to die is folded into mourning the living and the dead. It is a film about life and death, about paternity and about restituting the name for history. Fundamentally, it is a film about a writing of one's own name, and in the forgiveness of the paternal figure as an imminently historical figure, it is an always implicit writing that favors citation over that which is constructed explicitly in the autobiographical image.

Indeed, *Biutiful* materializes the autobiographical image from the very first words we hear spoken from beyond the grave by Uxbal's father, when he says: "¿Sabías que cuando los búhos mueren echan una bola de pelo por el pico?" (Did you know that when owls die, they leave a mound of hair in their bill?). These are words that will later be repeated, verbatim, by Uxbal's son while he is looking attentively at papers: a Family Record Book (Libro de Familia) and two photo-graphs that have been removed from Uxbal's father's tomb; one a portrait of his father and another of his father in the snowy forest with which the film opens. This is when the spectators know that Uxbal's father is dead and that the first scene of the film is actually the present narrative. The ring and the image of the owl (which we see in the opening scene) are the material objects, the links, that permit Uxbal to recognize his father and accept him warmly while also recognizing his father's story in himself, and in his children. Likewise, it simultaneously allows for a recognition of himself within a history of loss and exile that all history presupposes. We see this process unfold with some detail.

The film opens with a powerful and persistent image, a kind of after-image that remains in the eyes of the spectators until the end, when it reappears as an apparent repetition, but now acquiring its full meaning within a fundamentally temporal instability (is this the story's beginning or end?). It is an image-scene that, preceding even the title on a black screen, marks the beginning of the film in one single frame: the hands of a girl and a man lying in bed speaking of a diamond ring and telling its story. With an abrupt cut, this scene gives way to the scene of a snowy forest in which, still hearing the conversation between the two characters that now talk off-screen of the noise of the sea, we see a close-up of a dead owl, a mound of hair by its side, leaving, slowly, a path for the presence of an approaching young man to appear onscreen (it is also a moment in which we hear the girl call for her father, "papá, papá" [dad, dad]). This is the man we will later identify as Uxbal, or the father who places the ring in the child's hand. We see—and listen to—how the men of the forest speak of the owl, the noises of the sea, and of the wind; and we see, finally, how they light a cigarette, how the young man leaves, and how Uxbal (who the spectators have at this point yet to identify as this same young man) moves to follow him. A fade to black brings us to the title of the film we are about to see, a character preparing for death after having just learned he has a terminal illness.

At the end of the film, we recover the same image, the same scene, and the same words in faithful repetition: that is, the image of the father and daughter in bed looking at a diamond ring that, while telling his story, he puts on her finger, but only after we have already been through those preparations for death in the precarious and violent world in which Uxbal lives. Still, there is a fundamental difference, barely visible, between these two scenes (one has to rewind the film in order to confirm what is only a slight impression): the point of view, and the angle, of the camera are radically different. In the first image, the opening scene, the camera adopts Uxbal's point of view of lying on the bed with his daughter while putting the diamond ring that used to be her grandmother's on her finger. The spectator adopts Uxbal's gaze, looking from behind the hand with the ring and from within the scene he is seeing. At the end of the film, the camera adopts, or at first seems to adopt, an objective perspective, external to the scene, constructing it as though it were a frame the spectator sees from the outside, where we are able to observe both the father and the daughter with the ring. Here, the spectator recuperates the wake, the shadow the scene leaves behind, and recalls the empty moment that occurs through the abrupt cut of the first scene, leaving it suspended, and giving way to the scene that frames the snowy forest. This black instant—of emptiness—is now retrospectively filled with meaning while the spectators observe the final scene from the outside. The emptiness produced by the abrupt cuts between scenes, represented by a fade out (to black), marks the precise instant of Uxbal's death, his expiration.

In this repeating but varying scene we see, in the first iteration, the scene where he is now a corpse lying next to his daughter who plays with the ring in her hand, Uxbal fixedly observing, without blinking, and sitting in a chair that rests against a wall. The outside gaze of the spectator now corresponds, again, to Uxbal's gaze who is already looking in from the other side of life, the moment of his death. The spectator, however, has access to both Uxbal's corpse and to Uxbal after his death, where he is looking, along with the spectators, at the scene in which his death unfolds. We are reminded here of his daughter calling off-screen for her father, "papá, papá," during the fade to black that carries us into the forest. The camera situates itself within Uxbal's perspective here as well, but it is simultaneously situated in the scene (as corpse) and outside of it (observing himself already from death); as subject of the scene, now a corpse, and as a third-person perspective composing a way of seeing the scene. The after-image and the afterlife unveil themselves in all their fortitude as the power that propitiates the true autobiographical inscription: the moment of death as the moment of the subject's fullness; as the hospitable opening to one's own finality.

In other words, *Biutiful*'s narrative is the epitaph that allows him to recognize his own history and, at the same time, to inscribe in it his own legacy for the future. Such an autobiographical situation, however, is only capable of unveiling itself when exposed to the spectator's consciousness: that is, when it actively intervenes in making legible the instant of fusing into darkness, which, in retrospect, happens precisely at the moment of death. For Paul de Man, the autobiographical moment is produced "as an alignment between two subjects involved in the process of reading in which they determine each other by mutual reflexive substitution" (921). By way of the image and the temporal dislocation brought in its wake, this is an intensely specular moment in which the subjectivity of the spectator is absolutely conditioned by Uxbal's subjectivity, converting the two subjects into two autobiographical subjects who are, as consequence, the two participants in the bio-graphic inscription; an epitaph in all its senses.

Let us remember that for Paul de Man, the autobiographical is directed toward and from an absence of life, since "the dominant figure of the epitaphic or autobiographical discourse is . . . prosopopeia, the fiction of the voice-from-beyond-the-grave" (927). Understood in this way, *Biutiful* is not so much a film about self-redemption or of the other subjects who coexist within, and even form Uxbal's biography (the immigrants, the mentally ill, the dead, and so on). Rather, and above all, it is a film about the restoration of the intimacy that inscribes time as a radical responsibility toward mortality.

What, then, could be the strength of *Biutiful* as an autobiographical story? Would the autobiographical perspective resist or assume the political reason of a realist and sociological story seeking to represent violence and precariousness wherein the contemporary person lives? Where would we find that political reason, potentially transforming that which is contained, as I have tried to show, in an image of the afterlife that does not forget that other image of origin (the after-image)? In my essay, the after-image that fully unveils itself at the end of *Biutiful* uncovers the political proposal of a story structured around a desire for restitution that is available only once the spectator has come to occupy the same position as the corpse. In this sense, González Iñárritu makes us mediators between the living and the dead, like Uxbal, working on behalf of the after-image that Rancière would call a "pensive image": an image

> full of thoughts . . . encroached upon by a certain passivity . . . [that] contains unthought thought, a thought that cannot be attributed to the intention of the person who produces it and which has an effect on the person who views it without her linking it to a determinate object. Pensiveness thus refers to a condition that is indeterminately between the active and the passive. (107)

It is, following Rancière, "this tangle between several forms of indeterminacy . . . effect of the circulation, between the subject, the [director and the editor], and us, of the intentional and the unintentional, the known and the unknown, the expressed and the unexpressed, the present and the past" (114–15).

This is the pensiveness of an image that is retained in Uxbal's dead retina, reflecting the father putting the ring on his daughter's finger, the father and the son in the snowy mountain, the dead owl, all of which express in all its plenitude the function that Rancière gives to the image:

> the relationship between two operations that puts the unduly pure form or the event over-charged with reality outside themselves. On the one hand, the form of this relationship is determined by the artist. But on the other, it is the spectator alone who can fix the measure of the relationship; it is exclusively her gaze that

imparts reality to the balance between the metamorphoses of computer 'matter' and the staging of the history of a century. (128–29)

Uxbal's search moves toward the recovery and legibility of historical inheritance (encapsulated not only in the autobiographical inscription of one's own death, but also in recovering the figure of the father exiled for political reasons during the Franco years). It also inscribes the transformative power of hospitality toward that inheritance, that way of the father, which Uxbal passes on to his daughter. His search demands precisely the recovery of the subject's humanity, his historical reason for his being-in-time as a legacy that makes imperative the extracted significance of rupture, leaving the image charged with an excess of materiality, which is the realist and sociological story within *Biutiful*.

To conclude, this fullness, or this awakening to the meaning of legacy, is produced through the confluence of the gazes within the film, alongside the gaze of the spectator: from the place where nothing is perfectly clear within the film, where nothing is convincing and all action and all subjectivity are always interpolated in one zone of pure indetermination: the Chinese workers are bare life, zombies whose lives go by the symbol of the crematoria's chimneys or dead, beached whales, and Uxbal's spirituality is tinged with the commercial incentive of his family. Far from being home, it is estrangement, insecurity, and uncertainty that leads him toward extinction. The city is a space of unlimited violence whose subjects are lost while moving through an endless place of non-communitarian spaces. The testimonial quality of the film introduces, then, an intrinsically realist critical reflection and representation of the work ethic, of the family, of community, the human and post-human, and of banality and spirituality that make up the subjectivities of its characters.

But all of this nourishes Uxbal's story, while contaminating it via the spectator's gaze, through a cinematographic strategy that uses the after-image as a place in which the power of auto-bio-graphy emerges. Heterogeneous historical and temporal reasons emerge, then, through the confluence of historical record and the place where the spectator becomes an intrinsic part of the story; and they emerge through that pensive image loaded with thoughts not necessarily thought; in short, what comes together is a politics of memory, hospitable toward our dead and toward our living, and toward the relationship that exists between them and the future. *Biutiful* is a film that unveils and emerges from the inscription of autobiography understood as the impossible restitution of being-toward-death (Heidegger), as the essential kernel of all historical, communitarian, and, therefore, political knowledge.

NOTES

Thanks to Camila Moreiras-Vilarós for her excellent translation of this work.

1.   See Walter Benjamin's *The Arcades Project* and Jacques Derrida's *Specters of Marx*.
2.   See Mary Ann Doane's *The Emergence of Cinematic Time: Modernity, Contingency, the Archive*, particularly chapter 3.
3.   Also, see the question of restitution in Paul de Man's "Autobiography as De-Facement" where the author would consider the autobiography as the restoration of mortality through the name and the voice (prosopopeia) (930).
4.   I borrow this concept of the afterlife from a panel proposal that Patricia Keller presented at the MLA a few years back, wherein she states: Afterlife is a concept that alludes to the "promise and permanence of that which has been lost."
5.   This true historical knowledge can be compared to what Paul de Man calls the figure of reading or understanding.

WORKS CITED

Benjamin, Walter. *The Arcades Project*. Translated by Howard Eiland and Kevin McLaughlin, Belknap Press of Harvard University Press, 2002.

Bjerregaard, Peter, Anders Emil Rasmussen, and Tim Flohr Sørensen. "Introducing Materialities of Passing." *Materialities of Passing: Explorations in Transformation, Transition and Transience*, edited by Peter Bjerregaard, Anders Emil Rasmussen, and Tim Flohr Sørensen, Routledge, 2016, pp. 1–23.

De Man, Paul. "Autobiography as De-facement." *MLN*, vol. 94, 1979, pp. 919–30.

Derrida, Jacques. *Specters of Marx: The State of the Debt, the Work of Mourning and the New International*. Translated by Peggy Kamuf, Routledge, 2006.

Doane, Mary Ann. *The Emergence of Cinematic Time: Modernity, Contingency, the Archive*. Harvard University Press, 2003.

González Iñárritu, Alejandro, director. *Biutiful*. Roadside Attractions, 2010.

Harrison, Robert Pogue. *The Dominion of the Dead*. University of Chicago Press, 2003.

Heidegger, Martin. *Being and Time*. Translated by John Macquarrie and Edward Robinson, Harper Perennial, 1962.

Nancy, Jean-Luc. *The Inoperative Community*. Translated by Peter Connor, University of Minnesota Press, 1991.

Rancière, Jacques. *The Emancipated Spectator*. Translated by Gregory Elliott, Verso, 2009.

Resina, Joan Ramon. "The Concept of the After-Image and the Scopic Apprehension of the City." *After-Images of the City*, edited by Joan Ramon Resina and Dieter Ingenschay, Cornell University Press, 2003, pp. 1–22.

CHAPTER 8

What Do We Do with the Dead?

The Posthumous in Fernando León's *Amador*

Daniel García-Donoso

Otherness and marginality are recurring themes in the work of director Fernando León de Aranoa. *Barrio* (1998), *Los lunes al sol* (2002), and *Princesas* (2005) were praised for León de Aranoa's ethical preoccupation with segments of the population suffering exclusion at the hands of a culture that claims (and even celebrates) to be founded upon "human" or "humanitarian" values. The director's commitment to more democratic forms of understanding and coexistence has been analyzed by multiple scholars through the living bodies of men and women—adolescents, precarious workers and the unemployed, the sick, immigrants, racialized others, prostitutes, or the elderly—that populate the contemporary urban landscapes where his films are set.[1] It has been largely neglected, however, how the director's interest in marginalization connects in fundamental ways with his unwavering attention to death and dead bodies. After all, as Jean Baudrillard argues, death is modern society's primordial form of exclusion: "At the very core of the 'rationality' of our culture . . . is an exclusion that precedes every other, more radical than the exclusion of madmen, children or inferior races, an exclusion preceding all these and serving as their model: the exclusion of the dead and of death" (126).[2]

Amador (2010) is an exploration of contemporary dynamics affecting the exclusion of the dying and the dead, and this essay analyzes it as a turning point in the director's interest in the topic. The film traces the story of Marcela, a Peruvian immigrant living in Madrid whose unexpected pregnancy, right when the financial crisis is hitting the country hardest, pushes her to find a job in order to make ends meet. Marcela is hired temporarily to care for an elderly man named Amador while his only daughter leaves for the beach with her family during the summer. Initially reluctant to speak with Marcela, Amador slowly opens himself up to his caregiver and vice versa, starting a friendly relationship between the two. Midway through the summer, Amador dies but Marcela decides to keep it a secret in order to maintain her still meager pay at a time of enhanced precarity. By daily cleaning the house, bringing new flowers, and keeping Amador company while watching TV, Marcela's immaterial *labor* coalesces with a Freudian *work* of mourning (*Trauerarbeit*). By not discovering her secret, Marcela is also helping Amador to stay "alive," keeping him in a posthumous condition through the cultivation of a life with the dead other.

This essay will look at the idea of the posthumous to assess the centrality of death in Fernando León's film. The posthumous acts as a symbolic force underneath the film's composition, one marked by temporal structures of suspension and transition affecting the two main characters: Marcela as an expectant mother, and Amador as a dying man and, later, as a dead body. The posthumous, as I hope to demonstrate here, is not only a condition that affects the relationship between the human living and the human dead, but also one that permeates the material world of things in the film. More specifically, the second part of my analysis will concentrate on a series of particularly relevant artifacts (letters, puzzles, photographs) whose "life" is also impregnated by a posthumous quality and put on hold, demanding a human intervention for them to come back to life. The final section of the essay will discuss how Fernando León, through the corpse of Amador as a focal point, uses the posthumous to reflect on the cinematic art itself and its relationship with other media. The posthumous, then, can be proposed as a cinematic response to the moral and ethical dilemma posed by modernity's exclusion of the dead from our everyday life.

I understand the idea of the posthumous here in productive opposition to the concept of *conditio posthuma*, an idea advanced by philosopher Marina Garcés to talk about how time and death are experienced at the beginning of the twenty-first century. If the temporality of modernity was built upon the idea of history as linear and progressive (future equals reason, knowledge, freedom), and postmodernity opened the understanding of history to multiple times and *heterochronias*, "to the value of interruption, to the event, and to discontinuities," *conditio posthuma* for Garcés marks a regression: it is a return to "a new narrative, unique and linear: that of the irreversible destruction of our conditions of life . . ., not the realization of history, but its implosion" (5–6). *Conditio posthuma* happens in a historical time haunted by an experience of the idea of death as scandal and spectacle, a death that infringes on the life after which we have assumed that anthropological collapse is irreversible. Neglected by postmodernity's "the-future-is-now" mentality, death comes back in the form of an "apocalyptic dogma," an invasion of our cultural imaginary by zombies, vampires, and skeletons that speaks to the discomforting normality with which death walks with us in our everyday lives. As we become accustomed to death only as a catastrophe, Garcés warns, we forget "how to respond to real death—to the old and sick people who accompany us, to violated and murdered women, to refugees and immigrants who risk their skins to cross international borders." In short, *conditio posthuma* presents itself to us in the form of a "socially produced and culturally accepted death" (8) that reduces a politics of the possible to its absolute minimum.

From here, my analysis of *Amador* turns Garcés's idea of the posthumous on its head and looks at it as an enabling condition in times that are seemingly doomed. My interpretation of León de Aranoa's film emphasizes the structural and visual elements that question the temporality of inevitability through a posthumous engagement with the dead. Through both narrative and aesthetic strategies that call attention to the materiality of death, to its tangible and quotidian outcomes, the film emphasizes the need to incorporate a normalized experience of death that accommodates the dead to the world of the living.

What Do We Do with the Dead?

The corpse is the only material thing that remains of our loved ones when life ceases. A literal embodiment of the absolute otherness represented by the end of life, the human corpse is the depositary of an experience that we are unable to represent credibly, a form of temporal collapse that halts both reason and affect. What is a corpse? Is a corpse *still* human? How do dead bodies challenge what we understand by "human"? How can we ever assimilate that someone so loving to us is now something else, an accumulation of millions of minuscule processes of biological flux, decay, and decomposition forcing the living to act, to put them out of sight, to get rid of them? Within modernity's worldview, the bodies of the dead are devoid of function and, thus, they become the opposite of the *object*, or, in Julia Kristeva's terms, the elemental incarnation of the *abject*:

> The corpse, seen without God and outside of science, is the utmost of abjection. It is death infecting life. Abject. It is something rejected from which one does not part, from which one does not protect oneself as from an object. Imaginary uncanniness and real threat, it beckons to us and ends up engulfing us. (4)

Because of its absolute abjectivity, the corpse resists narrative and visual assimilation, and it unsettles cinematic representation. Even if slowly transitioning
into organic matter, inanimate bodies pose a challenge to cinema's imperative
of movement: they are un-cinematic matter. Fernando León's filmography is a
perfect illustration of this predicament, as death and corpses are often treated
in ways that are more elusive than anything else: the mute ambulance in *Sirenas*
(Sirens) (1994) that suggests the passing of the deaf grandfather at the end; the
grandmother's fake funeral in *Familia* (Family) (1996) as just another part in the
play performed by the family/troupe of actors; the tombs of Madrid's Almudena
cemetery in *Barrio* (Neighborhood), which Rai desecrates with his dance moves
as a prelude to his own being killed at the end; the flickering light that, in *Los
lunes al sol* (Mondays Under the Sun), indicates that the dead body of Amador,
who has thrown himself through the window, is lying on the invisible side of the
door canopy; or the protagonist's mother in *Princesas* (Princesses), whose demen-
tia makes her think that her defunct husband is still alive and sends her flowers.
These are all symbolic displacements that dodge the ever uncomfortable topic of
mortality and keep the camera away from the unmediated sight of dead bodies.

Many of these ideas around death, dying, and the influence of the dead over
the living converge and climax in León's fifth feature film. As we anticipated
earlier, *Amador* marks a turning point in the director's career as it puts death as
concept, plot event, and material outcome right at its center, and we can think of
at least two elements in *Amador*'s plot that may help explain this shift in León de
Aranoa's cinema.[3] The first one is the 2008 financial crisis, a global disaster with
necropolitical consequences where "death becomes ubiquitous in political imaginaries following massive breakdowns in basic life conditions" (Labrador Méndez
"Political"). It is the economic consequences of the crisis in the protagonist's life
that set the entire narrative in motion and partly motivate her actions. The second
element, which predates and engulfs the financial crisis, has to do with climate
change and its differential impact in the lives and deaths of vulnerable segments
of the population. In this regard, it is largely forgotten that the extreme heat wave
that swept Europe during the months of June–August of 2003 had a catastrophic
impact in Spain: the country's Instituto Nacional de Estadística reported that
there were almost thirteen thousand more deaths than the same period during the previous year (a 15 percent increase), with a disproportionate impact on
population over the age of seventy (1). High temperatures are a constant in the
film and, possibly, one of the reasons behind Amador's passing. We will see later
in our analysis of the film how these two elements influence the film's structure
and visual language; for now, let us emphasize how Fernando León weaves a

political and social narrative while simultaneously creates a personal, *auteur*-like universe that calls attention over his own understanding of the cinematic art.

By symbolically placing Amador's dying, then dead, body at the very core of his film, Fernando León is reflecting on cinema's historical relationship with death, as well as on the cinematic medium itself. From this perspective, the dying body and the corpse are embodiments of transitional subjectivities from the human to the nonhuman that question the centrality of the human in our cultural imaginaries as well as the temporal regimes of conventional fiction. Historically, the cinematic corpse has proliferated in popular film genres where death equals spectacle and/or an aberration. Zombies and vampires in apocalyptic and horror films, as well as dead bodies in the whodunit detective genre, become "active" corpses infused with a sense of exceptionality: *un*-dead creatures and unresolved murders embody the violation of the bourgeois status quo, automatically calling for the activation of exception mechanisms that seek to restore the administration of death to the sovereign. This dynamic is not very different from the Hollywood's vengeance film genre, where the structure is usually demarcated by death: a killing opens the plot and another killing brings it to closure. These narratives construct death as an unnatural phenomenon that can only be neutralized by vengeance as its natural counterpart, thus reinforcing the practice of sovereignty—the right to kill—as something that emanates from a sublimation of individual liberty.[4]

In an attempt to come to terms with cinema's fascination with death, Siegfried Kracauer argues that it is the camera's technical ability to capture the surface of things, its material essence, that explains this obsession with "[e]lemental catastrophes, the atrocities of war, acts of violence and terror, sexual debauchery, and death" (57). In this obsession, however, cinema's main goal is neither purely technical or phenomenological, nor is it a pursuit to overwhelm the senses. Faced with the dilemma of whether cinema should inhibit itself from the brutality of death, Kracauer says that cinema serves a higher ethical purpose: that is, to transform "the agitated witness into a conscious observer [where cinema's] lack of inhibitions in picturing spectacles which upset the mind . . . keeps us from shutting our eyes to the 'blind drive of things'" (58).[5] In the case of Fernando León's cinema and of *Amador* in particular, dying and dead bodies are not sensationalist, excessive, or apocalyptic corpses; rather, and in the spirit of Kracauer's ethical claim for cinema, they are material incarnations of the experience of passing, appealing to a sustainable economy of representation through a temporality that is commensurable with the capacities and proportions of everyday materiality.

In addition to this, the corpse in *Amador* is a physical medium wielding meta-discursive power. The stillness of the dead body represents a threat for an artistic form that, like cinema, is enamored with speed, change, processes, and movement. And yet movement in the cinematic image is only the result of an optical illusion that cannot excise itself from the radical stillness of its original artistic expression: the photographic still. As Laura Mulvey has argued, "[t]he stillness of the 'corpse' is a reminder that the cinema's living and moving bodies are simply animated stills and the homology between stillness and death returns to haunt the moving image" (88). The relationship between cinema and photography is one mediated by the posthumous, and Fernando León's film appropriates this idea to call the viewer's attention over the material quality of his own craft. If the presence of corpses in cinema recalls the uneasy cohabitation of life and death, of movement and stillness, within the boundaries of the celluloid strip, it also compels us to think of the relationship between death, the absence of life, and the persistence of matter. In this regard, matter is understood both as the trace that the dead leave behind—their bodies, their belongings—and as the tangible things and actions that the living elaborate upon the occasion of someone else's death. This preoccupation with the materialities of death transforms *Amador* into a cultural locus from which to conceive more democratic forms of representation that are not dependent on human-centric meanings.

Life and Death in Transition

Fernando León elaborates in *Amador* a response to the question of what to do with the dead and the dying. This response is done, first, by altering a stable perception of time and being through an intricate temporal structure that lies under a seemingly easy premise. Marcela, the film's protagonist, is an immigrant woman who has decided to abandon her partner Nelson and return to her native Peru after seeing how the financial crisis of the late 2000s has shattered her dreams of finding a better life in Spain. On her way to the airport, Marcela faints and quickly discovers that she is pregnant, which puts her return plans on hold as she resolves to give Nelson (and Spain) a second chance. This initial premise situates the main character in a time of multiple exceptionalities right from the outset. First, the financial crisis prompting the narrative action is a moment of exception with its own temporal disruption.[6] In addition, the abrupt end to Marcela's life in Spain and the accompanying feeling of failure transforms this time into some kind of ontological parenthesis (opening with her arrival in Spain, closing with her return to Peru). And finally, Marcela enters yet another temporality—pregnancy—which is itself a time of vulnerability and exception, an index of a time still to come, a future anterior, as well as a time in which a woman's sovereignty over her own body becomes even more challenged by both state and non-state actors. In sum, this accumulation of exceptionalities pushes the cinematic main action into a succession of temporal suspensions, advancing for the spectator a key to interpret states of *being* in the film, not as stable categories, but rather as states of *passing*. This idea will consolidate itself later in the film when Marcela starts working as a care assistant for Amador, an elderly man who is waiting to die at home; as we will demonstrate in our analysis, Marcela's pregnancy establishes a meaningful counterpoint with Amador's process of dying and ultimately his death, which creates the main temporal suspension and opens the film to a posthumous time.

Peter Bjerregaard and others have defined passing in a way that is particularly eloquent to understand the time structure affecting Marcela at the beginning of the film, as well as the ensuing encounter with the withering Amador:

> Passing is a matter of transformation, transition and transience. At the precarious and indeterminate borderlands of being and non-being, people, places and things are in motion across dubious, interstitial states of existence. Sometimes, these liminal entities are harnessed by the hope or even promise of a future, of a form of being beyond time, or they may be eclipsed by the prospects of dissolution. Even in the face of terminal existence, whoever or whatever makes the transition thus stands on the verge of emergence, either being subject to an inevitable metamorphosis or leaving behind a void filled with the potential for new beginnings. (1)

Marcela's immigrant status, coupled with minimal financial stability and unexpected pregnancy, puts her in a situation of heightened personal, material, and ontological contingency. "Where do you live, Marcela?" asks a nurse repeatedly during a visit to the hospital. Her unbreakable silence is a testament to her situation as a subject in transit, struggling to grasp a tangible form of existence.

In Baumanian terms, the "liquidity" of Marcela's existential predicament contrasts with the director's emphasis on two interrelated artifacts where ideas of time and passing acquire solid presence: the flowers (roses) that Nelson sells clandestinely through a network of immigrants in the streets of Madrid, and the refrigerator where Nelson and Marcela keep the flowers fresh at home. Because of the film's emphasis on the flowers' and the refrigerator's thingness, both can be said to work as "materialities of passing," embodying "the closest that humans may come to perceiving the fundamental spatiotemporal confines of their being" (Bjerregaard et al. 2). The flowers are one of the film's main leitmotivs, and one with clear posthumous resonances through the idea of fleeting time: from the classical invitation to seize the day (*collige virgo rosas*), to the suspension of death after they have been cut off. Nelson and Marcela make the flowers' posthumous life-extension possible with the application of an artificial air freshener (rose-scented), turning them into dead metaphors, into empty simulacra of their own selves. Conversely, the second artifact, the refrigerator, is used as an instrument to "freeze" the passing of time and keep the flowers alive. As "materialities of passing" that provide concrete visibility to states of passing, the flower-fridge pair establishes an interesting chiasmatic relationship with Marcela as an expectant mother: while she is carrying in her womb a creature expected to come to life within months, the refrigerator is an object-space where flowers are put after being "killed." This idea is emphasized early on in the film when Marcela wakes up terrified at night and sees the apartment's floor covered in water. Terrified that her waters broke or that she had a miscarriage, she quickly discovers that it is the fridge that broke down and is now leaking water. Additionally, the "alternative" use of the fridge to keep the flowers fresh can hardly conceal the fact that what the fridge is lacking is food. Void of its main content, the fridge is a displaced metaphor for the empty stomachs of thousands of Spaniards affected by the nutritional consequences of the crisis, a predicament that is even more noticeable through the contrast that those stomachs establish with Marcela's "full" stomach.[7]

The breaking down of the refrigerator moves the narrative toward the film's main plot, as Marcela is forced to get a paying job to help her and Nelson buy a new fridge. Shortly afterward, she finds a temporary position as the caregiver of Amador, a bed-ridden elderly man who lives alone in a small city apartment and spends the hot summer months completing jigsaw puzzles while calmly awaiting his final breath. Amador's daughter agrees to pay Marcela a meager five hundred euros/month to care for the old man on a full-time basis, an insulting pay when we learn that she and her family are spending the summer months in a beach town where they are building a vacation home. Marcela is a migrant worker in the informal domestic economy with no standards or benefits and, therefore, she is an individual relegated to a position of social invisibility. This becomes clear when Amador mutely refuses to acknowledge her presence in the home and "invisibilizes" her. Amador's neutralizing of Marcela's presence is a twofold defense mechanism against what she represents for him as a national: first, because as a care worker Marcela is perceived as a threat to ideals of independence in liberal societies (the ableist ideal of the fully functional body), and, second, as N. Michelle Murray has extensively studied in her book *Home Away from Home*, because "migrant women penetrate the home space and, through their care work, wield influence in familial and cultural life as domestic service workers," thus posing a "threat" to exclusionary and nativist conceptualizations of the homeland (133). By turning her presence into an unseeable and unspeakable "taboo," nationals

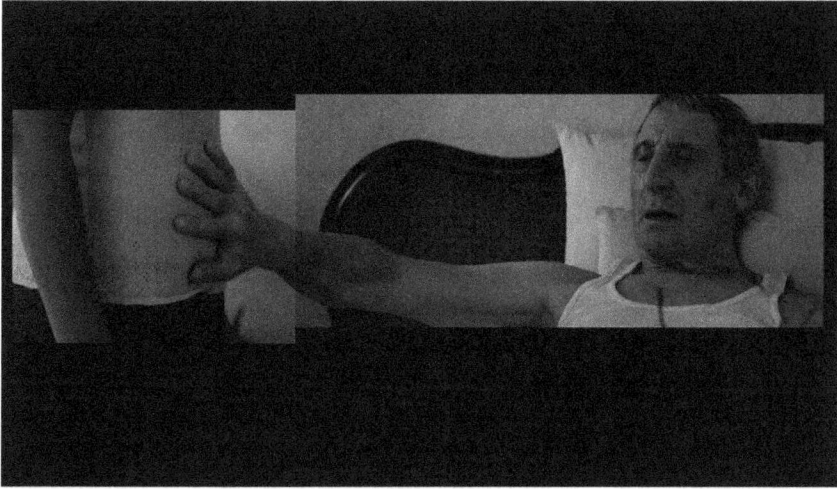

Figure 8.1. Amador's arm reaching out to bequeath his "life gift" to Marcela's baby, courtesy of Reposado P.C. and Film Movement

dismiss the fact that the assistance of immigrant workers is a necessary condition for them to maintain specific levels of life comfort and continue to live in a self-made fiction of national autonomy.

Simultaneously, if Amador's dismissive attitude invisibilizes Marcela, he too occupies a space of social invisibility and marginalization because of his old age and disabled condition. So the first part of the film develops along the gradual process of mutual recognition between two invisible subjects who share in forms of personal and social vulnerability. A chiasmatic relationship slowly re-emerges throughout this interaction as the film's core structural form, which culminates when Amador learns about Marcela's pregnancy: as Marcela nourishes her fetus transitioning toward life, she also takes care of Amador as he transitions toward death.[8] They become each other's materiality of passing, a reciprocal opportunity to grasp (literally, touch) the passing of time, particularly manifest when Amador lays his hand on Marcela's belly and talks to the baby: "¡Oye, tú, como te llames! Llegas tarde. Nos vamos a cruzar" (Hey, you, whatever your name is! You're late. We are going to miss each other). (Fig. 8.1) In a scene of intense emotionality, which brings to the fore the definitive realization that Amador has accepted the fate of death and is living in a posthumous manner, the verb that Amador utters ("cruzarse," meaning to cross paths with someone without seeing each other) perfectly verbalizes the chiasmus between beings in transition to/from life.

As Bjerregaard and others have said, "[t]he passage of time . . . emerges most dramatically and unambiguously in the encounter with the finality of bodily being—whether human or nonhuman—and assumes concrete form in practices connected with dying, death and decay" (2). Amador's conversation with the baby contains key aspects relating to how death assumes concrete form through a symbolic act of posthumous gift-giving: "Aquí ya no hay sitio para nadie" (The world is already full), Amador warns the baby. "Pero yo me voy ya y te dejo mi sitio. Tu madre lo va a guardar para ti. Es tuyo, acuérdate. Que nadie te lo quite" (But don't worry, I'm on my way out and I leave my spot for you. Your mother will save it for you. It's yours, remember. Do not let anyone take it away from you). From a formal perspective, León de Aranoa uses a panoramic shot (left to right) of Amador's extended arm with his open palm on Marcela's belly to evoke, on the one hand, Michelangelo's *The Creation of Adam*, thus turning Amador into a human, old, and exhausted version of God granting the gift of life (an association further emphasized by Amador's jigsaw puzzle, which shows a sky full of clouds reflected on a body of water); on the other hand, Amador's arm functions as a metaphorical umbilical cord through which his "gift" is transmitted. Both the hidden evocation of the Renaissance masterpiece and the physiological metaphor provide material support for the fulfillment of a symbolic exchange, which is in its turn necessary for death to materialize as well as a gift.

As Baudrillard explains, within a pure economic order characteristic of modern societies, death is reduced to meaninglessness as it is transformed into "a brute fact," into "natural, aleatory and irreversible death" (132). In contrast, forms of culture and sociality that maintain expressions typical of what he calls the "symbolic order," strive to provide death with a material substance that facilitates exchange, turning death into something "that is *given* and *received*," which, furthermore, allows for birth and death to be exchanged: "the opposition between birth and death disappears [as] they can also be *exchanged* under the form of symbolic reversibility" (132). Amador's gesture echoes Baudrillard's symbolic act, "which rids death of all the indifferent negativity it holds for us in the 'natural' order of capital" (166). When, shortly afterward in the film, death finally materializes and Amador passes away (about one-third into the movie), Marcela must confront a moral dilemma: if she communicates Amador's death to the family, she risks losing her job and her pay. The order of capital threatens with turning Amador's death meaningless, its exchange-value being absorbed by its use-value. Ultimately, Marcela decides to hide the news from Amador's daughter for as many weeks as possible to avoid being fired, but this occultation does not respond to an attitude of denial or "indifferent negativity," nor does it obey to immoral self-interest. Through a performance based on acting, Marcela productively and positively imbues Amador's dead body with posthumous life by keeping the body on the bed, returning every day to take care of the apartment, and sharing her life with Amador.

Two-thirds of the film happen, in a literal sense, posthumously, that is, after the death of the character that gives the film its title.[9] And the director reminds us of that by returning repeatedly to Amador's bedroom where we see his dead body covered with a bed sheet. As Margaret Schwartz has argued, "[a]s 'remains,' the corpse is a referential thing—it is the remains *of someone*. . . . [It] always references a human departure, a specific subject who has left it behind" (4). However, neither Amador's body nor his material belongings tell a complete story of his life, and we do not learn any more information than what was already available to us before his death: that Amador is a widower and has a daughter; that he occasionally enjoys the company of a prostitute, ironically named Puri; and that he maintains a written correspondence with Adela, a woman who lives in a retirement home in Galicia and whom we never see in the film. Frustrating conventional expectations, the rest of the film will leave unanswered a series of questions regarding Amador's life story, and will instead elaborate on how the life of the dead extends over the time of the living through the symbolic "contagion" of the posthumous to the material world of fiction.

This transference of posthumous value can be analyzed through a series of symbolic elements that are both intimately interrelated and meaningfully associated with death and the suspension of life through a shared disembodied quality. The first one is the written correspondence between Amador and Adela: Amador's last letter, posthumously sent by Marcela, never reaches her addressee since Adela has died in the interim, turning the letter into a message waiting for eternity to be delivered. The survival of Amador's letter in ghostly form is a clue to interpret the posthumous life of another piece of writing with even further-reaching implications for the film's structure: the farewell letter that Marcela writes for Nelson right at the beginning of the film. As we saw back then, Marcela had torn up this letter into pieces when she learnt of her pregnancy, thus putting on hold her plans to go back to Peru. But the letter has not "died," as she kept all the pieces in the false bottom of a tin box with her passport, some old pictures, and other valuables. This allows the letter to come back to life at the end of the film when Marcela discovers Nelson's infidelity and leaves the pieces—and the message— for him to reassemble.

The piecemeal, suspended quality of these letters connects them to two other objects in the film that have been disassembled. This time, however, the elements are not written but visual: a jigsaw puzzle, which Amador completes daily while resting on his bed, and a torn-up photograph. An amusing exchange between Marcela and Amador about the meaninglessness of doing puzzles opens the complex continuity between these two elements: "No entiendo que se tomen tanto trabajo de romper la fotografía en pedacitos. ¿Por qué no se la dieron con las

Figure 8.2, Not-so-pious portrait of Yolanda praying for the departed, courtesy of Reposado P.C. and Film Movement

piezas ya juntas?" (I don't understand why one would make the effort to break the photograph in little pieces. Why didn't they give it to you all in one piece?) asks Marcela. And Amador responds by making a meditation on the jigsaw puzzle as a metaphor for life. For him, a puzzle and a photography are the same thing, but they are different as well: "si haces tú las cosas salen diferentes, los rompeca-bezas y lo que no son rompecabezas. Todo" (if you do things yourself, then the results are different, puzzles and not puzzles. Everything). This gives Marcela an interpretive cue for her own predicament: it is a torn-up photograph (showing Nelson and Fanny, a younger friend of Marcela who also works in the flower business, holding hands in a very affectionate posture and looking at the camera) that will later confirm, its pieces having been reassembled, Nelson's suspected infidelity to Marcela. Devastated by this discovery, Marcela attempts to take her life by swallowing all the prescription pills that, to avoid the neighbors' suspicion, she had continued to buy from the pharmacy after Amador's passing. This sui-cide attempt constitutes a final ironic inversion of the puzzle as a life metaphor: if the pills can be considered to be small pieces that (medically) sustain life, they become the almost realization of death when put together.

Photography has a life beyond the relationship with the puzzles we just men-tioned. Photographs feature prominently in previous films by León de Aranoa (*Familia* and *Barrio*), where they function metaphorically as "corpses" in the way that Schwartz was referred to earlier: they are the "remains *of someone*," references to someone's past. Photography's mediatory nature in the director's aesthetic catechism, however, is not entirely reliable, but rather full of misleading traps. In *Barrio*, as Steve Marsh has cogently demonstrated, "photographs lie," laden as they are "with a kind of counterfeit or substitute affectivity founded upon a notion that they represent a strata in the family history that was once real" (174). In *Amador*, although most of the photographs are generic and with the camera always at a prudent symbolic distance, those that are invested with diegetic value must be approached with a healthy distrust toward the supposed sincerity they depict. One of them is the first communion portrait of a young girl (most likely Amador's daughter Yolanda) that is placed on top of Amador's bedroom dresser. (Fig. 8.2) This portrait is seen most distinctly when the camera shows, through the dresser mirror's reflection, the motionless body of Marcela on the bed after her suicide attempt. For a few seconds, we are able to see the innocent, smiling face of a girl in communion dress, her hands in prayer, in stark contrast with the image of Marcela's dying body next to the rotting corpse of Amador. The juxtaposition between photography and reflection in this shot creates an ironic effect that transforms the portrait into some kind of funeral votive showing someone *praying* for the soul of the departed/departing. Inevitably, this effect turns the angelical portrait of Yolanda into a satirical commentary on her manipulative, hypocritical, and not-so-pious attitude at the end of the film, when it is revealed that she's fraudulently *preying* on her dead father's pension to pay for her beach house.

Conversely, the photograph with the most diegetic value in the film—Nelson and Fanny's—does not lie. Rather, it reveals the sense of painful "truth" that the image re-presents, immediately turning Marcela's theretofore "real" relationship with Nelson (the one on this side of the photograph) into a lie. But beyond that, *Amador* invites the spectator to consider the relationship of photography with death and with the art of cinema. As instantiations of the photographic art, and regardless of their content, the photographs that we see in the film bear a meaningful association between death and the posthumous that has been extensively explored in theoretical discourse. Jonathan Auerbach synthesizes this multi-pronged connection through Roland Barthes's *Camera Lucida*:

> [F]or Barthes the moment the photo is snapped entails the self-mortification of the subject: "*Life / Death*: the paradigm is reduced to a simple click, the one separating the initial pose from the final print." "Whether or not the subject is already dead," he continues, "every photograph is this catastrophe." Yet the photograph for Barthes remains moribund not because of the fixity or falsity of the image; rather, photography always marks a "return of the dead" by virtue of the

absolute indexicality of the medium, which, he emphasizes, must always leave traces of past reality. (128–29)

As it was already noted, photographs in *Amador* lack the capacity to leave diegetic traces for the spectator. This, I would contend, is due to the fact that photographs coexist in the film with the lifeless body of Amador as a medium that portrays death in ways that are all the more real: photography's indexical power vis-à-vis the corpse's metonymical reference to death. Simultaneously, Amador's corpse exerts a haunting effect on cinema itself and, as per Mulvey's idea above, it concentrates the inanimate, ghostly presence of photography at the root of cinema, a stilled fragment within the continuum of cinematic time.

On a similar vein, Lesley Stern has explored in *Dead and Alive: The Body as Cinematic Thing* the performative impact that dead bodies have on the relationship that cinema establishes with time and the phenomenological materiality of reality: "bodies once living and now dead which somehow, in their corporeal materiality, exhibit a performative potential for conjuring a quality of cinematic thingness." Furthermore, Stern notes, they introduce "a mode of temporality that evoques [a] conception of quotidian rhythm. They appear to us, as do things, in a cinema characterised by a democratisation of things and persons" (4). This idea is key to analyze Fernando León's specific use of two techniques each in a relevant scene in the film to articulate a visual notion of the posthumous based on an enhanced materiality of things. The first one is the color palette deployed in the scenes inside Amador's apartment, a chronotope that couples domesticity and intimacy with different forms of temporal suspension in the film. The warm chromatic combination (yellows, oranges, and ochers) intensifies the sense of stasis brought about, first, by the deadly association of the summer season with heat waves and exponential death among the elderly, as we had noted at the beginning of this chapter. At the same time, these colors also contribute to the state of disrepair and past-ness of the space of the apartment, which N. Michelle Murray has extensively analyzed: "the dated décor in Amador's apartment suggests a bygone era and structural decay," intensifying the positions of isolation and marginality that both Amador and Marcela occupy in contemporary Spain (*Home* 146).[10] More important, the colors of the apartment elicit a feeling similar to that of looking at an old sepia picture and intensify the visual texture of the film, emphasizing the uncanny cohabitation of the photographic still within the celluloid frame and creating a dislocation between visual, historical, and narrative times.

Nowhere is this relationship more eloquent than in the scene portraying the death of Amador. In this scene, the meticulous use of camerawork translates in visual terms the cluttered temporality that follows the happening of death and

Figure 8.3. Framing Amador's dead body, courtesy of Reposado P.C. and Film Movement

the state of in-betweenness that Marcela goes on to occupy. This is conveyed first through what Barbara Klinger calls an "arresting image": usually associated with art films, arresting images are conveyed formally through an impeccable sense of composition that slows down the narrative *tempo* and absorbs the spectator's attention, "often appearing outside of time in a fantasy or dream-like dimension" (24). These formal aspects enhance the dramatic quality of the scene while over-shadowing its meaning. At the affective level, the arresting image has an "ability to stoke emotions in the audience that have been building through the film," but despite its power to function as "a focal point for emotions, this image does not typically provide sure resolution or catharsis [and] its emotional effects are both intricate and obscure" (24). *Amador's* arresting image occurs exactly the moment after Amador exhales his last breath and dies peacefully in bed. Despite being one of cinema's favorite clichés, life-to-death transitions are decisive moments in movie plots that the camera always fears: fixing on a lifeless body entails the threat of cinema's regression to the photographic still and its own dissolution. In Amador's dying scene, the director switches protagonicity to Marcela, who is reading at a small table at the end of the hallway across from Amador's bedroom, a suitable spatial metaphor for the idea of death as passage or transition. For twenty-five seconds, each distinctly marked with the ticking sound of a chiming wall clock over a Latin song being played on the radio, the camera very slowly zooms in on Marcela from Amador's bedroom. Feeling something eerie, a sensation conveyed through the painfully slow forward movement of the camera, Marcela stops turning the magazine's pages (another transitional metaphor) and

Figure 8.4. Marcela's passing to the other side, courtesy of Reposado P.C. and Film Movement

raises her eyes in the direction of the camera with a look of silent concern. Before the arresting image comes to an end, the clock starts chiming loudly, making a somewhat ironic announcement that the time of Amador has come and inaugurating the film's posthumous temporality.

The scene cuts then to Marcela, who, after an indefinite amount of time, enters the bedroom with a cup of tea and finds Amador's lifeless body on the bed. The camera fixates on Marcela's shocked reaction in a frontal shot that leaves Amador's body out of the frame. The director places her on the right side of the composition, leaving the open door of the room and a light switch on the left half of the shot. Indirectly haunted by the dead body we cannot see, each of those elements is a clear death metaphor—one pointing to the idea of departure, the other to the lights going out for him. As Marcela now becomes a witness to the death of Amador, she is also turned into a deferred mirror of the spectator's affective impasse from a few seconds earlier, when they witnessed Amador's exact moment of passing. This effect is formally enhanced by switching to a different camera angle that yields a most significant composition of the room through the use of a large mirror placed on the wall facing Amador's bed (which, I would contend, is an homage to Jean Cocteau's sustained use of the mirror in *Orphée* [1950] as a threshold connecting the world of the living with the underworld). (Fig. 8.3) With Marcela now to the left of the shot, the big bedroom mirror on the right allows us to observe Amador's body only indirectly through a blurred reflection. The shot is interrupted as Marcela flees the apartment in fear, not before the camera cuts to a close shot of Amador's hand still holding a piece of the puzzle.

When Marcela has gathered the courage to return to the apartment later, the director resumes the interrupted composition and asks the spectator for renewed attention to it. With a much calmer countenance this time, Marcela starts walking very carefully around the bed, in a move (left to right) that she had not dared to do earlier. (Fig. 8.4) This movement, swift but gentle, creates two most significant stills with powerful symbolic meaning: the first one happens when she almost imperceptibly slows her pace down to look at Amador. At this exact moment, Marcela's body obstructs Amador's reflection in the mirror, and it is now her figure becoming engulfed by the mirror's frame while remaining *outside* of it. The superimposition of Marcela over Amador's image places her in the center of the composition, suggesting the idea that Amador's gift has been finally given and it is Marcela (and her fetus) who occupy his place now. The second image happens three seconds later, after she resumes her passing movement and completes her transition to *the other side* of the room no longer looking at the bed but gazing forward in a somewhat phantasmal manner. This time, it is not Marcela but her reflection that appears *inside* the mirror. Marcela's passing in front of the mirror,

Figure 8.5. Marcela looking back to the dead, courtesy of Reposado P.C. and Film Movement

and the multiple illusions it creates, indicates her passing from the time of the living to a posthumous time, sharing in Amador's otherworldly space.

During this transition, we are also allowed to have a more complete view of the composition, one that calls attention to an old sepia-colored picture inserted in the frame of the mirror and whose generic content (two friends posing for the camera) does not seem to be connected to anything specific. However, that seemingly meaningless photograph becomes a fundamental piece: first, the shot's composition calls for a symbolic association between the photograph and the puzzle piece in Amador's hand (a photograph as the missing piece in Marcela's life dilemma); second, the photograph allows to compose a multi-framed image that includes the film shot, the mirror with Amador's reflection, the photograph itself, and the puzzle piece. These are all framed images with multiple temporalities and meanings, but they are all subjugated by a metadiscursive commentary on the intersection between photography and specular reflection as both indexical relationships with death (one metaphorical, the other real), as well as the relationship between cinema and photography as one mediated by death and the posthumous (and, in this case, literally through the corpse as medium).

Cinema's imperative of movement pushes forward the stilled temporality beckoned to by the corpse, eliciting the most evocative feeling of posthumousness in the film. As Jonathan Auerbach puts it, "cinema serves to perpetually postpone revealing the corpse that photographs inevitably instantiate" (131), a dictum that Marcela observes almost religiously as she covers Amador's body with a sheet for the rest of the film. Compelled by material (that is, financial) reasons, Marcela enters a race to keep Amador's body "alive" by attempting to stop time. Turned into a kind of postmodern Scheherazade—fiction as a mechanism to stop time and preserve, not one's own life, but someone else's death—Marcela accumulates a series of both practical and symbolic objects in Amador's bedroom: the roses (a common funeral decoration that symbolizes the idea of evanescence and fleeting time), the air freshener (which Marcela applies to both the roses and the body of Amador), the fan (which Marcela uses to keep the air as fresh as possible), and the TV (which she keeps running to avoid raising the neighbors' suspicions, and where we see Jordi Hurtado, a Spanish TV host who, in popular culture, is sarcastically referred to as being immortal). All of these objects are instrumental for Marcela to hold back time and conjure up the "afterlife" of Amador. In addition, the visual continuity between these objects and the lifeless body of Amador tinges the latter with a thing-like quality in front of the camera, his human boundaries getting blurred and becoming almost objectified.

Visually, the film will again invite the viewer to consider how desperately Marcela struggles with her own state of in-betweenness. When Marcela has already grown accustomed to a life with the dead body of Amador, a series of unexplained occurrences (open windows, moving fan, unfamiliar objects popping up in the home) instill in her an irrational fear that the ghost of Amador is playing with her as revenge for hiding his death and not giving him proper burial. To placate her own terror, she moves the mirror in Amador's bedroom to be able to "control" with her gaze the corpse of the old man from across the hallway. (Fig. 8.5) The carefully crafted composition of Marcela looking back toward Amador's mirror (and, therefore, toward death) as she slowly moves away from the bedroom through the hallway evokes the mythical image of Orpheus's look back at Eurydice. Portrayed numerous times throughout the history of Western art, this critical moment represents the tragic separation of the lovers and, following Orpheus's inability to follow the conditions imposed by Hades, the impossibility of bringing the dead back to life. The likeness that León de Aranoa's way of crafting this image bears to the classical myth suggests a deliberate attempt by Marcela to distance herself from Amador, but she proves herself again unable to break up with him. Following her emotional breakdown after she finds out about Nelson's infidelity, she attempts to end her life and reunite with Amador by lying down next to his dead body on his deathbed. The director's decision to show this moment, again, through the mirror's reflection will produce yet another instantiation of Marcela's inhabiting the world of the dead. Only, this time, to be interrupted by the unexpected visit of Puri, who brings Marcela back from the realm of the dead.

At the end of the film, Amador's daughter, Yolanda, returns from the beach with her husband and confronts Marcela about the death of Amador. To Marcela's surprise, however, Yolanda proposes to keep hiding the death of her father to continue cashing Amador's pension. Like Marcela, Yolanda and her family have been hit by the financial crisis and they also need the money, but for very different reasons: as opposed to Marcela's transformation of her immaterial labor into a work of mourning, Yolanda is only seeking to finish her family beach house. Furthermore, Marcela quietly discovers during the conversation that Yolanda and her husband (who is waiting outside while they talk) had known about Amador's death all along—she notices him throwing on the street a mint wrapping of the same kind that she had discovered in the apartment a few days earlier. Underneath a seemingly friendly agreement that puts both characters at an equal moral level, Marcela knows now that Yolanda is acting a role—and an utterly condescending one—in front of her. With this, the film frustrates the expectations of spectators thirsty for an easy and conciliatory ending, especially if it involves an immigrant "other" being pardoned by a national "self" as a precondition for turning both into partners in crime. Indeed, both sides make a questionable use of a dead body for economic purposes, but the film, based on Marcela's final gaze upon Yolanda and the tone of her voice, suggests Marcela's elevation to a plane of moral superiority. By revealing Yolanda and her husband as impostors, the film opens up to the possibility of redemption for Marcela's own performance, both in the sense of the lie that she lived with Nelson, and in the sense of the fiction that she will continue carrying out with Amador's body.

When the film ends, the spectator does not know if Amador's body has been or will be buried somewhere. After all, the financial crisis in Spain made even more financially burdensome for families to put their dead to rest in cemeteries or columbaries, intensifying the feeling that death had become a privatized affair (Congostrina). The film's closing scene, however, is packed with hidden meanings that deserve careful commentary with regards to the final destination of Amador's remains on a symbolic level. The scene shows Marcela sitting on a park bench with a suitcase next to her. Although the suitcase only appears briefly and the camera does not engage it in any special form (such as close up), it is possible to identify in this particular object a series of meanings related to movement, death, and containment mixed with hints of dark comedy. First, the suitcase stands as an index of the literal and symbolic voyage that Marcela is now ready to resume, reminding spectators of the trip back home that many immigrants who had arrived from countries like Bolivia or Ecuador were forced to do when the economic recession hit Spain (Cerrutti and Maguid 169–72). It is also true, however, that Marcela's immediate plans are never explicitly mentioned, and we should not automatically assume that she is going back to Peru as she intended at the beginning of the film. The suitcase also evokes the experiential

baggage, the cherished memories and the unique experiences that Marcela carries with her now. It speaks to the transformation of her identity as a migrant
and, in the face of death, it brings to mind Antonio Machado's famous luggage
metaphor: "Y cuando llegue el día del último viaje, / y esté al partir la nave que
nunca ha de tornar, / me encontraréis a bordo ligero de equipaje, / casi desnudo,
como los hijos de la mar" (102) (And when the day of the last journey comes into
sight, / and the boat which never returns is casting free, / you'll find me on board
and I'll be travelling light, / almost naked, like the children of the sea) (39). It is
precisely by virtue of Machado's alignment of the idea of luggage with death as
departure, that the suitcase finally becomes a new iteration of the materialities
of passing, awkwardly standing in resemblance to a tombstone that replaces the
physical resting place of Amador's remains, but also of a (portable) closet where
Marcela hides her skeletons. In sum, the suitcase is a reminder of the posthumous condition that Marcela now inhabits and a new form of matter that speaks
to the continuing, complementary temporality of the joint journey that Marcela
and Amador initiate.

As Bjerregaard and others remind us, a "healthy" grief does not necessarily
entail a complete severing of the ties with the lost ones, and holding on to the
dead does not necessarily lead to irreversible melancholia: "the bereaved tend to
establish 'continuing bonds' with the deceased. . . . Such ties are emotional and
material, and suggest that memory of that which has passed is not merely subjective or a temporal state of suspension, but can issue forth as a socially shared and
durable relationship" (13). Marcela's continuing bond with Amador shows how
cultural spaces for the posthumous open up possibilities beyond (and against)
the cultivation of disaster narratives. With *Amador*, Fernando León explores the
posthumous as a space of co-existence that incorporates both the living and the
dead; death as something not to be feared but embraced and looked in the face.
Amador is abandoned by his family, but he gets the privilege to experience death
in a domestic, quotidian environment, and in the company of others (human or
otherwise). Seen from León's personal lens, life after death is life with the dead
and life with death.

NOTES

1. For the immigrant as abject opposite of the purity of the national body, see Palardy;
    for León's interplay through the cinematic gaze to raise awareness about the social and
    institutional invisibility of marginal subjects, see Murray "Politics"; for the articulation
    of fluid, relational subjectivities to destabilize fixed ideas of identity, see Prádanos;

for the anticipation of new social and national configurations, see Cornejo Parriego and Domingo Amestoy; for the resignification of stereotypes of otherness, see Pérez.

2. Although relevant in a discussion about the exclusion of the dead, I am not referring here to marginalization for religious orthodoxy or political affiliation. In fact, the historical tendency in Spain to segregate "true" Catholics from unorthodox or atheists, as José Jiménez Lozano meticulously studied in *Los cementerios civiles*, could very well be seen as an action within the symbolic order. Death, and the exclusion of the *other* dead, is a mechanism that interprets a "natural" event within the realm of political theology.

3. Starting with *Amador*, Fernando León has consistently incorporated dead bodies in his films, as it is apparent in his later films *A Perfect Day* (2015), which opens with a corpse being pulled upward from the bottom of a pit, and *Loving Pablo* (2018), with countless scenes of explicit killings that portray the hardest years of drug-trafficking violence in Colombia.

4. Robert E. Watkins analyzes how the myth of American individualism has relied on a political narrative of revenge: "The vengeance ritually invoked in movies as a naturalized response to loss amounts to an effort to deny subjectivity, dependency, and vulnerability and reassert sovereignty and control over the unruly world of social relations" (2–3).

5. This is something that applies not only to lifeless but also to living bodies. León de Aranoa's frequent use of close-ups and extreme close-ups to frame the films' main characters indeed function as physical and symbolic approximations to their affective interiority (see Black 79). These visual techniques, however, compel the viewer to reflect on mortality, one's own and the other's, and to challenge the constructed nature of fiction. As Emmanuel Levinas theorizes,

> [f]ace of the other—underlying all the particular forms of expression in which he or she, already right "in character," plays a role—is no less pure expression, extradition with neither defense nor cover, precisely the extreme rectitude of a facing, which in this nakedness is an exposure unto death: nakedness, destitution, passivity, and pure vulnerability. Face as the very mortality of the other human being. (167)

6. Germán Labrador Méndez has spoken of a "temporality of crisis" to refer to "a distinct historical period (a chronotope), whose contours become visible in the shared awareness of finding oneself collectively exposed to a new distribution of biopolitical violence . . . a threatening articulation of macroeconomics over private individual spheres, which, if it is to be tackled, requires the public collective deployment of bodies, stories and common affects" ("Cannibal" 245).

7. By calling the spectators' attention to the temporal consequences of what Germán Labrador Méndez calls a "nutritional language of *the crisis*", the film brings to the surface "the fact that hunger and undernourishment [had] been erased from the Spanish democracy's collective imaginary" ("Cannibal" 245, 251).

8. Although not the focus of this essay, it is important to pay attention to how Marcela both reproduces and challenges cultural constructions of women as child bearers and caregivers of dependents, which become biological and cultural impediments for women's attainment of equal degrees of autonomy. This tension cannot be fully understood without Marcela's own road to independence after she breaks up with Nelson at the end of the film: the character not only embodies a caretaker of forms of life in transition but is herself an active life moving toward autonomy.

9. Spectators familiar with León de Aranoa's previous work are bound to notice that Amador is also the name of the character who dies by suicide in *Los lunes al sol*. If one adds to this that the character is played by the same actor (Celso Bugallo), then it becomes difficult to not see a sense of symbolic continuity at work between these two characters (widowers, Galician, living alone), to the point that it may very well be argued that *Amador* happens, in fact, posthumously in its entirety.

10. N. Michelle Murray analyzes how the home space in disrepair functions as a broader metaphor for the nation and the need for social regeneration, supported by the death of the national (Amador) and the arrival of new populations (Marcela and her baby). *Amador*, says Murray, "transmits the destruction of the past as Spain sallies forth toward an unclear, cosmopolitan future with diverse cultural elements" (*Home* 150). I believe, nonetheless, that the film invests more in visual terms to propose, not a clear-cut contrast or juxtaposition of times (past versus present/future), as Murray argues, but a dislocation of visual, historical, and narrative times brought about by the posthumous condition that haunts the film after Amador's death.

WORKS CITED

Auerbach, Jonathan. *Body Shots: Early Cinema's Incarnations.* University of California Press, 2007.

Baudrillard, Jean. *Symbolic Exchange and Death.* Translated by Iain Hamilton Grant, Sage, 1993.

Bjerregaard, Peter, Anders Emil Rasmussen, and Tim Flohr Sørensen. "Introducing Materialities of Passing." *Materialities of Passing: Explorations in Transformation, Transition and Transience*, edited by Peter Bjerregaard, Anders Emil Rasmussen, and Tim Flohr Sørensen, Routledge, 2016, pp. 1–23.

Black, Kyle. "La inmigración y la labor inmaterial en *Amador* (2010) de Fernando León de Aranoa." *Transmodernity*, vol. 7, no. 2, 2017, pp. 73–96.

Cerrutti, Marcela Sandra, and Alicia Maguid. "Crisis económica en España y el retorno de inmigrantes sudamericanos." *Migraciones internacionales*, vol. 8, no. 3, January–June 2016, pp. 155–89.

Congostrina, Alfonso L. "Colau crea una funeraria para reducir un 30% el precio del entierro." *El País*, 11 Nov. 2016.

Cornejo-Parriego, Rosalía. "Espacios híbridos, iconos mestizos: Imaginando la España global." *Letras Peninsulares*, vol. 15, no. 3, 2002, pp. 515–31.

Domingo Amestoy, Susana. "Postmodern Realisms: Memory, Family and the Collapse of the Nation in Fernando León de Aranoa's Films." *Collapse, Catastrophe and Rediscovery: Spain's Cultural Panorama in the Twenty-First Century*, edited by Jennifer Brady, Ibon Izurieta, and Ana María Medina, Cambridge Scholars, 2014, pp. 113–34.

Garcés, Marina. "*Conditio posthuma*." *The Great Regression*, edited by Heinrich Geiselberger, Polity, 2017, pp. 1–19.

Instituto Nacional de Estadística. "Defunciones según la Causa de Muerte 2003." *Instituto Nacional de Estadística—Notas de Prensa*, 24 Nov. 2005, pp. 1–7.

Jiménez Lozano, José. *Los cementerios civiles y la heterodoxia española*. Seix Barral, 2008.

Klinger, Barbara. "The Art Film, Affect and the Female Viewer: *The Piano* Revisited." *Screen*, vol. 28, no. 1, Spring 2006, pp. 19–41.

Kracauer, Siegfried. *Theory of Film: The Redemption of Physical Reality*. Oxford University Press, 1960.

Kristeva, Julia. *The Powers of Horror: An Essay on Abjection*. Translated by Leon S. Roudiez, Columbia University Press, 1982.

Labrador Méndez, Germán. "The Cannibal Wave: The Cultural Logic of Spain's Temporality of Crisis (Revolution, Biopolitics, Hunger and Memory)." *Journal of Spanish Cultural Studies*, vol. 15, no. 1–2, 2014, pp. 241–71.

―――――. "The Political Death of Live Bodies: Necropolitics and Radical Solidarity after the 2008's Crisis in Spain." Modern Language Association Convention, 6 Jan. 2018, Hilton Hotel, New York, New York. Session 601: Materiality and the Cultures of Death in Spain. Conference Presentation.

León de Aranoa, Fernando, director. *Amador*. Reposado Producciones, 2010.

Levinas, Emmanuel. *Entre Nous. Thinking-of-the-Other*. Translated by Michael B. Smith and Barbara Harshav, Columbia University Press, 1998.

Machado, Antonio. *Campos de Castilla*, edited by Geoffrey Ribbans, Cátedra, 1999.

―――――. *Campos de Castilla*. Translated by Patrick H. Sheerin, Junta de Castilla y León, 2011.

Marsh, Steven. "Tracks, Traces and Common Places: Fernando León de Aranoa's *Barrio* (1998) and the Layered Landscape of Everyday Life in Contemporary Madrid." *New Cinemas: Journal of Contemporary Film*, vol. 1, no. 3, 2002, pp. 165–73.

Mulvey, Laura. *Death 24x a Second: Stillness and the Moving Image*. Reaktion Books, 2006.

Murray, N. Michelle. *Home Away from Home: Immigrant Narratives, Domesticity, and Coloniality in Contemporary Spanish Culture*. UNC. Department of Romance Studies, 2018.

―――――. "The Politics of Looking in Fernando León de Aranoa's *Princesas* (2005)." *Studies in Spanish and Latin American Cinemas*, vol. 11, no. 3, 2014, pp. 241–53.

Palardy, Diana. "Lust and Disgust: The Rhetoric of Abjection in the Spanish Immigration Films *Bwana*, *Flores de otro mundo* and *Princesas*." *Bulletin of Hispanic Studies*, vol. 92, no. 7, 2015, pp. 826–40.

Pérez, Jorge. "El cine español viste a la otredad femenina caribeña: *Princesas* y la ética de solidaridad transnacional." *Cinema paraíso: Representaciones e imágenes audiovisuales en el Caribe hispano*, edited by Rosana Díaz Zambrana and Patricia Tomé, Isla Negra, 2010, pp. 104–127.

Prádanos, Luis I. "La mujer inmigrante latinoamericana en el cine español actual: Hacia una identidad cultural-relacional en *Princesas* (2005)." *Confluencia*, vol. 27, no. 2, Spring 2012, pp. 34–45.

Schwartz, Margaret. *Dead Matter: The Meaning of Iconic Corpses*. University of Minnesota Press, 2015.

Stern, Lesley. *Dead and Alive: The Body as Cinematic Thing*. Caboose, 2012.

Watkins, Robert E. *Freedom and Vengeance on Film: Precarious Lives and the Politics of Subjectivity*. I. B. Tauris, 2016.

CHAPTER 9

On Dying Colonialisms and Postcolonial Phantasies in Recent Spanish Cinema

N. Michelle Murray

Two recent epic films revisit Spain's past with Africa and Asia at specific moments of decolonization: *1898: Los últimos de Filipinas* (1898: Our Last Men in the Philippines) (Calvo 2016) and *Palmeras en la nieve* (Palm Trees in the Snow) (González Molina 2015).[1] Both films portray familial decline and colonial endings as associated plot points that gesture toward the films' broader concern with the state of the nation. This nationalist concern connects to the films' respective release dates—2015 and 2016—and the post-2008 economic, political, and social crises that unleashed a collective questioning about how to envision and conceive of Spain. Each 2010s film allegorizes the colony as a space of suffering and death inextricably linked to racialized others in Africa and Asia, yet simultaneously connected to the colonizing nation. Through these representations, the viewer perceives the symbolic force of the colony: along with its economic and social contributions to the colonizing nation, the colony serves as a space for both personal and national fulfillment. Both films thus evoke cultures of death in contemporary Spain, specifically, the distanced realm of the colony as a death-space that facilitates self-definition and transformation.

As the editors of this volume make note, dying bodies, ashes, and bones conjure up their own untimely temporality, and rites, flesh, and stone call upon the individual in several distinct manners that demand different avenues of theorization.

Intertwining these assertions with postcolonial scholarship that aims to "challenge the insularity of historical narratives and historiographical traditions emanating from Europe" (Bhambra 115), this essay examines representations of the colonies in *Últimos* and *Palmeras*. In both films, Spanish nationals travel to colonies in what I consider to be part of a mourning process. Once in the colonial space, they try to make sense of death that has affected them personally so that they may grieve appropriately and, consequently, thrive among the living. Through these journeys, the viewer perceives the extent to which the characters need colonial histories to endure. While Spain's historical dominance of the Americas is widely known, the mournful voyages under study occur in the Philippines in *Últimos* or in Equatorial Guinea in *Palmeras*; these settings broaden the understanding of Spain's colonial history to include nations in Africa and Asia frequently eclipsed by Spain's imperial designs in America from the fifteenth to nineteenth centuries. Through their travels, the protagonists overcome personal brokenness associated with the death of Spaniards to form new attachments of friendship and kinship problematically rooted in the death of the colonized.

The movies present the colonies as areas that contrast with Spain because of their necropolitics: these are lands where suffering and dying are commonplace and where death informs life. These relations reflect Michel Foucault's theory of biopower. For Foucault, biopower is the technological and political management of life; it is "a power that has taken control of both the body and life or that has . . . taken control of life in general—with the body as one pole and the population as the other" (253). Biopower thus hinges upon the state's social and political control of human life, with decidedly racist and colonialist undertones. Foucault introduces race into his discussion of biopower through the question, "Given that this power's objective is essentially to make live, how can it let die? How can the power of death, the function of death, be exercised in a political system centered upon biopower?" (254). Racism answers this query. Foucault states that racism is "primarily a way of introducing a break into the domain of life that is under power's control: the break between what must live and what must die. . . . That is the first function of racism: to fragment, to create caesuras within the biological continuum addressed by biopower" (254–55). These divisions potentially construct people and, by extension, the geographical areas associated with those people, as sites of life or death.

In "Necropolitics," Achille Mbembe draws upon Foucault's concept of biopower to theorize the aforementioned politics of death. Expanding upon Foucault's concern with life to analyze death and the wounded or slain body, Mbembe interrogates the death often associated with the colonies and racialized Others who exist there ("Necropolitics" 12). Mbembe explains, "In the economy of biopower, the function of racism is to regulate the distribution of death and to make possible the murderous functions of the state" (17). As Mbembe observes throughout the essay, the state not only wields the right to kill, but also to maim, to harm, to suspend life, to enslave, or to subjugate some bodies to various states of injury. Referring to slavery specifically, Mbembe theorizes the "spectacle of pain inflicted on the slave's body" wherein "[v]iolence ... becomes an element in manners ... aimed at instilling terror" (21). Death, which Mbembe notes is pivotal to the transatlantic slave trade of Africans and colonial designs in Africa (and elsewhere), forms part of a life-building process for European subjects rooted in the Western dialectical tradition. He contends that,

> The subject of Marxian modernity is, fundamentally, a subject who is intent on proving his or her sovereignty *through the staging of a fight to the death.* Just as with Hegel, the narrative of mastery and emancipation here is clearly linked to a narrative of truth and death. Terror and killing become the means of realizing the already known telos of history. ("Necropolitics" 20; my emphasis)

Here, the death inextricably linked to the colony gestures toward the life that defines the colonizer.

As my reading of the two films in question contends, colonialism and racial capitalism are predicated upon colonizers controlling death abroad. In this fashion, colonial relations manifest the underbelly of biopower, a necropower endowed with the right to kill and to exact violence against the colonized. In *A Critique of Black Reason,* Mbembe postulates that colonial power is "a *funerary* power that tended to reify the death of the colonized and deny that their life had any kind of value" (128). In both *Palmeras* and *Últimos,* mournful voyages cause Spanish nationals to travel to the colony and then *return* to Spain. Their routes underscore the extent to which European subjectivity emerges from colonial encounters. Referring specifically to the colonizers' control of death, Mbembe writes that "power is what was able to escape death and return from among the dead. For it is only in escaping death and returning from the dead that one acquires the capacity to make oneself into the other side of the absolute" (*Critique* 133). It follows, therefore, that in the films under study, after colonial voyages, Spanish nationals are able to overcome personal losses and form new affective bonds that enable them to survive the death that surrounds them.

For renowned historian Paul Gilroy, the colony is

> more than an extractive commercial operation. No longer merely a settlement, an adventure, an opportunity, a place for self-creation, self-discovery, and a space of

death, it can be recognized as a laboratory, a location for experiment and innovation that transformed the exercise of governmental powers at home and configured the institutionalization of imperial knowledge to which the idea of "race" was central. (46)

Gilroy acknowledges the colony's economic role, but signals its symbolic significance as a site through which colonizing peoples and nations came into being as subjects who constructed racial hierarchies and knowledges that stripped the colonized of their humanity and subjectivity. Colonies and colonized people, as a result, become the "nonself," "the unsayable," and "the concealed" (Khanna 5). Through this world- and border-making, knowledge about life and the self emerges from the social and symbolic death colonization projected onto overseas territories, which enables the national community to cohere.

Últimos and *Palmeras* also engage with death more abstractly as they represent decolonization or the virtual "death" of Spain's imperial designs in two specific nations. In these movies intended for a twenty-first-century audience, the former colony represents unresolved death, both for the Spanish nation and for nationals who embody it through synecdoche. Death as trope in these films gestures toward both unfettered colonial violence and the severed colonial relations that continue to haunt colonizer and colonized alike. My analysis of the films combines reading them as twenty-first-century portrayals of the death of the colony and theorizing the ways in which suffering and dying figure in these representations. My central argument is that the films resurrect a bygone imperial moment as a manner of coping with the economic and nationalist crises afflicting Spain of the 2010s. While representing the end of Spain's empire in 1898 and 1968, the films also resonate with the 2010s. Both movies embody a conservative, nationalist response to the attacks, both real and imaginary, against the sovereign nation and its attendant national identity: they resurrect Spain's colonial history and showcase injured and dead Black and Asian bodies as a mechanism to emphasize the life and prosperity of a nation immersed in crisis.

Últimos and *Palmeras* make the tensions of Spanish history, transnational cinema, and postcolonial issues evident in their connecting the Philippines and Guinea to Spain. While the producer Mercedes Gamero insists that her film *Palmeras* is "one hundred percent Spanish, in every sense" (AudioVisual451), since the crew and financing, among other elements are Spanish, her stance disavows the film's Colombian backdrop, African actors, and transcontinental plot. Indeed, her position reflects my assertion that the film advances nationalist principles at the expense of erased, disavowed, or even annihilated "foreign" elements that allow the nation to thrive. Contrasting with Gamero's view, as works that focus on

Spain's former colonies, both movies could be classified as "postcolonial cinema," a fluid category that unites postcolonial and cinematic studies. Sandra Ponzanesi and Marguerite Waller observe that "[a]mong Fanon's arguments about the urgent necessity of a new culture and a new human being, which grew out of his work on anti-imperial politics and psychoanalytic theory, it is his thinking about the gaze that is perhaps most pertinent to colonial/postcolonial cinema studies" (5). *Últimos* and *Palmeras* illustrate the ongoing significance of the colonizing gaze, specifically its reiteration through the cinematic apparatus, which allows white Europeans to establish themselves through perceived contrasts with distanced subjects in Africa and Asia.

Los últimos de Filipinas: From Death to Friendship

1898: Los últimos de Filipinas portrays the siege of Baler, a military conflict that transcended the end of the Spanish-American War. For 337 days, fifty-two Spanish soldiers, led by Captain Enrique de las Morenas, held the church compound of San Luis de Toledo, which they had transformed into a makeshift fortress, against the perceived threat of local Tagalogs led by the Filipino commander Colonel Calixto Villacorte in the Luzón region. Cut off from communication with Manila—232 kilometers away—and reluctant to believe perhaps falsified news reports offered by the indigenous population, the Spanish soldiers continued to defend the church in Baler until June 2, 1899, after the war had ended in 1898, with the Treaty of Paris, which stipulated the sale of the Philippines to the United States for twenty million dollars. At first, the United States had not planned to pursue interests in the Southeast Asian archipelago. Then, appealing to God and reason, President McKinley said it was America's duty to "educate the Filipinos, uplift and Christianize them" (qtd. in Miller 24). Infuriated, Spanish negotiators balked at "the immodest demands of a conqueror" (Miller 24). The twenty million dollars were officially offered for Spanish improvements to the island and, more symbolically, to assuage the nation after its defeat (24).

While it premiered in 2016, *Últimos* intersects with many important time periods. The first is the so-called Disaster of 1898, when Spain lost Cuba, the Philippines, and Puerto Rico as a consequence of the Spanish-American War. This defeat consolidated an era of imperial decline in which Spain's overseas holdings shrank considerably and signaled the supposed "end" of the Spanish empire.[2] Spain retained its colonies in sub-Saharan Africa and pursued a colonial war in the Maghreb to attain lands there. Narratives that invoke the 1898 date as the moment of all colonial loss must thus be resituated in light of that moment's symbolic force and the geopolitical realities of Spain's robust colonial position. According to Javier Krauel, "*foreign* critiques of Spanish colonialism coming from both rival imperial powers and present and former Spanish colonies cast Spanish colonialism as a project on the defensive. The more Spain lost its grip on the colonies and the world, the more insistent its affirmative repetition of colonialism became" (63). This issue is also pertinent to the films in question, which perpetuate particular Spanish political discourses that celebrate Spanish colonialism, its *difference* as a relationship of transnational friendship and kinship, and the colonizers' unwavering valor. Such discourses are reluctant to critique Spain's colonial position or colonialism more broadly as a flawed enterprise with problematic nationalist, racist, and sexist implications.

Últimos also revisits the 1945 production *Los últimos de Filipinas* (directed by Antonio Román) about the exact same subject matter.[3] The 1945 movie forms part of a corpus of Spanish films that glorify the imperial past and typify the propagandistic, nationalist cinema of the early years of the Franco dictatorship. The director, Salvador Calvo, insists *Últimos* is not a "remake": "Aquella era una película franquista que narraba las glorias del Imperio, y aquí lo que se cuenta son las miserias y lo dura que es la guerra" (EFE) (the first film was Francoist and narrated imperial glory, and what is told here is the misery and difficulty of war). Nevertheless, in its overarching themes, *Últimos* portrays the hardships of imperial-national-personal loss and emphasizes that both the soldier-protagonists and the empire they serve must negotiate how to assume the death of the colony as an essential feature of their lives. Indeed, *Últimos* is a film that not only features the difficulties of the colonial campaigns, but also the *fin-de-siglo* Disaster of precipitous colonial decline and national corruption. In this way, the film also intersects with the early 2010s moment of crisis.

Últimos depicts necropower in one of its most obvious articulations: colonial war. The movie begins with a massacre of Spaniards in Baler in October 1897, narrated in a voice-over. The 1945 film uses the same formal technique at the beginning of the film, leading Juan Enrique Gonzálvez Vallés to assert, "Este elemento narrativo es totalmente innecesario y sólo su objetivo propagandístico justifica su uso. La descripción del entorno de los españoles y lo que les acontecía en las Islas Filipinas no aporta nada nuevo a lo que dice la propia imagen" (57) (This narrative element [the voice-over] is totally unnecessary and only its objective as propaganda justifies its use. The description of the Spaniards' environment and what happened to them in the Philippines does not add anything new to what the image itself says). Thus, in its style and in its subject matter, the 2016 film shares qualities with the Franco-era piece known to be nationalist propaganda. The voice-over in the twenty-first-century version explains that a Spanish battalion was ambushed and slaughtered; only two men survived. The soldier-protagonists of the film have one mission: "recuperar aquel pueblo maldito y la grandeza de España" (recover that damned town and the greatness of Spain). Death is the axis around which the plot unfolds, specifically, the deaths of Spanish soldiers in the war that will lead to the loss of overseas territories. These deaths fuel the mission of the film's protagonists, who must not only avenge this defeat, but also defend the Filipino colony from the growing insurrection.

Allowing the Filipinos to take the land reminds the viewer of psychoanalytic theories of melancholia, since decolonization is, in a sense, equivalent to losing part of itself, and the Spanish nation-state cannot bear this territorial loss if it is to retain a problematic version of sovereignty premised on maintaining its overseas empire.[4] The soldiers' objective is directly connected to the nation-state's melancholia: that is, its inability to surrender the colony, problematically envisaged as a deathly, damned double that makes the glory of the metropolis possible. In *Últimos*, death is an equalizer. Spanish bodies are viewed as equally vulnerable as those of the Filipinos, and the Filipinos and Spaniards become one in death. At this point, the ultimate fear of the colonizing subject becomes clear: the subjection to death at the core of colonial necropolitics.

The film's themes of unconscionable loss and melancholia intensify through the protagonists' individual stories. When the new troops arrive in Baler, Lieutenant Martín Cerezo (Luis Tosar) confesses that he has lost his wife and daughter in Spain to tuberculosis. He has nothing left at home, so he vows that he will never leave the colony. The colony thus morphs into a substitute self-actualizing mission for the beleaguered soldier whose domestic life in Spain has fallen apart. The lieutenant's individual campaign of never surrendering functions as a compensatory gesture rooted in self-definition, and his mission reflects the more general colonial recuperation effort. Interestingly, to overcome death, he confronts it, even cloaks himself in it by enlisting in the colonial war. As a counterpoint to Lieutenant Cerezo, there is a young and naïve soldier named Carlos (Álvaro Cervantes) who is afraid to fight and die. Upon arriving in Baler, he gazes upon blood smeared on the wall from the 1897 massacre in horror. In a visual twist, the viewer learns that he prefers to paint, and his paintings soon decorate the church walls once covered in abject waste. Conceptually aligned with the colonial mission, Carlos's artwork ought to restore the original color and brilliance to the church structure. His art, furthermore, is a long-lasting cultural production that gestures toward the analogous immortality many soldiers seek in the Philippines through the eternal glory of hero status. With this fictional character, the film softens the imperial focus that otherwise permeates the plot. Moreover, through the characters' divergent approaches to death, the viewer apprehends the deadliness of the mission and the necropolitics governing colonial relations.

The soldiers face death in multiple forms in the Philippines. Baler itself is described as "damned," surrounded by dangerous jungles. In the colonial rebellion, lawlessness appears to reign, which contrasts with centuries of Spanish rule, supposedly marked by law and order. The "sanguinarios" (bloodthirsty) Tagalogs explicitly attempt to kill the Spanish soldiers to reclaim their land. Tellingly, none of the Filipinos are developed as characters. This feature resembles the 1945 propaganda film in which "[t]here is not the slightest interest in the waves of native 'Tagalogs' who are needlessly massacred so that Spaniards can quixotically display their courage in ennobling shots" (Kinder 153). In both films, the Filipinos serve as expendable bodies in the colonizing nation's relentless pursuit of power. Death is their defining characteristic either as murderers who slaughter Spaniards or those whose deaths enable Spanish colonial rule.

In addition to the Filipino fighters, there is one indigenous woman with a speaking role in the film, Teresa (Alexandra Masangkay). She personifies treachery and indecency. In Teresa's first appearance, the curmudgeon Sergeant Jimeno (Javier Gutiérrez) informs the troops that she is a prostitute who spies for the Tagalog insurrects, one of whom is her brother. Her beauty and her enthralling voice are captured in an allusion to the 1945 song "Yo te diré" (I will tell you), which reprises the Franco-era film's soundtrack. Teresa sings the three words in the song's title but refuses to sing the rest, leaving the men—and the audience that assumes their point of view—desiring more. In another telling scene, the Filipino commander mocks the Spanish men by inviting them to abandon their futile mission and to celebrate the end of the war. He strips Teresa and begins to have intercourse with her in front of them. Much like land that colonizers sought to conquer, Teresa's body represents the allure and danger of the colony for the Europeans. Here, Fanon's theory of the phobogenesis of race as a relation that stimulates anxiety is useful (117). Through Teresa, the viewer perceives the ways in which the colonizers may view the colonized through disgust and denigration, but also with potent relations of allure, exoticism, and desire (Hook 168). The film's gender tensions merit additional study, both the representation of Teresa as a gendered symbol of the danger intrinsic to the rebellious colony and of the soldiers who reflect the notion that "the military is where gender works most clearly in the service of colonialism. Empire has not only entailed the policing of bodies in the colonies, but has also directly impacted the gendering of Spain's national citizenry" (Chang 174). Throughout *Últimos*, as in *Palmeras*, erotic consumption becomes one form of colonial erasure, a mechanism that destabilizes boundaries and enables a treacherous Tagalog to destroy the Spanish army or enables would-be colonizers to penetrate and possess both lands and peoples.

My analysis of Teresa is limited to theorizing her role within a symbolic frame-work of death in the colony and critiquing her character's cinematic connections to the 1945 propaganda piece.

Along with the Tagalog rebels, their treacherous woman counterpart, and the overall lawlessness of the insurrection, the very flora and fauna of the colony portend death for the Spanish army. Corralled in the church in Baler, the men have limited access to food. They end up with contaminated provisions from Manila. The food infects them with beriberi, a crippling disease that ensues from vitamin deficiency. The scenes showing the men's disfigured bodies agonizing as a consequence of beriberi heighten the abject quality of the film, a characteristic already present in the initial massacre scenes rife with bloodshed. Social relations of colonialism, gender, and race thus become mapped out through abject scenes that signal the breakdown of borders and the reconfiguration of Filipino and Spanish society as a result of the colonial war.

Opium is another plant that functions to showcase the threatening *nature* of the Philippines. The parish priest, Fray Carmelo (Karra Elejalde), is addicted to opiates and his slow death by drugging resonates with theories of abjection. For Julia Kristeva, the fear of death infecting life is the height of abjection, which can be represented as a breakdown in bodily—and even national and social—borders (53). Abjection emerges in both films through the end of the colonial order; the works render these endings aesthetically in showcasing battered and beaten bodies, caught in the trappings of life and death, thus also reminding us of Mbembe's assertions about the spectacle of pain characteristic of necropower. Returning to the priest, his vocation complicates his portrayal as an addict and signals the abject status of religion, itself a tool of imperial control, at the "end" of empire. The film inscribes themes of death into the actual bellicose colonial history of Baler and the weary men defending themselves in the church. Entangling army and clergy in abject images in *Últimos*, the viewer sees the pillars on which the empire was established and on which it will die.

Unlike the 1945 movie, which unquestioningly exalts the last men in Baler as national heroes, the 2016 *Últimos de Filipinas* interrogates a besieged nationalism with frustrated soldiers asking "¿Qué ha hecho por ti España?" (What has Spain done for you?), and an impassioned debate about the sheer stupidity of a government that would sell the Philippines to the United States for a mere twenty million dollars, when it is clear that the symbolic value of the colony is priceless. As mentioned, the multi-million-dollar figure represents an attempt to ameliorate relations between the United States and Spain, with the Americans essentially paying for their victory. Lieutenant Cerezo also critiques the class dimensions of colonial war, telling Carlos, "España está llena de patriotas como [tu alcalde] don Gabriel, que mandan a otros [a la guerra] mientras ellos comen jamón de bellota" (Spain is full of patriots like [your town's mayor] don Gabriel. Those who send others [to war] while they eat fine ham). The Spanish deaths at the onset of the film are both real—the loss of actual life—and symbolic, expressed in a dying colonialism and strident critiques of the nationalisms underlying and undermining colonial rule. Ironically, in finally assuming these losses, the men return home, hailed as friends and heroes by the very Tagalogs who once wanted to slaughter them. The fatigued soldiers receive a special escort to the end of the Filipino commander's jurisdiction. He explains his kindness with the phrase, "Han sido cuatro siglos, teniente" (It's been four centuries, Lieutenant). He offers a viewpoint of colonialism as longstanding friendship and intimacy and, hence, appears to negate the war occurring only moments before. The legacy of the colony thus appears good and noble because of these men who bravely faced and conquered death in Asia so that they could return home to its antithesis, life, in Spain.

Palmeras en la nieve: From Death to Kinship

In *Últimos*, the Philippines as setting shows the vastness of Spain's empire. Africa, too, was pivotal to Spain's coextensive empire- and nation-building. After relinquishing its territories in Latin America and Asia, Spain led an aggressive colonial campaign in Morocco to acquire lands there and, hence, offset its losses in Latin America. At the same time, Spain retained its holdings in sub-Saharan Africa, specifically, in Equatorial Guinea. Africa thus became the continent through which Spain would attempt to reconstruct itself as a formidable empire during the twentieth century. So Spain's supposed uniqueness because of the Disaster of 1898 is debatable since Spain, like its European neighbors, took part in the land grabs of the twentieth century that would be termed the "European encounter with Africa" or "Scramble for Africa."

Michael Ugarte connects fictions of Equatorial Guinea to its colonization and subjugation. He writes: "the very area of Equatorial Guinea and its construction as a 'nation' (its geographic incongruousness with its islands not in direct alignment with its continental area) is due to a form of the heart of darkness: the 'idea' of creating national boundaries according to the will to perpetuate European political and economic power" ("Heart" 273). Paradoxically, as in the analysis of the friendship at the cornerstone of *1898: Los últimos de Filipinos*, both in *Palmeras* and broader colonial discourse, the fiction of friendship is also a vital element of discourse surrounding African colonization. It is a fiction of friendship because, much like the mapping that served European power, it purposefully misinterprets exploitation to facilitate domination. Mbembe explains:

> false knowledge of Africa is above all misunderstanding and fantasy. But here one fantasizes only in order to exclude, to close in on oneself. One fantasizes only to veil the kind of sovereign disdain that always accompanies claims that the Other is our 'friend,' whether the 'friendship' is real or imaginary, reciprocal or not. (*Critique* 71)

Hence, not only do colonial relations force the colonized into a sort of social death, this death remains rooted in the fantasies of intimacy, friendship, or even kinship that negate the violence integral to these dealings.

In tracing the lineage of the de Rabaltué family of Pasolobino, Huesca, and their contact with Guinea, *Palmeras* makes visible the tensions of necropolitics and an imagined kinship that necessarily negates the violence of the colony. Upon the death of Jacobo (Alain Hernández), his daughter Clarence (Adriana Ugarte) learns that her family has been sending money regularly to the island of Fernando Poo in Equatorial Guinea, where the men in her family had worked until the nation's independence. She intuits they have additional family members there. Combining Clarence's twenty-first-century investigation with events occurring from 1953 to 1970, the film shows the enduring legacy of the colony for this particular Spanish family. Clarence confirms that her uncle, young Kilian de Rabaltué (Mario Casas) raised a family with a Guinean woman named Bisila-Daniela (Berta Vázquez).[5] The romance, however, is fleeting. They both endure violence because of their love, and their family is eventually split apart.

Billed as a holiday film—released on December 25, 2015—and a love story, *Palmeras* contradicts its generic conventions in featuring unfathomable violence that is frequently intimate in nature and a structuring element of the de Rabaltué family's narrative, especially their history in the colonies. It is eventually revealed that Clarence's father Jacobo raped Bisila and possibly fathered her son Laha-Fernando (Michael Batista). The money the family sends ensures Bisila's survival and also finances Laha's study in Spain, showing the ways that twenty-first-century migration issues overlap with the colonial past.[6] After uncovering her secret family in Guinea, Clarence brings Laha and Iniko (Djedje Apali), Laha's half-brother and Clarence's lover, "home" to Aragon in an attempt to incorporate them into the family, an endeavor undeniably complicated by the *blood* history that both unites and divides them. With the term *blood*, I am specifically referring to the shared history of colonial violence that becomes a shared familial bond, ostensibly of love.

The violent scenarios in *Palmeras* illustrate the ways that death informs life in the colony, a distanced outpost of the colonizing nation yet an essential component of its self-fashioning. The colony is an essential site of necropower, expressed in *Palmeras* through whippings, stabbings, hangings, shootings, rape, and exploitative work arrangements that resemble enslavement. These work scenarios are pivotal as they are the origin from which colonialism implicates bodies in its matrix of power by subjugating people to states of life that border on death. As the renowned writer Donato Ndongo points out, in his native Guinea, in addition to expropriating all colonial lands, the Spaniards imposed stringent work laws that operated to enrich the Spanish government and Spanish colonizers at the expense of African people (122, 130). The sheer Otherness and negative affects Mbembe described as integral to characterizing Africa thus contribute to a culture in which suffering and bloodshed continue to serve as the defining elements of Europe's former colonies there.

As in *Últimos*, assuming and conquering death in colonial space also lies at the crux of *Palmeras*, which casts colonial dynamics through interpersonal ones. The death of the protagonist's father Jacobo spurs Clarence's voyage to Guinea, where she unearths long buried family secrets. In *Palmeras*, as in *Últimos*, abject scenes signal the troubling of the boundaries between Europeans and Africans, boundaries that nevertheless remain intact despite these moments of ambiguity. These dynamics could also reflect the blurriness of cultural difference in Spain, which has both served as a proximate Other for northern Europe all while insisting upon the Otherness of populations in Africa and Asia. For instance, the men of the de Rabaltué family envision themselves as Africans while downplaying their roles as Europeans-Spaniards and colonizers of Bioko. In fact, they claim they are workers, much like their African counterparts who earn a living by hiring themselves out for a pittance to the Spanish business owners. Even Clarence upholds this idea in the twenty-first century, insisting that her father and uncle were "empleados de finca" (farmhands) not colonizers. Material realities and the symbolic force of necropower prove these claims false as they all receive obvious privileges as white men in Guinea. They each have an African "boy" to do their bidding, and the viewer sees Jacobo and Kilian attacking Africans brutally, with impunity, in the film. This African status in the film is also gendered, reflecting the dynamics of the colonial enterprise. Kilian and Jacobo's friend Julia is instructed not to compare herself to the Africans; similarly, in the twenty-first century, Africans repeatedly call Clarence a white girl and push and shove her in Bioko as a contemptuous response to her presence there.

Kilian is the chief figure through which a problematic doubling occurs. Kilian was born in Guinea in 1934 and first returns in 1953; his father insists that he was born there and this is his home, despite the years he has spent in Spain. He cannot speak the Bubi language, and while attempting to learn it, his brother Jacobo notes he only needs to master violent phrases like "I will hit you" to survive on the island. The language lesson avers the extent to which the colony remains a site of unfettered violence carried out by Europeans such as the men in his family. Envisaging himself as a native son, Kilian wants to discover "la Guinea indígena, la auténtica, si es que queda algo de ella" (the indigenous, authentic Guinea, if anything remains of it). He associates a true Guinea with the Bubis, who he embraces as his people. In this formulation, both the European colonizers and Africans who are not Bubis (such as the Corisqueans, Nigerians, Fang, Ndowé) inhabiting Fernando Poo erode its *purity*.

Woman and colony are intimately linked in Kilian's perspective. The prostitutes he encounters are not only corrupt, but this impurity directly relates to their culture as miscellaneous Africans who are also not Bubis; the Bubi purity takes form through the character of Bisila. Bisila is the name of a mythical figure in Bubi culture that was later appropriated by Claretian priests and transformed into a Marian figure (Nuestra Señora or Virgen de Bisila). The plot reflects the symbolism of her name as Kilian hopes to possess this woman to similarly possess an African authenticity that reflects the truth of the continent and his heritage. In the twenty-first century, Clarence embraces a similar colonialist methodology of possession. Anne McClintock notes that "[c]olonial photography, framed as it was by metaphors of scientific knowledge as penetration, promised to seek out the secret interiors of the feminized Orient and there capture as surface, in the image of the harem woman's body, the truth of the world" (124). In McClintock's account, photography, integral to acquisition of colonial knowledge, is fueled by a desire to *control* bodies, lands, and resources—all feminized in many colonial accounts—that is, justified with racist, sexist, and nationalist rhetoric. It is not coincidental that upon arriving to Guinea, Clarence takes photographs of the plantation where her ancestors worked, until locals inform her that it is not allowed. Clarence and Kilian's shared missions, despite the temporal differences, are to know themselves through Africa; and for both, African lovers come to symbolize their control and domination of unknown land and people.

Bisila and Kilian's difficult relationship underscores its impossibility. On Kilian's first day at work, he sees Bisila singing and crying among the cacao trees on the plantation. She disappears, and he soon hears sexual noises; the scene creates suspense as the viewer imagines he will see Bisila, the object of his desire, with another man. Instead, Gregorio, a cruel overseer, is having sex with a prostitute he refuses to pay. The cheat admonishes Kilian telling him never to veer off the plantation's path again, as he wouldn't last "en la selva" (in the jungle). In this scene,

Bisila serves as a *clear* contrast to the abused prostitutes and dangerous jungles in Guinea. I use the word "clarity" intentionally here, as both Bisila and her father Osë (José María Kimbo) are inexplicably lighter than every other African in the film except for biracial children like her son Laha. This phenotypical presentation aligns them with whiteness and suggests their goodness in colonial racial hierarchies connected to skin color. By the same token, the implied darkness of the jungles and of the darker-skinned Africans forms part of their threat. Another key figure in this portrayal is Lady Sade (Brigitte Emaga), a dark-skinned and voluptuous sex worker that other characters describe as powerful and dangerous, with no further explanation. In the colony, she serves as an inexplicable threat to Kilian and Bisila; and in the post-colony, she has the same mysterious function with their children. By violently pointing at Clarence and Iniko on the street and holding Clarence's face to look at her, she supposedly conveys to the viewer the clear and present danger she embodies. Through these visual linkages connecting dark and ostensibly ominous women, the jungle, and the crying and suffering Bisila, Kilian apprehends the danger of Fernando Poo and seeks to regain control of this space through a relationship with Bisila.

The fleeting moments of joy between Kilian and Bisila literally occur on the backs of suffering or dead black bodies. After a month of watching his son frequent nightclubs and consort with prostitutes along with his brother Jacobo and Jacobo's buddies Dick (Mark Schardan) and Pao (Xabier Deive), Kilian's father, Antón de Rabaltué (Emilio Gutiérrez Caba), intervenes. He eventually takes Kilian to see a traditional wedding ceremony of the Bubis. Much to Kilian's surprise, he learns Bisila is the bride of an African man named Mosi (Fanor Zapata). Bisila's marriage does not deter Kilian, although all are aware of the awful consequences of besmirching one's purity within the Bubi culture. When their mutual friend Gustavo is attacked, they are finally able to bond in the plantation hospital where Bisila works. Gustavo's attack is ambiguous; witnesses note it could've been carried out by resentful Europeans angry over the imminent decolonization or excessively violent Africans carrying out decolonization. The film collapses African and European in this scene, now through violence that problematically equates colonization and decolonization. Moreover, the imagery of Gustavo's suffering emphasizes the ways in which Bisila and Kilian's love takes shape through the abused black body: there is Gustavo's bloodied body and the threat of Bisila's harsh punishment if their affair is revealed.

While Gustavo's battered body is a primal image in the scenes initially linking Bisila and Kilian romantically, Mosi's dead body forever unites them. These bodies in the grips of death further affirm the extent to which colonized African others endure the necropolitical subjugation Mbembe theorizes. After his wife's rape, Mosi seeks vengeance against the three European men involved: Jacobo, Dick, and Pao. Mosi tortures and hangs two of the perpetrators, but Jacobo manages to shoot and kill the Guinean man. The shooting itself and the events leading up to it heighten the aforementioned tensions of Kilian's African/European splitting. Kilian attacks his brother Jacobo, repeating that he has raped "mi mujer" (my wife), a flawed classification as Bisila is still married to Mosi. Kilian states that he ought to kill Jacobo, "porque sería mucho menos doloroso de lo que Mosi pueda hacer contigo" (for this would be much less painful than what Mosi would do to you). Here, he becomes a conflicted double for Mosi, since both men's commitment to Bisila is bound up in an unconsummated revenge plot against his lover's rapist. Unlike Mosi, Kilian cannot kill Jacobo because of their brotherhood—an overt allusion to their familial bonds and a subtler, flawed reference to their shared European whiteness—which tempers his anger. Along with other statements that convey his anxieties around cannibalism and the violence of decolonization, Kilian's discourse evinces the Eurocentric limits of his aspirations to an "Africanness" he desires yet simultaneously considers ferocious and appalling. Interestingly, his declarations espouse the very concerns European travelers cited—such as nudity, cannibalism, polygamy, witchcraft—in justifying their civilizing role (Alás-Brun 164). The eventual shooting complicates Kilian's African splitting. Kilian and Mosi coincide in frame, and Jacobo shoots at them blindly. Both men fall, but only Kilian rises while Mosi has perished from the gunshot wound. The shooting scene ultimately ends with Kilian commanding his brother to get off "mi isla" (my island), a mandate that leads the viewer to realize that his sexual conquest of Bisila has finally given him the African authenticity he desires. Indeed, Mosi's death seems logical and even produces a disturbing moment of relief in the movie, since it frees Bisila to marry Kilian, who may finally attain a sense of belonging in Africa. The film proves that in the logics of the colonial death-space, it is colonized people who must repeatedly suffer and die for Europeans to become subjects.

Much like the broken domestic life of Lieutenant Cerezo in *Últimos*, destroyed families are central to *Palmeras*. Kilian and Bisila's marriage falls apart once Guinea's independence movement takes hold, and all Spaniards must leave as part of decolonization. Along with Jacobo's death in Spain, the movie takes Kilian's painful separation from Bisila in Guinea as the initial scene and the orienting event of the film. These representations enter into a matrix of broken attachments and unrecoverable losses for Clarence and her cousin Daniela (Kilian's daughter, who shares Bisila's Spanish name) who, like the viewer, must attempt to make sense of this history of colonial death. With this perspective, the film further erases Bisila as a subject, although it is her pain that advances the storyline.

From its inception, the movie's plot develops around Clarence mourning her father's death and investigating her family's past. When she lands in Malabo, she goes directly to her grandfather's grave, where she is astonished to discover fresh flowers in a powerful image combining death, life, and remembrance. Even the name "Clarence" evokes African death to fuel European life. While in Bioko, Iniko shows her the volcano Clarence Peak, which dominates the scene and occupies most of the frame. These formal qualities avow the landmark's potency despite its supposed irrelevancy. Clarence stares at it in wonder, unaware that she was named for this African point. She despondently notes that it is "un volcán extinguido" (an extinguished volcano) and Iniko corrects her, saying that the volcano is not extinct, but dormant; only it knows how *alive* it is inside. Indeed, in contrast to the dead Africans seen throughout the film, Clarence remains intact and even thrives, having conquered this Otherness to define herself.

Bisila's relationships highlight the tensions of colonial dead functioning to fuel European life. Indeed, Bisila's conversation with Clarence offers the insight she craves into her family's history. One disturbing instance of this pattern occurs when Bisila must comfort a crying Clarence while revealing her rape by Jacobo, Clarence's father. This scene shows the limits of colonial friendship, a "friendship of compassion, of empathy and sympathy shaped by encounters with Black suffering" (Mbembe, *Critique* 74). Indeed, the intimacy of the scene emerges from Bisila's violation. What's more, Clarence's crying makes the viewer concentrate on her sympathy rather than Bisila's victimization. Clarence has also invaded Kilian's privacy by reading his diary to receive the first half of the story and justifies her acts claiming "esta también es mi historia" (this is my story, too), appropriating the colonial struggles of those who came before her.

The continual focus on Clarence undercuts the African storytelling essential for the movie to occur. Bisila is rendered voiceless in a narrative ventriloquism that reaches problematic heights at the end of the film. When Clarence returns to Spain, she sings a song that Bisila has taught her; the song delights her uncle Kilian, who, in his ongoing delirium, begins to have visions of a young Bisila as his niece carries out a performance essentially predicated upon stealing Bisila's voice. The strangest part of this scene is that within the film's logics, Bisila could've traveled to Spain to sing the song herself; yet for some reason, Clarence has chosen to do so. Later, when Bisila receives an envelope from Spain perhaps informing her of Kilian's death, she commits suicide by walking into the ocean, which the film has spent nearly two hours portraying as "el mar que termina recibiéndonos a todos" (the sea that welcomes us all). The sea has served as the site of Bisila and Kilian's marriage; Clarence and Iniko's sexual encounter; and a site of perpetual return and belonging through ongoing allusions to turtles laying eggs on Bioko. These references to the sea in the film express natural logic and peace as antithetical to the corrupt structures of human society. Bisila's final moments consolidate this oceanic representation in underscoring this colonial death as an act of peace and self-fulfillment. The cool blue of the sea occupies most of the frame, functioning in chromatic harmony with her blue gown.

The synchronized death scene at the end of *Palmeras* is nefarious. Kilian never dies on film, unlike Bisila, whose suicide is a narrative device that avows she must only exist for her European counterparts, specifically, Kilian, and the intended European audience that craves a happy ending through an imagined meeting in the afterlife. These elements of the form and plot reveal the extent to which the democratic nation still clings to the sacred, theological, patriarchal, and colonial structures of the dictatorial era that preceded it. Most important, Bisila's death directly connects to the topic of death at the heart of this volume. In my reading, her death can be understood in necropolitical terms: not only has her life been suspended in a visual spectacle of violent abeyance through threats, rape, assault, and work exploitation seen throughout the movie, her life has also principally served to further a broader European project of subject formation for the de Rabaltué family members and the intended audience who ought to identify with them.

Bisila's death strongly connects the colonial subject matter of *Palmeras* with today's migration issues as Africans and Arabs perish in *pateras* attempting to gain entry into Europe. Intensifying the film's connection to cultural productions that treat European immigration and assimilation, the final scene shows Bisila's sons traveling to snowy Huesca where they will form deeper connections with the de Rabaltué family and perhaps attempt to remain in Spain. The sons trek through the snow like Jacobo and Kilian before them and arrive at the de Rabaltué home. There is a final sequence in which they look at a family tree of which they are spectral absences, while their African forbears are the colonial dead who have made these ghosts possible. In fact, the "palmeras en la nieve" referenced in the film's title are not Laha and Iniko, but Jacobo and Kilian, the previous generation of colonizers whose violence transformed their nations and, now, their families. As I stated earlier, blood unites and blood divides. Viewing the blood and waste of abjection and degraded, abject bodies, as film critic Tina Chanter postulates, is a part of a process of social cohesion that usually conforms to the logic of patriarchy, capitalism, or colonialism (3). The combination of Bisila's death and the sons' gazing upon a family tree in a frigid European terrain where they figure as "nonself," "the unsayable," and "the concealed"—to use Khanna's terminology—in the tree image only serves to consolidate the film's narrative technique of exposing the ways colonial narratives rely on the often-violent erasure of the Other to frame European existence. Finally, the de Rabaltué women attempt to incorpo-rate these men into their family through positive affective bonds of love, albeit with sexually tense undertones that remind the viewer of the erotic fascination and penetration pivotal to the colonial enterprise. The potential family unit that emerges at the end of *Palmeras* not only uncritically exoticizes and romanticizes the Africans, but also elides the violence and bloodshed that has brought them into the picture, all while removing them from the official family narrative of the tree. As in the friendship somehow instituted in the siege of Baler, in *Palmeras*, the family conceals the colonial dead who have made possible a far more lucrative relationship rooted in the human capital flight of intelligent youth like Laha and the ongoing exploitation of Africans as migrants in twenty-first-century Spain.

Colonial Death and Postcolonial Crisis Cinema

To what extent do these films grapple with the issues of Crisis plaguing Spain of the 2010s? Regarding the panorama of films produced during the crisis, Dean Allbritton writes, "The types of cinema produced under such conditions vary as dramatically as the experiences of being a politically, economically and physi-cally vulnerable citizen" (103). It is my contention that the deaths at the crux of each story enter into the necropolitical logics whereby European life sallies forth from colonial suffering, loss, and death. My analysis of death in *Últimos* and *Palmeras* is twofold. First, national death appears to resolve itself through voyages to the death-space of the colonies where melancholy attachments are healed, and Spaniards are able to mourn. The national dead are the axes around which the plots unfold in both films: dead Spaniards propel an investigative or explanatory journey to a bygone colonial past, and during these voyages, nation-als attempt to comprehend the present. Second, both films re-present the "death" of the colony. Intertwined with the aforementioned narratives of self-fashioning and self-actualization wrought from the pursuit of a bygone past in the colony is the narrative of the colony's separation from Spain. The self-fashioning here is key, as Baler supposedly represents the initial moment of Filipino friendship with Spain. In fact, in 2003, the Philippines became the only country to celebrate its former colonialism when it enacted Philippine-Spanish Friendship Day, a national holiday connected both to the siege of Baler and the Philippine's unique economic relationship with Spain, one of its largest trade partners. *Palmeras* also suggests that the Guineans and Spaniards in the movie will be partners for life through their singular familial saga and potential romances.

The temporalities of the films are key: both represent decolonization—in

1898 and in 1968—during the twenty-first century. The watershed moments of independence from Spain joins up with the 2010s reality. I return to an insightful quote from Krauel: "The more Spain lost its grip on the colonies *and the world*, the more insistent its affirmative repetition of colonialism became" (63; my emphasis). While Krauel refers to the nineteenth century, a similar process is at work in these twenty-first-century cinematic productions that showcase violence and bloodshed to frame friendly, familial relations with former colonies. Bringing colonial history into the twenty-first century meshes with the more individualized plots wherein the protagonists are searching to recover a loss or yearning for the past. In this way, both films illuminate the extent to which the necropolitical colony as concept endures to facilitate the self-fashioning of the former colonizers. The films reflect the ways that the world remains haunted by colonialism and empire. These hauntings are the impulses behind the films, with each one focused on community formation through death.

NOTES

1. *Palmeras en la nieve* is based on the homonymous novel by Luz Gabás, published in 2012. This essay does not take into account the novel, only the 2015 film.
2. For a broader discussion of Spain's complex role as a metropolis even after losing most of its colonies, see Blanco and Tsuchiya.
3. The Siege of Baler was the focus of a double episode on the popular Spanish television series *El Ministerio del Tiempo*. This episode proposes that disease led to the defeat at Baler more so than the rebel army. The conflict is also portrayed in the Filipino romance drama *Baler* (directed by Meily 2008).
4. For a further explanation of empire and nation-building in Spain's history, see Martin-Márquez.
5. Some Bubi characters have two names: a Spanish one and an indigenous one. I list the African and Spanish names with a hyphen the first time I mention a character with two names, and then I only use the African one.
6. For a more detailed analysis of the colonial relations underlying Guinean migration to Spain, see Ugarte, *Africans in Europe*.

WORKS CITED

Alás-Brun, Montserrat. "The Shattered Mirror: Colonial Discourse and Counterdiscourse about Spanish Guinea." *Arizona Journal of Hispanic Cultural Studies*, vol. 8, 2004, pp. 163–76.

Allbritton, Dean. "Prime Risks: The Politics of Pain and Suffering in Spanish Crisis Cinema." *Journal of Spanish Cultural Studies*, vol. 15, no. 1–2, 2014, pp. 101–15.

AudioVisual451. "Mercedes Gamero habla sobre 'Palmeras en la nieve.'" YouTube, 17 Dec. 2015.

Bhambra, Gurminder K. "Postcolonial and Decolonial Dialogues." *Postcolonial Studies*, vol. 17, no. 2, 2014, pp. 115–21.

Blanco, Alda. "Spain at the Crossroads: Imperial Nostalgia or Modern Colonialism?" *A Contracorriente: Una Revista de Historia Social y Literatura de América Latina*, vol. 5, no. 1, 2007, pp. 1–11.

Calvo, Salvador, director. *1898: Los últimos de Filipinas*. Sony Pictures Home Entertainment, 2016.

Chang, Julia. "Becoming Useless: Masculinity, Ability, and Empire in Nineteenth-Century Spain." *Unsettling Colonialism: Gender and Race in the Global Nineteenth-Century Hispanic World*, edited by N. Michelle Murray and Akiko Tsuchiya, State University of New York Press, 2019, pp. 173–202.

Chanter, Tina. *The Picture of Abjection: Film, Fetish, and the Nature of Difference*. Indiana University Press, 2008.

EFE. "Empieza el rodaje de 'Los últimos de Filipinas,' una visión humanista del fin del Imperio español." *RTVE*, 5 May 2016.

Fanon, Frantz. *Black Skin, White Masks*. Translated by Charles Lam Markmann, Pluto Books, 2008.

Foucault, Michel. *"Society Must Be Defended." Lectures at the Collège de France, 1975–1976*, edited by Mauro Bertani and Alessandro Fontana, translated by David Macey, Picador, 2003.

Gilroy, Paul. *After Empire: Melancholia or Convivial Culture?* Routledge, 2004.

González Molina, Fernando, director. *Palmeras en la nieve*. Warner Bros., 2016.

Gonzálvez Vallés, Juan Enrique. "'Los últimos de Filipinas' como ejemplo de las nuevas relaciones internacionales del régimen franquista." *La imagen del Franquismo a través de la séptima arte: cine, Franco y posguerra*, edited by David Caldevilla Domínguez, Vision Libros, 2012, pp. 41–66.

Hook, Derek. "Fanon and the Libidinal Economy." *Re(con)figuring Psychoanalysis: Critical Juxtapositions of the Philosophical, the Sociohistorical, and the Political*, edited by Aydan Güerce, Palgrave Macmillan, 2012, pp. 164–83.

Khanna, Ranjana. *Dark Continents: Psychoanalysis and Colonialism*. Duke University Press, 2003.

Kinder, Marsha. *Blood Cinema: The Reconstruction of National Identity in Spain*. University of California Press, 1993.

Krauel, Javier. *Imperial Emotions: Cultural Responses to Myths of Empire in Fin-de-Siecle Spain*. Liverpool University Press, 2014.

Kristeva, Julia. *Powers of Horror: An Essay on Abjection*. Translated by Leon S. Roudiez, Columbia University Press, 1982.

Martin-Márquez, Susan. *Disorientations: Spanish Colonialism in Africa and the Performance of Identity*. Yale University Press, 2008.

Mbembe, Achille. *A Critique of Black Reason*. Translated by Laurent Dubois, Duke University Press, 2017.

————. "Necropolitics." Translated by Libby Meintjes, *Public Culture*, vol. 15, no. 1, 2003, pp. 11–40.

McClintock, Anne. *Imperial Leather: Race, Gender, and Sexuality in the Colonial Conquest*. Routledge, 1995.

Meily, Mark, director. *Baler*. Viva Films, 2008.

Miller, Stuart Creighton. *Benevolent Assimilation: The American Conquest of the Philippines, 1899–1903*. Yale University Press, 1982.

Ndongo-Bidyogo, Donato. *España en Guinea. Construcción del desencuentro. 1778–1986*. Ediciones Sequitur, 1998.

Ponzanesi, Sandra, and Marguerite Waller. *Postcolonial Cinema Studies*. Routledge, 2011.

Tsuchiya, Akiko. "Introduction." *Empire's End: Transnational Connections in the Hispanic World*, edited by Akiko Tsuchiya and William G. Acree, Jr., Vanderbilt University Press, 2016, pp. 1–13.

Ugarte, Michael. *Africans in Europe: The Culture of Exile and Emigration from Equatorial Guinea to Spain*. University of Illinois Press, 2010.

————. "Spain's Heart of Darkness: Equatorial Guinea in the Narrative of Donato Ndongo." *Journal of Spanish Cultural Studies*, vol. 7, no. 3, 2006, pp. 271–87.

Part III: Stone

CHAPTER 10

A Stone That Makes Them Stumble

Mining the Lithic in Manuel Rivas's
O lapis do carpinteiro

William Viestenz

In the Gospel of Matthew, Christ, after relating a set of parables to chief priests and Pharisees, analogizes the Kingdom of God to a "stone that the builders rejected." Those unfortunate enough to stumble on this formerly repudiated cornerstone "will be broken to pieces; and it will crush anyone on who it falls" (Matt. 21.42–44). Biblical exegetes, the most prominent being René Girard, have gestured toward the complex significance this and other passages in Judeo-Christian scripture assign to the concept of *skandalon*, or stumbling block, in relation to violence, civil fracture, and mechanisms, such as scapegoating, that aim to curb societal unrest through the deaths of innocent victims. *Skandalon*, a Greek term conceptually related to the way Christ metaphorically uses stone in the above passage from Matthew, refers to impediments that cause one to stumble, or to a snare that not only impedes movement forward, but tightens the more one struggles to escape the grasp of whatever it is that trips one up. *Skandalon* is thus a lithic concept that merges stony materiality with human culture, a phenomenon seen explicitly in the term being the etymological root of the notion of scandal, not only in the narrow sense of a public humiliation, but in the broader understanding of how the insistent attachment to prohibited and restrained desire, whether on an individual or a collective scale, leads to discord and the repetitive interruption of historical progress.[1]

Manuel Rivas's critically celebrated novel *O lapis do carpinteiro* (The Carpenter's Pencil), published in Galician in 1998 and widely translated thereafter, has become an important text for better understanding a range of problematics that have adhered to post-Francoist Iberian culture in the last several decades. In broad strokes, the novel recounts the companion relationship of a prison guard, Herbal, and a doctor, Daniel Da Barca, as the two coexist on both sides of the ideological spectrum over the course of the Spanish Civil War. The novel, set in the 1990s and told through retrospective narration, is an important touchstone for studies concerning historical memory of the Francoist dictatorship, documenting "la magnitud de la tragedia y el sentido apocalíptico que caracteriza este episodio de la historia de España" (Tasende 298) (the magnitude of the tragedy and the apocalyptic sense characterizing this period of Spain's history). In addition to supplementing the historical record, the novel has also been shown to illuminate the deontological dimension of spectral haunting (Loureiro 149–50); the subversive function of humor in novels of memory (García-Donoso, "La risa"); and the interconnection between the act of narration and identity transformation (Folkart), to name a few sophisticated examples. This essay proposes to investigate an aspect of the text that has not received a sustained level of attention: namely, the integral function that stone, as both an agentive object and anchor for theorizing culture, fulfills in the text as a catalyzing participant in human social assemblages. On the one hand, stone operates as a material support and mediator for human intentionality in the text, thus speaking to the porousness of the human body as it meshes with and is catalyzed by the objective world assembled around the self. It is also a crucial mediator in human efforts to inscribe the past, at once supplementing the finitude of flesh but also projecting a scalar range that upends the centrality of humanity's historical presence. In its multi-textured engagement with the lithic, *O lapis do carpinteiro* also emphasizes that stone is the basis for the thinkability of important conceptual phenomena, especially the aforementioned notion of the *skandalon*, that speak to the political crisis and the historical repetition of violence integral to Rivas's narrativization of the Spanish Civil War. In the pages that follow, I will demonstrate the multifaceted role of the lithic in *O lapis do carpinteiro* by first commenting on the text's innovative focus on the way material flesh and stone merge in order to anchor society and establish temporal foundations for cultural narrative and memory. In the second half of the essay, I will emphasize the importance in the novel of various phenomena associated with the lithically rooted notion of *skandalon*, especially scandal, the stumbling block, and the scapegoat.

Stone works as a corrective to the finitude of human flesh threatened by the inevitability of death, as it provides a lasting foundation for the cities and architecture that exceed the lifespans of any individual human subject. In Rivas's novel, the Falcona prison is one striking case, as its presence effortlessly outstrips many of the persecuted lives of its prisoners, and the narrator makes special mention of its mossy, stone walls: "as paredes do cárcere eran de lousas pintadas de carriza" (25) (the prison walls were slabs of stone coated with moss) (15).[2] In addition, stone is a means of inscription and instigator of memory: in Rivas's novel, the graphite embedded within the carpenter's pencil insistently reminds Herbal of his role in the death of the artist and the life of Daniel Da Barca. In addition, the artist employs a jagged shard of tile to transpose the faces of his fellow prisoners into a notebook before being given the more serviceable graphite-laden pencil. Stone also serves as a surface of inscription, with the prime case being the granite façade of the Pórtico da Gloria overlooking the Falcona prison yard where the Maestro Mateo in 1188 AD sculpts a vision of Christ's redemption as seen through the apocalyptic framework of St. John. Thus it is tempting to assign to stone a merely instrumental role as first the writerly means by which human beings undertake aesthetic creation and inscription of the past and secondly as the passive, receptive screen on which such works of expression are projected. Rivas, both in *O lapis do carpinteiro* and elsewhere, instead attempts to transcend a facile opposition between active culture and passive nature in arguing for the catalytic role that both humans and stones affect upon one another in the moment of their mutual entanglement.

Bruno Latour offers a sophisticated critique of viewing nature as uniquely transcendent and culture as a phenomenon immanent to human communities. Latour, in demonstrating the intellectual profit of deconstructing the nature/culture divide, argues that a certain strain of social analysis ascribes absolute passivity to objects, making them "mere receptacles for human categories" (52) and "the white screen on to which society projects its cinema" (53). In Rivas's work, the stony figures populating the Pórtico are material objects that, far from passively reflecting cultural symbolism, are actually set in motion as a response to human engagement, a sentiment he alludes to both in *O lapis do carpinteiro* as well as while interpreting a poem by Rosalía de Castro as part of his 2009 acceptance speech upon entering the Real Academia Galega. In *Follas novas*, the poetic voice, upon contemplating the twenty-four *ancianos músicos* sitting atop the central arc of the Pórtico da Gloria, exclaims: "¡védeos!—parece / que os labios moven, que falan quedo / os uns cos outros" (Look at them!—it looks like / their lips are moving, that they are talking softly / to one another). The voice next asks: "¿Estarán vivos? ¿Serán de pedra / aqués sembrantes tan verdadeiros, / aquelas túnicas maravillosas, / aqueles ollos de vida cheos?" (54) (Are they actually alive? Those faces that seem so real, / are they really made of stone? / Those marvelous gowns? / Those eyes so full of life?). Rivas's response to the poet concerns the catalyzing function of literary creation, or more precisely, what he describes as the openings of the mouth of literature: "Se a pedra abre os labios no Pórtico da Gloria, como nos di Rosalia, é porque está a abrirse a boca da literatura cos [sic] cancioneiros" (12) (if stone opens lips in the Pórtico da Gloria, as Rosalía tells us, it is because the cancioneiro's mouth of literature is opening). Stone, which in its seemingly immobile natural state appears indifferent to human affairs and exists at a scalar temporal level that overwhelms calendrical history, is catalyzed into action in the Pórtico as it is drawn into and meshed with cultural production— the opening mouth of literature—which itself is a vehicle for creating an assemblage of human and, in this case, lithic components.

At the same time, the magnitude of lithical scalar time is precisely what draws human beings into the activities that use granite, graphite, shale, and other mineral elements in order to preserve the historical record and supplement the meager duration of living flesh through storytelling and archival inscription. Stone, in other words, likewise catalyzes important cultural practices in the same manner that *a boca da literatura* instigates sculpted lips into motion as it draws lithic materiality into assemblages with human actants. Jeffrey Jerome Cohen echoes this phenomenon via a notion he calls "lithic provocation." In Cohen's analysis of medieval stories, one encounters the suggestion that "rock is a perpetual catalyst, summons, force. A primal element, stone invites us to gigantic temporal frames, to spaces populated by vast figures who seem monstrous but reveal a surprising intimacy. It compels us to ponder our brevity and intensifies our desire to send messages to far cultures, inciting creativity, spurring art" (86). Stone not only instigates contemplation of death but makes possible the kinds of aesthetic activities that allow participation in human communities beyond an individual lifespan. In the artist's reinscription of the Pórtico da Gloria in *O lapis do carpinteiro*, the cathedral's lithic summonsing comes at a moment of intense awareness of the brevity of human life, as the pencil employed by the artist is passed down from its previous carpenter owner, Marcial Villamor, prior to the latter being executed for syndicalist sympathies and not long before the former suffers the same fate. In such an environment of imminent danger, the artist's sense of finitude increases proportionate to his obsession with inscribing a record of his and his colleagues' existence: "E a medida que pasaban os días co seu ronsel dos peores presaxios, máis se concentraba el no caderno. Mentres ous outros parolaban, el retratábaos sen acougo" (31) (as the days went by, trailing the worst omens in their wake, the painter concentrated more and more on the notebook. While the others chatted, he tirelessly copied down their features) (24–25). The material objects that comprise the social assemblage surrounding the prison mediate the painter's archival preservation of the endangered Republican prisoners.

The Pórtico da Gloria, in this sense, is certainly a "marco simbólico" (Tasende 298) (symbolic framework) through which Rivas allows the reader to comprehend the magnitude of the Spanish Civil War in Galicia and to interpret the hermeneutical function of individual characters in the novel, such as reading the doctor Daniel Da Barca through the Prophet Daniel. The pencil, for its part, is a mnemonic container infused with the agglutination of "la imagen de la identidad gallega" (the image of Galician identity) and operates as a "símbolo material" of "historias-mitos de iden-tidad" (Aguado 290) (material symbol [of] mytho-histories of identity). However, the function of these materialities cannot be reduced to symbolism alone; the Pór-tico, for example, reinforces how the unique arrangement of material objects and nonhuman lives that aggregate in a given space catalyze cultural practice, thereby "opening the mouth of literature," and will inflect and add texture to how human beings tell stories, project history into the future, and intuit the possibility of future realities that remain in states of latency.

Stone, with its lithic provocations, is as agentive as human subjects, and as its entanglement with cultural production intensifies, material reality becomes less lifeless, more imbricated with the course of human history, and expressive of its own state of motion and transformation.[3] For Rivas, objects are neither passive receptacles nor natural entities that overdetermine and imprison "the soft and pliable wills of the poor humans" (Latour 53). Materialities like the Pórtico or the sculpted wood of the carpenter's pencil better resemble an inflecting agent as they are both social and natural at once; or more precisely, they resemble what Latour, following on a theory developed by Michel Serres, calls "quasi-objects." Serres specifies that objects have the potential to exert a subjectifying func-tion and thus fuse in an ontological merger with the human agent that handles them. Serres uses the example of a hammer, which is both a tool to be picked up and utilized to carry out intentioned work projects but is also a quasi-object that designates "a subject who, without it, would not be a subject"; "the hand is no longer a hand when it has taken hold of the hammer, it is the hammer itself" (30). *O lapis do carpinteiro* often references the fusion of the human body with contiguous objects that share an intimate cohabitation with the human sub-ject. At its outset, the novel foreshadows the human/object enmeshment most explicitly demonstrated with the carpenter's pencil in its opening representation of an aged Da Barca, who has returned to Spain from exile in Mexico after the death of Franco. The peacefulness of the opening scene is upended through the intimate cohabitation of Da Barca's infirm biological body with a technological apparatus including a mask and oxygen tube; the luminosity of Da Barca's body makes it as if "o paciente estivese conectado a un xerador" (10) (the patient were connected up to a generator) (2).

The life support attached to Da Barca magnifies, at the same time, the manner in which material reality, including, most prominently, that supported by stone, extends the scope of human temporal duration and gives life a renewed vitality. Another example comes in the second half of the text, as Da Barca and Herbal travel from A Coruña on a train transporting tuberculosis patients to Porta Coeli. As the train advances, the passing landscape leads the doctor to reflect on the artist's aesthetic representation of fisherman at work: "os pescadores estaban cativos das mesmas redes que capturaban os peixes. Chegou un momento en que os corpos se fragmentaron. Brazos fouce. Ollos de mar. Pedras do rostro" (118) (the fishermen were captive of the very nets that seized the fish. It reached the point where their bodies fragmented. Sickle arms. Sea eyes. Face stones) (124). On the one hand, Da Barca's admiration for his friend's aesthetic is an implicit critique of Romantic understandings of landscape, where nature is valued as an object to be consumed pictorially. In Latourian terms, the Romantic landscape is a symbolic construction that passively reflects the ideological pretensions of the town and city, as though it were a white screen to be imputed with cultural content that transcends its own limited opening to the world. Da Barca's recollection also emphasizes the manner in which the workers' bodies are fragmented according to the subjectifying forces exerted upon them by an array of quasi-objects. Similar to how Gilles Deleuze and Félix Guattari will argue that a wasp collecting pollen transforms into a becoming-orchid (and the orchid into a becoming-wasp), the fishermen's arms fuse in a chain of ontological continuity with the sickle; the eyes with the sea; the faces with stones.[4] As with Serres's hammer, these objects are tools intimately tied to the labor value of extracting produce from the sea but as quasi-objects they also exert a subjectifying force on their handlers, transforming the latter into becoming subjects.

Rivas speaks more at length of a similar entanglement of human flesh and stone in an essay that expounds upon the petroglyphs of concentric circles and other figures that dot the Galician landscape. Given their provenance from the Bronze Age, dating back approximately six thousand years, Rivas highlights the stones' enigmatic nature: "Podrían ser mapas topográficos que indicaran cómo estaba distribuida la población; hay quien piensa que serían mapas astrales . . . pero en realidad no se sabe bien qué es lo que cuentan" ("El cuervo" 10) (They could very well be topographic maps that would indicate how the population was distributed; some believe that they are astral maps . . . but in reality nobody really knows what they communicate). Rivas, in spite of such archaeological doubt, argues with assurance that "desde luego se trata de un relato. Quien veía las piedras transmitía una historia verdadera" (10) (of course it's about a story. Whoever saw those stones was telling a true story). In the artist's enmeshment with the Pórtico da Gloria in *O lapis do carpinteiro*, the intended, verifiable mean-ing instilled originally in the façade by Maestro Mateo is less important than how the sculpted stone operates as an instigator for the inscription of memory, which uses the basic structure of Mateo's creation as a point of departure. For Rivas, the Bronze Age petroglyphs fulfill the same function: "los círculos concéntricos de los petroglifos nos permiten un mirar ensanchado, un ser en expansión, sin límites, que incluye las dimensiones de la memoria y de la imaginación, de las leyendas y de los sueños" (12) (the petroglyphs' concentric circles allow for a widened vision, a being in expansion, without limits, which includes the dimensions of memory and the imagination, of legends and of dreams). The petroglyphs and the façade of the Pórtico da Gloria together instigate the opening of the mouth of literature. The uncertainty, or indecipherability, of the stories the stones were originally sculpted to convey grants license to the exercise of individual memory and imaginative flight.[5]

Stone, at the same time, is inherently ambivalent, for as much as it provides the material support for preserving stories and memories, it nevertheless retains its own geological and cultural history, the scope of which minimizes the tem-poral significance of the relatively short life of the engaged human subject. In his discussion of Galician petroglyphs above, Rivas emphasizes stone's resistance to revealing the totality of its secrets. Elsewhere, in his novel *Os libros arden mal* (Books Burn Badly), Rivas notes the ambivalent nature of material reality: "Había, sí, estas dúas percepcións que facían especial un cadro ou un poema. Unha, o falar das cousas. O captar o falar das cousas . . . A outra, o calar das cousas. O seu agochar. O seu ausentarse. O seu baleirar. A súa perda" (107) (Here were two perceptions that made a picture or a poem seem special. One, the speaking of things. Capturing the speaking of things. . . . The other, the falling quiet of things. Their hiding. Their being absent. Their emptying. Their loss) (69).[6] *O lapis do carpinteiro* suggests that human subjects may very well be the agent of this loss; for example, with each passing of the carpenter's pencil onto a new subject, with it ultimately ending up in the hands of Maria da Visitação, the migrant worker in the prostitution club Herbal manages, the history of the object's previous own-ers fades. The stone that comprises the Pórtico da Gloria itself leaves behind a natural history the moment Maestro Mateo sculpts the granite, and the exact providence of the granite has only recently been verified.[7] More nefariously, the falling quiet of nonhuman reality is, for Rivas, also an effect of damage to the environment.[8] Cohen notes that stone in particular, due to its temporal scale extending the limits of story far beyond normal durations, invites contempla-tion of the limits of communicating across time. Similar to Rivas, he ruminates on the subject while referencing petroglyphs and wonders "how far back ancient messages, abetted by stone's material endurance, might extend; probing whether writing necessitates words, or if lithic architectures and other nonverbal petroglyphs (including the fossilized remains of various life forms) can communicate across obliterating sweeps of time" (78). The "sunken" histories that no longer reach human comprehension in the petroglyphs as well as the vanished histories that are obscured with each passing on of the carpenter's pencil are only truly lost if one is taking an anthropocentric perspective, as all of these narratives remain inscribed in the life history of the objects, whether there are humans around who are able to decipher the traces. In the end, stone both marks the possibility of archival transmission and the excessive surplus of history that will always render any understanding of the past incomplete and defer its meaning, a notion that Derrida well establishes in "Archive Fever."[9]

In their capacity to tie together sweeps of time that would otherwise obliterate the continuity of human narration, stone and other material objects that bear historical inscription are able to function as stumbling blocks that disrupt official narratives of history. In a convincing summary, Tasende puts forth that Rivas's recreation of the Pórtico da Gloria "subvierte la visión unívoca e indisputable del pasado oficial y desmantela todo el entramado mítico creado por los forjadores del franquismo" (309) (subverts the univocal and indisputable vision of the official past and dismantles the entire mythic framework created by the architects of Francoism). In addition, the spectral haunting occasioned by Herbal's attachment to the pencil is an additional source of stumbling, insistently keeping present the ruptures of a silenced past in the present and calling out in an ethical demand for the (re)construction of "el sujeto humano como responsabilidad por la muerte del otro" (Loureiro 150) (the human subject as responsible for the death of the other). As García-Donoso further argues, the "secular mythology" invented by the prisoners via the Pórtico da Gloria satirically contests the attempted sacralization of Francoism's crusade via "la profusión de mitos heroicos y religiosos con los que el franquismo institucional, mezclando proclamas falangistas con doctrina católica, construiría su imaginario durante la dictadura" ("La risa" 212) (the profusion of heroic and religious myths with those that institutional Francoism, blending Falangist proclamations with Catholic doctrine, will construct its imaginary during the dictatorship). In these critical readings, the intersection of Herbal and the carpenter's pencil scandalizes the forced erasure of historical memory in compelling the former prison guard to recollect the perspective of those victimized by the regime. In a broader sense, the pencil gestures toward any material object or residue from the past that operates as a *skandalon*, causing one to stumble in the effort to move forward, or transition, toward a non-Francoist democratic future without first accounting for the specters of the past.[10]

As René Girard has argued, *skandalon*, as Christ uses the term in the Gospels, is less a material object and more another subject with whom one enters into an antagonistic rivalry for a shared mimetic desire. I will next put forth that stone is hermeneutically significant to understanding *O lapis do carpinteiro* not only in regards to human-object entanglement but also as a conceptual root for understanding the forms of social reciprocity that both precipitate and quell violence. Girard argues that human desire only exists through the attempted imitation of other human subjects, who easily turn into rivals when desires cannot be shared or are blocked. The "mimetic model," in the course of the process of blocked desire, exerts a "special form of temptation, causing attraction to the extent that [he] is an obstacle and forming an obstacle to the extent that [he] can attract" (*Things* 416). Scandal stems from the idea that the more a model attracts and tempts, the stronger feelings of resentment simultaneously arise. Competition for shared objects of mimetic desire not only scandalizes the model-acolyte binary but has the potential to provoke social fracture: "scandal is always a relationship of doubles . . . the passive object of scandal becomes an agent of it and contributes to its diffusion. That is why Christ says, 'woe to the man by whom scandal comes,' for his responsibility can extend to many people" (418). As Girard later argues, the only path for defusing a large-scale mimetic crisis of desire—which has the potential to cause "cultures to perish, to fall back into the chaos from which they came" (*The One* 15)—is to provoke a victimary mechanism by which the ire of all sides can be redirected toward a scapegoat figure. More precisely, "the initial proliferation of scandals leads sooner or later into an acute crisis at the climax of which unanimous violence is set off against the single victim, the victim finally selected by the entire community" (*I See Satan* 30). The scapegoat is an innocent victim whose blamelessness is never made explicit as the community reconciles around the shared destruction of a liminal social figure who exists within, but often at the margin of, the social. In Girard's reading, Christ's crucifixion is crucial as it lays bare the hidden truth of the victimary mechanism. The Gospels reproduce "the archaic structure of sacrifice in order to stand it on its head . . . since the victim is not guilty, he no longer has the power to absorb violence" (*The One* 63).

Throughout *O lapis do carpinteiro*, scandal insistently adheres to both the Herbal-Daniel dyad but more generally associates with a wider range of Da Barca's activities as he moves through various prisons and hospitals. Girard asserts that scandal always begins as a question of doubles, and indeed Herbal is described in multiple parts of the text as Da Barca's shadow. The first instance comes as Herbal volunteers to trail Da Barca prior to the latter's imprisonment: "Durante unha longa tempada fun a súa sombra. Seguira as súas pegadas coma un can de caza. Era o meu home" (37) (For a long period I was his shadow. I tracked him like a gun dog. He was my man) (29). Herbal's attraction to Da Barca's is not undertaken in fulfillment of the responsibilities of his post, but stem from an innate desire that "lle saía de dentro. Podería dicir que ía tras del coma un can doente, cheirando os seus pasos. El odiaba ao doutor Da Barca" (41) (You could say he had followed him like a sick dog, sniffing out his footsteps. He hated Doctor Da Barca) (35). Da Barca, in the classical function of a mimetic rival, simultaneously attracts and repulses. Fittingly, Herbal's pursuit of Daniel is also predicated on a form of mimetic desire on the part of the guard, who sees in the doctor a way to remain connected to a woman, Marisa Mallo, for whom he has held a longstanding but unsatisfied infatuation. The doctor, as a stone that makes Herbal stumble, also blocks libidinal fulfillment at the same time that he serves as a model of desire for the guard, transforming Mallo's character into a kind of Lacanian *objet petit a*. To the extent that desire, as a permanent lack, is only legible through the modeling of what others possess, Herbal cannot easily undo the attachment to his mimetic rival, which explains his initial effort, at the artist's urging, to preclude Da Barca's death in Santiago by having him transferred to A Coruña. It also explains Herbal's ambivalence about following through with executing Da Barca after having put in a transfer to follow the doctor to A Coruña, as his uncle's voice echoes in his mind prior to pulling the trigger: "Preferiría non facelo, compañeiro" (55) (I wish I didn't have to, friend) (49). To the extent that Da Barca attracts, he obstructs; to the extent that he obstructs, he attracts, and due to this paradox Herbal remains attached, as a shadow, to Da Barca throughout much of the novel's plot. That Herbal ultimately volunteers to form part of the firing squad the night of Da Barca's selection confirms the basic framework of Girardian mimetic desire, as Daniel's conversion into a scandalous rival precipitates a persistent and increasingly aggressive form of antagonism until such point that the stumbling block is dispatched.

While there are a number of similarities between the Prophet Daniel of scripture and Daniel Da Barca, the most salient for this reading is how both are invariably tempted, but ultimately resist, becoming scandalized. Chapter 6 of the Book of Daniel emphasizes the prophet's immunity to scandal at multiple points. Darius the Mede moves to appoint Daniel as president of his kingdom, provoking other officials to search for possible scandals to derail the king's plans. However, "they could find no grounds for complain or any corruption, because he [Daniel] was faithful, and no negligence or corruption could be found in him" (Daniel 6.4). Later in the chapter, Darius prohibits the worship of God under penalty of being cast into a den of lions. Daniel, refusing the order, and the temptation to secure his own life at the expense of betraying God, continues to pray but is spared when thrown to the lions through divine intervention. Earlier in the gospel, the prophet's associates also prove to be immune to scandal, as three men, Shadrach, Meshach, and Abednego are thrown into a fiery furnace after refusing to worship Nebuchadnezzar's golden idol. The flames, naturally, envelop their guards and spare the three Jewish men. Rivas's Da Barca, of course, is also spared certain death in surviving being executed at short range and demonstrates a perilous fidelity to his ideals in the most threatening of circumstances.

Da Barca's return from death ultimately serves to illuminate the inner truth of the scapegoating mechanism, placing him on a firm plane with the Christ figure in relation to mimetic crisis and the reformation of political authority. García-Donoso has observed the Da Barca-Christ connection, noting the pencil's link to the profession of carpentry with which Christ was associated. In addition, "las escenas de Da Barca como centro de atención en arengas políticas o las discusiones con sus compañeros de presidio en la Falcona pueden leerse como trasunto de las predicaciones de Jesús en el templo y de las charlas con sus discípulos" (*Escrituras* 233) (the scenes with Da Barca as the center of attention during political harangues or discussions with his prison mates en la Falcona can be read as a repetition of Jesus's preaching in the temple or conversations with his disciples). Da Barca's attachment to scandal further solidifies his resemblance to the Christ model. It is scandalous, initially, that Da Barca survives his execution, which itself begets an increasing array of new stumbling blocks for the Regime. The failure of his clandestine death sentence inspires more scandal, as "polo visto, ten dobre nacionalidade e pode armarse unha boa" (57) (it would seem he has double nationality and the whole thing could get quite out of hand) (52). And indeed, once he is court martialed and sentenced to die again, "desatárase unha campaña internacional para acadar o seu indulto" (60) (an international campaign was under way for him to be granted a reprieve) (55). While immune to scandal on his own merits, Da Barca nevertheless transforms into a stumbling block that scandalously disrupts, in a repetitive way, the normal functioning of the Francoist machine of discipline and punishment. To emphasize this point, during the discussion of Da Barca's case and its potential to spiral into more scandal, the governor walks to his window and in the distance sees that "preto da Torre de Hércules, un canteiro cicelaba cruces de pedra" (57) (near Hercules Tower, a stonemason [was] chiseling stone crosses) (52), a very explicit reference to both the lithic roots of the *skandalon* concept as well as to the Christ model, with the sculpted rock taking the form of a cross. The concern that everything could "get out of hand" gestures toward Girard's contention that scandal tends to multiply, as a form of negative reciprocity, and lead to widespread social crisis.

The natural response to ceasing the snowball effect and restoring the sovereign order of the system is to find a substitute victim, or scapegoat. Naturally, in the same conversation in which the authorities outline the problematic nature of Da Barca's case, the conversation shifts abruptly to Da Barca's prison mate, Dombodán, who is also due for execution: "Pero todos sabemos que é retrasadiño. Parvo de Cotolengo" (57) (But we all know he's just a bit retarded. The village idiot) (53). Dombodán, in other words, matches the profile of the scapegoat. As a prisoner accused and convicted of Republican sympathies, he can stand in plausibly as a substitute for Da Barca, yet is innocent and wrongly accused. Finally, he is a marginal member of society, with the theoretical assumption that these qualities will make his death more acceptable to a wide swath of the community.

In theory, carrying out Dombodán's execution could curtail the course of scandal instigated by Da Barca by reasserting the Regime's binding sovereign mandate. In an effort to derail the invocation of the scapegoating mechanism, Da Barca, over the course of his trial, does not speak in his own self-defense but rather defends Dombodán, emphasizing his innocence: "Iso son eu, señores do tribunal, un inocente. Dombodán, O'Neno . . . O nome de Dombodán resoou coma un artefacto nas tripas da sala. O presidente do tribunal ergueuse desencaixado e mandou calar ao doutor Da Barca botando man do sabre" (62) (That, gentlemen of the tribunal, is I, an innocent. Dombodán, The Kid. Dombodán's name echoed like a firework in the belly of the courtroom. The presiding judge rose to his feet, visibly shaken, and ordered Doctor Da Barca to be quiet, laying hand to his sabre) (58). Da Barca continues to operate as a block that makes the Francoist penal system stumble, a fact referenced here with his words being compared to an explosive device internal to the body of justice. His address to the court makes explicit the substitutive nature of Dombodán's execution: Da Barca not only intervenes on behalf of Dombodán, but also speaks ironically as if he were him, merging the two men's identities into one. That the shaken judge immediately reaches for his "sabre" is a clear reference to the nineteenth-century conservative theorist Juan Donoso Cortés, who in his "Discurso sobre la dictadura" advocates "una dictadura del sable" (261) (dictatorship of the sabre) in order to preserve absolutist monarchy and reconfirm the preeminence of sovereign power over the rule of law. In a striking parallel, Rivas's later novel Os libros arden mal also features a magistrate, named Ricardo Samos, who pens a graduate thesis on Donoso Cortés and later becomes infatuated with the most well-known jurist of the German Third Reich, Carl Schmitt, who himself was influenced by Donoso Cortés's ideology.

Da Barca's ability to declaim publicly the innocent nature of the scapegoat, and thus scandalize the process of centering retribution on a single victim for the purposes of stabilizing the Francoist sovereign rule of order, also highlights the Girardian distinction between negative and positive reciprocity. Girard puts forth that in a situation where rivalry has escalated, drawn in other competitors, and joined forces with other scandals, the original objects of desire are forgotten and replaced with "reciprocal violence." Once this form of all pervasive violence takes root, the differences between the combatants, which would have been marked initially by the nature of their shared objects of desire, tend to vanish: "in rivalry, everyone occupies all the positions, one after another and then simultaneously, and there are no longer any distinct positions" (*Things* 299). Beneficent reciprocity, on the other hand, is represented for Girard in the Christ figure, and instead of being based on reciprocal violence it is marked by love and positive imitation. Both forms of reciprocity share in common the ability to transcend difference in a uniting force, despite each achieving radically divergent results. Da Barca, in effect, not only rejects the possibility of displacing reciprocal violence onto a scapegoated victim, but also provokes benevolent reciprocity from his antagonists with his unfailing commitment to justice, such as the Mercedarian nun, Mother Izarne, in the Porta Coeli hospital, or the military sergeant who allows the doctor and Mallo to spend the night together in a hotel in Vigo. While unable to instigate the type of beneficent reciprocity that would challenge the harsh Manichaean duality of the Francoist worldview, and thus cause the differentiation between Nationalist and Republican sides to dissipate in a benevolent form of national reunification, Da Barca nevertheless points toward an alternative politics that is able to think beyond violence as a remedy for a fractured body politic.

Da Barca's explicit critique of the substitutive nature of scapegoating conceptualizes death as the ultimate guarantor of individual singularity. Dombodán is unable to stand in for Da Barca as his individual death represents the one aspect of his identity that cannot be given over to another. This structure recalls how Martin Heidegger theorizes Dasein. As Heidegger argues, "*no one can take the other's dying away from him . . .* insofar as it 'is,' death is always essentially my own" (230; original emphasis). Da Barca reaffirms the "ownmost possibility" of existence in refusing to allow another subject—Dombodán—to have his right to death stripped away from him as a scapegoated stand-in for the punishment of another. Da Barca's critique of the Regime's substitutive treatment of death is linked to the way in which he scandalizes, or disrupts, the flow of the judicial and ideological apparatus. Death, as Heidegger continues, has a "nonrelational character" that "individualizes Dasein down to itself" and precludes that the subject be "overtaken by the existence-possibilities of others" (252–53). In the novel, as Da Barca proclaims the centrality of death to singular existence, he halts the efforts of Francoist ideology to mobilize the lives of the defeated for the purposes of its own "existence-possibilities."

In conclusion, *O lapis do carpinteiro* offers the reader a deeply textured analysis of the complex relationship between stone and human flesh. On the one hand, this essay first showed how Rivas represents the human body as a porous entity that fuses, in a mutually subjectifying way, with the material world around it, with stone playing a particularly pivotal role as a quasi-object that conditions and mediates the way memory and culture are transcribed. Human intentionality, for its part, is able to infuse vitality into stone, making a seemingly inert element spring to life and become an active member of the community. In addition to serving as a foundation that stabilizes and anchors culture and historical remembrance, stone is also the lithic underpinning for important concepts, most notably the *skandalon*, that speak to the emergence and curtailing of violence through the destruction of flesh. Through the example of Da Barca, Rivas is able to elucidate the relationship between scandal, reciprocal violence, and the use of scapegoating, while at the same time offering to the reader political alternatives to approaching political and cultural difference. A lithic reading of the novel, moreover, helps bring to light prominent intellectual threads related to ecology, post-humanism, and sovereignty that become more prominent in Rivas's subsequent work in the first decade of the twenty-first century, with his activism in relation to the *Prestige* disaster and close attention to Carl Schmitt and the notion of political exception in *Os libros arden mal* being two clear examples.

NOTES

1. David McCracken notes that an exact translation of *skandalon* is difficult because the original concept has been broken up and fragmented into a number of different words. As a brief genealogy, McCracken writes,

    > the Greek *skandalon* became the Latin *scandalum*, which became the English *scandal*, but in spite of the similarity no one would argue that they mean the same thing. In the verb form, the Latin *offendere* is close to the Greek *skandalon*, both mean "to cause to stumble," and both have found their way into English . . . *Offense* still conveys a warning of results to the offender, but it also increasingly conveys the challenge that must be endured by the person who has been offended . . . regardless of the consequences to the offender. (6)

2. English translations are taken from Jonathan Dunne's edition of the novel. Unless noted, translations are mine.

3. Timothy Morton makes this point particularly lucidly in presenting his concept of "enmeshment": "All life forms are the mesh, and so are all dead ones, as are their habitats, which are also made up of living and nonliving beings. . . . We drive around using crushed dinosaur parts. Iron is mostly a by-product of bacterial metabolism.

So is oxygen. Mountains can be made of shell and fossilized bacteria" (29).

4.   For more on the becoming-relationship of the wasp and the orchid, see Deleuze and Guattari (10).

5.   Folkart lucidly ties object entanglement to the opening up of desire for narration. More specifically, she argues that the pencil operates as a symbol of "creation and change" (308) and is linked to Herbal's evolved desire to participate in an "intercultural encounter" and be understood as a subject (311). However, the pencil in Folkart's reading is limited to "symbolic agency" (311), which overlooks the catalytic provocation of the object's material reality.

6.   The English translation is from Dunne's edition of the novel.

7.   In 2011, for the purposes of restoring parts of the Pórtico, engineers needed to locate an exact match of the stone originally used to construct the façade. The location had been a mystery until a resident of Vrins wrote to ask that the team analyze the old quarry near the town. The resident had reported that it was common in the area to refer to the quarry as "a Canteira da Catedral" and in the end samples of the stone matched that of the Pórtico ("La cantera").

8.   Rivas, for example, calls the Spanish government's response to the *Prestige* oil spill an attempt to impose "la invisibilidad" (invisibility): "el verdadero ruido de la marea negra fue el silencio. El paréntesis de silencio abrumado del mar, entre el antes y el después de su mugido acusatorio" (*A cuerpo abierto* 256) (the true sound of the oil slick was silence. The parenthesis of the sea's overburdened silence, between the before and after of its accusatory bellow).

9.   Derrida argues that the "archontic principle" of the archive is one of consignation, which involves the "gathering together [of] signs" (10). That said, while the word archive shelters within itself the concept of arkhe, and the principle of foundation it suggests, "it also *shelters* itself from this memory which it shelters: which comes down to saying also that it forgets it" (9).

10.   In 2006, Rivas weighed in on a similar concept rooted in the lithic in reference to the "Caso Bono" in which a government delegate, Constantino Méndez, resigned in the wake of the unlawful imprisonment of two Partido Popular militants who were accused of assaulting the socialist Minister of Defense, José Bono. Rivas links the scandal to the notion of "scruple," which he notes is limited normally to "una china en el zapato y que se le despida con disculpas o sin más miramientos" ("Scrupulus") (a pebble in the shoe that is brushed aside with apologies or without further consideration). Rivas, also emphasizing the historical roots of scruple as a form of stone used for currency exchange, notes that in this case, scruple acquired a moral dimension with the potential to irritate and disrupt those who exercise power. The notion of scruple, like that of *skandalon*, reinforces the interest Rivas shows in *O lapis do carpinteiro* in stone serving as a foundation both for material reality as well as for the conceptualization of social thought.

WORKS CITED

Aguado, Txetxu. *Tiempos de ausencias y vacíos*. Universidad de Deusto Press, 2010.

Castro, Rosalía de. *Follas novas*. Akal, 1985.

Cohen, Jeffrey Jerome. *Stone: An Ecology of the Inhuman*. University of Minnesota Press, 2015.

Deleuze, Gilles and Felix Guattari. *A Thousand Plateaus: Capitalism and Schizophrenia*. Translated by Brian Massumi, University of Minnesota Press, 1987.

Derrida, Jacques. "Archive Fever: A Freudian Impression." *Diacritics*, vol. 25, no. 2, Summer 1995, pp. 9–63.

Donoso Cortés, Juan. "Discurso sobre la dictadura." *Ensayo sobre el catolicismo, el liberalismo y el socialismo. Otros escritos*. Planeta, 1985, pp. 241–62.

Folkart, Jessica. "On Pencils, Places, and the Pursuit of Desire: Manuel Rivas's *El lápiz del carpintero*." *Revista de Estudios Hispánicos*, vol. 40, no. 2, 2006, pp. 297–315.

García-Donoso, Daniel. *Escrituras postseculares: Sedimentos de la religión en la narrativa española (1950–2010)*. Biblioteca Nueva, 2018.

_____. "La risa del fantasma: Humor y memoria en *El lápiz del carpintero* de Manuel Rivas." *Romance Studies*, vol. 33, no. 3–4, November 2015, pp. 208–17.

Girard, René. *I See Satan Fall like Lightning*. Translated by James G. Williams, Orbis, 2008.

_____. *The One by Whom Scandal Comes*. Translated by M. B. DeBevoise, Michigan State University Press, 2014.

_____. *The Scapegoat*. Translated by Yvonne Freccero, Johns Hopkins Press, 1986.

_____. *Things Hidden since the Foundation of the World*. Translated by Stephen Bann and Michael Metteer, Stanford University Press, 1987.

Heidegger, Martin. *Being and Time*. Translated by Joan Stambaugh, State University of New York Press, 2010.

"La cantera que surtió al Maestro Mateo." *El País*, 3 Jan. 2011.

Latour, Bruno. *We Have Never Been Modern*. Translated by Catherine Porter, Harvard University Press, 1993.

Loureiro, Ángel. "La vida con los muertos." *Revista Canadiense de Estudios Hispánicos*, vol. 30, no. 1, 2005, pp. 145–58.

McCracken, David. *The Scandal of the Gospels: Jesus, Story, and Offense*. Oxford University Press, 1994.

Morton, Timothy. *The Ecological Thought*. Harvard University Press, 2010.

New Oxford Annotated Bible, edited by Michael D. Coogan, Oxford University Press, 2007.

Rivas, Manuel. "A boca da literatura: Memoria, ecoloxía, lingua." Real Academia Galega, 2009.

_____. *A cuerpo abierto*. Alfaguara, 2008.

_____. *Books Burn Badly*. Translated by Jonathan Dunne, Vintage, 2011.

_____. "El cuervo de Noé y los árboles de Ítaca." *Voces de Galicia: Manuel Rivas y Suso de Toro*, edited by Sadi Lakhdari, Indigo, 2012, pp. 9–15.

_____. *O lapis do carpinteiro*. Xerais, 1999.

_____. *Os libros arden mal*. Xerais, 2006.

_____. "Scrupulus." *El País*, 13 May 2006.

_____. *The Carpenter's Pencil.* Translated by Jonathan Dunne, Overlook Press, 2002.

Serres, Michel. *Genesis.* Translated by Geneviève James and James Nielson, University of Michigan Press, 1995.

Tasende, Mercedes. "La guerra civil española como apocalipsis: La función del Pórtico de la Gloria en *El lápiz del carpintero.*" *Alba de América*, vol. 23, no. 43–44, 2004, pp. 297–31.

CHAPTER 11

Encounters between Memories and the Present

The Muslim Cemeteries in Contemporary Spain

Jordi Moreras and Sol Tarrés

Introduction

Memory, according to Maurice Halbwachs, is social (37). To this, Pierre Nora adds that any attempts at a recuperation of memory presupposes the instrumentalization of the past in the present (8). And Paul Connerton thinks that it is necessary to apply historical reconstruction to social memory in order to limit as much as possible the arbitrariness with which it is created (13–14). Memory, both the one that is recovered and the one that is selectively forgotten, confronts us with our society's contradictions in the present. Memory is enunciated when it is possible to locate it or relate it to a given space, in which certain historical episodes were lived. The topographic dimension of memory allows us to recall the past. But at the same time, memory is expressed in terms of loss, through the expression of feelings provoked by the disappearance of people with whom an affective and/or emotional bond is established.

The interaction between place and affect is a good starting point for our approach to the existence of Muslim cemeteries in contemporary Spain. These are often considered evidence of a higher degree of cultural and religious pluralism in contemporary Spanish society, but it is worth remembering a fact that often goes unnoticed: out of the thirty Muslim cemeteries that exist today in Spain, seven of them were created during the Civil War (1936–1939) to bury the Moroccan soldiers who died fighting for Francisco Franco's army. From here, it may be asked whether it is possible to reconcile the recognition of funerary otherness in Spain with the fact that some Muslim cemeteries are a heritage of the Civil War. In this essay, we will take the case of Muslim funeral spaces to approach the idea of funeral otherness and its recognition in the present from the point of view of the recuperation of a part of Spain's history that has not yet been incorporated into recent collective memory initiatives. If cemeteries are recognized as spaces for remembrance, how can we refer to current Muslim burial spaces without recognizing that some of them are the result of a time—the Civil War and the dictatorship—whose traumatic memory is yet to be properly acknowledged and coped with? Some of the situations that Muslims experience today with respect to their willingness to bury their deceased in Spain, we believe, have to do with what may seem contradictions arising from the past to the present.

The Memory of the Deceased

Halbwachs suggests that there is a relationship between collective memory and space, allowing individuals from the same community to connect with a shared memory in more meaningful ways. In this process of memory reproduction, spaces that are considered sacred play an even more significant role:

> The believer entering a church, cemetery, or other consecration place knows he will recover a mental state he has experienced many times. Together with fellow believers he will re-establish, in addition to their visible community, a common thought and remembrance formed and maintained there through the ages. (151)

In Western societies, cemeteries are spaces where the remains of our loved ones find a place to rest, and where we remember them. They order the space and the time after death, and they demand that the living maintain the memory of the deceased. The sacralization of funeral spaces contributes to a further endurance of memory, as it turns the visit to the deceased into a religious obligation. Although each individual's death is unique, cemeteries establish a conventional sense of what a "good death" means: that is, a proper death according to social conventions. Furthermore, cemeteries claim for themselves a certain monopoly as memory spaces. But cemeteries are no longer the only spaces where memory of the deceased is produced, as other spaces of death have also become places of expression for social mourning: from the spontaneous memorials generated by individual accidents (Allué), or those emerging after traumatic collective events, such as attacks or tragedies where there are human losses (Doss; Sánchez Carretero), to the spaces of exhumation of graves of the disappeared during the Civil War (Fernández de Mata; Ferrándiz, "Autopsia"; "Exhuming").

It is therefore important to understand other forms of tribute to the memory of those with whom we do not have a direct relationship of ancestry or descent. The "policies/politics of death" (Casquete and Cruz) range from the definition of material and immaterial heritage (Michonneau; Cruz), to the cult of political leaders (Box; Ucelay-Da Cal) and state funerals (Ben-Amos), or the enduring memory of the fallen in state-sponsored military campaigns. As such, these exercises of collective memory become significant because those who deserve to be remembered come to represent, in one way or another, the condition of the group; their memorialization becomes an act of affirmation of one's identity. Paul Connerton insists on the performative nature of social commemorations as a mechanism to reinforce a specific group's identity. In the case of those cultural expressions with a funeral dimension, he emphasizes the use of a "liturgical language [that] makes special use of 'us' and 'those'" (58), and establishes a link with those who are remembered, while creating a distance from those who are considered guilty of that loss. There are several examples that can be provided in this sense: from popular reactions against gender-based murders, to expressions of mourning after an air travel tragedy, or mobilizations condemning terrorist attacks. The act of mourning, then, is no longer limited to a single social space, and public commemoration of death has overflown the walls of cemeteries to be present in many spheres of social life.

In the case of Spain today, many municipalities have passed initiatives to honor in their cemeteries those who died in the Spanish Civil War, by installing memory plaques or erecting commemorative motifs. These memory acts are intended as forms of reparative justice and compensation in the face of existing monoliths and mausoleums that had already been dedicated during the dictatorship to those who fought on the winning side. Other local authorities have opted for a restorative exercise of grouping all those who died during the war, regardless of their side. In any case, it is important to note that Francoist mausoleums occupy an indisputable centrality in many cemeteries, whereas democratic attempts to repair the memory of the "other fallen" have had to occupy a more secondary space. This leads us to talk about the spatial meanings observed in cemeteries, and about the ways in which distinctions and separation between tombs have been defined throughout history.

The Separation between Graves

The configuration of the modern cemetery has traditionally meant the removal of funeral spaces from social life (Urbain 148). This process of urban and symbolic peripheralization, argued for in terms of hygienic reasons, not only implied the displacement of cemeteries from the space occupied by the living in Western societies, but it also ended up determining its internal organization. In 1787, King Carlos III issued a Royal Cell ordering the construction of cemeteries *extra muros* (that is, outside the cities), citing hygienic and sanitary reasons. Cemeteries were still spaces consecrated by the Church and ecclesiastical officials retained the authority over who could—or could not—receive ecclesiastical burial, which in practice meant that cemeteries could not accommodate the bodies of those who did not participate in the Catholic faith. With the new law, however, municipalities took responsibility for funeral services, which was the first step toward the secularization of funeral spaces. In 1831, King Fernando VII issued a royal order authorizing the creation of segregated cemeteries for non-Catholics, whose burial had been banned until then by canon law. Except in very specific cases, the new regulation did not become widespread practice, and the usual way to resolve these situations, as José Jiménez Lozano documents in *Los cementerios civiles*, was to enable "un rincón del cementerio municipal o católico, o se enterraba al 'indigno de sepultura eclesiástica' junto a la tapia del cementerio, bien por la parte interna o bien por su lado exterior" (102) (a corner of the municipal or Catholic cemetery, or [to bury] those "unworthy of ecclesiastical burial" next to the wall of the cemetery, either on the inside or on the outside). In practice, civil cemeteries "se convirtieron en un vaciadero de desechos o en agrios eriales abandonados y de aspecto hosco y desolado por su reducido tamaño y su inmenso abandono" (103–4) (became dumping grounds for debris or abandoned wastelands with a gloomy and desolate aspect due to their reduced size and absolute abandonment).

Historically, the Catholic Church argued that the inclusion of "civil cemeteries" meant the desecration of a space that was considered sacred. When in January of 1932 the government of the Second Republic signed a decree to secularize all cemeteries, the ecclesiastical authorities spoke of the undesirable "pollution" that the creation of civil cemeteries entailed. The Cardinal of Barcelona, Francisco Vidal y Barraquer, expressed this feeling in the following terms:

> Conviene advertir que solo en caso de sepelio de un infiel o de un excomulgado, previa sentencia condenatoria o declaratoria, queda violado o profanado el cementerio, es decir, la santidad del lugar queda manchada, de manera que no se puede dar sepultura a otros, hasta que no sea reconciliado el cementerio. (22–23)

(In the case of the burial of an infidel or an excommunicated person, after a conviction or declaratory sentence is issued, the cemetery is violated or desecrated, that is, the sanctity of the place is stained, resulting in the impossibility to bury others until the cemetery is sanctified.)

The question about the existence of civil cemeteries was not only raised in doctrinal terms, but it also applied to those who had not agreed to receive ecclesiastical obsequies in life. In the explanatory memorandum of the bill (drafted in December 1931), where the unification of civil and religious burials was justified, it was stated that "ser disidente, era motivo de sanción aún en la hora de la muerte, pues como tal se ha venido considerando la privación de enterramiento en sagrado" (qtd. in Fernández de Velasco 285–86) (being a dissident was sanctionable even at the time of death, because the deprivation of burial in consecrated ground has been considered as such). With the new legislation, the walls that separated both types of burials were suppressed, and it was now possible to access the civil sections from inside the cemetery. In addition, the new Republican regulation also recognized the singularity of the English cemeteries and established that only inhumations of people of the same nationality and religious confession as those of the cemetery's founders could be performed there.[1] This criterion was also extended to the Hebrew and Muslim cemeteries of Ceuta and Melilla. In December 1938, the Franco regime returned to the Catholic Church part of the management and maintenance of the municipal cemeteries as sacred spaces, but it did not eliminate the sections that had been intended for civil burials. These sections ended up receiving the deceased of other religious traditions (like Protestants or Jews). Discretion, and not anonymity, set the criteria that maintained these "different" sections, within the predominant Catholic symbolic homogeneity.[2]

José Jiménez Lozano defends the thesis that civil cemeteries, due to the failure of political secularization in Spain, become a space reserved for the dissidents of religious (Catholic) and cultural (Spanish) orthodoxy, that is, those who had challenged an entire society, its traditions, and its sentiments. Hence, those who were buried in them dragged the stigma of being different in both life and death:

En la mente popular, ser enterrado 'como un perro' se asimila en los mismos proverbios populares a ser enterrado 'como un judío, 'como un moro, 'como un hereje, y todas estas expresiones se han usado en el habla popular para señalar la misma realidad de un enterramiento civil, sin la presencia de la liturgia católica. Y eso aunque no se tenga fe. Porque es que quedan como rotas o heridas las normas sociales de la tribu; hay una descastificación, una violenta ruptura con los valores convenidos, e incluso estética, y sentimentalmente resulta intolerable esa ausencia de liturgia funeral. (222)

(In the people's mind, being buried "like a dog" is assimilated into the same popular proverbs as being buried "like a Jew," "like a Moor," "like a heretic." And all these expressions have been used in popular speech to indicate the same reality of a civil burial, without the presence of the Catholic liturgy. This is so even if you do not have faith [in the Catholic Church]. Because the social norms of the tribe are left broken or wounded in a way; there is a de-castification, a violent rupture with conventional values, and even aesthetically and sentimentally this absence of funeral liturgy is intolerable.)

After four decades, Franco's municipal burial ordinance was repealed during the democratic transition and a new legislation was passed instituting nondiscrimination for religious reasons in relation to funeral rites, the possibility of establishing chapels or places of worship, and a mandate to reestablish the physical connection between civil enclosures and the rest of the cemetery. The changes also opened the possibility for non-Catholic religious confessions to have reserved spaces in municipal cemeteries to bury their members according to their respective funeral traditions. This has created what seems to be a contradiction: the defense of the principle of nondiscrimination for religious or ideological reasons at the time of receiving funeral rites necessarily entails the creation of differentiated spaces of burial. The separation between graves is argued on doctrinal principles, according to which it is mandatory to establish a separation between remains. Examples of Jewish and Muslim traditions are cited, based on the requirement that their graves cannot be mixed with those of other religious convictions. The non-mixicity to which these doctrines refer is taken for granted, but it must be taken into account that, first, this criterion is applied within the framework of societies where such traditions are a majority (and therefore, differentiation is carried out with respect to other traditions that, as in the case of the Maghreb countries, end up having their own cemeteries) and, second, that doctrinal adaptations are proposed to allow for burials to be carried out according to specific needs.[3] The argument in favor of differentiated spaces has been presented as a way to integrate and normalize religious diversity in cemeteries, despite the fact that these were much more inflexible with the limits imposed by certain funerary practices with respect to current legal regulations.[4]

The issue of the separation between tombs has been recently brought back to the fore in Spain. The administrative framework that regulates the recognition of cultural and religious diversity proposes a response to what decades ago was a subject of intense debate. Given this set of circumstances, we would like to study the status of Muslim cemeteries in contemporary Spain based on four concrete examples (two of them from the Civil War period and two from more recent historical contexts) to probe a series of issues about the assumptions and rationale behind the recovery/reunion with respect to a specific memory.

The Military Cemeteries of the Civil War

In November 2014, a large group of Muslim protesters marched in front of the townhall of Griñón, south of Madrid, where a Muslim cemetery was created during the Civil War. They protested against the municipal decision to temporarily close the cemetery in an attempt to regularize the inhumations that took place there. The history of this cemetery dates back to November 1936, when a wealthy landowner gave the Francoist army a piece of land so that Moroccan soldiers fighting on the Madrid front could be buried. A field hospital had been set up in that same locality, and the wounded soldiers who eventually died there could be readily buried in what would later be called a "cementerio militar musulmán español" (Spanish Muslim military cemetery). After the war, the cemetery would remain the property of the Ministry of Defense, which, at the end of the 1970s, transferred its management to the Moroccan Consulate in Madrid. From then until today, much criticism has been levelled at the consular delegation regarding its lack of attention and inability to systematize the inhumations in this place. For some years, the cemetery was practically saturated. In 2011, the Guardia Civil (Civil Guard) sent a report to the Griñón City Council informing that burials there did not comply with local funerary regulations, with some of them being made directly in the ground without a coffin. Three years later, and after the Moroccan Consulate repeatedly refused to take over the administrative management of the cemetery, the Ministry of Defense signed the transfer of its management to the local city council for a period of fifty years. In the document, the Ministry of Defense reserved an area to bury Muslim soldiers who die in service, and the agreement also contemplated the possibility of erecting a funerary monument as tribute to the military service people whose remains are buried there. The temporary closure of the cemetery represented the first municipal management of this funeral space, and it proposed the compliance of future burials with existing sanitary regulations, the construction of twenty-two new horizontal tombs, as well as the opening of a competition to hire funeral services that would be privately managed.

The demonstration of November 23, 2014, was convened under the slogan "Nos cierran el cementerio, nos abren las heridas" (They close our cemetery, they open our wounds), and some of the banners carried by the protesters read "Nuestros muertos tienen derecho" (Our dead have rights) and "No hay ni donde caerse muerto" (This is no place to drop dead) ("Musulmanes"). Despite the proclamations vividly delivered by the protesters (who also demonstrated in front of the Ministry of Justice in Madrid a few days later), a significant fact must be highlighted: the Griñón City Council exposed the Moroccan Consulate's administrative mismanagement of the cemetery and stated that it was no longer possible to carry out a census or gather any information regarding the identity of the people buried in the cemetery due to the high number of burial sites that did not have tombstones. It also seemed that, until the City Council intervened, protesters had not been concerned with the dignity and memory of those who had been buried in the Griñón cemetery. In the background of this controversy, there was an internal conflict between the Muslim representations in Spain, but it showed the extent to which Muslim communities in Spain have not engaged in the recovery of a recent memory, responding to the demands of the present.

The creation of cemeteries to bury the Moroccan soldiers who fought in the Francoist army was a logistical decision that was taken among other types of accommodations for the specificities of this troop. Around the different units of the army composed of Muslim soldiers, different services were set up (De Madariaga; Sánchez Ruano; Tuma). As in the case of Griñón, many of these cemeteries were located next to military hospitals in which wounded Muslim soldiers were assigned to specific pavilions. Rosa María De Madariaga provides a noncomprehensive list of Muslim hospitals (Seville, Granada, Jerez de la Frontera, Sanlúcar de Barrameda, Cádiz, Villafranca de los Barros, Zafra, Plasencia, Toledo, Medina del Campo, Zaragoza, Salamanca, Valladolid, Leganés, Griñón, and Avilés), to which one should add the ones we have consulted in the Military Archive of Ávila (Palencia, Zamora, León, Talavera de la Reina, Burgos, Toro, Cáceres, Baños de Montemayor, and Béjar). Cemeteries were not always set up next to every hospital, and some of the bodies were transferred instead to hospitals where military commanders had established a specific space to bury Muslim soldiers, often next to the local cemeteries (as in the case of Granada, Seville, León, or Zaragoza, one of the most important military hospitals during the war, since it had to attend the wounded in the Battle of the Ebro and the campaign in Catalonia). Also, the documentation consulted in the Military Archive of Ávila indicates that these hospitals remained active once the military conflict ended, and some of them (such as the ones in Zamora, León, or Toro) were open until 1950.

A more detailed analysis of the documentation generated by the Intervention of Moroccan Affairs in Spain (the army's administrative unit in charge of the colonial

Figure 11.1. Muslim cemetery in Talavera de la Reina (Toledo), photograph courtesy of S. Tarrés

Figure 11.2. Muslim cemetery in Barcia (Asturias), photograph courtesy of J. Moreras

troops during the Civil War) indicates that not all Moroccan soldiers fallen during the war were buried in Muslim cemeteries: some were interred in other locations depending on the contingencies of the battles. Not all the information referring to the number of Muslim cemeteries created during the Civil War was available at the time, and information was also incomplete on whether they were properly fenced and separated from the local Catholic cemetery (AGA, Box 81/1114, "Asuntos marroquíes en España: Cementerios musulmanes en España"). To remedy this, the commander of the Intervention sent a letter to the civil governors of each Spanish province on March 16, 1940, where he asked them to list the towns where Moroccan soldiers had been buried during the war. The commander's missive was adamant that the data be as accurate as possible, "ya que se trata de organizar este asunto de cementerios musulmanes rindiéndoles el respeto debido" (since this is about organizing the issue of Muslim cemeteries showing the respect that is owed to them). In the following months, all this information was transmitted to the Intervention office, but it is unclear whether it was used to compile a comprehensive report. We do know, however, that the information provided by each civil governor was very scarce and disparate.[5] It is important to note that not all Muslim cemeteries have remained until the present, and some of them, like those in Talavera de la Reina and Barcia, have become vestiges of a more or less forgotten past. (Figs. 11.1 and 11.2)Likewise, the seven cemeteries that have remained to this day are not always located in the same space where the fallen Muslim soldiers were buried. The cemeteries of Seville (1987), Granada (2003), León (2010), and Griñón (1978) are still in the original location, but those of Córdoba (1992), Zaragoza (2002), and Burgos (2009) were moved somewhere else (we indicate in parenthesis the dates of re-inauguration).

The Muslim Cemeteries Today

This section will discuss the cases of two cemeteries from the Civil War period and two cemeteries built in the 1990s to respond to the needs of an increasingly important Muslim community in Spain. All of them illustrate how local funerary spaces have adapted to a more plural and diverse social reality by enabling spatially differentiated burial locations. The contrast between the past and the present configuration of some of these cemeteries shows as many seeming contradictions as the fact of understanding and recognizing the diversity that exists also in funeral rituals (Moreras and Tarrés, "Cimetières" and "Topografía").

The cemeteries of Seville and Granada were the first funerary spaces created at the beginning of the Civil War, which may partially explain why they have been infused with a sense of "recovered spaces" for the collective memory of the Muslim communities living in these Andalusian towns. In the cemetery of Seville, inaugurated in 1936, only a few soldiers (not more than five, according to some sources) were buried, due to the fact that this city was occupied by the Francoist army in the first month of the war. After the war, the cemetery was closed by municipal authorities in 1944 and the land was used to store maintenance tools for the municipal cemetery (Valencia; Tarrés, "Ritos").

The cemetery is located in the northwest corner of the municipal cemetery of San Fernando, next to the outer wall. It has an independent entrance and is connected to the municipal cemetery by a back door. In the cemetery's official plan, this section is called "Arab cemetery." The entrance to the cemetery was designed by the municipal architect Francisco Pérez Bergal in *neomudéjar* style, and it consists of a wooden door under a pointed horseshoe arch with geometric decoration, and a hip roof with ceramic tiles. (Figs. 11.3 and 11.4) Above the door, the decoration consists of two lances, each on separate vases, crossing Islamic crescent moons. Inside, the cemetery was subdivided into an entrance area, which had a space for the ritual washing of the deceased and twelve tombs for adults marked with bricks on the ground; and a second space, separated from the first by a wall with the founding plaque, with seventy-two spaces for graves of adults, and a palm tree pointing toward Mecca (*quibla*).[6] The tombs are oriented perpendicularly with respect to the entrance of the plot. With an initial area of 200 square meters, the cemetery today has an area of 650 square meters, and capacity for just over one hundred graves; in the last expansion (2017), a general ossuary was added.

In 1983, the Islamic Community of Seville-Umma (the first Muslim community that was organized in the city and consisting mainly of Muslim converts) requested for the first time that the necropolis be reopened. After a long period of initiatives, proposals, and negotiations, the city council nulled the 1944 closure decree in 1987, thus becoming the first Muslim cemetery that reopened in the post-Francoist era. In the agreement between the City Council and the Islamic Community, it was established that the Muslim cemetery would be governed by the general norms of the municipal cemetery of San Fernando, which also assumed the administrative direction and supervision of municipal services. The Islamic Community of Seville-Umma assumed the management of the place in perpetuity, and its leaders took possession of its keys. This cemetery is reserved only for Muslims residing in the city of Seville, and burial is performed without a coffin, under a provision allowed by a 2001 decree of the Andalusian regional government that protects this type of burial based on religious reasons. The small size of the cemetery, coupled with the increasing number of Muslims in the area, has led to the formation of a civic platform demanding the construction of a larger Islamic cemetery that can also serve the entire metropolitan area.

The Muslim cemetery of Granada, known as the Rauda, is located in a park managed by the Council of the Alhambra and Generalife and was also inaugurated in 1936. With an extension of about 4,500 square meters, its central section holds close to a hundred tombs that contain the remains of unidentified Moroccan

Figure 11.3. Main entrance to the Muslim cemetery of Seville, photograph courtesy of S. Tarrés
Figure 11.4. Connection between the Muslim Cemetery and the Municipal Cemetery, photograph courtesy of S. Tarrés

Figure 11.5. Main entrance of the cemetery of Granada, photograph courtesy of J. Moreras
Figure 11.6. Various styles of tombs, photograph courtesy of S. Tarrés

soldiers who died in the area during the civil war. After the war, the cemetery ceased to function and remained abandoned for decades, until several communities of Muslim converts began to demand the opening of this space in the 1970s (Tarrés and Rosón). Despite the opposition of the municipal authorities, these communities began to use the site clandestinely in the 1980s, and some notable people (like Muhammad Asad, an Austrian convert and cofounder of the state of Pakistan) were buried there during that time.

After a long negotiation with local authorities, an agreement was signed in 2002 between the city council, the Islamic Council of Granada, and the funeral company EMUCESA to resume operations (Rosón). The cemetery did not officially reopen until 2009, when a new space for tanatopraxia, waiting rooms, toilets, and an administrative area were added. The cemetery houses a total of 577 tombs, all of them directly on the ground without a coffin. The agreement also establishes the use of the plot for a renewable term of seventy-five years, and it mandates that only Muslims residing in the city of Granada and its metropolitan area can be buried there. The management of the cemetery is shared between the local Muslim community, which takes care of the practical and religious aspects (such as washing and shrouding, taking care of the tombs, and the performance of funeral rites), and the municipal funeral company, which assumes the administrative management. As part of the land managed by the Council of the Alhambra and Generalife, and in accordance with current patrimonial legislation, specific emphasis is made on the cultural use of this space as an Islamic garden and on being open to the general public several days a week. (Figs. 11.5 and 11.6)

In 1997, the city council of Barcelona signed with representatives of several Muslim entities (Islamic Center of Religious Formation, Wright Protection Association, Catalonia-Lebanon Association, and Catalan-Palestine Association) an agreement to set up a plot of 552 square meters in the cemetery of Collserola for inhumations performed according to the Islamic ritual. This agreement recognized that some of these rituals, such as the washing and shrouding of the body, could be carried out at the home of the deceased, who then would be transferred to a mosque where the religious ceremony could be held. Unlike the case of Andalusia, current Catalan regulations mandate that the burial be done with a coffin, and this is also reflected in the agreement. The works of adaptation and construction of the tombs were funded by the Muslim community, and, at present, this facility performs between twenty and thirty inhumations per year.

In this cemetery, the Islamic plot is separated from the rest of the funeral areas by a row of cypress trees. (Figs. 11.7 and 11.8) The tombs have a uniform and very simple design, and they are organized in three bodies below ground level (as a vertical underground niche). This fact, along with the obligatory use of coffins, has generated some disagreement within members of the local Muslim community. Criticism has also been directed toward how inhumations are being managed by the Islamic Center for Religious Formation. At the root of these controversies is each party's willingness to manage the cemetery, since the main Muslim groups in the cities (the Pakistani and Moroccan communities and converts) do not consider to be represented by the organizations that signed the 1997 agreement. As a way of compensating, the city council of Barcelona promoted the creation

Figure 11.7. Islamic plot in the cemetery of Collserola (Barcelona), photograph courtesy of J. Moreras
Figure 11.8. Detail of wake with epitaph in one of the Islamic tombs, photograph courtesy of J. Moreras

of a Muslim funeral home in the Montjuïc cemetery in 2007, which was made available to the Muslim communities in the city.

Although the Islamic plot of Collserola was configured initially as a funerary space at the service of the city of Barcelona, it has ended up serving the entire Catalan region for several years. In recent times, as a logical result of the demographic growth of the Muslim community in Catalonia, other reserved plots have been opened in municipal cemeteries for the burial of Muslim dead (Moreras and Solé, *Espais*). The preference toward the repatriation of the remains of the deceased to their regions of origin for burial (mainly in the cases of Moroccans and Senegambians), which may be understood as a way to maintain cultural ties with their places of origin, explains the lack of a continuous demand from community representatives—except in the case of Muslim converts—to have new specific funeral spaces (Moreras and Solé, "Genealogies"). However, and due to demographic changes in these groups, the number of inhumations of fetuses and dead infants has increased, so new alternatives were sought to avoid reaching a situation where graves that were mainly intended for the burial of adults could be saturated. In light of this, the city council of Barcelona proposed to increase the number of Islamic tombs, including some particularly designed for children, using for the first time the niches that are typically used for the deceased of other confessions (although only those oriented toward Mecca).

The cemetery serving the city of Bilbao is located between the municipalities of Derio and Zamudio, and has an area of 208,000 square meters, containing about 28,600 tombs. The creation of a Muslim plot in this cemetery was the result of an agreement signed in October 2008 between the funeral municipal services of Bilbao and the Union of Islamic Communities of the Basque Country (UCIPV). Following the recommendation made by the Ararteko (Ombudsman of the Basque Country) in its annual report to offer reserved spaces for Islamic burials in municipal cemeteries, this agreement made it possible for Muslims living in this region to bury their dead according to Islamic rites. With an area of 450 square meters and a capacity for about fifty tombs, the Muslim plot is located in the northern part of the Derio cemetery and attached to the outer wall, bordering the old civil cemetery. This plot is located in a discrete area, with no particular visible signals, and it has two access doors: one from the inside and one from the outside (which is the only one used for burials). (Fig. 11.9) This criterion was required and specified in the agreement between the funeral services of Bilbao and the Union of Islamic Communities of the Basque Country. Although the location of this plot is not indicated on the official plan of the cemetery (following a security criterion by the cemetery's managers), each tomb is marked with the same type of stela present in all cemetery tombs; unlike the previous ones,

Figure 11.9. Interior and exterior access doors to the Muslim plot in the Bilbao cemetery, photograph courtesy of J. Moreras
Figure 11.10. Interior of the Muslim plot in the cemetery of Bilbao, photograph courtesy of J. Moreras

however, it does not include a *lauburu* (a curved-arm cross that is one of the hallmarks in traditional Basque funerary imagery), but a simple number. (Fig. 11.10)

The agreement with the UCIPV establishes the right to use this land for seventy-five years. For each year of concession, the Muslim community must pay an annual cost of about six thousand euros. The workers of the municipal cemetery carry out the excavation and preparation of the tomb, while the Muslim representatives are in charge of the preparation and handling of corpses, in accordance with existing sanitary norms. Only those Muslims born or residing in the city of Bilbao can be buried here. Recently, authorities responsible for the municipal cemetery have had to face a series of difficulties. First, the Muslim community has not been able to meet the annual maintenance costs of the plot, mainly due to its members' preference for the repatriation of the deceased to their country of origin. And second, the cemetery is only being used to bury fetuses and children, using tombs for adults, which represents a problem of space use. Due to this, it has been necessary to carry out some remodeling of the tombs to adapt them to this unforeseen use.

Conclusion: The Constants of Separation

Paolo Montesperelli argues that societies learn to remember but not to forget, despite the fact that "pueden deteriorarse las huellas de la memoria, los objetos, los instrumentos a los que confiamos la conservación de la propia memoria. Cuando se destruyen las formas de exteriorización de la memoria colectiva, entonces se cierne sobre un grupo, o sobre toda la sociedad, el riesgo de una amnesia colectiva" (51) (the traces of memory, objects, the instruments to which we entrust the preservation of our own memory can deteriorate. When the forms of externalization of collective memory are destroyed, then the risk of collective amnesia looms over a group, or over the whole society). In Spain, as in other societies, cemeteries come to materialize the expression of collective memory. They are the manifestation that, as a society, we conspire against the oblivion of both our loved ones and of those public figures with whom we share our history. But if we are to be fair to our past (and to our present), we must recognize that not all memories fit in cemeteries. And the proof of this in Spanish society continues to be the debate over the exhumation of the remains of those who were victims of the violence during the Spanish Civil War.

This essay aimed to address an example of the paradoxical contrast between the ongoing recuperation of a part of the past (and it is uncertain if it will be included in some form of collective memory), and the expression of a funerary diversity that demands social recognition and a place in these spaces of remembrance.[7]

We believe that an analysis of cultural diversity in funerary heritage is useful to show meaningful contrasts between past and present, and not only as an argument to propose measures in favor of the current management of this diversity.[8] The case of Muslim cemeteries in Spain is significant in our opinion because two different logics converge around them: on the one hand, the recovery of a past that remains controversial, and in which the figure of the Moroccan soldiers who fought in the Francoist army is still subject to a number of prejudices (Tuma); on the other hand, an administrative action that springs from the gradual recognition of religious pluralism.

The cases explored in this essay force us to reconsider the ways in which a given society determines how and where "their" dead, as opposed to those "other" dead, should be buried. Historically, individuals and collectives have been "buried apart" based on the way they lived (homosexuals, criminals, or the sick), professed their faith (people with nonmajority cultural or religious affiliation), or died (suicide). To attempt to answer this question inevitably brings us back to understanding the reasons behind the controversies that turned cemeteries into spaces of social exclusion and segregation. In this regard, separation was something that generated intense social and political debate in Spain decades ago, and which is now considered good practice in terms of the recognition of religious pluralism. The priorities of the present may seem to postpone the claim of a collective memory of the past by Muslim communities in contemporary Spain. The demand made by Muslim representatives to have reserved/distinct burial spaces represents a plausible—and legal—exercise of seeking recognition of their own specificity. Plots reserved for Islamic burials, whether recovered from the recent past or newly created, are located within cemetery spaces in a distinctive way with respect to the rest of the tombs. These plots may use elements intended to enclose the space (such as tree hedges, fences, or groupings), and others that serve to establish a clearer separation (such as doors, walls, or fences), thus defining different areas for different bodies.

In our opinion, it is possible to discuss quantitatively the degrees of separation that these elements create, but the fact remains that they actively contribute to segregate between dead people, and to raise the feeling that these may be spaces that are not only unique but also isolated (this is even more noticeable when they have a separate entrance from outside the cemetery, as in the cases of Seville and Bilbao). How can we reconcile this separation in the present with the fact that this was already proposed by Cardinal Vidal y Barraquer in the 1930s in a controversy about the incorporation of the so-called civil cemeteries, in order to provide them with an independent entrance? As it was suggested at that time, having a direct entrance from the exterior would mean avoiding the confluence of religious symbols. This is an argument that is repeated today and requested by representatives of Muslim communities. More attention needs to be paid to new questions arising from this separation (which favors again a kind of "communitarization of the deceased" by grouping them according to their cultural and religious uniqueness), as it happens now within the spatial framework of municipal cemeteries that are legally defined as secular spaces.

In sum, spaces for Islamic burial in Spanish cemeteries inherit the condition of discretion and reserve that were restricted for civil cemeteries or cemetery sections for non-Catholics. Within each cemetery's topography, these plots are located within peripheral areas, thus accentuating even more the reserved character of what was already subject to guardedness and restraint. In addition, understanding the current meaning of the low profile of certain spaces for differentiated burials necessarily entails recognizing and assuming what this fact represented in the past. Without this exercise of historical memory, it will be difficult to establish the basis for a gradual recognition of a fundamental right to religious liberty, such as having a dignified death according to one's convictions. An exercise through which the Muslim communities in Spain should be able to elaborate a collective memory, "seen from within," as Maurice Halbwachs affirmed (86).

NOTES

This essay is part of the research project "Memories of Africa: Rebuilding Spanish Colonial Practices and their Traces in Morocco and Guinea" (HAR2015–63626-P / 2016–2018), directed by Dr. Yolanda Aixelà (IMF-CSIC Barcelona), and with the participation of Professor Jordi Moreras.

1. The first "Cementerio inglés" (English cemetery) was inaugurated in 1830 in the city of Málaga, followed by different cemeteries, initially linked to the consulates of Great Britain, in those cities and towns where the British had business (commerce, mining, and so on). In those places where these segregated cemeteries were made, other foreigners of non-Catholic confession were also buried (see *Gaceta*).

2. We have reflected elsewhere on the configuration of a funeral heritage of religious minorities in Spain, indicating how the discrete presence of symbologies different from Catholic ones did not prevent their presence inside the public cemeteries (Tarrés and Moreras, "Patrimonio").

3. Islamic doctrine prohibits burying a Muslim among tombs of other religions. This is why Islamic jurists recommend Muslims living in non-Muslim countries to have a designated space to bury their dead. But appealing to the principle of necessity (*darura*), which implies above all the obligation to bury the deceased, some jurists allow burial in non-Muslim cemeteries (Abu-Sahlieh).

4. For instance, see Generalitat de Catalunya's *Recomanacions per a la gestió de la diversitat religiosa en l'àmbit dels cementiris* (2009) and Fundación Pluralismo y Convivencia's *Manual para la gestión municipal de la diversidad religiosa* (2010).
5. Huelva and Tarragona offer two very clear examples. In the first case, the information was sent to the Intervention on April 9, 1940:

> Only in the city of Aracena and in the antitubercular sanatorium of said city, Army lieutenant Paniel Bent Woter, a native of Sierper [*sic*] (Spanish Morocco), died on December 16, 1939. His death was registered in Book 29 of the Deaths Section in the municipal court of the abovementioned city of Aracena, receiving burial in the cemetery of this town.

> In the case of Tarragona, it was sent on April 16: "Soldiers buried in: Cabacés, Paula, Rasquera, Prades, Tarragona, Reus, Gandea, Vilabella, Bot, Mora de Ebro, Salomó, Amposta, Capafons, Horta de San Juan, La Figuera."

6. The plaque is written in Arabic and Spanish and commemorates the cemetery's inauguration in 1936, with the Marqués of Soto Hermoso as city mayor.
7. Rachel Carmen Ceasar has shown the contradictions that arise in the exhumation of deceased Spaniards and Moroccans who died in the Civil War.
8. Despite this, in recent years we have combined both approaches (Moreras and Tarrés, *Guía* and "Patrimonio").

WORKS CITED

Abu-Sahlieh, Sami A. Aldeeb. *Cimetière musulman en Occident: Normes juives, chrétiennes et musulmanes.* L'Harmattan, 2002.

Allué, Marta. "Memorials espontanis: Gestos de dol davant les grans tragèdies." *Revista d'Etnologia de Catalunya*, vol. 43, 2018, pp. 24–36.

Archivo General de la Administración (AGA). Box 81/1114, "Asuntos marroquíes en España: Cementerios musulmanes en España."

Ben-Amos, Avner. *Funerals: Politics, and Memory in Modern France (1789–1996).* Oxford University Press, 2000.

Box, Zira. "Rituales funerarios: Culto a los caídos y política en la España franquista. A propósito de los traslados de José Antonio Primo de Rivera." *Políticas de la Muerte: Usos y abusos del ritual fúnebre en la Europa del siglo XX*, edited by Jesús Casquete and Rafael Cruz, Los Libros de la Catarata, 2009, pp. 265–98.

Casquete, Jesús, and Rafael Cruz, editors. *Políticas de la Muerte: Usos y abusos del ritual fúnebre en la Europa del siglo XX.* Los Libros de la Catarata, 2009.

Ceasar, Rachel Carmen. *At the Crossroads of Love, Ritual, and Archaeology: The Exhumation of Mass Graves in Contemporary Spain.* 2014. University of California-San Francisco, PhD dissertation.

Connerton, Paul. *How Societies Remember*. Cambridge University Press, 1989.

Cruz, Rafael. "El sabor fúnebre de la política española entre 1876 y 1940." *Políticas de la Muerte: Usos y abusos del ritual fúnebre en la Europa del siglo XX*, edited by Jesús Casquete and Rafael Cruz, Los Libros de la Catarata, 2009, pp. 73–105.

De Madariaga, Rosa María. *Los moros que trajo Franco: La intervención de tropas coloniales en la Guerra Civil*. Ediciones Martínez Roca, 2002.

Doss, Erika. *Memorial Mania: Public Feeling in America*. University Chicago Press, 2010.

Fernández de Mata, Ignacio. "Demediados y desajusticiados: Los conflictos de la memoria como antesala de la reparación y la justicia." XII Congreso de Antropología. León, September 2011. Conference Presentation.

Fernández de Velasco, Recaredo. *Naturaleza jurídica de cementerios y sepulturas*. Editorial Revista de Derecho Privado, 1935.

Ferrándiz, Francisco. "Autopsia social de un *subtierro*." *Isegoría*, vol. 45, 2011, pp. 525–44.

_____. "Exhuming the Defeated: Civil War Mass Graves in 21st-Century Spain." *American Ethnologist*, vol. 40, no. 1, 2013, pp. 38–54.

Gaceta de Madrid, 12 Apr. 1933, pp. 102, 278–82.

Halbwachs, Maurice. *The Collective Memory*. Translated by Francis J. Ditter Jr., and Vida Yazdi Ditter, Harper Colophon, 1980.

Jiménez Lozano, José. *Los cementerios civiles y la heterodoxia española*. Taurus, 1978.

Manual para la gestión municipal de la diversidad religiosa. Fundación Pluralismo y Convivencia, 2010.

Michonneau, Stéphane. "¿Lugares de la memoria o memoria de los lugares? Estrategias discursivas para expresar un trauma." *Políticas de la Muerte: Usos y abusos del ritual fúnebre en la Europa del siglo XX*, edited by Jesús Casquete and Rafael Cruz, Los Libros de la Catarata, 2009, pp. 149–67.

Montesperelli, Paolo. *Sociología de la memoria*. Ediciones Nueva Visión, 2004.

Moreras, Jordi, and Ariadna Solé. *Espais de mort i diversitat religiosa: La presència de l'islam als cementiris i tanatoris catalans*. Generalitat de Catalunya-Departament de Cultura, 2014.

____. "Genealogies of Death: Repatriation among Moroccans and Senegalese in Catalonia." *Transnational Death*, edited by Eerika Koskinen-Koivisto, Samira Saramo, and Hanna Snellman, Studia Fennica, 2019, pp. 118–35.

Moreras, Jordi, and Sol Tarrés. *Guía para la gestión de la diversidad religiosa en cementerios y servicios funerarios*. Observatorio del Pluralismo Religioso en España, 2012.

_____. "Les cimetières musulmans en Espagne: des lieux de l'altérité." *Revue Européenne des Migrations Internationales*, vol. 28, no. 3, 2012, pp. 13–26.

"Musulmanes de Madrid condenados a no ser enterrados." YouTube, 23 Nov. 2014.

Nora, Pierre. "Between Memory and History: Les Lieux de Mémoire." *Representations*, vol. 26, Spring 1989, pp. 7–24.

Recomanacions per a la gestió de la diversitat religiosa en l'àmbit dels cementiris. Generalitat de Catalunya, 2009.

Rosón, Javier. *¿El retorno de Tariq? Comunidades etnoreligiosas en el Albayzín granadino*. 2008. Universidad de Granada, PhD dissertation.

Sánchez Carretero, Cristina. *El archivo del duelo: Análisis de la respuesta ciudadana ante los atentados del 11 de marzo en Madrid*. Consejo Superior de Investigaciones Científicas, 2011.

Sánchez Ruano, Francisco. *Islam y guerra civil española: Moros con Franco y con la República*. La esfera de los libros, 2004.

Tarrés, Sol. "Musulmanes en Andalucía." *¿Y tú (de) quién eres? Minorías religiosas en Andalucía*, edited by Rafael Briones, Fundación Pluralismo y Convivencia-Icaria Editorial, 2010, pp. 289–347.

____. "Ritos funerarios en el islam: la praxis entre los musulmanes de Sevilla." *Zainak*, vol. 28, 2006, pp. 429–46.

Tarrés, Sol, and Jordi Moreras. "Patrimonio cultural funerario. Los cementerios de las minorías religiosas en España." *Geopolíticas patrimoniales. De culturas, naturalezas e inmaterialidades. Una mirada etnográfica*, edited by Beatriz Santamarina, Editorial Germania-Asociación Valenciana de Antropología, 2017, pp. 247–63.

____. "Topografía de la otra muerte: Los cementerios musulmanes en España (siglos XX-XXI)." *Religio in labyrintho*, edited by José J. Caerols, Sociedad Española de Ciencias de las Religiones-Escolar y Mayo Editores, 2013, pp. 309–21.

Tarrés, Sol, and Javier Rosón. "¿Musulmanes o inmigrantes? La institucionalización del islam en España (1860–1992)." *Revista CIDOB d'Afers Internacionals*, vol. 115, 2017, pp. 165–85.

Tuma, Ali al. *Guns, Culture and Moors: Racial Perceptions, Cultural Impact and the Moroccan Participation in the Spanish Civil War (1936–1939)*. Routledge, 2018.

Ucelay-Da Cal, Enric. "Enterrar al ciudadano o el tránsito que para el tránsito. El gran funeral público del prócer en la Barcelona ensanchada (1900–1939)." *Políticas de la Muerte: Usos y abusos del ritual fúnebre en la Europa del siglo XX*, edited by Jesús Casquete and Rafael Cruz, Los Libros de la Catarata, 2009, pp. 129–69.

Urbain, Jean-Didier. *L'archipel des morts: Le sentiment de la mort et les dérives de la mémoire dans les cimetières d'Occident*. Payot, 1998.

Valencia, Rafael. "El cementerio musulmán de Sevilla." *Ilu. Revista de Ciencias de las Religiones*, 1995, pp. 263–70.

Vidal y Barraquer, Francesc. *La secularització dels cementiris*. Foment de Pietat, 1932.

CHAPTER 12

The Forensic Eulogy

Science and Invented Traditions in the Commemoration of Republican Dead from the Spanish Civil War

Layla Renshaw

Introduction

The Spanish Civil War (1936–39) was triggered by a military coup headed by General Franco against a democratically elected leftist government known as The Popular Front. Recent studies suggest that 175,000 to 200,000 people were killed away from the battlefields and in the first decade of Franco's dictatorship (Ríos et al.; Preston). Under the dictatorship, there was a strong prohibition against the public mourning or commemoration of the defeated Republican dead (Graham 320). Spain's transition to democracy in the 1970s was characterized as the pact of silence, reflecting a perceived necessity to draw a line under the past (Aguilar 151).

A radical shift in Spain's prevailing memory politics has been observed since 2000 with the founding of the Association for the Recovery of Historical Memory (ARMH), which spearheads the activities of a diverse range of Republican memory campaign groups (Ferrándiz, "Return" 7; Silva and Macías). A primary focus is the investigation of Republican mass graves, and the exhumation, identification, and reburial of Republican remains. The work of ARMH in communities throughout

Spain has triggered a massive popular engagement with the question of the war dead (Fernández de Mata, "Logics" 2528). As individuals explore their family's or community's Civil War history, and re-evaluate Franco's legacy in present-day politics and society, Civil War memory has also become the focus of intensive scholarly work, creative responses in literature and film, and legislative responses to grapple with the status of the dead and the rights of their descendants (Ferrándiz, "Exhuming" 53; Ferrándiz and Baer).

This essay will examine the representations of the Republican dead that accompany the reburial ceremonies in which these human remains are re-interred within cemeteries in their communities. The dramatic re-emergence of long dead relatives in the extraordinary circumstances of a mass grave exhumation has no precedent for most people. Individuals and communities must endeavor to mark this process meaningfully with words, symbols, and actions that constitute newly invented traditions of commemoration and mourning (Renshaw, *Exhuming* 192). The enduring trauma of Spain's war, dictatorship, and transition to democracy has created a representational vacuum around the Republican dead, which persists even at the moment in which their families, communities, and the country as a whole are most intently focused on them. Aspects of the past cannot be broached even within a community intent on mourning the dead, recovering their memory, and transmitting it to posterity. Exhumation opens up new representational spaces and opportunity for new discourses on the past to be made and contested. The investigations generate a wealth of new physical and visual manifestations of the past in the form of objects, human remains, photographs, mementoes, and scientific reports (Renshaw, "Scientific" 63). Yet despite this moment of apparent opportunity, the actual representations of the dead made in the reburial ceremonies often remain muted and narrowly curtailed.

Decades after the Civil War, the passing of time, coupled with the breakdown in the transmission of detailed biographical or personal memories of the dead, means that the kind of conventional representations of the dead associated with funerary rites are problematic. There are deeply ingrained prohibitions on the recounting of narratives concerning the violence and murder that occurred in small communities, meaning that these narratives cannot form part of the memorial process, and receive little explicit representation in the investigative process as a whole. There is a similar widespread wariness around representing the ideology and politics of the dead due to sentiments of culpability and guilt inculcated by the dictatorship (Cenarro 170). Furthermore, confusion often surrounds the precise nature of the dead Republicans' political identities or affiliations. There is a loss of political heritage from those Left-wing movements that might otherwise have furnished the imagery, pageantry, or rhetoric associated with the dead and their cause. The use of traditional Catholic funerary rituals is also problematic given the highly charged and divisive nature of state religion in the war, dictatorship and in current memory politics.

These factors all contribute to a representational vacuum, and I argue here that instead of the possible representations enumerated above, the "recovery of memory" becomes a self-referential act, meaning the scientific processes by which the bodies were located, recovered, and identified form a major part of the newly invented traditions that surround this category of the dead. This results in the newly invented tradition that I characterize as the "forensic eulogy," in which the scientific analysis of the dead becomes a form of expressing post-mortem care for the dead (Crossland, "Acts" 103). The conventional associations of forensic science—neutrality, impartiality, and irrefutability—are crucial in navigating the many tensions that surround the representation and commemoration of the Republican dead.

This essay is based, in part, on ethnographic fieldwork I conducted in a number of communities across Spain, including in Asturias, Extremadura, Andalusia, and, primarily, in the Burgos Province in Castile Leon between 2003 and 2008. Informant names, and some place names, have been changed to ensure the anonymity of the contributors. The essay also draws on the more recent ethnographies and critical social analyses by a number of authors currently working in Spain.[1] Some observations offered here may be particular to their time and place, but nonetheless, they provide critical insights on how the scientific investigation of atrocity feeds into the social and affective processes of mourning and memory.

Post-Memory, Self-Censorship, and a Representational Vacuum

It is useful to reflect on the kind of subject matter and detailed content that might be expected to form the basis of representations of the dead made during their commemoration and reburial, in order to highlight precisely what *cannot* be represented about the dead and identify the reason why these representations are impossible in so many families and communities. It might be expected that in an attempt to remember the dead on either a collective or individual level, and bring to mind the events of their deaths, certain key themes would be referenced in these ceremonies. These might include the personal biographies and intimate histories of the dead, perhaps recalling milestones in their life, aspects of their character, persona, or profession. Given the collective nature of the great majority of these ceremonies and the collective identity that binds them as Republicans, it might be expected that their political ideology or activities would be represented. Finally, the timeline surrounding their deaths, the rationale for why they were targeted, and some reference, on an individual or collective level, to who killed them might be considered integral to the fostering of a lasting memory of the events being commemorated.

Instead, a representational vacuum and profound impossibility surrounds these strands of memory in many communities in Spain. Even the sequence of radical acts constituted by exhumation is not sufficient to challenge the impossibility of what can be said about the past. Although these acts achieve a form of rupture, changing both the physical and symbolic status of the dead, and although the exhumation process elicits a great number of speech acts, in the form of testimony, memorialization, and scientific discourse, a surprising amount of content remains unsaid. These are significant lacunae that are relevant to understanding the form of commemorative practices and forms of memorialization that are characteristic of the current wave of mass grave exhumations in Spain.

The twin themes of who was responsible for the killings and the rationale for why the victims were targeted are scrupulously avoided in almost every discourse, public and private. Even when expressing bitterness or anger about the injustice of these killings, these are voiced in very abstract forms, often as fatalistic tautologies about "evil" in the world, not targeted at specific perpetrators, or grounded in specific episodes. Collective terms for the perpetrators are used such as "los que mandan," those in charge, or "bosses." Some collective nouns make a moral judgment, such as "los sinvergüenzas" (the shameless ones), or the fatalistic "los que pudieron" (those who could) and the related comment, those who killed "porque pudieron" (because they could). When a narrative account draws close to the theme of the perpetrators, distancing mechanisms can be noted, sudden references to events that occurred in other places, switching the narrative voice from a firsthand account, to a second, or even thirdhand report. The reported crimes from elsewhere are less dangerously close. The culpability surrounding the crimes is attenuated by separating out the guilt of those shadowy figures who ordered the killings, and those who just followed orders.

The investigative paradigm that is employed surrounding these graves closely mirrors a forensic investigation and actively tries to elicit as much empirical information as possible from survivors, witnesses, descendants, and the wider community. Yet despite this, the investigators themselves often largely operate within the conventions of self-censorship, particularly around the naming of perpetrators and the political reasons for why individual victims were targeted. In this way, they respect the sensitivities of the informants, but also leave some silences about the past unchallenged.

There is a dominant discourse surrounding the contemporary exhumations that borrows from other transitional justice movements and other global precedents of post-conflict investigation (Rubin 100). However, the discourse of human rights in Spain often focuses on the rights of the dead, *as dead bodies*, and the rights of the descendants of the dead to recover and mourn the remains (Moon 62). This casts the primary injustice as the mass grave itself, which consigns the dead to clandestine or anonymous burials. This can preclude a focus on the original crimes of abduction, extrajudicial detention, torture, and killing that thousands of these victims suffered. These crimes, which led to the formation of the mass graves, are referenced but often in a notably oblique or fragmented way, while the urgent necessity of recovering the bodies, and the collective disgrace that this has not yet been done, is foregrounded, both in the discourse of ARMH, and in the testimony and reflection of relatives and survivors.

There is little acknowledgment, and little apparent "folk memory," of the kind of grassroots political and social initiatives in which many of the murdered Republicans were engaged during the 1930s. The ideological divisions of Spain's Civil War and the tumultuous years preceding it remain a topic of extreme sensitivity to many older and middle-aged Spaniards. Invoking these divisions explicitly is seen as threatening to the post-transition version of a pacted democracy. The form of political repression enacted under Franco's dictatorship also characterized Republicans as profoundly evil and threatening to Spain. A strategy to malign the Republicans was to depoliticize the ideological conflict, reframing it as a moral and spiritual crusade, and masking the substance of the Republic's policies and achievements. Francoist propaganda also promoted guilt by association, punishing whole families for the perceived ideological sins of their Republican relatives, drawing on tropes of heritability, taint, and contagion in "othering" the enemy (Rodrigo 10; Ryan 245). When investigating mass graves in small communities, there is a frequently asserted claim by descendants that the victims "weren't political," and the related assertion that the killing of their relative was inexplicable, the result of collective madness, or even a mistake. This shows a deeply inculcated mechanism of self-protection, an attempt to defend the reputation of the dead, and by extension the family as a whole. This can make it problematic to represent any kind of coherent collective political identity during the commemoration of these deaths.[2] It is also problematic to represent individual political biographies, such as party affiliation, trade union activism, or the holding of public office, as so much of this biographical detail has been repressed, and its public representation may be a source of anxiety for descendants, or even be taken as an acknowledgment of "guilt" by some.

In many communities, there was considerable overlap between the wealthiest and most powerful families, those groups sympathetic to Franco, and those coordinating violent political repression. In small rural communities still dominated by inherited wealth, and the enduring influence of well-connected families, the political situation of the 1930s is obviously a sensitive topic. In many places, there will be a strong correlation between the influential families of the 1930s, and those still dominant today. To explore these power relations, and their central place in explaining the repression that occurred, comes dangerously close to an indictment of the perpetrators, and by extension, may come uncomfortably close to challenging power relations in the present day. A common trope I noted in public discourse about the perpetrators is to invoke the church, priests, or monks as primary instigators of repression, or as particularly morally responsible. This is a complex, layered trope in narratives of Civil War violence, but I argue that attributing guilt to the church effectively masks the other economic and power relations that led to these killings, many of which still pertain in the present day. It avoids individually identifying those responsible, as priests can be identified as representatives of a faceless institution, rather than belonging to a named family, and most significantly, priests do not have direct biological descendants living in these communities today.

The way in which the Civil War and the dictatorship have resulted in the profound obliteration of the identities of the dead, and the degree of anguish this has caused among the living, is most apparent when considering personal or intimate memory of the dead. In many families, particularly the direct descendants of the dead, a state of post-memory exists. This can be characterized as an awareness of loss and grief, and the absorption of these emotions, without a firsthand, intimate memory of what was lost (Hirsch 106). The only surviving descendants must have been very small children when they lost their parent. In some cases, they arrived posthumously, born after their father was killed. The conditions of the dictatorship curtailed most normal modes of communication surrounding the dead. No public mourning permissible, and even in the privacy of the family home, there was an intense fear of surveillance and denunciation amongst Republican families. Adults feared that children could betray the family by speaking about the dead or perpetuating enmity in small communities. The stigma and marginalization experienced by the children of Republican families transmitted shame and anxiety about their family history. The descendants of murdered Republicans were raised by the bereaved and traumatized survivors of these killings. In this climate, children were naturally wary of asking difficult questions.

In many poorer households, or following wartime displacement and looting, families had very limited access to portrait photos and mementoes of the dead. Those that existed featured in very muted ways in memorial practices within the home. Speech about the dead was often highly bounded and formulaic, such as naming them in bedtime prayers, or wordlessly kissing a photo, and was devoid of biographical content (Renshaw, *Exhuming* 132). This lack of intimate knowledge of the dead leaves some descendants profoundly bereft, as it is experienced as a double loss. It also invoked complex feelings of shame and guilt, as they were unable to truly share in the grief of others (such as their mothers) and unable to perform the filial duty of remembering their murdered parent. In the investigative processes that I observed, those forensic practitioners and oral historians gathering testimony about the dead must approach this dearth of memory with extreme sensitivity, as it has the potential to be very traumatizing to those elderly participants engaging in the recovery of their parent's body (Fernández de Mata, "Rupture" 300). On a more complex level, it is also threatening to the whole premise and rationale of the current Republican memory campaign, predicated on the idea that memory can be "recovered," and gains much of its moral and legal authority from the participation of the descendants. When the deep-seated discomfort and ambivalence that surrounds the bond between living and dead is exposed, this is potentially destabilizing to both the individual relatives and the wider Republican memory project. This strongly shapes the representational vacuum observable in the emerging memorial practices and the way these vacuums are filled.

"Socialist Rituals": Tensions between Political and Religious Iconography in the Reburial of Republican Dead

This section will explore the tensions between two competing visions of the words, ritual practices, images, paraphernalia, iconography, and monuments that should be used to commemorate the Republican dead. This tension surrounds whether the primary point of reference should be the religious iconography of conventional Spanish Catholic funerary rites, or iconography of the Spanish Left, including the Republican tricolor flag, and communist, socialist, or trade union banners, slogans, songs, and even gestures such as the clenched fist salute. As a Civil War, there is not the same recourse to a national iconography that might accompany the repatriation or public commemoration of the war dead of other conflicts. In areas with a particularly strong, autonomous regional identity (and where that regional identity is broadly compatible with Republican memory), regional iconography is employed to reflect the identity of the dead and their descendant community. However, for many Spaniards with Left-liberal sympathies, the iconography of the centralized Spanish state, particularly the National flag, has explicitly conservative and Right-wing overtones. Zahira Aragüete-Toribio remarks on this striking absence of both state involvement and nation-state referents in the current reburials of Republican dead, making it very differ-ent from most other ceremonies commemorating war dead ("Negotiating" 6–7). This absence leaves religious and political symbols as the possible alternatives to structure collective memorialization.

One of the main barriers to resolving the tensions between political and reli-gious iconography is the lacunae in memory explored in the preceding section. There is often little detailed knowledge surrounding the political biographies of the dead, such as the exact nature of their party affiliation, their ideological beliefs, or their degree of commitment and activity. Equally, the personal reli-gious convictions of the dead are often unknown. This is frequently an area of stubborn silence (or active obfuscation) within family memory. Furthermore, the political and religious identity of their living relatives may be completely at odds with those of the dead. Given the role of the relatives in driving the exhu-mation process and giving a vital moral and legal authority to the contemporary Republican memory campaign, family consent and contributions are essential in determining the form of the reburial ceremony. Even if memory campaigners or the expert practitioners coordinating these exhumations have a strong vision of the "right" way to memorialize the dead, they cannot ride roughshod over the relatives and communities with whom they work. The inclusion or exclusion of religious and political imagery can stir deep passions and provoke deep angst. The words and ritual acts accompanying a reburial are performative, designed to confer a new symbolic status upon the dead and bring eternal rest. Even the emerging or "invented" burial practices that accompany these exhumations are still functioning as vital rites of passage that must command a collective confi-dence in their efficacy, to lay the dead to rest and bring some closure to the living. The social and metaphysical stakes are very high (Verdery 31).

Among the many speakers I observed and interviewed, there was an acute aware-ness that the reburial should properly "honor" the deceased, meaning it should accurately and authentically reflect their values and beliefs. Yet this remained an elusive question. There was also a recognition by most memory campaign-ers that the wishes of living descendants and societal pressures for a normative burial might override a consideration of the deceased's particular biography and ideology. These tensions are articulated very expressively in the following quote from a lead campaigner in the Foro por la Memoria, a Republican memory group aligned with the hard Left, who explicitly traced an ideological heritage from the Spanish Left of the 1930s. As I quoted elsewhere:

Si quieres respetar su memoria, y este hombre es de izquierdas, lo normal es, lo correcto es, que haya un tipo de ritual distinto y socialista. Luego si la familia quiere llevar un cura, que la familia haga lo que quiera, primero tiene que haber un ritual colectivo que respete el pensamiento y las ideas de los muertos, porque por eso lo mataron. Eso es revisionismo histórico. Si dentro de cien años, si a todos los muertos asesinados por Franco los dejan bajo una cruz, van a pensar que todos los muertos eran de un solo bando, y fueron asesinados por ser católicos. (Mariano, Foro campaigner, Madrid qtd. in *Exhuming* 206)[3]

(If you want to respect his memory, and this man was a socialist, the right thing to do is use socialist rituals. Later the family can do whatever they want, but the collective ritual has got to be a ritual in keeping with the ideas that he professed, because he died for those ideas. This is historical revisionism. If, in a hundred years, all the dead killed by Franco are lying buried under crosses, they are going to think that they were killed for being Catholics.)

Here the contrast between religious and "socialist ritual" is presented very starkly. The imperative to reflect the Republican cause is strengthened by the observation that the dead not only lived by those ideals but died for them. Furthermore, the phrase "historical revisionism" is a statement that the dead were avowedly *not* Catholics, and that the use of Christian iconography not only fails to reflect their full identity as Republicans but actively traduces it. Informed by his own political convictions and historical knowledge, the Foro campaigner speaking here has a particularly polarized view of Republicanism versus Catholicism. For him, they are mutually incompatible. However, for many relatives of the dead throughout Spain, and for many other Spaniards in the 1930s, the opposition is much less clear-cut. While secularism, and even a vehement anticlericalism, constituted important strands of Republican ideology, the lived reality for many (in the past and present) is a more syncretic and socially accommodating belief system, blending ideological, spiritual, and cultural elements in nuanced ways.

These tensions were demonstrated in my recording of a meeting convened among all relatives of the dead who had engaged with a mass grave exhumation in a rural community in Burgos Province. The meeting was called to plan all the details of the reburial ceremony, including burial location, monument, structure, and content of the ceremony, and who would officiate or have a formal role. The place of religion, in terms of the involvement of a priest, entering the church, and the inclusion of prayers and hymns was a central topic of debate. The meeting was opened by a local Republican memory campaigner who suggested a number of options:

ARTURO. Ir dando la dirección de cada familiar y el teléfono. Una vez que estén aquí los cuerpos hay más de una forma de llevarlos al

cementerio, y también tenéis que pensar que es lo que quiere cada
uno, en unos sitios se ha hecho un homenaje al ayuntamiento, en
otros sitios te ponen la película de cómo los han identificado, otros
desde la iglesia, hay que consultar. ¿Dónde se hace?

INTERLOCUTOR 1. Yo no soy religioso, pero entre lo que yo opino y lo
que opine otra persona prefiero que se haga lo que opina esa otra
persona, a mí no me ofende que vayan a la iglesia.

SANTI. Les mató la iglesia, sus ideas no eran religiosas. No creo que quisi-
eran un entierro católico.

HIJA DE LAURA. Se puede ofender a otras personas, lo que ellos pensaban
quizá no es lo que los herederos piensan hoy, tenemos que ser más
tolerantes.

CLAUDIA. Hay momentos que hay que plantarse. Tienes que saber hasta
dónde puedes ceder. Yo trato de no imponer nada a nadie.

SANTI. Murieron por defender sus ideas.

INTERLOCUTOR 2. El día que se muera mi padre tendré que ir a misa por
no ofender a mi madre, yo lo tengo claro. Cuando ellos desaparez-
can se acabaron las misas.

INTERLOCUTOR 3. Me parece una falta de respeto a la gente que está en las fosas.

HIJA DE LAURA. Muchos de los muertos eran religiosos.

INTERLOCUTOR 2. Estaban dando muestra de una tolerancia, aunque no
les sirvió para nada.[4]

(ARTURO. Get the address and telephone number of every family. Once
the bodies are here there is more to do than just carry them to the
cemetery. In addition, each of you has got to think about what you
want. In some places they made a homage in the town hall, in other
places they showed a film about how each of the bodies had been
identified, others went to the church. There's got to be consultation.
Where will you do this?

SPEAKER 1. I'm not religious but it doesn't offend me if they go to the church.

SANTI. The Church killed them, their ideas weren't religious. I don't believe
they would have wanted a Catholic burial.

LAURA'S DAUGHTER. This could offend other people, perhaps what the
dead thought is not what their descendants think today. We've got
to be more tolerant.

CLAUDIA. There are moments when you have to put your foot down. You
have to know when you can compromise. I try not to impose anything on anybody.

SANTI. They died to defend their ideas.

SPEAKER 2. The day my father dies, I will have to go to mass so as not to offend my mother, I know this for sure. When [my parents] are gone, no more mass for me.

SPEAKER 3. It seems to me to be a lack of respect for those in the graves.

LAURA'S DAUGHTER. But many of them were religious.

SPEAKER 2. They were tolerant of religion, even though it didn't do them any good.)

At no point in this planning meeting was there any discussion of the specific political affiliations of the dead, nor the suggestion that these qualities could form the content for a new commemorative act. It must be remembered that a significant proportion of those awaiting reburial had held public office, as councilor or mayor, under the Popular Front government, and others held roles in the Casa del Pueblo and the predominant trade unions of the period. There was little doubt that the majority of the dead in this grave had been killed for their politics. The word Republican was not used at all in this phase of the meeting. Most people were measured and restrained in their vocalizations within this public forum, but a few left the meeting visibly angry and dissatisfied. The stark comment by Santi that "the Church killed them" was met with strong approval even among those who did not speak up. One attendee said upon leaving: "Voy a enterrarle en mi jardín antes de ir a la iglesia" (I'll bury him in my garden rather than take him to the church).

The eventual format for the reburial ceremony in this particular community reflected compromises and accommodations. Similarly, Aragüete-Toribio observed in her fieldwork in Extremadura, that the development of these ceremonies was characterized by negotiation between families at every stage, finding common ground so that an appropriate memorial form could emerge ("Negotiating"). After the caskets containing the bodies were processed through the streets, they were taken to the village cemetery where a priest was waiting. A key informant told me that a young priest, not directly attached to this community, had been invited to officiate, as he was perceived as a liberal and inherently more sympathetic to the exhumation. By meeting the bodies in the cemetery, the question of whether to physically enter the church was circumvented, and the possibility of a longer religious service or mass was avoided. However, a significant proportion of those attending refused to enter the cemetery while the priest was present, and some relatives of the dead did not wish the bodies to enter either. The result was that a large group gathered by the gates of the cemetery, smoking, and making anti-clerical comments. Others commented more neutrally that they felt the prayers were a moment for the family only, particularly as the space around the grave was so crowded, and so they hung back, in deference. This division at the cemetery gates, of a previously united group of mourners, rendered the still-divisive nature of religion highly evident.

The repeated mention of a "family moment" was reference to the fact that it was primarily relatives of the dead, particularly the elderly, who wanted a priest, whereas the coordinators, campaigners, and expert practitioners would have preferred no religious content. The priest's words were brief but conciliatory; he pronounced the standard formula used when committing a body into the ground and led a prayer around the graveside. The rest of the attendees entered the cemetery once he had stopped speaking and stepped away from the grave. As if to balance out the religious content, a short speech on the theme of injustice was made, stating that all the dead had died defending democracy and that their democratic ideals should be upheld in the present. Although this invocation of democracy touched upon the politics behind these killings, it did so in the most neutral, ahistorical, and abstract terms possible, with no mention of Republicanism or any Leftist ideology.

The Forensic Eulogy

The term forensic eulogy is used here to mean a commemorative act structured around an account of the investigation into the mass grave, and the presentation of scientific findings from the investigation, particularly the supposed identity of the dead. I argue that the format of the forensic eulogy is particularly effective, and even expedient, in the specific historic, cultural, and political setting that shapes Spain's Civil War memory. It fills the representational vacuum outlined in section one and is a "third way" between the political and religious rituals outlined in section two. Forensic practices have strong positive associations with rationalism, empiricism, modern progressive techniques, and neutral objectivity.[5] This perceived objectivity provides a welcome antidote to the anxiety, prevalent in post-transition Spain, that all engagement with the past must descend into intractable and partisan claims and counter-claims. Yet despite the perceived neutrality of this investigative paradigm, the forensic eulogy also facilitates an intense sensory engagement with the many aesthetic and affective affordances of the mass graves, the dead, and their possessions.

To return to events observed in rural communities in Burgos, it is useful to revisit the comment of one of the ARMH coordinators, Arturo, when spelling out the options for how to commemorate and rebury the dead: "in some places they made a homage in the town hall, in other places they showed a film about how each of the bodies had been identified, others went to the church." In reality, a number of reburial and commemoration ceremonies I observed throughout Spain blended aspects of all three options, but with detailed account of how the dead were recovered and identified being a central, structuring element in the ceremony. This shows how the scientific work is not simply a necessary precursor to the symbolic and emotional closure, normally associated with funerary rites, but has become integrated with them on a continuum of post-mortem care (Renshaw, "Forensic" 221).

The resulting reburial ceremony in that community is described here, with a more detailed account I have given elsewhere (*Exhuming* 211). All the skeletons recovered from a large mass grave had been placed in individual sealed boxes with a cloth over each. The boxes had been assembled in front of a stage in the town hall, which was full of relatives of the dead, their supporters in the local community, Republican memory campaigners, expert practitioners, and journalists. The event began with a summary of how the exhumation had been initiated and had gained momentum locally, thanking key individuals. Then a short film was screened showing the discovery and exhumation of the mass grave. The stage was taken by the lead forensic anthropologist who had authored the report on the identification of the forty-six bodies, Jorge, who projected an extensive PowerPoint presentation onto the screen behind the bodies. Jorge endeavored to explain the principles of human identification using the analysis of skeletons and objects, but in layman's terms that engaged his audience. He also had to announce which bodies had been successfully identified and which had proved impossible to identify, news that elicited a great deal of excitement and emotion. The majority of the closest relatives, most engaged with the exhumation process, already had this information. However, this ceremony took in a much larger constituency than those who were already actively engaged with the process, and everyone attending was eager to hear the outcome. To have the report condensed verbally and presented visually brought home its significance to the audience, even those who had been briefed, as was made evident by their emotional responses.

After running rapidly through some scientific background on forensic approaches to age, sex, stature, and skeletal markers of disease and injury, Jorge projected a results table showing the number assigned to each skeleton and the presumed identification, with varying degrees of certainty expressed. Jorge's analysis and report represented a considerable technical achievement. Deprived of the financial resources of a criminal investigation and with so little reliable antemortem data to refer to, Jorge had conducted a painstaking and systematic analysis, and by a series of logical deductions had achieved remarkable success in identifying the dead. Around one-quarter of the forty-six bodies have been confidently identified, a further twelve had been tentatively identified, and the remaining names had been assigned the numbers of the multiple skeletons considered to be biologically "compatible" with what was known of that individual.

The projection of this "results" slide caused a pulse of excitement around the room. I noted an elderly couple who had not participated thus far, grasping each other's hands when their relative's name was announced. He appeared to be restraining his urge to go straight to the stage and find his box. The audience craned their necks to look at the boxes, with fresh eyes, and see if they could discern their own relative's remains. It was extremely moving to observe people experiencing the emotions raised by this encounter, not simply with the recovered bodies in their caskets, but with the recovery of a unique individual, yet attempting to contain their reactions, within the confines of a public event. In the moment of revealing these results, it briefly seemed that some long-lost relatives had entered the room. The presence of the dead, and the well of feelings for them among the living, became suddenly palpable.

To explore this invented tradition of the forensic eulogy it is useful to consider in greater depth the depictions of the exhumation itself, the role of the expert, and the kinds of physical evidence that are foregrounded when explaining the scientific work. Considering the film footage of the exhumation, it is striking to note the tight representational focus, shallow time depth, and self-referential quality of the whole event, which could more accurately be called a commemoration, or celebration, of the investigative process itself, rather than a memorialization of the war, dictatorship, or the lives of the dead. The depiction of the exhumation process, showing the open grave and the bodies in situ, showed the expert practitioners at work, reiterating their role and contribution. It also showed the bodies at their most abject and disturbing, some lying layered or contorted on the ground, and it was able to wordlessly reference the violence of these deaths, without explicitly describing the killings. The sight of the mass grave also powerfully communicated the structural distance that had been bridged by this process, bringing the bodies from a clearing in the woods to the town hall, from marginalized to valorized. The massed and tangled bodies, partly occluded by soil, also underscored the logistical achievement of their recovery and identification, bringing order and dignity to the dead, against all odds.

The explanation of how the various identifications were achieved entailed a sustained scrutiny of large-scale projected images of bodies and objects from the grave, now cleaned and photographed in laboratory conditions, so their form and details were much more readily apparent than when viewed in the ground by visitors to the grave site. Significantly, a number of black-and-white portrait photos of the dead Republicans, taken of them in life, were also shown as part of this technical explanation. The identifications were based, in various ways, on the matching of ante- and post-mortem evidence through a triangulation between bodies, objects, and photographs. Thusly the presentation necessitated an immersive engagement with the dead via a number of material registers, presenting them for the assembled audience in various ways. Existing mementoes of the dead, primarily portrait photos contributed by relatives of the dead, were brought into assemblage with the discoveries of the forensic investigation, changing the meaning of these photos, and drawing the relatives in. The aesthetic charge of both the human remains and the portrait photos was heightened, and changed, by being juxtaposed with each other in the presentation, as the links between ante- and post-mortem features were explained.

The sustained engagement with the material possessions of the dead also has a particular aesthetic and emotional impact, more so as their material qualities are rendered much more visible in a presentation than in the grave. Skeletal tissues, particularly the rather abstruse features routinely used in the estimation of age and sex in the skeleton, can seem blankly homogenous, remote, or hard to relate to the qualities of a living person. The sternal rib end or a pubic symphysis may be highly revealing to a trained forensic anthropologist but offer little point of visceral or emotional connection, or comprehension, to the relatives of the dead and the wider community attending this ceremony. Similarly, the sight of amassed skeletons in the grave can elicit horror, moral outrage, and a comprehension of the scale of the crime, yet they do not usually elicit a deep sentiment of mourning or empathy for the individual dead. In this way, personal possessions are often more effective indices of the lives lost.[6] The preservation of an object such as a comb, watch, or belt means they are less radically altered than a skeleton that has lost its flesh. The suite of objects associated with the dead are similar to things that any one of us might wear or carry on their person and so they powerfully convey the specificity, individuality, and reality of that past life. As an informant in Spain who had witnessed many exhumations, including those of his own family members, reflected, "una bota es más humana que un hueso" (qtd. in Renshaw, *Exhuming* 159) (a boot is more human than a bone).

The remains and objects also eloquently conveyed their complex histories. They have a particular patina of age and decay that speaks of their time in the grave.[7] The aesthetic of these objects and their recognizably mid-century provenance is a powerful connection with the existing repertoire of images of the 1930s. They speak of a particular period, yet many materials, such as a plastic comb or a coin, are so close to the present-day form as to produce a jolt of recognition and familiarity, reminding us that these events are very close to our own time. In this way, the objects manage to be both archaeological and contemporary. The mundane, often humble, nature of the objects is also a fundamental part of their emotional power. This speaks of horror interjecting itself into the commonplace. Of civilians, going about their daily lives, and having those lives suddenly shattered by violence (Sturkin 21).

Reflecting upon the aesthetic and affective power of these objects, helps to comprehend the efficacy of the forensic eulogy, the type of representational vacuum it has come to fill in the Republican memory project, and the precise representations of the past afforded by the public presentation of forensic evidence. It is vital to engage with the aesthetics of these objects and images, precisely because the whole premise of the forensic eulogy is that it is *not* an aesthetic and affective representation of the dead. Rather, it is framed as a "necessary" engagement predicated on the functional, utilitarian value of this material as "evidence." The paradigmatic associations of neutrality, objectivity, and practical necessity circumvent the defenses of viewers who might be wary of aestheticized depictions of the dead. Profound taboos and uneasiness around representations of the Republican dead are more effectively assuaged by this kind of pragmatic, technocratic focus on the dead as evidence. Furthermore, the representation of bodies and objects under the auspices of a scientific presentation is very effective in sidestepping potential critiques from opponents of exhumation, namely the accusation of exploitative representations of the dead, by politicizing the powerful images of mass graves, or romanticizing the Republican dead.

As described in the account above, the revelation of the identities of the dead was an intense peak in the collective emotion of those assembled for the reburial, and a point of palpable catharsis in the ceremony. It is unsurprising that the moment in which a human identity is reconstituted from an undifferentiated mass, and the crime of consigning a body to oblivion is undone, is powerful for those who witness it, particularly those with a biological or affective connection to the dead. However, the material affordances of these objects and images shown in the forensic eulogy are also a significant part of this catharsis. As the condition of post-memory necessitates the recovery or construction of traces of a lost past, whose loss can then be mourned, the representation of bodies and objects from the grave enables a focus of mourning for the great majority of mourners assembled at the ceremony, who will have no firsthand knowledge or memory of the dead. In the ceremony described here, I observed that the revelation of identity proved deeply affecting, even to those individuals who at the beginning of the investigation that individualizing the dead through scientific identification was *not* of primary importance to them.

A more complex point relating to post-memory and catharsis in the forensic eulogy resides in the conceptualization of forensic evidence as a kind of magic trick. This is not in any way to contend that the scientific practices are deceitful, nor to be glib about the emotional impact of receiving forensic evidence about a loved one. However, there is something of a magical aura about the way many forensic analyses are conducted. Tiny, unpromising, and seemingly inconsequential details may be transformed, via the expert gaze or analytical equipment, into profound revelations such as the identity of a body, or the events surrounding their injury, death, or disappearance (Crossland, "Clues" 75; Renshaw, "Forensic" 230). The quality of a magic trick is attained because of the seemingly incommensurate scale and register between something unimportant, such as a fingerprint, single hair, or drop of blood, and the magnitude of the answers that this evidence may ultimately reveal. The rapid presentation of a chain of connections that leads to a forensic identification, particularly those revelations that rest on small or hitherto concealed features, can induce a sense of vertigo when they are explained. The presentation of these results is arresting and suspenseful, adding to the sense of relief and catharsis. Far from being dry, the presentation of this technical work engages the imagination of those assembled in profound ways. This is particularly true when the aspects that are selected for presentation being those most accessible, readily apprehended, technically impressive, or intellectually satisfying.

As a corollary to this, the highly contingent nature of forensic evidence has its own emotional force. That the bodies and objects were once thought lost, or that the small but significant pieces of evidence contained within the skeletons or objects could so easily have been damaged or overlooked, makes the successful discovery of graves and the successful identification of bodies even more impactful. Particularly given the long history of repression and denial in Spain, these feel like successes that have happened against all odds. In some cases, the discoveries seem so dependent on chance as to feel miraculous. It leaves the impression that the dead are willingly giving up their secrets and are collaborating in their recovery and the restitution of their identities (Renshaw, "Forensic" 232). In the post-memorial context, this sense of a collaboration is of profound significance to the emotional impact of the ceremony and of the exhumation as a whole.

There is also a more prosaic reason to foreground science in commemorative acts for the Republican dead, as it clearly instills confidence and conveys the authority of those undertaking the exhumation work, and by extension, the wider Republican memory project. This is not a charge that those undertaking the work are cynically using their expert status as a source of power in their interactions with relatives of the dead, or local communities. In all the projects I encountered, the interactions were a model of sincere engagement and open communication.

However, the contemporary Spanish exhumations are almost unique in that they have reached a scale of activity and a quality and proficiency of evidence collection and reporting, yet with no overarching authority, such as a tribunal or truth commission taking responsibility for outcomes and impact of this work.

Thousands of bodies have been unearthed and are on the move between mass graves, science laboratories, and cemeteries, all without any central investigative organization to oversee it. The legal framework surrounding these bodies has evolved but remains piecemeal. It can be destabilizing for relatives of the dead to take responsibility for such a radical act as unearthing the dead. It can induce profound anxieties over whether the outcomes are reliable, whether exhumations best serve the dead, or should they be left to rest in peace. The public representations of both the exhumation and laboratory work can assuage these anxieties. It underscores that those conducting the work had the technical authority to do it, and the investment of their physical and intellectual labor (almost always on a voluntary basis) confers a type of moral authority, too. The idea of exposing the dead and moving them, decades after death and burial, can be shrouded in taboo, as potentially violent, even obscene. The forensic framing or dressing of the grave site, with expert practitioners delicately and methodically at work, the sterile environment of the lab, and the professional photos of bodies and objects with scales and labels in view, defuse the potential violence of opening up the graves, and recasts it emphatically as a form of post-mortem care.

Invented Traditions and the Genre of Atrocity

As media depictions of mass grave exhumations have become more common, showing atrocities from around the world, the layperson has become more attuned to decoding these images. Alfredo González-Ruibal notes that images of mass grave exhumations have cemented themselves in the collective imagination of the Spanish public (94), while Ariel Dorfman notes the universalizing or "globalizing" visual vocabulary surrounding the investigation of death and disappearance (255). Visual commonalities subtly situate Spanish exhumations in a lineage of other mass graves, globally. This reinforces the discourse of the contemporary Republican memory campaign in Spain, seeking to borrow from international precedents of transitional justice. The transnational turn in Spanish memory politics is receiving increased scholarly attention, with Marina Montoto Ugarte arguing that with a growing engagement with transnational law, there is an accompanying "circulación internacional" (international circulation) of key structuring concepts such as victim and victimhood (1). The transnational turn is increasingly reflected not only in forensic protocols and standards, but in the commemorative acts adopted in Spain, and the merging of science and ritual is part of this turn.

The forensic eulogy is part of an iterative cycle whereby memorial practices already associated with other historical atrocities are adopted or adapted in order to commemorate the newly recovered Republican dead. At the same time, the selection, reproduction, and circulation of certain images of the bodies and objects from Spanish exhumations closely mirrors the canon of images already associated with other conflicts. These practices in image production implicitly lay claim to historical and political parallels, which, in turn, makes the co-opting of universalized memorial practices seem more fitting to the Spanish context. Alejandro Baer and Natan Sznaider identify a nexus of representational borrowings, or symbolic references, that link the Spanish Republican memory campaign, the Dirty War in Argentina, and the Holocaust (33). Due to a series of chronological, cultural, and ideological connections, they identify these two periods of atrocity as fundamental reference points in the development of the Republican memory movement.

The forensic eulogy is an invented tradition that entails a deep sensory and visual engagement with the black-and-white portrait photos of the dead, with images of amassed human remains in the grave. In particular, the forensic eulogy entails a sustained engagement with the personal possessions and ephemera of the dead, all material culture dating to the 1930s, including glasses, shoes, and fragile hand-written documents. These mundane possessions are fundamentally changed in meaning and become icons of an atrocity through the radical way they have become separated from their owner, their normal use coming to an abrupt end. Such radically bereft objects, gathered on a massive scale during the extermination of Europe's Jews, have become indices for the dead and disappeared. We are extremely well-versed in reading possessions with a similar provenance and patina as shorthand for an individual life cut short by catastrophe. The aesthetic and affective alignment of these killings with the Holocaust, a near-universal byword for evil, is a profound challenge to the muted way that Civil War violence was conceptualized during Spain's transition to democracy. It is part of the radical reclassification of the mass graves in the popular imagination achieved by Spain's Republican memory campaign over the last twenty years. The bodies and objects contribute to a visceral, intuited sense of the historical parallels concerning destruction, loss, and injustice, rather than an intellectual argument about the historical connections between the Civil War, the Holocaust, or the Dirty War.

The reburial ceremony detailed in the previous section can be situated in a wider genre of atrocity, drawing on the aesthetics of a universalized memorial culture. A young cellist had been invited to sit in the cemetery and play mournful classical music while the individual boxes of skeletonized remains were interred together. When I spoke to the local ARMH coordinator who had overseen the planning of the reburial, he explicitly said that classical music was chosen to overcome the "problem of singing." This meant the very real risk of spontaneous singing of political anthems or slogans, versus a competing religious contingent singing a hymn, or intoning a prayer. Instead, the wordless music, not grounded in any particular Spanish tradition, filled a representational space with something seemingly neutral. However, it was not entirely content-free, as something of the melody and timbre of the cello music made an aesthetic appeal to representations of World War II, specifically, the Holocaust. The aesthetic resonance with the Holocaust was confirmed when some of the activists did an exaggerated impression of the cello music and joked that "it was like a scene from Schindler's List." I guessed that this frustration was primarily because the effect of the music, drowning out Republican anthems, was readily apparent to those familiar with these ceremonies. Also, by referencing a big-budget Hollywood film, the attempt to stage-manage the event, and even to stage-manage emotions, was critiqued as inauthentic. For those activists immersed in Civil War history, and the politics of the Republican memory campaign, the obvious reach for pathos had descended into bathos. Yet the wider response of those assembled at the reburial was one of strong approval. The mournful music was praised as moving, "fitting" to the ceremony, and evocative of "the past."

Many of the possible representations of the dead that might be made during exhumation and reburial remain highly contentious and potentially divisive. There are deeply ingrained prohibitions against publicly recounting the violence that occurred in small communities. There may be ambivalence around the ideology of the dead, and the political affiliations that might otherwise have furnished the imagery, pageantry, or rhetoric used in commemoration. Normative funerary rites, drawing on Catholic tradition, are also problematic for the Republican dead, and a potentially divisive topic amongst the surviving relatives. The result is a representational vacuum, and so the recovery of memory becomes self-referential and performative. The scientific processes by which the bodies were recovered and identified are a safe repository for the memorial impulse, and so form a major part of the invented traditions used to commemorate the Republican dead.

The format of a forensic eulogy, in which film footage, photographs, and scientific reports from the investigative process become a central element of memorialization, has a number of important effects on the way the dead are remembered. By being primarily self-referential, it enables a redemptive narrative around these graves, celebrating the collective achievement of families, communities, and expert practitioners in these exhumations, which are truly remarkable examples of grassroots social action. This redemptive ending reframes the longer narrative arc of civil war, dictatorship, and the failure to recover these bodies in the democratic transition. The forensic eulogy also entails a deep engagement with the strong aesthetic and affective powers of bodies and objects from the graves. It frames this sensory engagement in terms of evidential value, thus circumventing resistance, and deflecting a charge of the emotional or political "exploitation" of the dead. While carrying associations of neutrality and objectivity, the forensic process reframes these bodies and objects in subtle and complex ways, conferring new emotional and memorial resonances upon them. Some of these aesthetic and affective affordances are specific to the Spanish context, while some reference an increasingly universalized discourse on human rights and the memorialization of atrocity.

NOTES

1. See Aragüete-Toribio *Archive*; Bevernage and Colaert; Ribeiro de Menezes; Ríos and Etxeberria

2. See Ledesma and Rodrigo on the challenge of commemorative equivalence between the two sides.

3. For further discussion of this interview, see my book *Exhuming Loss* (206).

4. Unless otherwise noted, my recording.

5. For discussions that problematize this, see Crossland, "Evidential" 121; Keenan and Weizman 66; Rosenblatt 18.

6. See Clark for a more comparative discussion of the diverse objects that become icons of atrocity.

7. See Ferrán or Torres for powerful examples of this.

WORKS CITED

Aguilar, Paloma. *Memory and Amnesia: The Role of the Spanish Civil War in the Transition to Democracy*. Berghahn Books, 2002.

Aragüete-Toribio, Zahira. *From the Archive to the Grave Producing History in Spanish Civil War Exhumations*. Palgrave Macmillan, 2017.

_____. "Negotiating Identity: Reburial and Commemoration of the Civil War Dead in Southwestern Spain." *Human Remains and Violence*, vol. 1, no. 2, 2015, pp. 5–20.

Baer, Alejandro, and Natan Sznaider. "Ghosts of the Holocaust in Franco's Mass Graves:

Cosmopolitan Memories and the Politics of 'Never Again.'" *Memory Studies*, vol. 8, no. 3, 2015, pp. 328–44.

Bevernage, Berber, and Lore Colaert. "History from the Grave? Politics of Time in Spanish Mass Graves Exhumations." *Memory Studies*, vol. 7, no. 4, 2014, pp. 440–56.

Cenarro, Angela. "Memory beyond the Public Sphere." *History and Memory*, vol. 14, no. 1–2, 2002, pp. 165–88.

Clark, Laurie Beth. "Mnemonic Objects: Forensic and Rhetorical Practices in Memorial Culture." *Memory and Post-War Memorials: Confronting the Violence of the Past*, edited by Marc Silberman and Florence Vatan, Palgrave Macmillan, 2013, pp. 155–73.

Crossland, Zoe. "Acts of Estrangement. The Post-Mortem Making of Self and Other." *Archaeological Dialogues*, vol. 16, no. 1, 2009, pp. 102–25.

_____. "Evidential Regimes of Forensic Archaeology." *Annual Review of Anthropology*, vol. 42, 2013, pp. 121–37.

_____. "Of Clues and Signs: The Dead Body and its Evidential Traces." *American Anthropologist*, vol. 111, no. 1, 2009, pp. 69–80.

Dorfman, Ariel. "The Missing and Photography: The Uses and Misuses of Globalization." *Spontaneous Shrines and the Public Memorialization of Death*, edited by Jack Santino, Palgrave Macmillan, 2006, pp. 255–60.

Fernández de Mata, Ignacio. "The 'Logics' of Violence and Franco's Mass Graves: An Ethnohistorical Approach." *International Journal of the Humanities*, vol. 2, no. 3, 2004, pp. 2527–35.

_____. "The Rupture of the World and the Conflicts of Memory." *Unearthing Franco's Legacy: Mass Graves and the Recovery of Historical Memory in Spain*, edited by Carlos Jerez-Farrán and Samuel Amago, University of Notre Dame Press, 2010, pp. 279–303.

Ferrán, Ofelia. "Grievability and the Politics of Visibility: The Photography of Francesc Torres and the Mass Graves of the Spanish Civil War." *Memory and Postwar Memorials: Confronting the Violence of the Past*, edited by Marc Silberman and Florence Vatan, Palgrave Macmillan, 2013, pp. 117–36.

Ferrándiz, Francisco. "Exhuming the Defeated: Civil War Mass Graves in 21st-Century Spain." *American Ethnologist*, vol. 40, no. 1, 2013, pp. 38–54.

_____. "The Return of Civil War Ghosts: The Ethnography of Exhumations in Contemporary Spain." *Anthropology Today*, vol. 22, no. 3, 2006, pp. 7–12.

Ferrándiz, Francisco, and Alejandro Baer. "Digital Memory: The Visual Recording of Mass Grave Exhumations in Contemporary Spain." *Forum: Qualitative Social Research*, vol. 9, no. 3, 2008.

Graham, Helen. "The Spanish Civil War 1936–2003: The Return of Republican Memory." *Science and Society*, vol. 68, no. 3, 2004, pp. 313–28.

González-Ruibal, Alfredo. "Museums and Material Memories of the Spanish Civil War: An Archaeological Critique." *Public Humanities and the Spanish Civil War: Connected and Contested Histories*, edited by Alison Ribeiro de Menezes, Antonio Cazorla-Sánchez, and Adrian Shubert, Palgrave Macmillan, 2018, pp. 93–114.

Hirsch, Marianne. "The Generation of Postmemory." *Poetics Today*, vol. 29, no. 1, 2008, pp. 103–28.

Keenan, Thomas, and Eyal Weizman. *Mengele's Skull: The Advent of a Forensic Aesthetics*. Sternberg Press/Portikus, 2012.

Ledesma, José Luis, and Javier Rodrigo. "Caídos por España, mártires de la libertad: Víctimas y conmemoración de la Guerra Civil en la España posbélica (1939–2006)." *Ayer*, vol. 63, 2006, pp. 233–55.

Montoto Ugarte, Marina. "Las víctimas del franquismo en 'La Querella Argentina': Luchas por el reconocimiento y nuevas desigualdades." *Papeles del CEIC. International Journal on Collective Identity Research*, vol. 1, 2017, pp. 1–25.

Moon, Claire. "Human Rights, Human Remains: Forensic Humanitarianism and the Human Rights of the Dead." *International Social Science Journal*, vol. 65, 2014, pp. 49–63.

Preston, Paul. *The Spanish Holocaust: Inquisition and Extermination in Twentieth-Century Spain*. Harper Press, 2012.

Renshaw, Layla. *Exhuming Loss: Memory, Materiality and Mass Graves of the Spanish Civil War*. Left Coast Press, 2011.

———. "Scientific and Affective Identification of Republican Civilian Victims from the Spanish Civil War." *Journal of Material Culture*, vol. 15, no. 4, 2010, pp. 449–63.

———. "The Forensic Gaze: Reconstituting Bodies and Objects as Evidence." *Mapping the "Forensic Turn": Engagements with Materialities of Mass Death in Holocaust Studies and Beyond*, edited by Zuzanna Dziuban, New Academic Press, 2017, pp. 151–71.

Ribeiro de Menezes, Alison. *Embodying Memory in Contemporary Spain*. Palgrave Macmillan, 2014.

Ríos, Luis, and Francisco Etxeberria. "The Spanish Civil War Forensic Labyrinth." *Legacies of Violence in Contemporary Spain: Exhuming the Past, Understanding the Present*, edited by Ofelia Ferrán and Lisa Hilbink, Routledge, 2016, pp. 44–68.

Ríos, Luis, et al. "Patterns of Perimortem Trauma in Skeletons Recovered from Mass Graves from the Spanish Civil War (1936–1939)." *The Routledge Handbook of the Bioarchaeology of Human Conflict*, edited by Chris Knüsel and Martin Smith, Routledge, 2014, pp. 621–40.

Rodrigo, Javier. *Hasta la raíz: Violencia durante la Guerra Civil y la dictadura franquista*. Alianza, 2008.

Rosenblatt, Adam. *Digging for the Disappeared: Forensic Science after Atrocity*. Stanford University Press, 2015.

Rubin, Jonah. "Transitional Justice against the State: Lessons from Spanish Society-Led Forensic Exhumations." *International Journal of Transitional Justice*, vol. 8, 2014, pp. 99–120.

Ryan, Lorraine. "The Sins of the Father: The Destruction of the Republican Family in Franco's Spain." *History of the Family*, vol. 14, 2009, pp 245–52.

Silva, Emilio, and Santiago Macías. *Las fosas de Franco: Los republicanos que el Dictador dejó en las cunetas*. Temas de Hoy, 2003.

Sturkin, Marita. "The Objects that Lived: The 9/11 Museum and Material Transformation." *Memory Studies*, vol. 9, no. 1, 2016, pp. 13–26.

Torres, Francesc. "The Images of Memory: A Civil Narration of History. A Photo Essay." *Journal of Spanish Cultural Studies*, vol. 9, no. 2, 2008, pp. 157–75.

Verdery, Katherine. *The Political Lives of Dead Bodies: Reburial and Postsocialist Change.* Columbia University Press, 1999.

◆ CHAPTER 13

De-metaphorization of "the Other" in the Wake of Modern Biopolitics

A Reading of Jesús Carrasco's
La tierra que pisamos

Pedro Aguilera-Mellado

A Kate, por todo lo incontable.

The other is not the possible. So it would be necessary to say that the only possible invention would be the invention of the impossible.

JACQUES DERRIDA, *PSYCHE: INVENTIONS OF THE OTHER*, 44

On a previously unseen scale, the global nature of the circulation of mortality as well as the status of uncountability of disappeared bodies—or in other words, the disappearance of death itself—determines the contemporary status of death for human existence. In what follows, I argue that under the current flexible pattern of the global accumulation of capital, the so-called "disenchantment of the world" continues toward its exhaustion, *but* it is simultaneous to, and inseparable from, the processes of the re-enchantment of the world that turns capitalism into a religion that administers death and manages our existence like never before. These processes accelerated in the context of the Spanish nation-state since 1959, and they are now urging us to reconsider the biopolitical diagnosis and therefore its necropolitical emendation in a fully globalized capitalistic society.

It is not that both biopolitical and necropolitical paradigms are no longer certain; rather, by having precisely unfolded to their territorial and technical limits, they invite us to think beyond the ontological presupposition of force (of force as being, of politics as being) that both paradigms still fall into. This presupposition has recently been recognized by Gareth Williams, who, grappling with Foucault's notion in the present global "technification" of life and Gramsci's notion of hegemony, states:

> Biopolitics not only remains consciously blind to the ontological problematic; it is that blindness reconverted into the socialization of the everyday and the sociologization of political thinking itself. It therefore posits, on one side, the technologically mediated subordination of the workers' body reconverted into the calculability of the value of life on a previously unseen and unimaginable scale, and, on the other, the relation between the political and its ontological presuppositions to the extent that it is itself the subtraction of the relation between life and death from every ontological presupposition in favor of the absolute economization and circulation of mortality in the name of the extension and reproduction of surplus value. (8–9)

This leads Williams to propose that "all contemporary thinking of the limits of the political would do well to consider the possibility of a post-Gramscian and of a post-Foucauldian inflection, in such a way as to think both the limits of and between hegemony and biopolitics" (9). Although this certainly requires further discussion that will not fit into this essay, the modern risk of dwelling within hegemony and biopolitical (and therefore also within the *necro*political) paradigms will expose us to the "socialization of the everyday and sociologization of political thinking itself" (8). I claim that this is precisely the limit or "ontological end" that Jesús Carrasco's 2016 novel *La tierra que pisamos* (The Earth We Tread) signals. By doing so, it sets up a fundamental point of inflection in contemporary Spanish narrative by posing death at the center of a possible resistance to the administration of bodies that now capitalism enacts at a global scale. Only on its surface is this novel about early modernity and the birth of colonialism, or about the Holocaust, or about the Spanish Civil War, or about a particular so-called migratory crisis within a particular region of the planet. The novel also deals with the modern processes of labor and the present worldwide displacement of bodies, but more crucially, *La tierra que pisamos* engages with the principle of general equivalence that underlies and sustains all of the above during the modern longue durée of (and current scattering in the present day) capitalism as the ultimate religion on our planet. As a response to that, I claim that, through this novel, finitude appears as the forgotten kernel of our existence beyond or besides the becoming political of life, and as the only trace beyond or besides biopolitical (or necropolitical) naming. This is perhaps the only undeniable equivalence that is again and again concealed and exposed by the deployment of the principle of general equivalence. By setting some distance from an accumulative relation to death and from a naming that only ever converts each singular existence into another number for the processes of accumulation and bio-politization, Carrasco moves away from the question of death from the Spanish nation-state to a global problematic, allowing thus a more sophisticated engagement with the question of death, mortality, and planetary finitude.

In Carrasco's *La tierra que pisamos*, Spain at the beginning of the twentieth century has been conquered by and annexed to a northern Aryan European empire of unseen proportions, possibly Germany. The military elite of the reigning power chooses Extremadura, in the west of Spain, as the place of solace for the generals and provosts who bravely fought during the "occupation" and "pacification" of the Spanish territory. The main figure and narrator of the novel is Eva Holman, the wife of a Iósif Holman, a former colonel of the sixth battalion of fusiliers of the expanding Empire and now bedridden war hero incapable of surviving on his own. His sanguinary personality, though, remains, since he is verbally abusive toward his caring wife. Eva progressively feels regretful about her past life and realizes the despicable qualities of Iósif's personality. One morning, an unknown man shows up in Eva's garden. He stands quiet and still. As soon as Eva sees the stranger, she grabs a shotgun and warns him: "No puede estar aquí. . . Ésta es una propiedad particular" (16–17) (you cannot stay here, this is private property). But the stranger remains undaunted and still. Jesús Carrasco leaves the reader uncertain about this stranger for several chapters: we don't know who the stranger is, where he comes from, or what language he speaks. We do not know who this other is. Eva becomes more and more curious about him; she asks the stranger questions, she even feeds him, but the stranger remains silent. Eva considers reporting the presence of the stranger to the military garrison in the area: "se llamará a su patrón para que lo recoja en el cuerpo de guardia. Antes, será azotado por el verdugo militar" (they will take him to his master, or their guardians will flog him), she thinks, as this is the usual procedure in the colony. "También puedo matarlo yo," Eva hesitates, "cogeré la escopeta y le volaré la cabeza" (Or, maybe, I could shoot him myself. . . I'll grab the handgun and shoot him in the head). Despite the interruption that the stranger's arrival produces in Eva's daily life, however, she keeps hosting him.

Eva tries to obtain the name of this stranger. After a few thwarted attempts, she mutters her own name in front of him and, suddenly, the stranger replies: "*Leva*" (39). We cannot know if he is echoing Eva's name or if his name is Leva. *Leva* is the Spanish word for military levy; as a verb, it means to start or wage war. It also refers to a mechanical piece that in combination with others may put a machine into motion. It may also mean to impose a tax on something. But Eva does not know for certain Leva's name or identity, Eva only really begins to know Leva when she takes a piece of paper from the pocket of Leva's unattended jacket. The note is a letter of recommendation written by Adrien Boom, a retired lieutenant. The lieutenant and Eva initiate a correspondence, and Eva gets to know that Leva was the lieutenant's servant. In fact, the jacket belongs to the lieutenant, who gave it to Leva. The lieutenant oversaw a timber forest in northern Europe, one of the many exploitations that the Empire uses to sustain its economy, and Leva was a worker in that area and later a personal secretary to the lieutenant. Leva, then, is a worker, a prisoner, a personal secretary of the lieutenant, and a stranger to Eva.

Gradually, Eva narrates her daily encounters with Leva, which also enables a secondary and simultaneous fiction that recounts Leva's life and introduces the reader to colonial life in Spain under the rule of the Empire. On one occasion, Eva recounts seeing bodies that are being transported through the streets of Badajoz and someone from Olivenza mentions that her town has been bombarded—in an explicit reference to Carrasco's own hometown in Extremadura, also bombarded during the Spanish Civil War. Through Eva's conscious and unconscious narration, we glean a very accurate description of the processes of primitive *expropriation*, of *despojo*, that enabled the accumulation of capital during the colonial and territorial empires; Carrasco's empires ironically include Spain as a center colony that is now subsumed under a northern European empire and prey to the same patterns deployed by the alliance of the crowns of Castile and Aragon in the Americas, the Philippines, Northern Africa, and Guinea since 1492. Eva speaks about this directly:

> vamos a lugares remotos del planeta y allí nos establecemos, tanto da si en desiertos o junglas, como si siguiéramos en nuestras campiñas. Al principio embelesamos a los indígenas con oropeles y ellos nos traen yuca o café. Más tarde les pedimos que nos lleven de la mano a la roca donde consiguen ese metal con el que perforan sus lóbulos. Luego metemos allí máquinas, capataces con látigos y los indígenas ya no salen a acariciar nuestras pieles blancas. (92–93)

> (We go to remote places of the globe and we establish ourselves there and, regardless if we are in the desert or in the jungle, we just go there and live there as if we were living in our own yards. At the beginning, we captivate the indigenous people with glitter [*oropeles*], and they bring us yucca or coffee. After this, we ask them to take us to the source of their metal that they transform and use in their earlobes. Then we introduce our technology and foremen carrying whips, and then the indigenous people do not come to us anymore)

What we read here is what Karl Marx calls "the secret of primitive accumulation": the history of an expropriation, says Marx, "written in the annals of mankind in letters of blood and fire" (875). This is the history of the processes of expropriation: namely, of war and colonialism that triggered in modern times the transformation of feudalist societies into capitalist ones. Progressively, "the slaves are newly freed men by becoming sellers of themselves, only after they had been robbed of all their own means of production, and all the guarantees of existence afforded by the old feudal arrangement" (875). In the passage above, Carrasco elaborates on the beginnings of modern societies, which were built on the creation of the other as a sheer owner of value (such as mineral resources), whose expropriation (*Ausraubung*) enabled the accumulation of capital during the longue durée of modernity. In the novel, Eva tells us of "[m]iles de seres sojuzgados y transportados igual que animales de una punta a otra del continente. Hacinados entre alambres de espinos y vigilados desde torretas de maderos desbastados" (99) (thousands of beings subjugated and transported like animals from one end of the continent to the other. They are heaped within hawthorn-made wires and they are watched from turrets made of devastated pieces of timber). It was this construction of the other as a labor-wager in the name of value, as an owner of his work force as a commodity in the name of another race and class, this "racialization of the other," that enabled the cultural foundation of a capitalist logic of economy, originally possible only through the custody and displacement of bodies, that is, the accelerated setting into motion of biopolitics in modern times.

The custody and the displacement of bodies is paradoxically the kernel of the creation of the *oikos*, of the house and economy of the sheer imperial unfolding. Leva underwent this deportation of bodies (this de-localization or deterritorialization) when he was transported from Extremadura to work in a timber forest in northern Europe and made part of a group of prisoners that were transported back to Extremadura to build a road. The passengers, however, do not know where they are going, multiple stops take place during the trip and prisoners are forced to get in and off the vehicle. This is an example of the absolute unpredictable life determination experienced by the prisoner-workers who are violently transported, *displaced, put into circulation*, with an economic purpose. Eva tells us that these prisoners are confined to the church of the town, where they sleep and are concentrated when they are not made to work on the infrastructures of the area:

> Al principio Leva piensa que es el azar quien gobierna su nueva vida. Quién sube o quién baja, generalmente, viene determinado por un dedo que indica sin un sentido aparente. *Lo mismo da si el elegido es anciano o joven, si procede de un país o de otro. Paran, señalan, y la gente es arrastrada por las tablas y, a veces, cuando el elegido no se decide, es echado a patadas por sus propios compañeros de cautiverio,*

del mismo modo que hace el organismo sano cuando expulsa al cuerpo extraño. Con los días se dará cuenta de que no es el azar sino la violencia la que se ha hecho cargo de su destino. Viven los que son capaces de golpear a otro para hacerse con su comida, arrancándosela de las manos o sacándosela de la boca si es preciso. Viven los que aguantan de pie y no sucumben al cansancio que los empuja al suelo, donde *ya se acumula un sedimento de cuerpos.* (52; my emphasis)

(At the beginning, Leva thinks that fate governs his life. Who gets on and off the transportation is usually determined by a pointing finger, without making obvious sense. *It does not matter if the one pointed to is old or young, if he or she comes from this or that country. They stop, point to someone, and people are then dragged over the ground. Sometimes, when the person chosen hesitates, his fellow prisoners will kick him out, in the same way that a healthy organism expels alien bodies. Day after day, he will realize that it is not fate but violence that governs his destiny. Those who can hit each other to get food, only those who can take food out of others' hands or even others' mouths will survive.* Only those who remain standing and do not succumb to fatigue will not end up on a floor that is *already accumulating a sediment of bodies.*)

The singularity or particular condition of each prisoner does not affect the custody and transportation of each individual body. Violence is the force that drives or determines the lives of the prisoners, as a way of destiny, or so says Eva. The objective of this violence is the production of value at the cost of amassing corpses. Dr. Sneint, the doctor of this local territory of the empire, explains, as recounted by Eva, what this empire makes out of "the earth we tread," which Dr. Sneint calls "campos de trabajo" (working fields). Dr. Sneint confesses that he was confined in one of those fields, and that he worked in the extraction of kaolin. Eva explains how Dr. Sneint remembers "cientos de hombres que vio morir por las aspiraciones del mineral triturado. 'Todo allí era blanco: las piedras, y los pulmones de los hombres'" (99) (hundreds of men that he saw die because of the inhalation of crushed minerals. "Everything was white in there: the plants, the stones, and the lungs of men".)

We now know that the custody and displacement of bodies has the ultimate aim of sustaining the Empire and its economy at the expense of the devastation of ecosystems in the name of value extraction. In other words, it is the "biopolitization" of politics what sustains Capitalism and reproduces a certain hegemony or power relationship. Each day of tree falling, the forest goes back some feet, and each new day is a carbon copy of the previous one, "ni los soldados ni sus mandos parecen haberse dado cuenta de ello, guiados por una lógica según la cual, cuanta más madera sea extraída en el menor tiempo, más posibilidades tendrán de ascender por las tripas del Imperio" (128). (Nobody seems to have noticed this after so many and similar full working days. The soldiers or their commanders seem to have missed this, since they are guided by a logic that says that the more wood they extract in the least time possible, the more the possibilities to climb through the innards of the Empire.)

This logic of extraction and its subsequent devastation of nature, the colonial and expropriating origins of this empire without a name, as well as the de-re-localizing and always-unpredictable custody and transportation of bodies determine the relationship between life and death. We are therefore no longer talking about Spain only, or a particular nation, but about a notion of Empire that is the concealment of just another name for the extractive, sacrificial, and de-territorialized globalization that no longer adheres to a particular nation-state nor has an "outside."[1] In other words, the sociological "disenchantment of the world" and loss of "conventional" religious followers goes hand in hand with a phenomenon explored by Walter Benjamin in his 1921 essay "Capitalism as Religion": "Capitalism is entirely without precedent, in that it is a religion which offers not the reform of existence but its complete destruction. It is the expansion of despair, until despair becomes a religious state of the world in the hope that this will lead to salvation" (289).[2]

The different ways of existence presented by Carrasco in his novel in-distinguish workers from refugees or from prisoners, and in a fundamental gesture, the novel hints at the secret of the sacrificial religion of capitalism, whose only horizon is the destruction of the planet, the expansion of despair without an "outside," the circulation of excess, and the "even more," *item more*, of violence: *sevicia* is the Spanish term of this "excess of violence" coined by Carrasco in his novel (178, for example). Unlike localized concentration camps during the Holocaust, this unleashed devastation of nature only ceases in the novel when the forest is gone, not after the defeat of the hegemonic Aryan European empire and the closure of concentration camps. In the novel, the devastation provoked by the prisoner-workers will continue elsewhere after the closure of this or that particular camp (project, timber forest, settlement, and so on). In this sense, ecocriticism cannot be a trend or a "focus" within the cultural critique, since our very existence is determined by this destructive faith of "anything goes" of capitalism as religion or sacrificial construction of existence. In a text entitled *La Comparution* (The Appearance), the French philosopher Jean-Luc Nancy thought that this sacrificial horizon of capitalism is enabled by the "principle of general equivalence," defined by Nancy as "a principle that sustains that 'anything goes,' as long as all forms of existence are regulated by the universal unifying principle of value" (Nancy and Bailly 115; my translation).

The custody and transportation of prisoners, the relocation of workers, the use of a labor force that is captive, the use of captives as a labor force, the value of experience as "qualified labor-force [*mano de obra cualificada*]," the extraction of resources throughout the world and the resulting devastation of nature, the ethnification of the other and attitude of supremacy of the Aryan Empire toward the other (as we read in the resentful words of Iósif), security, and immunization are *all* deployments of the principle of general equivalence that tends to join everything in terms of value, which is the underlying principle of Jesús Carrasco's writing in *La tierra que pisamos* and what puts together the original empire with the global world of Capital today. The general equivalence is another name for the force of being (for being as force) that explains the complexity and the rupture of temporality (with a particular age or epoch) of this book. Only on its surface is this novel about early modernity and the birth of colonialism, or about the Holocaust, or about the Spanish Civil War, or about a particular so-called migratory crisis within a particular region of the planet. The novel also deals with the modern processes of labor and the present worldwide displacement of bodies, but more important, *La tierra que pisamos* engages with the principle of general equivalence that underlies and sustains all of the above during the modern longue durée (and present scattering) in present-day global capitalism, of capitalism as the ultimate religion on the present civil war of planetary dimension. In *La Communauté affrontée* (The Confronted Community), Jean-Luc Nancy states that: "The present state of the world is not a war of civilisations. It is a civil war: it is the internal war of an enclosed city, of a civility, of an 'urbanity,' which are in the process of fanning out to the very limits of the world, and, because of this, spreading to the extremity of their own concepts" (23). Hence, the underlying in-distinguishing of different ways of existence (or concepts such as refugee, migrant, worker, or prisoner) is nevertheless determined by the same principle of equivalence, value reproduction, and the *hopeless-faith* of destruction. This principle of general equivalence is enabled by the supremacy or will to power that goes along with it. Eva reveals this supremacism at the beginning of her encounter with Leva, when Eva confesses that there is not room among them "para los holgazanes, los pusilánimes y los cobardes" (for the idle, the fainthearted, or the coward), stating that "si hemos alcanzado un lugar hegemónico en la historia ha sido porque hemos sabido expulsar a los débiles. Una bandera tan grande como para albergar a los pueblos del mundo. Un solo Dios verdadero. Un solo rey" (55–56) (If we reached this hegemonic place in history, it is because we have known how to expel the weak. A flag big enough to harbor the peoples of the world. One true God. Only one king).

This will to power and mastery that guarantees the reproduction of value is even more clear with the phallocentric and patriarchal violence of Iósif's language, the once war hero, now bedridden husband of Eva. "Puta, seguro que te acuestas con él" (66) (you whore, I am sure you sleep with him), says Iosif referring to Eva and Leva's bond. Iosif's abusive words speak of the internal violence, the familiar violence that perpetuates the violence of this (imaginary and vague) ultimate *imperio*, and that allows the circulation and determination of the human as material finitude in the name of value and in a global—and therefore not only territorial—scale.

At the end of *La tierra que pisamos*, in a fundamental gesture, Leva, the stranger, is not saved or redeemed by anyone. There is no redemption for him; nor is there an end for the reigning Empire. Instead, we read how the *corpses* of all the *others* are buried in mass graves that they themselves had previously excavated. There are only two moments of coming together: not between Leva and Eva Holman, but between Leva and his deceased wife, Teresa, and Leva and his daughter, Lola. Here is the first "encounter," between Leva and Teresa:

[A]lgunas noches, mientras duerme, grita y se convulsiona. Alguien que no es Teresa, que no tiene su cara ni su cuerpo, que ni tan si quiera es una mujer, puede que ni un ser humano, camina sobre cenizas. No es posible distinguirla del fondo, pues sus ropajes son del color del grafito. Tampoco oír sus pasos, amortiguados por la alfombra gris. Pero hay un momento, un instante apenas perceptible, en el que su piel refleja el fulgor final de ascua a punto de apagarse. Entonces cree reconocer a ese alguien que no es Teresa pero que participa de su mismo ser. El manto de grafito ya no es igual porque, al despertar, aunque no pueda ser consciente de ello, hay algo en él capaz de volver a prender fuego. (230)

(Some nights while sleeping, Leva yells and trembles. Someone that is not Teresa, who does not have Teresa's face or body, and which is not even a woman or perhaps even a human being, walks over ashes. It is not possible to distinguish that person from the background because her robes are like those of the graphite on the ground. It is impossible to discern her steps, which are softened by a grey rug. But there is a moment, there is an instant hardly noticeable in which her skin reflects the final glow [*fulgor*] of an ember nearing its extinction. It is then that Leva seems to recognize someone who is not Teresa but who participates in Leva's being. The mantle of graphite is no longer the same because at his awakening, and although Leva can hardly be conscious of it, there is something on him that can turn into flame.)

Despite the disappearance, and *instead of* a concrete and epiphanic other, there is a flame, there is an ash or a glow that burns at the unlikely threshold of consciousness and unconsciousness and that opens another relationship with the other that is neither represented nor metaphorized (in other words, that is neither mastered nor determined) in the plot of the novel. Unlike material bodies, status of ashes is different from that of flesh. In *L'Époque de la Disparition. Politique et esthétique* (The Epoch of Disappearance: Politics and Aesthethics), Jean-Louis Déotte and Alain Brossat analyze the characteristics of the disappearance of bodies, considering ashes (*les cendres*) as the marks of an interruption or opening:

> Ashes mark the interdictions and obstacles that are insurmountable to their own transmission. They put into play an unproductive memory, a memory purely and simply destroyed. We cannot build anything upon the memory of a genocide, we cannot build someone with the memory of a genocide. Ashes show the empty or dead area that humanity should never know, an area that however humanity has known and that humanity will continue to know. (55; my translation)

There is an encounter, then, with the other that is somehow impossible within the representable other(s). In addition to this encounter (that is not an encounter, or that *is* an encounter in an impossible form), Leva finds her daughter Lola, in this case, while crawling through the mud in which all of the dying bodies and corpses of the "Huerto de las Guindas" lie. After many years without her, Leva finally finds the body of his daughter Lola. He hugs Lola's dead body and feels "como si hubiera encontrado, entre los muertos, una nueva familia" (264) (as if he had found, among the dead, a new family). *The community of those who are going to die* and *have been* named, administered, circulated, exploited, and finally buried as *others, because* they are others.[3] The novel does not end with restitution, redemption, or salvation: Leva's life, the life of those without a proper or certain name, will continue as it has been. Eva finally speaks about Leva, affirming that Leva will soon abandon those bodies . . . that his brothers will see him leaving, and that he will be beaten until losing consciousness, and "luego, todavía inconsciente, te subirán en un camion con destino desconocido y, en el lugar remoto al que irás, tendrás que levantarte, cargado como un Atlas, y volver a ese lugar" (265) (Afterward, and while you are still unconscious, they will drive you toward an unkown destiny and, from that remote place, you will have to wake up again, loaded as the Atlas, and return to this place).

There is no redemption, then, just more circulation and dispersion of bodies under the principle of general equivalence that has determined Leva's existence. In fact, the novel closes with Eva coming back to her husband Iósif out of the sheer charity and compassion that the Christian faith of the empire instilled in her. In the final scene, Eva returns to El Huerto de las Guindas where all of the mass graves are, and there Eva pronounces the closing words of the novel:

Solo necesito saber que estáis aquí debajo y que hay una hermandad entre vuestros cuerpos. Toda la vida huyéndonos. Toda la vida tapando la piel de las mujeres, hurtándoles a los niños las caricias. Y ahora, apagados los alientos, irónicamente mezclados. ¡Qué hermosa hubiera sido esta cercanía en otro tiempo! Hombres, mujeres, ancianos, niños, familiares, amigos, desconocidos, reunidos. Juntos los cuerpos en una aleación indestructible. Quizá, como dicen, en algún momento fuimos uno. No un solo cuerpo, sino un solo ser. Nosotros, los árboles, las rocas, el aire, el agua, los utensilios. La tierra. (268)

(I only need to know that you are there underneath the earth, and that there is a bond among your bodies. We have spent all our lives avoiding each other. We have spent all our lives covering the skin of our women and stealing caresses from our children. And now, there you are, with your breath off, ironically mingled. How beautiful this proximity would have been in another time! Men, women, elderly people, relatives, friends, unknown people, all gathered together. All the bodies together in an indestructible alloy. Maybe, as they said, we were all one once upon a time. Not just a sole body, but a sole being. We, the trees, the rocks, the air, the water, the utensils. The land.)

Contrary to Eva's final words of nostalgia and humanistic hope (as a form of sad passion, as another horizon of a "re-enchantment of the world" at the end, in which we are all *already* united and are part of nature), the novel has abundantly shown that neither romanticism nor humanism could possibly rise from these ashes and piles of bodies; Eva returns to Iósif, and Leva will again be put into circulation under the many names of the other. There is no "once upon a time" for human history. The only human bond that we can infer from *La tierra que pisamos* is that of those who died, who are going to die, and/or who are mortal. Finitude is what we (do not) share. After reading about the circulation of bodies in the name of value, after reading the constant naming and *metaphorization* of "the other" (like in the name of the filial or theological humanism), its re-creation and essentialization in the name of value, we learn that no "wishful thinking," no nostalgia, no romanticism is possible when speaking of the other. Finitude then appears as the forgotten kernel of our "living-together," as the only trace beyond or besides biopolitical and necropolitical naming; it does not saturate our existence except in its very possibility. Existence equals mortality. This is perhaps the only undeniable equivalence that is again and again concealed and exposed by the deployment of the principle of general equivalence. From early primitive expropriation to present-day migrations and refugee crises, capitalism uncovers its secret as a religion that overdetermines our mortal existence: overdetermining, or always predetermining, our relationship with each other and with our finite planet, as if we and our planet were infinite.

After reading this novel, one wonders if every form of discrimination through naming—in the naming of a nation, gender, or race, even in the name humanity—is but a naturalism and ultimately a form of colonialism. How, then, does one cultivate a culture without colonialism? Or how does one build a friendship or love *outside* of the confines of our *phalo-logo-centric tradition* of friendship toward the other (here, represented by Eva vis-à-vis Iósif and Eva vis-à-vis Leva)? How, then, does one live and think otherness, or with the other, without the attribution of names, without or beyond attribution *qua* attribution? If it is true that globalization is the de-territorialization of the principle of general equivalence, its sheer attempt to become "more and more global" proves that it cannot be totally global, that power and its absolutization of value cannot be total. There is a unifying principle of general equivalence that in its selfsame scattering proves that there can also be unpredictability and singularity, exception or suspense in the complete and absolute unification of everything under value.

I mentioned at the beginning of this essay that when Leva arrived at the threshold of the Holman home for the first time, Eva aimed a shotgun at him, urging the stranger to get out of the property. Later in the novel, Eva shoots Leva but immediately takes care of him, the stranger, and fights against her inner self, against everything that she has learned with and from the sanguinary Colonel Iósif, her husband. Eva's relationship with Leva has gradually changed, and she takes the newly injured stranger to the clinic where Dr. Sneint heals him from the wound that she herself inflicted. This is a major transgression of the law, for Eva is not only feeding Leva but is now taking him (*"one of them,"* one of *the others*) to the hospital, which is an expressly prohibited and prosecutable crime under the totalitarian and anonymous regime. As matter of fact, Eva is summoned by the town consul who interrogates her about whether it is true that she is hosting a "lugareño" (native) in her home (222). If found guilty, Eva will be locked up in prison and her properties confiscated, but she does not deny the charges and admits to the accusation. With this gesture, Eva signals the abyss of difference within the law. This is the beginning of Eva's responsibility by means of a dissident and inventive rupture with respect to authority, tradition, orthodoxy, rule, or doctrine that begins with a self-questioning (Derrida *Gift*, 29). She is now distancing herself from herself, at first by taking a step away from Iósif, her blood-stained husband. In one scene, Iósif falls and is now lying on the floor, and Eva thinks: "Por un instante me visita la antigua Eva y siento que mi deber es ayudarle" (172) (For a moment, the old Eva is visiting me, and I feel the obligation to take care of him). But she does not take care of her repressive husband. Why does she, instead, keep transgressing the law and *de*-identifying with her own culture? She asks herself the same question, why she saved "one of them," why she paid attention to the stranger Leva if she did not even know his name: "no conozco tu nombre y ya no recuerdo ni el timbre de tu voz, pues únicamente te he oído hablar una vez" (234) (I do not know your name and I barely remember the sound of your voice, since I have only heard you talking once).

It is Leva's silence that sparks Eva's narration as the opening to another relationship with the stranger, one still however pre-determined by a theological "sense of guilt" and an inherited humanistic moral. She oscillates between a humanistic epiphany: "si no lo denuncié nada más verle fue por la fascinación de su presencia" (If I did not enounce him when I first saw him, it was because I was fascinated by his presence), and a substantiated deontology of moral-power: "si no lo hago ahora es porque hay algo que nos une y debo tratar de averiguar qué es antes de que los soldados entren y se lo lleven, como se llevaría un basurero los desechos de una cocina" (121–22) (If I do not do it now, it is because there is something that unites us, and I must try to figure out what it is before the soldiers find him and take him as one would take kitchen waste to a dump). Eva narrates the inner conflict with her own language and herself, with her own culture and (in) the face of another that shakes her home or *oikós* (*oikotés*, home, economy, or stability) to its foundations. The other, the stranger, the foreigner is for Eva what for the whole *oikos* (the Empire of *La tierra que pisamos*) is a prisoner, a barbarian, a worker, a beggar, an indigenous subject, a migrant, a vagabond, Eva the wife, a refugee, the idler, the gregarious man, or the "gloomy people," to name but a few *figures of the other* that are circulated on the grounds of general equivalence. Leva's silence and Eva's astonishment reveal that our culture is somehow originally and ultimately colonial, a system of codes under the principle of general equivalence. In *Monolinguism of the Other, or the Prosthesis of Origin*, Derrida affirms that: "every culture founds itself through the unilateral imposition of some 'politics of language.' Mastery begins, as we know, through the power of naming, of imposing and legitimizing appellations" (39). Facing Leva's silence reveals for Eva that what is at stake with naming and with the logocentric logic under it (ultimately, with the principle of general equivalence) is but the very same question of the other, of otherness, of alterity and the constant risk of its metaphorization. The functioning of Carrasco's Empire (of Europe once, of globalatinization now) and Eva's own double bind with her own culture as well as with the other has put at stake the so-called concept of European humanism. This humanism declares that something always already unites us, that we are all already one for the other while it puts into circulation the other under the unifying principle of value during the longue durée of modernity, from early modern Empire to present fully globalized capitalism. There is then still the risk of an alterity in which the other is but a value to be redeemed, or the risk of trumpeting a humanism that is an undercover theology (the other as a possible epiphany, the other as another name for God or an alleged common ground), or the risk of another as a subaltern that *we* (under a surreptitious will to power or mastery) allow—or do not allow—to speak. There is the threat of approaching the other out of guilt or out of sheer *duty*, as another name for a cultural and colonial violence that overdetermines our relationship to others. There is also the overdetermination of the other in the name of peace. Eva early on in the novel says: "desde que España fue pacificada, se podría decir que este es un lugar seguro" (109) (Since Spain has been pacified, we could say that this is a safe place). "Since," here, means since Spain was occupied and determined by the Empire, either at the end of the Spanish Civil War (1939) or at the beginning of the inclusion of Spain under the umbrella of the United States and the global Pax Americana during the late 1950s. In Leva's letter of recommendation written by the retired lieutenant Adrien Boom, which Eva found in Leva's jacket, the lieutenant stated that Leva will be of great help as a farmer (48). This is a clear example of the other as an economic or calculated other, of a recommendation of value, or just another example of a figure of the other that does not shake the *oikos*: the other as a calculated other (worker, slave, foreigner, stranger, and so on).

These figures of the other, captives in town, are a group of filthy captives that resemble a group of lunatics who have been destroyed by lust or possessed by visions from another world, and who are taken in lines to a "final solution" or final holocaust. In a scene that resembles Goya's *Black Paintings*, the prisoners are forced to walk wearing hoods. All the prisoners are taken to the Huerto de las Guindas, a garden now transformed into a mass grave of dead and piled-up dying bodies. Some of the bodies are alive, and others have been burned in the massive fires that every so often take place in the Empire:

Ven arder la pira a cierta distancia, sin saber que ese olor quedará para siempre tatuado en sus mentes. El fuego envolviendo crepitante la masa descoyuntada, caramelizando pieles y ropas hasta fundirlas. Leva aparta la mirada, pero en su mente ya solo flotan, como pavesas, las piernas mordidas del niño. Un niño que, de algún modo, es también hijo suyo (90).

(Some of the people look at the burning pyre from a certain distance, without knowing that the smell will remain tattooed in their minds forever. The fire wraps the crackling and dislocated mass of corpses, turning skins and clothes into caramel until complete melted. Leva looks away, but in his mind, he sees the legs of a kid floating. It is a kid that somehow is also his son.)

This is the version of a final solution in the novel, in which the disappearance of bodies and death signals that the highest risk of disappearance is the disappearance of death itself, in which the biopolitical and necropolitical controls over life unveil their own extremities and limits, perhaps even suggesting another response or a response other than the counter-biopolitical or counter-necropolitical response within hegemony. This is not just a power that controls the subjugation of lives and deaths (through GPS, or radar, or tele-technology), a power that takes life or allows to live, or that makes life and allows to die, but the spatial range of this power is now also foreign to internal or state legality. In other words, even the biopolitical and necropolitical controls over secularized bodies reach their limits and at the same time fade in globalatinization. Upon reaching a global and de-territorialized status, the biopolitical and necropolitical paradigm over life and death signals by means of a symptom the necessary end of its own ontological presupposition as, in the introductory words of this essay, "the absolute economization and circulation of mortality in the name of the extension and reproduction of surplus value" (9). This is the juncture where *La tierra que pisamos* leaves us.

In *On Cosmopolitanism and Forgiveness*, Derrida calls "impossible forgiveness" the possibility of interrogating the "absolutization of value" that contraposes normal, normative, and normalizing globalization: "It would be necessary to interrogate from this point of view what is called globalization, and which I elsewhere call globalatinization—to take into account the effect of Roman Christianity which today overdetermines all language of law, politics, and even the interpretation of what is called the 'return of religious,' *No alleged disenchantment, no secularization comes to interrupt it. On the contrary*" (32; my emphasis). It is in this precise sense and in the context of the re-enchantment of the world after the so-called disenchantment of the world that Jesús Carrasco's novel stands as a shared *cri de cœur* about finitude, as a certain work of literature that remains intolerable to the intolerance of theological-political systems and the saturation of the geopolitical processes in its becoming worldwide.[4]

Finally, in *Cosmopolitanism and Forgiveness*, Derrida also mentioned that: "We are all heirs, at least, to persons of events, marked somehow or another by crimes against humanity" (29). In July 2017, the Netherlands—the same state that funded the writing of *La tierra que pisamos*—was found responsible for the deaths of 350 Muslim Bosnians in Srebrenica during the UN mission of July 1995 ("Srebrenica"). In 2014, 3,419 dead bodies were found in the Mediterranean Sea, perishing on their way to Italy, Greece, or Spain. The report of the International Organization from Migration of that year released that the nation-state of Spain received (and is therefore co-responsible for) around 20 percent of the annual deaths that take place *between* borders on the entire planet (Castellano). There is no possible other, then, as long as it is calculated, administered, excluded, or even invented and domesticated to our own culture. Let me conclude with a rather long quote on the so-called other from Derrida's *Psyche: Inventions of the Other*:

> The invention of the other is not opposed to that of the same, its difference beckons toward another coming about, toward this other invention of which we dream, the invention of the entirely other, the one that allows the coming of a still unanticipatable alterity, and for which no horizon of expectation as yet seems ready, in place, available. Yet, it is necessary to prepare for it to allow the coming of the entirely other, passivity, a certain kind of resigned passivity for which everything comes down to the same, is not suitable. Letting the other come is not inertia ready for anything whatever. No doubt coming of the other, if it has to remain incalculable in a certain way aleatory (one happens upon the other in the encounter), escapes from all programming. But this aleatory aspect of the other has to be heterogeneous in relation to the aleatory factor of a calculus, and likewise to the form of the undecidable that theories of formal systems have to cope with. This invention of the entirely other is beyond any possible status; I still call it invention, because one gets ready for it, one makes this step destined to let the other come, come in. The invention of the other, the incoming of the other; is certainly not constructed as a subjective genitive, and just as assuredly not as an objective genitive either, even if the invention comes for the other—for this other is thenceforth neither subject nor object, neither a self not unconscious. To get ready for this coming of the other is that can be called deconstruction. It deconstructs precisely this double genitive and, as deconstructive invention, itself comes back in the step [*pas, paso*]—and also as the step [*pas, no*]—of the other. To invent would be to "know" how to say "come" and to answer the "come" of the other. Does that ever come about? Of this event one is never sure. (39)

The other constructed or identified within the regime of the same (of the representable, of an essence, of general equivalence) would still fall under the biopolitical, necropolitical, and hegemonic-counterhegemonic paradigms and their subtraction of the gap between life and death that lies beneath modern societies, as Gareth Williams's words signaled at the beginning of this essay. After *La tierra que pisamos*, there is no hope, no romanticism, no story, no infinite redemption that is possible or humanism of the other or in the name of the other, yet there is the *impossible* opening to prepare for an entirely finite other that it is not, and no longer, the other as a hidden God or the name of a body-value, in other words: that is not the other as a metaphor. It may be just the reminder of a flame or an ash.

The invention of the impossibility of the other or an impossible invention. Not an inertia but an occupation that suspends the creation, calculation, and circulation of the other in the name of something else, including in the name of the other.

NOTES

1.   There are several veiled references to the history of Spain in the novel; in particular, certain passages of the novel could perfectly refer to or express the violence(s) of the Spanish Civil War, Francoism, or the current CIES (the Centers for the Internment of Foreigners, or Centro de Internamiento de Extranjeros). For more on the CIES in contemporary Spain, see Ramajo.
2.   For a brief cultural and sociological view of the Spanish Catholic Church's loss of both followers and wealth, see Bayona.
3.   I take this absolutely striking expression from Brogan.
4.   I am here paraphrasing the end of Derrida's *Politics of Friendship*: "Is not literature today, in the saturation of a geopolitical process of a becoming-worldwide [*mondialité*], the very thing which remains intolerable to the intolerance of the theological-political systems for which, the idea of democracy having no unconditional virtue, no speech, can elude the space of theological-political authority?" (303).

WORKS CITED

Bayona, Eduardo, "Crisis en la Iglesia: Misas vacías, 4.200 parroquias sin cura y 7.000 frailes y monjas dejan de cotizar." *Público*, 6 Apr. 2017.

Benjamin, Walter. "Capitalism as Religion." Translated by Rodney Livingstone. *Selected Writings. Vol. 1. 1913-1926*, edited by Marcus Bullock and Michael W. Jennings, Belknap Press, 1996, pp. 288–91.

Brogan, Walter. "The Community of Those Who Are Going to Die." *Heidegger and Practical Philosophy*, edited by François Rafful and David Pettigrew, State University of New York Press, 2002, pp. 237–47.

Brossat, Alain, and Jean-Louis Déotte. *L'Époque de la Disparition. Politique et esthétique.* L'Harmattan, 2000.

Carrasco, Jesús. *La tierra que pisamos.* Seix Barral, 2016.

Castellano, Nicolás, "España suma más del 20% de las muertes en las fronteras del planeta." *Cadena SER*, 2 May 2018.

Derrida, Jacques, *Monolingualism of the Other, or the Prosthesis of Origin.* Translated by Patrick Mensah, Stanford University Press, 1998.

_____. *On Cosmopolitanism and Forgiveness.* Translated by Mark Dooley and Michael Hughes, Routledge, 2001.

_____. *Politics of Friendship*. Translated by George Collins, Verso, 2005.

_____. *Psyche: Inventions of the Other*, vols. 1–2, edited by Peggy Kamuf and Elizabeth Rottenberg, Stanford University Press, 2008.

_____. *The Gift of Death*. Translated by David Wills, University of Chicago Press, 1995.

Marx, Karl. *Capital: A Critique of Political Economy*, vol. 1. Translated by Ben Fowkes, Penguin, 1990.

Nancy, Jean-Luc. "The Confronted Community," translated by Amanda Macdonald, *Postcolonial Studies*, vol. 6, no. 1, 2003, pp. 23–36.

Nancy, Jean-Luc, and Jean Christopher Bailly. *La Comparution*. Christian Bourgois éditeur, 1991.

Ramajo, Javier, "Miedo, violencia, muerte: Un informe recopila la 'bienvenida' de España a los migrantes encerrados en Archidona." *Eldiario.es*, 7 June 2018.

"Srebrenica: Dutch State Partly Responsible for 350 Deaths." *BBC News*, 27 June 2017.

Williams, Gareth, "In the Wake of Leviathan: From Biopolitics to Posthegemony." *Paradigmi. Rivista di Critica filosofica*, forthcoming.

Politics, Arts, and Disrupted Death Rituals

Luis Martín-Estudillo and Nicholas Spadaccini

One could say that the symbolic treatment of death is one of the most universal manifestations of what entails to be human, as the members of our species tend to have a clear prescience of their own demise. Moreover, for many of us working in the areas of Spanish literary/cultural studies, it could even be argued that Spain is a particularly fruitful site for its study. One thinks of Jorge Manrique's *Coplas* from the Middle Ages, the numerous representations of death in the early modern period (especially with its characteristically baroque *vanitas*), the images of death and bullfighting in the works of Francisco de Goya or Federico García Lorca, and the notion of wisdom as knowledge for death (complementing science as knowledge for life) in Miguel de Unamuno, and Pablo Picasso's *Guernica* during the Spanish Civil War, to mention some of the most prominent cases in the national canon. Throughout the centuries of Spain's history, various works of art and literature have dealt with the topic of death in ways that have attracted attention both within and outside of the European context. Moreover, that very corpus has contributed decisively toward the shaping of an image of the country and its people that offers a pointed contrast to the stereotype of a hedonistic vitalism.

The prevailing perception of Spaniards being passionately involved with death originated largely in the early modern period, when the immense power accumulated by the Spanish crown was to contribute to the creation of gory narratives based on the perception of certain events, among them, the stories of Felipe II's treatment of his son Carlos, the darkest actions of the Inquisition, and the most violent episodes of the conquest of the Americas, some of which reverberated in the imagination of Spain's rivals, who used those accounts as effective tools of anti-Spanish propaganda. Even for observers who were more sympathetic toward the Iberian nation, death played a fundamental role when engaging it—one thinks, for instance, of Ernest Hemingway's fictions. In any case, what stands out in many of the creations linking conceptualizations of Spanishness and death are the imbrications of the political and the funerary, with art serving as a mediating element.

While the present volume focuses on contemporary Spain, it might be useful to frame the discussion about death historically by reflecting upon two of the defining (and deadliest) moments in the nation's history and how they were represented by two of the country's most influential artists: Francisco de Goya and Pablo Picasso. The first created a series of engravings known as *The Disasters of War* (1810–1814), when the Spaniards' War of Independence from the French brought an unprecedented sense of brutality and national awareness. Goya's long-term employer, the Bourbon royal family, had left the country in agreement with Napoleon Bonaparte, who cunningly exploited their internal feuds to place his brother Joseph on Madrid's throne. While the aging artist contributed work to welcome the new rulers, who implemented reforms that were close to his liberal ideals—including measures such as the 1813 abolition of the Inquisition (reinstated in 1814 and abolished definitively in 1834)—he was taken aback by the fierce local resistance to the foreign leaders and the brutal repression exercised by Bonaparte's troops, events that were captured brilliantly in engravings that he produced secretly on reused or deficient plates. A deliberate meditation on war and its devastating consequences—both material and moral—transcends the prints' apparent urgency, which stems from an alleged direct observation of the incidents depicted. The images also show that the end of the hostilities did not mean a restoration of civility and dignity, as the defeat of the French brought about a reactionary backlash, and the invaders' brutality was used for decades as an excuse to reject the ideals of *liberté, égalité, fraternité*. Notwithstanding Goya's political ambivalence (which he was at pains to refute later on), his ethical stance remains pristine in these images: human suffering, horror, and bestiality are laid bare for the careful contemplation of anyone daring to watch. Death is profusely represented in the form of gruesome images depicting dismembered bodies as piles of corpses that survivors can barely manage to bury. "It cannot be seen," states one of his inscriptions—yet it *must* be seen, Goya's collection asserts, even if it was to take a long time to be made widely visible, as the series was first printed and disseminated in 1863, thirty-five years after the artist's own passing in France.

Goya's series has largely been regarded as a model for the representation of the worst consequences of political conflicts and it still exerts a powerful influence today. It is telling that in 1937, during the height of the Civil War, the government issued a new edition of the prints with two main goals: funding the Republican cause and sending a powerful reminder of its plight to a group of international dignitaries that included Winston Churchill, Joseph Stalin, and Eleanor Roosevelt. Moreover, a map detailing the bombings of Madrid by the Nationalist army was appended to the prints. In the meantime, Pablo Picasso was at work on his *Guernica* (1937), in implicit dialogue with Goya's precedent, following a commission from the Republican government.

As the role of the new work was meant to be propagandistic, the commission stated that it had to engage politics explicitly, a dimension that Picasso had not explored in his career until he created his then-recent *The Dream and Lie of Franco*. Like Goya, Picasso put the suffering of civilians in the limelight. *Guernica* exposes the sudden destruction of their dwellings and daily habits and, most tragically, the death of innocent victims. While some representatives of the Republican forces objected to the painting's lack of specificity regarding the situation in Spain, the general public quickly hailed it as a denunciation of the atrocity of war and as an icon of pacifism. Most importantly for the type of contributions analyzed in this volume, Picasso's work set a new priority in the relationship between cultural production and death: the political associations of the issue could no longer be ignored. The lasting, global impact of *Guernica* would defy the Franco regime's attempts to whitewash its image during the following decades. The painting was a somber reminder of the origins and nature of the dictatorship as the government insisted on a folkloric, vitalistic self-fashioning of the country aimed at attracting tourists and gaining the acceptance of Western powers.

In some ways, the conflicts between the forces of change and reaction that first stirred during the Peninsular War, or War of Independence, had found a different expression in the 1936–39 Civil War, a fratricidal conflict that deeply scarred the nation and was to prompt political and legal actions in ways that continue until this day. And while the vast number of people who lost their lives during the war were not always unaware of the cultural and political implications of those clashes, the symbolic appropriation of their deaths, and the material management of their bodies, were to mark the decades that followed. This management of the funereal included cases as diverse as the treatment of the remains of fascist leader José Antonio Primo de Rivera (which were carried on foot from Alicante to Madrid, accompanied by members of Falange and a display that included a torchlight parade), the purposeful neglect, debasement, or self-interested use of the corpses of the defeated by the victors, and the complex issues associated to the burial of North-African Muslim soldiers hired by the Nationalists. Many of these issues are tackled in this volume of Hispanic Issues by exposing the complex articulation of death as personal tragedy, societal issue, and cultural product. Through an analysis of archival documents, films, photographs, novels and a range of well-known theoretical texts, essays in this volume manage to engage various debates about death while considering the larger narratives that have sprung forth since the 1936–39 Civil War, especially, though not exclusively, the memorialization of those killed along political lines.

The date of 1959, when the Valley of the Fallen was inaugurated, is a useful starting point for the volume's main focus. The exhumation of the dictator in October 2019 could be seen as a moment of closure for a period in which the fatal consequences of the Civil War and the ensuing dictatorship haunted the nation. Yet this issue was not resolved with the removal of Franco's remains from public grounds, as thousands of corpses are still missing. The disappearance of those murdered for political reasons during the conflict and its immediate aftermath remained largely unresolved until it came to occupy a relevant space in the public imaginary with the debates about historical memory that emerged in the 2000s. Such a debate has lingered, more or less visibly, during a particularly dynamic period in the modern history of Spain as it underwent a formidable transformation in virtually along political, economic, and social lines.

The country's transition to democracy also came at the expense of justice, as the amnesty approved by the government meant that the perpetrators of the political crimes of the dictatorship did not have to face penal consequences. As the face of the nation changed and new challenges and customs arose, the public and cultural management of death presented novel forms. One can point to greater concerns for human rights, including the abolition of the death penalty and greater awareness of police torture. Rapidly changing attitudes toward the Catholic Church implied variations in the ways families dealt with the passing of their loved ones after centuries of apparent immobility in this regard. The devolution of powers to the regions, some with national aspirations, fostered their own cult of the dead. The unprecedented prosperity for certain segments of society and the more uncertain future for others more prone to the effects of economic crises was manifested in differential life expectancies, which questioned the extent to which the local version of the welfare state had succeeded in its mission to provide greater equality among citizens. The arrival of new immigrants and the growing international mobility of Spaniards brought along diverse conceptions of dying. At the time of the writing of this afterword, an act regulating euthanasia was being approved in parliament. These issues overlapped with other fundamental problems such as violence toward women, a feminicide whose scale finally shook the complacent attitudes of many citizens who pressured the government to take action.

The recent (and ongoing at the time of writing) Covid-19 pandemic brought death to the fore again, after decades in which it had been "pushed further and further out of the perceptual world of the living," as Walter Benjamin alerted us almost a century ago, when he quoted a sobering motto that he saw in Spain, where he ended his life in 1940 after attempting to escape fascism: "There used to be no house, hardly a room, in which someone had not once died. (The Middle Ages also felt spatially what makes that inscription on a sun dial of Ibiza, *Ultima multis* [the last day for many], significant as the temper of the times" (93–94). Yet this estrangement of death, which Benjamin associated with modernity, has continued to evolve. The Covid crisis brought death back to places where it had not been visible for a long time, or into spaces which had been kept insulated from it for being somewhat improper. Among the most striking images of the pandemic for a global audience were those of an ice rink in Madrid and refrigerated trucks in New York used as temporary morgues, and visual images of acres upon acres of land in Brazil used as impromptu burial sites. The crisis also highlighted a different kind of connection with the other through the imposition of a rationalization of space, a distance from the other's body, a rearrangement of relations—a kind of exile. In an interview by Walter Veltroni, Benedetto Carucci Viterbi, a leading Rabbi of Rome, recalled an interpretation of creation which saw the human being as bifrontal and androgynous, "a separation and distancing that helps the process of identification." Yet he went on to suggest that, within the context of later phases of the pandemic, less reflexive and tolerant than the first, that process could well manifest itself in an "exclusive and excluding identitarian drift and descend into suspicion of the other," something, one might add, that certain political forces have not discouraged.

The pandemic disrupted relationships and brought about a new realization of the fragility of human beings and their cultural constructs. It also revealed particular vulnerabilities among certain demographics, among them, the elderly in congregate care, people of all ages with serious pre-exiting medical conditions, people in service-oriented jobs for whom working from the isolation of their homes is impossible, and populations with inadequate access to health services, especially undocumented immigrants, minority populations, and the poor of all races and ethnicities. In Spain, as elsewhere, people died alone, away from their loved ones, and the normal rituals of burial were severely disrupted, with traumatic consequences for those left behind. The Covid crisis also brought about pandemic fatigue and a lack of trust in institutions for alleged lack of transparency, an issue that created rancor within the European Union regarding equitable access to vaccines amidst special deals made with pharmaceutical companies by some of the Union's most powerful members (Germany, for example) and its ex-member, the United Kingdom.

Another consequence of the politics of life and death in the time of Covid was the exacerbation of tensions between two kinds of principles: that of democracy—often messy and chaotic— and that of competence under the tutelage of a hierarchy of technocrats under the guise of predictability and order. Finally, as Jürgen Habermas pointed out in a recent interview, the pandemic has tested "the willingness of each of us to accept, in consideration of others as well as ourselves, a certain number of restrictions and, for many professions, personal risks" (Blin). To be sure, during the health emergency Spain did not seem to descend into the type of extreme politization that happened in the U.S. under the unscrupulous and self-serving Trump presidency, with the connivance of conspiracy-oriented hard-right politicians, radical groups, certain segments of the mass-media system, and the fragmented public sphere overloaded with a multiplicity of social networks that often served as echo chambers. Yet the comparison with the last months of Trump's rule cannot obscure the fact that the behavior of the Spanish political class was very far from exemplary even as they dealt with the most serious crisis the country had faced since the Civil War.

The editors of this volume remind us that the concepts of death and culture "bear an inextricable relationship to each other" and argue, through Derrida, that "there is no culture without a cult of ancestors, a ritualization of mourning and sacrifice, institutional places and modes of burial." The Covid pandemic has once again brought death to the forefront on a global scale. And while there is an evident inextricability of the relationship between death and culture, the health emergency (which, hopefully, will be attenuated and eventually resolved through extensive global distribution of vaccines) seems to have altered the more traditional modes of ritualization of mourning. As with other areas of life, such as work and travel, the pandemic has had an undeniable impact on the attitudes toward death and dying. Those grieving had to renounce the solace of proximity. In Spain, for example, participation in funerals was limited to three attendees and an officiant. It remains to be seen to what extent the new approaches are here to stay. What is less doubtful is that different artistic forms (from literature to the visual arts, including the now seemingly ubiquitous television cable and streaming series, which entertained so many people during the long periods of confinement), will play an important role in the shaping of alternative models of funerary practices and mourning that do not necessarily align with institutional religion.

WORKS CITED

Benjamin, Walter. "The Storyteller: Reflections on the Works of Nikolai Leskov." *Illuminations*, edited by Hannah Arendt, translated by Harry Zohn, Schocken Books, 1969. pp. 83–109.

Blin, Simon. Interview with Jürgen Habermas. *Libération*, 30 Jan. 2021.

Veltroni, Walter. "Il rabbino: 'Il sentirci fragili alla fine ci aiuterà a riscoprire gli altri,'" *Corriere della Sera*, 30 Nov. 2020.

EUGENIA AFINOGUÉNOVA is professor of Spanish at Marquette University. Her research covers modern and contemporary Iberian cultures, with a special emphasis on museums and the tourist industry. She has published extensively, from essays on the tourist community in Andalusia to the relationship between film and travel, to the status of Picasso's *Guernica* after the Catalan Revolution. She is the coeditor of *Vademecum del cine iberoamericano: Métodos and teorías* (2016), and the author of *The Prado: Spanish Culture and Leisure, 1819–1939* (2017), which was translated into Spanish as *El Prado: La cultura y el ocio (1819–1939)* in 2019. She has also worked in digital and visual projects on museums and travel culture.

PEDRO AGUILERA-MELLADO is assistant professor of Spanish at University of Notre Dame, where he teaches and researches on modern and contemporary Spanish literature and culture, with a particular focus in the deconstruction of modern ideas and culture. Recent publications include: "'Trazo Sacrificial,' Capital y Guerra Global Contemporánea: Apuntes sobre María Zambrano y *Las Variaciones Guernica* (Guillermo G. Peydró, 2012)" and "'Goyesque Gaze': Image, Violence, and Dignity-Potency." He is currently working on a book manuscript titled *Modernidad infrapolítica: Fines de la representación, la modernidad y la subjetividad en la modernidad ibérica.*

ANTONIO CÓRDOBA is associate professor of Spanish at Manhattan College. He has published *¿Extranjero en tierra extraña? El género de la ciencia ficción en América Latina* (2011) and coedited *The Sacred and Modernity in Urban Spain: Beyond the Secular City* (2016). He has published essays on Spanish and Latin American science fiction and horror film and literature. He is currently working on a manuscript tentatively titled *Exhausted Futures: Science Fiction and the Limits of the Political Imagination in Contemporary Spain.*

ANA FERNÁNDEZ-CEBRIÁN is assistant professor at the Department of Latin American and Iberian Cultures at Columbia University. Her research focuses on the important historical shifts pertaining to ideological production and the transformations of the public sphere from the Second Republic to late Francoist Spain. Her forthcoming book, *Fables of Development: Capitalism and Social Imaginaries in Spain (1950–1967)*, examines cultural fictions and collective social life at the time—the 1950s and 1960s—when Spain turned from autarky to industrial and tourist development. She has published numerous essays on literature, cultural studies, film, and media.

DANIEL GARCÍA-DONOSO is associate professor of Spanish at Catholic University of America. He has published *Escrituras post-seculares: Sedimentos de la religión en la narrativa española, 1950–2010* (2018) where he examines the presence of religion and religious questions in a representative corpus of contemporary Spanish narrative fiction as an expression of a post-secular culture. He is also coeditor of *The Sacred and Modernity in Urban Spain: Beyond the Secular City* (2016) and the author of a number of articles on Spanish literature and film. He is currently working on a book-length project on the cinema of Fernando León de Aranoa.

PATTY KELLER is associate professor of Spanish and comparative literature at Cornell University. Her research and teaching interests are located at the intersection of literature, photography, critical theory, political philosophy, cultural studies, cinema, and media studies. She is the author of *Ghostly Landscapes: Film, Photography, and the Aesthetics of Haunting in Contemporary Spanish Culture* (2015), which examines the relationship between image production, ideology, and spectrality. Weaving together close readings of three distinct media from Spain's fascist and post-fascist periods—documentary newsreels, art films, and conceptual photography—this study explores the interpretive possibilities of visual constructions of loss in contemporary culture. She is currently working on a new project titled *Photography's Wound: Exposing Belief in Times of Uncertainty*, a study of contemporary photography, ethics, and structures of belief.

ANGEL LOUREIRO is emeritus professor at the Department of Spanish and Portuguese at Princeton University. His books include *The Ethics of Autobiography: Replacing the Subject in Modern Spain* (2000) and *Mentira y seducción: La trilogía fantástica de Torrente Ballester* (1990). He has edited volumes on autobiography for *Anthropos* (1991), *Suplementos Anthropos* (1992), and *Journal of Interdisciplinary Literary Studies* (1994). He has also been the editor of *Joseph Blanco White, "The Examination of Blanco by White," Revista de Estudios Hispánicos* (1999); *El gran desafío: Autobiografía, feminismos, postmodernidad* (1994); and *Estelas, laberintos, nuevas sendas (Unamuno. Valle-Inclán. García Lorca. La Guerra Civil)* (1988).

ANNABEL MARTÍN is associate professor of Spanish, comparative literature, and women's, gender, and sexualities at Dartmouth College. She is also the founding director of the Gender Research Institute at Dartmouth and the cofounder of the Jahjaga Foundation in Prishtina, Kosovo. She is the author of *La gramática de la felicidad: Relecturas franquistas y posmodernas del melodrama* (2005), the editor of *Humanities: Gender in Times of Crisis: A Multidisciplinary Conversation* (2017), and the coeditor of "Reconciliation and Its Discontents," a special number of *Dissidences: Hispanic Journal of Theory and Criticism* (2012). She has also written extensively on Iberian cultures. She is currently studying the cultural context surrounding the end of ETA terrorism in Spain and the role the arts play in processes of reconciliation in her manuscript *Rest in Peace: The Basque Political Contours of the Arts*, a collaborative project with Basque artists Bernardo Atxaga, Julia Otxoa, Ricardo Ugarte, Luisa Etxenike, and Helena Taberna, among others.

LUIS MARTÍN-ESTUDILLO is professor of Spanish and Collegiate Scholar at the University of Iowa, specializing in modern and contemporary Spanish literature and culture. He has also published broadly on early modern topics, European studies, and visual culture. He is the executive editor of *Hispanic Issues* and *Hispanic Issues Online* and codirects the literary journal *Iowa Literaria*. His latest books are *The Rise of Euroskepticism: Europe and Its Critics in Spanish Culture* (2018; winner of a National Endowment for the Humanities Open Book Award in 2020) and *Despertarse de Europa: Arte, literatura, euroescepticismo* (2019). His next book, *Goya and the Mystery of Reading*, is forthcoming.

CRISTINA MOREIRAS-MENOR is professor of Spanish and women's studies at University of Michigan. She is the author of *Cultura herida: Literatura y cine en la España democrática* (2002) and *La estela del tiempo: Imagen e historicidad en el cine español contemporáneo* (2011). She has published extensively on authors and filmmakers from Teresa de Jesús and Rosalía de Castro to Álex de la Iglesia and Mario Camus, and focused on violence and memory, violence and the state, critical regionalism, the Spanish Civil War, the Francoist Dictatorship, and the Transition to Democracy. She is the editor of a monographic issue for *Journal of Spanish Cultural Studies* titled "Critical Interventions on Violence." She is working on two book projects: *Galicia y sus fronteras: Escritores, márgenes y el canon nacional (siglos XIX y XX)* and *Spanish Documentary and the Politics of Critical Regionalism*.

JORDI MORERAS is a researcher and part-time professor at the University Rovira i Virgili (URV) and teaching collaborator of the Open University of Catalonia

(UOC). In 2002 he joined the Secretariat of Religious Affairs of the Generalitat de Catalunya, where he worked as head of studies until 2004. As an independent consultant, he has collaborated with public and private Spanish and international institutions. He is the author of different monographs on Muslim communities in Spain, such as *Musulmanes en Barcelona: Espacios y dinámicas comunitarias* (1999), *Imams d'Europa: Les expressions de l'autoritat religiosa islàmica* (2005) and *Identidades a la Intemperie: Una mirada antropológica a la radicalización en Europa* (2019), among others. He is also the editor of *Socio-antropología de la muerte: Nuevos enfoques en el estudio de la muerte* (2019).

N. MICHELLE MURRAY is assistant professor in the Spanish Department at Vanderbilt University. Her research and teaching focus on contemporary Spanish literature and film. Her first book, *Home Away from Home: Immigrant Narratives, Domesticity, and Coloniality in Contemporary Spanish Culture* (2018), studies representations of immigrant women as domestic workers in contemporary Spain. She has also published a number of articles and book chapters on contemporary Spain. She is the editor of *Studies on Migration in Spanish and Latin American Literature and Film*, a monographic issue of the *Vanderbilt e-Journal of Luso-Hispanic Studies*, and coeditor of *Unsettling Colonialism: Gender and Race in the Nineteenth-Century Global Hispanic World* (2019). She is currently working on a manuscript entitled *Migrant Markets* that explores migration, political economy, and trafficking in the Southern Mediterranean.

LAYLA RENSHAW is associate professor in forensic science at Kingston University. Her research and teaching expertise combine forensic sciences and social sciences in the study of death and burial, with a strong focus on post-conflict and human rights investigations. She has produced several publications on this topic. She was an assistant archaeologist with the United Nation's International Criminal Tribunal for former-Yugoslavia, working on the exhumation and identification of war victims in post-war Kosovo. She has also worked in a consultative capacity for a number of UK police constabularies, working on human identification. One of her primary research areas is the impact of recent and ongoing exhumations of mass graves from the Spanish Civil War. On this topic, she published *Exhuming Loss: Memory, Materiality and Mass Graves in the Spanish Civil War* (2011).

ELIZABETH SCARLETT is professor of Spanish at the Department of Romance Languages and Literatures at Buffalo University of SUNY. Her research focuses on Spanish literature, film, and media. She has published *Under Construction: The Body in Spanish Novels* (1994) and *Religion and Spanish Film: Luis Buñuel, the Franco Era, and Contemporary Directors* (2014). She is also the coeditor of *Convergencias Hispánicas: Selected Proceedings and Other Essays on Spanish and Latin American Literature, Film, and Linguistics* (2001). Her articles, essays, and book chapters cover a wide range of topics and periods in modern and contemporary Iberian cultures, ranging from Gertrudis de Avellaneda to Clara Serra, Javier Marías, Miguel Bosé, and twenty-first-century zombie films.

NICHOLAS SPADACCINI is professor emeritus of Spanish and comparative literature at the University of Minnesota-Twin Cities. He has published books, critical editions, articles, and collective volumes on the literature and cultures of Spain's early modern period, and has coedited two volumes of literary/cultural criticism on Colonial Latin America. His most recent published volumes (coedited) are *New Spain, New Literatures* (2010), *Hispanic Literatures and the Question of a Liberal Education* (2011), *(Re)reading Gracián in a Self-made World* (2012), *Memory and Its Discontents* (2012), and *Writing Monsters: Essays on Latin American and Iberian Cultures* (2014). He is the founding editor of Hispanic Issues and Hispanic Issues On Line (HIOL).

SOL TARRÉS is a social anthropologist that conducts research and teaches at the Department of History, Geography, and Anthropology at the University of Huelva. She focuses on Islamic religiosity in Spain and on the culture of death. She has coauthored *¿Y tú (de) quién eres? Minorías religiosas en Andalucía* (2010) and *Encuentros: Diversidad religiosa en Ceuta y Melilla* (2013) and coedited *Patrimonio cultural inmaterial y funerario de la diversidad religiosa en España e Iberoamérica* (2019). She has written extensively on funerary urban spaces and culture in Spain.

WILLIAM VIESTENZ is associate professor in the Department of Spanish and Portuguese Studies and the Institute of Global Studies at the University of Minnesota Twin Cities. His research focuses on modern Iberian literature and culture, topics on which he has published numerous essays. He is the author of *By the Grace of God: Francoist Spain and the Sacred Roots of Political Imagination* (2014) and the coeditor of *Ethics of Life: Contemporary Iberian Debates* (2016) and *The New Ruralism: An Epistemology of Transformed Space* (2014). He is the editor of *Catalan Review* and is currently working on a second book project entitled *Beasts of Burden: Bullfighting and Other Eruptions of the Creaturely in Modern Spain,* which studies the relationship between animal symbolism and political sovereignty, ethics, and human rights.

INDEX

Page numbers in *italic* indicate figures.

www.ingramcontent.com/pod-product-compliance
Lightning Source LLC
Chambersburg PA
CBHW020455270326
41926CB00008B/610